CONTENT ANALYSIS

Other works by the same author:

A Biography of Caius Marius, Proceedings of the African Classical Associations, 1961.

Bureaucracy in Traditional Society, Coronado Press, 1972.

A Catalogue of the Roman and Related Foreign Coins in the Collection of Sir Stephen Courtauld, University Colleges, Rhodesia and Nyasaland, 1963.

P. Terenti Afri Hecyra, Classical Association of Rhodesia and Nyasaland, 1964, (English Edition).

Translations into English:

A. P. Vacolopoulos, *A History of Thessaloniki*, Institute for Balkan Studies, 1963.

John the Lydian, *De Magistratibus*, Coronado, 1971.

Content Analysis

A TECHNIQUE FOR SYSTEMATIC INFERENCE FROM COMMUNICATIONS

T. F. CARNEY

Professor of History
University of Manitoba

B. T. BATSFORD LTD London

87148

First published 1972

© University of Manitoba Press 1972

Published in Canada by University of Manitoba Press,
Winnipeg, Canada

Printed in Canada for the publishers
B. T. Batsford Ltd, 4 Fitzhardinge Street, London W1H 0AH

ℝ   ISBN 0 7134 2007 3

*Grateful acknowledgement is made to the Alumni Association of the
University of Manitoba for financial support in the publication of this
book.*

iv

TO BARBARA

Contents

List of Diagrams

BIBLIOGRAPHY OF SHORT TITLES
and General Notes on Books Cited

I BIBLIOGRAPHY

The following abbreviations refer to books which are very frequently cited. Some are works written specifically about content analysis; some contain applications of the technique; others involve matters related to content analysis.

Bureaucracy in Traditional Society: T. F. Carney, *Bureaucracy in Traditional Society: Romano-Byzantine Bureaucracies Viewed from Within,* Coronado, 1972.

* C.A.C.: R. W. Budd, R. K. Thorp and L. Donohew, *Content Analysis of Communications*, Macmillan, 1967.

Centuries of Childhood: P. Aries, *Centuries of Childhood: A Social History of Family Life,* Vintage ed. 1965.

(*) *Communication Content*: G. Gerbner *et al, The Analysis of Communication Content*, Wiley, 1969.

"Content Analysis"; B. R. Berelson, "Content Analysis" in G. Lindzey (ed.), *Handbook of Social Psychology*, Addison-Wesley, vol. 1, 1954, pp. 488-522.

(*) *Content Analysis*: O. R. Holsti, *Content Analysis for the Social Sciences and Humanities*, Addison-Wesley, 1969.

Meaning and Mind: R. F. Terwilliger, *Meaning and Mind: A Study in the Psychology of Language*, Oxford U.P., 1968.

North, *Content Analysis*: R. C. North *et al, Content Analysis: A Handbook with Applications for the Study of International Crisis,* Northwestern University Press, 1963.

Social Class: D. Lawton, *Social Class, Language and Education*, Routledge and Kegan Paul, 1968.

"The Changing Picture of Marius": T. F. Carney, "The Changing Picture of Marius in Ancient Literature", *The Proceedings of the African Classical Associations*, 10, 1967, pp. 5-22.

* *The General Inquirer*: P. J. Stone *et al, The General Inquirer: A Computer Approach to Content Analysis*, M.I.T. Press, 1966.

The Image, K. E. Boulding, *The Image: Knowledge in Life and Society*, Ann Arbor ed., 1961.

The Image of the City: K. Lynch, *The Image of the City*, M.I.T. Press, 1960.

The Open and Closed Mind: M. Rokeach, *The Open and Closed Mind: Investigations into the Nature of Belief Systems and Personality Systems*, Basic Books, 1960.

Trends: I. de S. Pool, ed., *Trends in Content Analysis*, U. of Illinois Press, Urbana, 1959.

** Maccoby, *Readings*: E. E. Maccoby, T. M. Newcomb and E. L. Hartley, eds., *Readings in Social Psychology*, Holt, Rinehart and Winston, 1958.

II   GENERAL NOTES

A bibliography of works cited in the notes will be found at the end of the book. In the notes themselves, I have followed the normal practice of citing the full particulars of date and publisher only at the first mention of a book. Subsequent references cite author and title only. The following points concerning some of the books in the Bibliography of Short Titles may be of interest.

* Books asterisked are those which are most commonly used in the teaching of content analysis, as reported by Barcus (see "Education in Content Analysis: A Survey", *Communication Content*, p. 546). Barcus's list of most commonly used books also includes:

H. D. Lasswell, D. Lerner and I. de S. Pool, *The Comparative Study of Symbols*, Hoover Institute Studies, Series C: Number 1; Stanford U. Press, 1952 (cited in this book by reference to individual symbols studied).

(*) Clearly, *Content Analysis* will also be included in all future coursework bibliographies. It is the up-dated version of Berelson's classic, incorporated as such in a major social science reference work. Equally clearly, *Communication Content*, successor to *Trends* and like it a milestone, will also become required reading for students of content analysis.

** When trying to acquire the technique of content analysis, readers of a Liberal Arts background may find it helpful to have a social science reference work available. Sometimes an unfamiliar expression or mode of thought will occur in connection with a study employing content analysis. Or maybe social science techniques, theories or findings are referred to by a content analyst. A reference work which has in practice repeatedly been found useful for supplying such background information is the set of readings edited by Maccoby, Newcomb and Hartley.

Introduction

This is a work of despecialization, in two ways. Content Analysis is nowadays a specialism within a specialty. It is a highly developed special purpose technique used by experts, and it is generally found largely within the disciplines of Communications, Political Science, Psychology and Social Anthropology. This book tries to show that the technique is intelligible to the non-expert, and that it is applicable in *any* discipline which has to deal with written materials or literature. To do this job, the special terminology of content analysis has been, I hope, rendered into plain English. And the practical uses to which the technique can be put have been set out in terms as plain and basic as the matters under discussion would allow.

Content analysis is a technique which aims to improve the quality of the inferences we make. It is based on analyzing communications, be they verbal, written or even pictorial. It analyzes by objectively and systematically picking out characteristics in specified parts of those communications. And it involves demonstrating how these characteristics are related to our inferences. Most of us, presumably, have had qualms about the tricks our attention and memory can play when we are reading impressionistically. This book is written for people who want to be objective and systematic when they are reading in search of evidence on which to base a case. For content analysis ensures that *all* relevant material (*contra*, as well as *pro*) is collected in our reading. And it relentlessly forces awareness of the way we go about making inferences from such reading.

For detailed analysis of what we read, the only training most of us ever get is in précis writing at school. We go through life acquiring ever greater sophistication in regard to concepts. But we make do, for analytical purposes, with our school-day skills in précis. Content analysis is a technique evolved in the adult world of literary criticism, newscasting, military intelligence and psychiatry. It is the sequel to précis and moves our analytical skills on to a new level. Instead of the various little analytical ruses we tend to acquire by dint of rule-of-thumb experience, it provides us with a well-thought-through *system* for the analysis of complex bulk communications. This system is geared to the kind of information retrieval problems we have so commonly to deal with in our everyday lives. Content analysis is thus of enormous and quite basic significance.

My experience is that two kinds of people have been particularly interested in content analysis. One kind consists of final year students or beginning postgraduates in Arts. Such students keep telling me that they wish they had been informed about the technique earlier. It would have helped them enormously in their earlier student days, they invariably say. (It can be used on anything from an essay to a Ph.D. thesis.) Anyone who is working hard on documents gradually works out for himself something like this technique, in its more rudimentary forms. But this 'working out' can take years. So it is quite irritating to discover that what is involved is a technique which can be taught in a matter of weeks. Consequently, the book aims to fill this felt need. It is primarily aimed at students, both undergraduates and graduates, particularly those in Arts courses.

But there is a second kind of person who shows keen interest in the technique. This is the sort of person who is aware that the Social Sciences are currently reshaping our thought-world. Everyday experience indicates that it is increasingly impossible to assess social phenomena without knowledge of social science concepts and techniques. It is quite difficult to read through the welter of social science publications so as to attain an overall grasp of a technique like content analysis. For the boundaries between this technique and other approaches are becoming daily more blurred. Inevitably, additional background information must be acquired. Specialist works on content analysis, for instance, assume that readers already know how to perform multivariate analysis. This book is written with this problem, and second kind of reader, very much in mind.

So it has an important secondary aim, as well as an important secondary target audience. Its primary aim is to make content analysis more quickly and easily understandable and more widely known. For it is simply because content analysis is not much known that it is not much used currently—outside the Social Sciences. The secondary aim of the book, on the other hand, is to show in a practical way how various social science techniques can be used in literary, historical or humane studies. This information should enable a reader to identify the variety of social scientist he should approach, if he wants to acquire further skills particularly appropriate to his own concerns. Many students, in my experience, are much helped by having the ice so broken for them.

Clearly, the book assumes that the Arts and Social Sciences are interrelated, not inimical. Such assumptions are not shared by all Arts scholars. Nor is the introduction of what may be seen as a radically new approach likely to pass without objection. Heavy intellectual investments in the Conventional Wisdom are, after all, at stake. So the book has to take a third audience tacitly into account.

Its members cannot, experience indicates, be won over by 'diplomatic' presentation of this book's subject matter. Moreover, diplomatic presentation produces unnecessary complexity in setting out what is already a difficult subject. Account has been taken of this third audience mainly by outlining criticisms which have, in my experience, come from traditionalists and intuitivists. Such are the criticisms most likely to come the way of the readers for whom this book is intended.

This review of stock criticisms occurs in chapter 1, which attempts to indicate the benefits to be gained from using the technique. Chapter 2 is fundamental for an understanding of the technique: it sets out what content analysis is — not an easy undertaking, as the technique has developed through and into a variety of forms. Chapters 3 and 4 contain background material. Chapter 3 attempts to outline what is currently known about communications phenomena, and 4 sets out to appraise the 'new look' in Psychology. Current applications of content analysis presume familiarity with such things. Chapter 5 deals with sampling, a matter of basic importance in content analysis.

Chapter 6 contains the kernel of the book. It sets out the details of how one goes about the business of analyzing a text systematically and objectively. It further relates each kind of analysis to the kinds of inferences which that analysis renders possible. Chapter 7 explains the basic essence of multivariate analysis. For, unless the influence of one factor can be offset against another by employing a multivariate layout, it is not possible to conduct a content analysis. Chapter 8 goes on to indicate ways of applying multivariate analysis, and other patterned forms of inquiry. Chapter 9 sums up. It shows how the insights and approaches discussed in the preceding chapters are brought together when a content analysis has to be conducted. The appendix discusses various ways in which content analysis can be used to help everyday notetaking, a side issue about which students are always asking questions.

Men far better qualified than I have written books on content analysis (and you will find them mentioned frequently in this book). I have really only one qualification for writing it. I can — in fact I regularly do — teach it, to students from a variety of disciplines. And I can teach it fairly quickly and effectively (within my limits). Now, all the handbooks on content analysis are written by social scientists, and mostly by distinguished ones at that. These men control more, and more sophisticated, techniques for the analysis of social events than most of us can readily imagine. It is hard for them to forget the whole interlocking complex of concepts with which they are so familiar and start off from scratch in explaining the technique to a non-social scientist. What is 'scratch' for them tends to be some distance from where the rest of us are standing. Hence my advantage: I am not so far from scratch that I cannot remember only too well what it felt like to be standing there.

Earle Barcus, who is the authority on the teaching of content analysis, has recently reported that the technique is relatively little known, and considered to be of great difficulty, even in the Social Sciences.* What makes me think that this book will alter things in Arts? Well, first, I know of no other book on content analysis specially written by an Arts scholar for people in the general Arts area. Secondly, this book is quite modest in its aims. It simply hopes to make a beginner out of someone who, before reading it, knew nothing about the technique. It is like first gear in a car: it gets you started. Once you are off, you can soon move up to the high performance gears and areas. But without this first stage, it is not possible for a general reader to reach them. Don't take my word for it: try the latest handbook on content analysis (*The Analysis of Communication Content*) for yourself.

I'm a classicist, of sorts; an ancient historian. If you try to introduce content analysis into a field like Classics, you will not find that the Establishment hastens to incorporate it within the Conventional Wisdom. Indeed, if I had had to hold down a job in a Classics department while working on it, I probably could not have produced this book. The price of my freedom of inquiry has been eternal vagabondage. So clearly I have some rather special thanks for those who have supported me.

This book is dedicated to my wife, who has stood cheerfully by me in all my changes of jobs, countries and disciplines, calmly organizing the aftermath of a move from a tenured position or a drop in rank. The University of Manitoba has provided a uniquely supportive environment which enabled me to bring the work far on the way to completion. Two deans, Bill Sibley and Lloyd Dulmage, backed me strongly when I most needed support. Colleagues in the History department continued trusting their methods course to me. The students of that course proved at one and the same time to be my keenest critics and most vocal champions. Gordon Leckie, acting director of the university press, backed the embryo book — an act of considerable bravery, for most of its reviewers may well come from the third variety of readers mentioned above. The Canada Council, and in particular the Killam Award, provided a grant which gained for me

* See "Education in Content Analysis", pp. 539-54 of *Communication Content*, and especially pp. 549-53.

the time which has made it possible to write the book. A number of Council officers have shown great interest and understanding, but I cannot fail to record my particular gratitude to Madame Erica von Conta and Monsieur Robert Cournoyer. Without the support which I have received from the above, there would have been no book.

My intellectual debts are, as the book makes clear, great. It is difficult to know where to start; one meets so many fascinating people, with all sorts of amazing abilities. In the Center for International Studies at the Massachusetts Institute of Technology, Harold Isaacs taught me about images, Dan Lerner about 2 x 2s, Ithiel Pool about communications, and Fred Riggs about models. The work of the communications specialist George Gerbner has had a great influence on me. His findings are of arresting significance and his approach to content analysis opens up a whole new range of fresh applications. I must express my gratitude for the friendliness and helpfulness which he has shown, right from my first letter — from the rustic depths of Sussex and from a complete unknown. I would also like to express my indebtedness to the publishers' readers, and in particular to Professors F. E. Barcus and O. R. Holsti, for their constructive and illuminating criticisms. The final version is much the better, thanks to their scholarship and judgement.

There have always been fellow classicists who have encouraged me: Ernst Badian, Sister Kathleen O'Brien, Harold Reiche and Lynette Thompson in America; Edwin Judge and Godfrey Tanner in Australia; and here in Britain Robert Browning, Eric Handley, and Frank Norman. Peter Burke, the historian, is another friend who helped and encouraged.

These are not the only people who provided inspiration or encouragement, of course: a moderately full list would take another page. But, in fairness, I have to mention those to whom my debts are greatest. Just do not think that they are responsible for my inadequacies. I managed those on my own.

I would like to thank the following publishers for allowing me to quote short extracts from their publications: Addison-Wesley and Prof. O. R. Holsti (who allowed me to quote from page 14 of O. R. Holsti's *Content Analysis for the Social Sciences and Humanities*); the Macmillan Company (who allowed me to quote a definition from B. R. Berelson's *Content Analysis in Communication Research*); and the Association for Educational Communications and Technology and Dean G. Gerbner, for a diagram, figure 2 from p. 177 of G. Gerbner, "Toward a General Model of Communication", *AV Communication Review*, 4, Summer 1956. I would also like to thank the

editors of *Mosaic* for allowing me to reproduce a diagram which originally appeared in an article of mine in Volume 1, Part 1, of that journal.
My thanks go also to the Canadian Broadcasting Corporation, for
allowing me to recast, as chapter 4, what was originally a talk produced
for their 'IDEAS' series.

  I would also like to thank Mrs. Janice Gill for making a typescript out of a monumentally difficult manuscript. I owe it to her
that the notes are attached to their proper places, an achievement
for which I am sure I will not be the only one to be grateful.
Miss Leo Barclay helped cope with the flood of retyping caused by
revisions. Mrs. Janet Cameron brought the book into a final typescript
form when, engulfed again by teaching and other duties, I was beginning to despair that it could be done. To all these ladies, my thanks —
especially to Janet for her gentle bullying.

T. F. Carney,
August, 1970
Birkbeck College & the
Institute of Classical Studies,
University of London,
and
The University of Manitoba.

1

Weighing Opinions: Have *You* Any Scales?

A Basic Technique for
Systematic Inference from Communications

PROBLEMS

Suppose there is a group discussing a member of a football team. One member of the group claims that the rest are wrong in their poor opinion of the player. He argues that a prominent sportswriter in a certain influential paper is biased against the player and has influenced and misled the group. He cites three separate occasions on which, he asserts, the sportswriter has interpreted events unfairly. Someone else in the group immediately counters by recalling two occasions on which the sportswriter was — in this speaker's opinion — unduly *favorable* to the player. This second speaker claims that the sportswriter is a man of strong views, but a man who assigns praise and blame without fear or favor; that he is, in fact, fair. The whole matter now becomes merely a conflict of opinions unless someone comes up with an objective method of checking the sportswriter's comments for bias. Can you name or describe such a method?

Or suppose that a teacher or professor has been giving an account of what a certain writer thought of a particular matter — young people in Victorian society, let us say. The lecturer does have passages from the writer's works which bear out what he claims. But we are still not wholly convinced. Maybe the lecturer is biased. Maybe there is a less subjective way of assessing a writer's picture of such things than that which he has used. How good can we be at intellectual self-defence? What steps would the lecturer have to take in such a case before he could claim to have marshalled all relevant facts? Is it possible to tell when facts have been so poorly gathered together in such a case that any generalization based on them is just so much hogwash?

Most of our information comes to us at second hand. It comes in such a constant stream and in such huge volume that we generally have to rely on some authority or other to assess and synopsize it.[1] But we should know how to sift through masses of bits of information for ourselves if we want to. And we should also know how to appraise the way in which our 'authorities' go about their assessments and synopses. It is no use mistrusting anyone over thirty if it is impossible to tell when elders are trying to mislead and when they are not. He who knows how to use the technique of content analysis can be his own critic of radio, T.V. and press. The technique was initially evolved for just such a purpose.[2]

Also, if you know how to use the technique, instead of merely *suspecting* that a speaker hasn't done his homework, you can easily work it out — and tell him exactly why you are giving him such poor marks for that homework!

APPLICATIONS OF THE TECHNIQUE

Take some other examples of cases where the technique is useful. Suppose there is a choice of any one of three textbooks as background for a course. There is a way of quickly and methodically comparing what each has to offer. Do you know it? It could save expense and inconvenience, by enabling selection of the best one first time. Or suppose the task is to write an essay comparing Jones's biography of someone or other with Smith's biography of him. Thirty pages can be spent stringing together brilliant observations on how Smith differs from Jones on this point and that — and still, at the end of it all, the reader is left confused as to basic overall differences between Smith's interpretation and Jones's. Or a way of systematically contrasting one biography with another can be evolved, taking so much time in doing so, and making the writer so exhausted mentally[3] that a very limp and half-baked little essay indeed eventually results. Or use may be made of the work others have done on how to carry out such comparisons.

---

[1] This phenomenon has been termed 'the two-step flow' of communications. For a readable and significant book on this and related topics, see E. Katz & P. Lazarsfeld, *Personal Influence: The Part Played by People in the Flow of Mass Communications*, Free Press, 1955.

[2] See B. Berelson & M. Janowitz, eds., *Reader in Public Opinion and Communication*, Free Press, 1950, p. 263 (section 6, which follows, gives some excellent illustrative examples). For a more extensive survey of the development of the technique (but without illustrative examples) see *The General Inquirer*, pp. 21-23.

[3] See J. S. Bruner *et al*, *A Study of Thinking*, Wiley, 1956, chapter 4, "Selection Strategies in Concept Attainment", especially pp. 81-2.

In this case a suitable form of analysis for the Smith-Jones biographies[4] can be selected and the guts of the matter set out concisely in ten well foot-noted pages. What *does* happen in your case?

Look at this another way. Suppose the textbook chosen describes the climate of opinion at a critical point quite differently from another textbook. How is it possible to go about assessing and criticizing each description? Historians, literary and otherwise, are fond of depicting the 'mood of the times'. It may be felt that the depiction produced by some famous historian and pressed upon readers is distorted by that historian's prejudices.[5] But to translate feeling into conclusively-argued criticism involves knowing exactly how to go about reconstructing the 'mood of the times'. Those who do not have lots of company — including historians, famous and otherwise. Everyone can choose between being bemused by a history or literature textbook, like a rabbit by a stoat, or using it with discernment, like an ant milking an aphis. Outdated information is useless; so there is a need to be able to tell which bits of information are outdated. Content analysis will help enormously in this regard.

What is involved is, in short, a set of basic analytical skills which should be in the possession of anyone who wishes to make controlled use of written materials.[6] Think a moment. How many Arts students have been taught any technique for systematically extracting data from texts since they did *précis* at high school? Probably few. They have gained appreciation of new and powerful *concepts*, but they are most likely still battling along without suitably updated *technical* skills. Undergraduates in disciplines such as Political Science, Psy-

---

[4] The bibliography at pp. 265-77 of *The General Inquirer* will give some idea of the different kinds of problems and applications to which the technique has been put. This is, however, merely a skilful selection from a much larger number of studies: there were more than 1700 in 1959, 75% produced after 1940; *ibid.* p. 23. Section 2 of *The General Inquirer* contains some well-chosen illustrative samples.

[5] On "the basic problem of bias in history books" see E. H. Dance, *History the Betrayer: A Study in Bias*, Hutchinson, 1960, chapter 2, especially pp. 45-7. For a detailed study of the effects upon the history taught of the unconscious preconceptions held by its teachers, see A. B. Hodgetts, *What Culture? What Heritage?* Ontario Institute for Studies in Education, 1968, pp. 19-21 (cf. 31-4); 24-5 (& 99), and 35, n.3.

[6] Indicated by Harold Lasswell's classic little study "Why be Quantitative?" See H. D. Lasswell, *Language of Politics*, Stewart, 1949 (now available in an M.I.T. Press re-issue of 1965), chapter 3 (this study also appears on pp. 265-77 of the Berelson & Janowitz *Reader* of note 2 above). The findings are clear that impressionistic reading, in practice, does lead to overlooking relevant material: see *Content Analysis*, p. 151.

chology, Anthropology and Sociology are introduced to content analysis and other such techniques as a matter of course. Why should the
other side have all the good tools? Does a questionnaire or a folktale
really call for more skill in analysis than a Shakespearean play?

By 'a' set of analytical skills I do *not* mean 'the' set. In an analytical
tool kit, content analysis is, as it were, the hammer. A craftsman will
not get far with only a hammer — but he will not get far without one
either. Mention of a hammer, however, brings uncomfortably to mind
Kaplan's "law of the instrument". Give a child a hammer, and he will
suddenly find that everything needs hammering.[7] There are so few
well-elaborated analytical techniques known to Arts scholars that they
tend to overuse those they have. Ancient historians, for instance, use
prosopography (a form of élite studies) in and out of season, very
largely for this reason. There is no suggestion here that content analysis is an all-purpose tool, merely that, as it is basic, you should have
it to use if you need it.

In fact, as this book will show, acquaintance with content analysis
should lead to acquaintance with other techniques. It is one of a battery
of tools. Its use should lead to further additions to the rather meagre
analytical tool kit generally possessed by literary and historical craftsmen. (If you do not think this tool kit is meagre, try naming five
analytical techniques for detailed investigation of written materials.)
It is true that this learning will involve gaining some general acquaintance with work in the Social Sciences. But it is becoming increasingly
ridiculous to stay within the sometimes rather oddly defined boundaries
of one peculiar academic discipline, ignoring relevant work in adjacent
disciplines. To some, interdisciplinary awareness necessarily implies
superficiality. But there is no reason why administrative convenience
(in the form of each university department controlling 'its' discipline) and the structure of knowledge must inevitably coincide neatly
in their divisions.

DEFINITIONS OF THE TECHNIQUE

A rounded view is necessary, because mastery over a tool comes only
when its weaknesses are known. To guard against overuse, it is
important to know when not to use a technique. Sometimes another
technique can do the job in hand better. To know this involves knowing

[7] A. Kaplan, *The Conduct of Inquiry: Methodology for Behavioral Science*,
Chandler, 1964, p. 28.

[8] See B. R. Berelson, *Content Analysis in Communication Research*, Free
Press, 1952, p. 18. Probably readers will find the shortened version "Content
Analysis" (see list of short titles) easier to come by: see pp. 488-9 there.

about the other techniques. But first things first. Start by knowing what this technique is, and what it can do. Then look at its limitations. There are various definitions, for the technique is constantly being reviewed and elaborated. Chapter 2 will describe how. For the moment a rough outline will do to go on with.

Berelson (1952)[8] initially defined it as

> "a research technique for the objective, systematic and quantitative description of the manifest content of communication."

However, communication has since come to be seen not as separate messages held stationary for analysis by being 'frozen' into print, or speech, but as a flow of interactions (Lasswell's "who says what, in which channel, to whom, with what effect?")[9]

Consequently, content analysis came to be seen by Budd, Thorpe and Donohew (1967)[10] as

> "a systematic technique for analyzing message content and message handling . . . the analyst is concerned not with the message *per se*, but with the larger questions of the process and effects of communication."

This definition suggests that, as things stand, a little about related techniques such as modelling and multivariate analysis has to be known to make the fullest use of this technique.

It also means that a major concern of content analysis must be the drawing of inferences. Nobody can argue from a communication to its effects without making inferences, for instance. In fact, it is precisely this concern which distinguishes content analysis from an index, a concordance or a précis. Content analysis always involves relating or comparing findings to some standard, norm or theory. It does so to discover latent attributes (in describing a communications flow, for instance) or to infer characteristics (in analyzing personality from writings which set out that person's perceptions). Hence the definition which, of late, keeps coming to the fore:

> Content analysis is any technique for making inferences by objectively and systematically identifying specified characteristics of messages.[11]

---

[9] See Lasswell, "The Structure and Function of Communication in Society" in L. Bryson, ed., *The Communication of Ideas*, Harper & Row, 1948, p. 37.

[10] See *C.A.C.*, pp. 2 & 4.

[11] *Content Analysis*, p. 14.

But perhaps a better way of defining the technique is by explaining what it does. Think of a spotlight held unfalteringly, as a patch of light of uniform size, on one particular danseuse in a can-can line-up right through the show, in spite of all her movements. Now think of reading through a set of novels with a question about their author in mind. You start by looking for one set of things and gradually, unconsciously, revise this set as your familiarity with the writer grows. You are not always equally diligent, during the course of any one interrupted day or of some particularly boring chapters, in looking for everything in that day's 'set of things'. Your span of attention thus expands in some areas and contracts in others. Your focus of attention sometimes sharpens, sometimes blurs, flickers or wavers. When you have finished, it is difficult to say just where you have looked and for what.

PURPOSE OF USING THE TECHNIQUE

There is nothing unusual about this; our minds are so constituted that they balk at this kind of drudgery. If we are to focus unwaveringly, we need discipline. This is what content analysis imposes. It forces us to be very conscious about just what we are looking for, and why we are looking for it — about what is sometimes called our frame of reference. It also forces us to hold this frame of reference steadfastly. Content analysis is a way of asking a fixed set of questions unfalteringly of all of a predetermined body of writings, in such a way as to produce countable results.

In a way content analysis is like a rake which has a range of heads with various arrangements of teeth. We use it to rake in all of the objects which a particular set of teeth is designed to catch, from all of the area we are raking. The teeth are chosen to suit the objects we want to rake in and the terrain from which we have to rake them. Two things are worth noting. First, a new rake is not needed for each new job of raking. The variety of available heads can be tried. When you think about it, why should anybody redo all the work which experts have put into coping with analytical problems of this kind? Not everyone is good at, or interested in, devising complex analytical procedures. Those who are not may well blunt the edge of their attention and energy by having first to cope — probably in only a mediocre fashion — with this chore. Knowledge of this technique thus enables augmenting analytical skills by using the pooled experience of people who *are* good at, and interested in, such things. It also permits concentration of efforts where they do most good. Secondly, the rake does not unconsciously select only those objects which are of interest to us, or which suit our views. It does not get sidetracked towards objects on which the writer has lavished attention, missing inconspicuous ones. *Everything* of the appropriate size or shape sticks in its teeth. We are left with a smoothly raked patch of ground in front of us and an assortment of stones at our feet. The area raked is clear for all to see, and we have got all the stones out, *all* the material with which to build our castle in the air.

The technique, in its multivariate form, also enables the sorting out of a mass of different sorts of things quickly and systematically. Multivariate analysis is the analysis of how two or more things go together. In essence it involves modifying one detail, or aspect, of a thing to see what effect this one change has upon the whole. It is thus a very basic form of analysis, and many techniques assume knowledge of it or incorporate it. Content analysis is one of these.

Imagine that someone gives you a huge bag of marbles. Some are large, some are small. Some are glossy, some are mat. All are green, but some have blue marks on them, whereas others have yellow marks. In some cases the marks are in the form of streaks, in other cases they are in the form of blotches. You have to work out how many different types of marble there are (i.e. large, glossy, blue streaked ones; small, mat, yellow blotched ones, etc.) and how many there are of each type. How would you go about doing this? It is actually very simple, if you know how. Few Arts scholars do. Try it out on a few of them.

The illustration is a trivial one. But the point behind it is not. If an historian is properly to assess the 'climate of opinion' at any period, he has to correlate many more (and much more varied) data than this. It follows that, if he is not able to sift data in the less complicated case, he will not be able to do so in the more complex one. And, in case anybody thinks the illustration too divorced from the 'reality' with which an historian has to deal, consider the following problems.

ILLUSTRATIVE EXAMPLES

The Emperor Hadrian had more than 1100 issues of imperial coinage struck for him, in four metals, during a twenty years' reign which falls into at least four major periods. How may the coins be grouped so as to discover what kinds of messages the Emperor is putting out to the various levels of society in each period? The voluminous coinages of the emperors who precede and follow him will have to be considered, to separate what is peculiar to Hadrian's policy from what is common to imperial propaganda in general at this time. In fact Hadrian appears to have reacted against the public relations themes of his predecessor, the Emperor Trajan. But his own public relations are promoted with varying intensity. The beginning and end of his reign, for instance, saw an intensification of activity — to counter current scandal mongering at the beginning and to refurbish his image at the end. Hadrian was an emperor who emphasized the role of the provinces within an Empire seen as a commonwealth. The Anatolian massif along with the Levant was predominant herein, with the older, more established provinces next in emphasis and the Dambian zone — something of a trouble spot — third. The metal which acted as medium for the largest number of his messages was orichalcum; the most favoured combination of metals was the triad gold-silver-orichalcum: he seems to have addressed himself primarily to the middle (to upper) majority.[12]

This form of enquiry, which involves depicting interrelationships in some form of matrix, is very convenient and frequently used. For instance, one historian checked natural history encyclopedias of different dates to see what changes they indicated in knowledge related to various kinds of animals, both domestic and wild — native, foreign and legendary.

The sixteenth century differed markedly from the thirteenth in the increase in informed scientific information involved. Another checked the minutes of the Royal Society at different points in the seventeenth century to record its changing emphases. There emerged: purely scientific research, topical, applied research, and research which clearly had practical applications though the researcher did not dwell on them. Less than half of the articles were devoted to pure research; in fact, marine transport was the dominant preoccupation, just leading military applications, followed by mining. Another checked through 100,000 letters written by nineteenth century railroad executives to see how different concerns (business ideas, managerial issues, relations with other bodies, social problems, etc.) were treated at different points. A literary scholar used this format in a case of disputed author-ship. Several different categories of noun were defined. Then their frequencies in the works of the two writers each thought, by a different school, to be the author of the document were compared with their frequencies in the document itself.[13] From this it became obvious that one of the two (Jean Gerson) was not at all likely to have been the

---

[12] See Carney "Political Legends on Hadrian's Coinage: Policies and Problems", *The Turtle* 6 (5), 1967, pp. 291-303.

[13] See *The General Inquirer*, pp. 51-52, and *Content Analysis*, pp. 109 (& 85-86).

author, whereas the other (Thomas à Kempis) was.

Or take the case of an archaeologist. He has dug at, or has write-ups of forty different sites from five areas around the Mediterranean and Black Sea. The sites contain from six to ten levels, involving some fifty-odd forms of artifacts in up to eight different styles for each one. He can date all of the levels in some of the sites, some of the levels in the others. He wants to find out who traded with whom and when. How should he correlate the data? If he does not know how to arrange and rearrange the data to check his hypotheses, he will simply be overwhelmed by their abundance, like a mouse with a sack full of grain streaming over it.

COMMON CRITICISMS OF THE TECHNIQUE

Possibly the most daunting experience that a newcomer to content analysis is likely to have will occur during his first one or two discussions of the technique with people who turn out to be traditionalists. The degree of emotion and hostility with which such people can react is virtually unbelievable until you have experienced it. In practice, the criticisms most commonly levelled against the technique by such people are based on misconceptions. These misconceptions generally concern what the technique is or the limits of the possible in documentary analysis. Some criticisms however are shrewd. It is best to know one variety of criticism from the other. And you will want to know what they are before you decide whether to invest time in acquiring the technique.

A balanced view of all these criticisms can be attained only with an intimate understanding of content analysis, weaknesses as well as strengths. They are discussed more fully in the summary at the end of the book. But, in case this is thought to be begging the question, a brief indication of the main lines of reply to the commonest criticisms is given at this point. You are likely to think more deeply about the issues involved if you do so at leisure rather than during a heated verbal altercation. Moreover, mulling over these criticisms is another way of seeing what is involved in content analysis. For it compels thinking about the limits of the possible in analyzing written materials.

One point should be clearly grasped at the outset. Skill at content analysis is of a wholly different nature than rhetorical skill. Debating skills are real, measurable even (by content analysis), and take time to acquire. They have taken centuries to evolve, after all. That is why they are so effective. Once manoeuvred on to ground of an expert debater's choice, you may well be lost. For instance, content analysis is a skill, like bicycling. So the sensible line of response to the "It's only what we all do" type of objection is *not* to debate the first principles/philosophy of bicycling. It is to produce the bicycle and say: "Then show me — *now*."

A better illustration, perhaps, of how a debater can set the stage for a debate involves the stereotypes concerning intuition and method. Thus discussion of content analysis often proceeds with its critic contrasting the brilliant intuitive (Arts) mind with that of the unimaginative, plodding methodologist. But analytical incompetence is no guarantee of intuitive brilliance. People can be good at both — or neither — simultaneously. And the Arts have no monopoly on brilliant intuitions. This antithesis is a piece of debating sleight of hand. Unthinkingly accepted, it will work havoc in subsequent discussion. Deeper understanding of the problems involved in literary analysis can be achieved only by moving discussion away from this points-scoring level of debate.

The commonest objection occurs in the form of the question: "But isn't this just an overelaborate way of doing what any good historian/literary scholar does intuitively anyway?"[14] It is true that certain scholars, working with great rigor in their specialized fields, have evolved something like some earlier forms of this technique. This was the case with some Germanic source-criticism in Classics, for instance. But it is extraordinarily difficult to unearth half-a-dozen studies conducted with anything like the rigor of a content analysis in any given field. Try. For in fact there is no *general* appreciation of the range and interconnectedness of the problems involved in conducting a common or garden content analysis. Try people out with one or two of the problems mentioned at the beginning of this chapter. People who are aware of these analytical problems rarely ask the above question, in fact. They tend to go straight into detailed questions on specifics, to see if the technique will help them. The common lack of appreciation of a flexible technique of wide general applicability lurking behind the methodological rigor of this or that great scholar has a consequence.[15] People in the general Arts area are still taking years of

[14] See for example the comment of H. Bloch ("A Revolution in Classical Scholarship?" *Journal of Hellenic Studies* 88, 1968, p. 136): "students of literature and historians have for generations pursued 'content analysis' as a major aim of their professions" (following a statement that "content analysis has nothing to contribute").

[15] See "Resources and Strategies in Different Areas of Application" in *The General Inquirer*, pp. 52-53 & 57-58. It is noteworthy that, although an historian made a major contribution to the major review of content analysis in the 50s (Garraty, in *Trends*), history did not so feature in the major review in the 60s.

advanced work to pick up by trial and error a technique which can be taught to beginners in a matter of weeks.

Perhaps an analogy will clarify the position. Even before Freud, great novelists and playwrights saw deeply into the workings of the subconscious. So, in a sense, everybody knew 'all' about those workings. 'All' that Freud did was was to make them a public fact. He gave ordinary people the concepts and techniques with which to discuss and evaluate those workings. In consequence, after him everybody knew about them in a qualitatively different way. So it is with the analysis of written materials following the work of the content analysts.

To use this technique with ease, there is need to be at least acquainted with what is sometimes termed the 'new look' in psychology. A brief survey of some of its findings in regard to selective perception will make it clear what is meant. Psychology is not to be equated with Freudian psychoanalytic theory, which seems to be practised nowadays almost solely in schools of literary criticism. In the last twenty years psychologists, working on how we perceive and learn things, have given us new ways of thinking about and assessing personality. The significance of these insights and methods of assessment is still but little recognized in the Arts and Humanities area. Some term those who try to introduce a little method into their work 'methodologists', and those who are committed to traditional impressionistic ways 'intuitivists'. A gulf yawns between methodologists and intuitivists. This book does not attempt to gloss over this issue. It is written with the assumption that, if you are working in an area in which the insights of the Social Sciences are useful, you had better know something about those insights.

Another objection is that certainty is not attainable by content analysis any more than it is by impressionistic reading, so that the extra labor is pointless. This is a useful red herring for a hard-pressed intuitivist with debating skills. It shifts debate to the topic of whether complete objectivity is possible. If it is seriously meant, this objection, when taken to its logical conclusion, means that only subjectivity is possible. It follows that many forms of literary analysis and literary criticism, for instance, can be only empty playing with words. Complete objectivity is not possible. But the question as to whether anyone can reach an unattainable ideal is merely a rhetorical one. In fact, analyses are strung out at various points along a *continuum* running from utter subjectivity to complete objectivity. In real life the question is whether one method of analysis is closer than another to the objectivity end of this continuum. What participants to a debate or dispute require is a method of analysis which both can agree upon because it is impartial.[16] And there can be no doubt that content analysis is far superior to reading for impression on this score (objectivity/impartiality). There can also be no doubt that it involves far more work than reading for impression — but critics do not dwell on the dangers in corner cutting.

The difference between a content analysis and an impressionistic study is as follows. In both cases the researcher immerses himself in studies of the writer's works and background until familiarity is gained. At this point the impressionist commences writing; he aims, after all, to put forward a credible account only from his viewpoint. The content analyst has still to envolve and then test his analytical infrastructure, and to conduct a rigorous investigation of the text. Only after these two further stages can he commence writing. But then he is aiming to produce findings that will stand independent inquiry by others.

Another objection is that all content analysis does is to gather facts; the making of inferences from those facts is not governed by the technique — or *any* technique, for that matter. This objection is true, but irrelevant. Before you make your inferences you have to pass all relevant facts (or as many as you can get) under review. So you will use whatever technique gives you all relevant facts (or as many as can be got). Besides, content analysis involves running a cross-check on the inferences which you draw from the facts it gives you; it has built-in controls upon the validity of your final findings.

Yet another objection is that content analysis is meant for use in the Social Sciences, and therefore it is not suitable for use in Studying Literature. Now logically such an objector cannot tell that 'it isn't suitable' until he knows what 'it' is. And he obviously does not know what content analysis is, or he would know that it is actually being used in studying subjects like history and literature.[17] At the opposite extreme is the apparently tough-minded objection that

[16] The facts of the matter are that it is often important to be able to assess documents impartially and objectively enough for others to be able to accept the assessment as a basis for joint action. For a dramatic illustration, see Lasswell's "Propaganda Detection and the Courts" in *Language of Politics*, pp. 173-232. More recently, in the Cuban Missile Crisis, analysts kept plotting the intensity and frequency of statements in the Soviet media. A 'fever curve' of dramatic increases on both counts developed. Only when the Russian missile-carrying freighter turned off course did things begin to abate, indicating that de-escalation was imminent. (Verbal communication at a conference.)

[17] For a discussion of its use in history see chapter 6 in *Trends* (J. A. Garraty on "The Application of Content Analysis to Biography and History"). For an

content analysis claims to be 'scientific' and so is mere pretentiousness. But this book does not claim that content analysis is 'scientific', merely that it is based on practical experience and that it works.

This criticism is worth thinking further about because it assumes a common, but very narrow, definition of what 'scientific' means: argument by deductive logic from universal 'laws' as first principles. This is indeed the most rigorous form of reasoning known. But it can be applied only when the subject matter allows. About 5% of our human experience, at most, falls into this class. With a definition like this, medical science can be defined as 'not scientific'. The facts of the matter are that there are logical ways of reasoning about probabilities, and most of our reasoning concerns probabilities. These are the *only* ways to reason 'best' about probabilities. Content analysis is in accordance with them. Before starting to analyze social phenomena, it is as well to know what kinds of analysis are actually possible.[18] Most people do not. This objection belongs in the never-never land where 'what is ideally desirable' may be found.

Another objection is that content analysis, by focusing attention, restricts it. But any form of inquiry, even the most impressionistic, restricts attention. The choice is between restricting it consciously or unconsciously. If you are conscious of what you are doing, you will be more aware of restrictions. And with content analysis you are highly conscious. This generally cannot be said of impressionistic or intuitive approaches.

Yet another objection is that a written document, by its very nature, is only part of the total 'message' conveyed, and so content analysis cannot deal with it. For, by the time the stage of 'Will you put that in writing?' has been reached, what has passed is so charged with emotion as to make every phrase of the subsequent document pregnant with hidden significance. This is true. In fact it is a truism: *all* forms of inquiry into documents are restricted by this fact. Thus it is a general constraint, not a criticism of one specific method. Content

application to literature see A. B. Ellis and F. A. Favat "From Computer to Criticism: An Application of Automatic Content Analysis to the Study of Literature", chapter 23 of *The General Inquirer* (on Huckleberry Finn), and Holsti's comments on "literary detectives" at *Content Analysis*, pp. 85-87. For an application to all three together see M. U. Martel and G. T. McCall, "Reality-Orientation and the Pleasure Principle: A Study of American Mass-periodical Fiction (1890-1955)", in Dexter & White, *People, Society and Mass Communications*, pp. 283-333.

18 These limits are well set out in E. J. Meehan, *The Theory and Method of Political Analysis*, Dorsey, 1965; see chapters 3 to 4, and note especially pp. 49 & 123-4.

analysis can tell things about a document that the writer of that document was not aware of. In fact, through content analysis a deeper and more detailed case study of a document can be made than is generally possible through an impressionistic approach. Also, content analysis attempts to analyze documents by setting them in their context in a flow of communications. So background factors, such as those intimated here, are forced into the foreground.

Finally there is the criticism that subjectivity is built into the actual procedures of content analysis. This is an insider's criticism, not that of an intuitivist. You have to know a lot about content analysis before you can identify specific weak points: it is the content analysts themselves who make this criticism. This criticism involves an overgeneralization, but it is valid in some respects. Though some forms of content analysis (for example, of frequency and contiguity) are very rigorous, others (of intensity, for instance) are less so. It is these 'others' which are being called in question. But content analysts generally use more than one form at a time to offset this.

The facts are that one wide range of applications of this technique produces results which outside or further evidence shows to be valid. For instance, in World War II it was possible to calculate how success-ful military intelligence had been in anticipating or interpreting enemy action from content analysis of enemy communications. Success was impressive: 101 out of 119 inferences (better than 5 out of 6) in one two-month period.[19]

Another range is known inherently to involve more subjectivity. It is easy to damn the whole technique by concentrating criticisms upon the latter range. In actual practice we have to cope with the job in hand with the best tools we have. Demanding ideal tools is a posture found only among those criticizing in the abstract. Now analysis can be only as 'objective' as the subject matter and the questions to be posed will permit. In practice, the 'best' analysis of a given document is that analysis which is as rigorous as circum-stances allow. The trick is to know just how much objectivity circumstances allow. And people keep finding ways of being objective in situations where this was once not thought possible. The answer to this criticism therefore is that it is partly true, but it is becoming less so as the technique evolves. The 'bugs' are being worked out of the machinery, as it were.

When you think over all these objections, two things become clear. First, when all the objections are gathered together, it becomes ap-

[19] See *Content Analysis*, p. 70.

parent that content analysis is being criticized uniformly for its lack of rigor. The implication is that it does not cope as well as some other way could. But no 'other way' is ever mentioned. The hard fact is that there *is* no other way. Quite simply, content analysis is the best technique we have for doing this kind of thing. Methodically speaking, it is content analysis or nothing. Impressionism or intuitivism is the negation of method. Especially in the heat of debate, it can fail to be noticed that every criticism levelled against content analysis applies, with additional force, to impressionistic approaches. These do not seriously try to meet the real difficulties indicated by the objections levelled against content analysis. If we are going to analyze documents in the ways described at the beginning of this chapter (and we all, inevitably, will, some time or other), and if we want to do so as logically as possible, there is no alternative but to use content analysis.

The second thing that becomes clear involves objectivity, or the limits of the possible, where analysis of written material is concerned. Whatever the method employed, objectivity is obviously an ideal goal rather than something normally attained. Content analysis does not ensure absolute objectivity, though relatively it is far more objective than impressionistic approaches. So it is as easy to overclaim on its behalf as it is to overcriticize. The fact that, in its field, it is the best tool we have should not blind us to its imperfections. There is a more comprehensive discussion of these elsewhere in the book. But a brief account will be given here.

LIMITATIONS OF THE TECHNIQUE

The technique is limited by the following constraints. Of their nature, the materials on which it must work tell only part of the story behind them. The technique can focus only on some of their aspects in any one study. 'Scientific' deduction is not normally possible, and so the inferences of content analysis are probabilistic. These are constraints, of course, which apply to any form of analysis of communications. Limitations specific to content analysis are as follows.

A content analysis will produce data in answer to a question. But it will not produce the question. And, if the initial question is a poor one, the content analysis will turn out to be mere busy work. There is little need to tell a content analyst that it takes brilliant intuition to think up a question. As he knows only too well, all the technique does is make that question 'operational', that is, capable of being tested in some way which will show whether the data do or do not support it. He also knows, from experience, that a content analysis is only as sensitive as he himself is. For the more he knows about the subject, about the written materials, and finally about content analysis itself, the better his investigation. A content analysis can be conducted only when much is known about the subject matter and background of the inquiry. Content analysis is an art. As such, it cannot be better than the craftsman who employs it. To change the tool in our simile, the greatness of his sculptures is owed to Michelangelo, not to his chisel. But he could not have done them if he had only his finger-nails to work with.

To sum up: impressionistic reading and inferring produces slipshod results. Content analysis gets infinitely better results, but at the cost of infinitely more painstaking labor. True, some forms of content analysis involve less work than others. It is easier to perform a word count or a count of spatial and typographical emphases than it is to do a count of the occurrence of a complicated theme, for example. But the kind of inference possible is related to the kind of content analysis employed. Simple, straightforward counts most often allow only simple, straightforward inferences. The benefits to be gained have to be offset against labor costs involved. Sometimes these are prohibitive, given the actual time at the analyst's disposal.

Besides, sometimes the materials involved are too flimsy or un-representative for analysis to have a chance of producing valid results. This limitation applies to an impressionistic study too, of course; but, in the case of a content analysis, there is no escape from the fact. If the sample is unsound, the findings will be too, however skilfully they are produced. To put it bluntly, you cannot always use content analysis.

Much depends on the nature of the question which you want to ask. Some questions are simply too fuzzy to be redefined in such a way as to allow any form of 'counting'. These are few. More frequently the difficulty is that a question may involve the use of themes as units for counting. Sometimes themes can be most difficult to identify uniformly. Yet they can easily become distorted if broken down into their component parts for sure identification. A balance has to be struck between two things. One is the rigorousness with which counting is done, and hence the certainty that absolutely everything is identified accurately. The other is the significance of the things being counted. Typically, significant findings go with in-depth analyses, and these rarely involve counting what is obvious and thus easily countable. Skill in applying content analysis can make a great deal of difference in this respect. It can mean being able to manoeuvre until a more rigorous form of content analysis than seemed initially possible can be employed.

'Balance' is in fact the operative word. Use of content analysis calls for judgement. There is need for the ability to say 'no' when a project is impracticable. Even more important is the self-discipline to keep striving for a better question and a better way of posing it. Standards, too, must be very carefully chosen. For inferences can be only as good as the standards or theories against which data are compared. This quest can well involve lengthy foraging expeditions into new fields or related disciplinary areas, if the study is a major one. Devising a content analysis generally involves far more time than is normally budgeted when someone with an Arts background undertakes an inquiry. You get more out of your content analysis only because you have to put so much more into it.

ADVANTAGES OF THE TECHNIQUE

Let us conclude by answering the question "what use is content analysis?" at a general level. First, you can be sure what you have been looking for and where you have been looking for it. This sureness about facts is the basic advantage conferred by the technique. Using it, you adopt an investigative frame of mind: instead of seeking facts to prove or disprove an hypothesis, you are simply recording details each in itself too insignificant for you to be able to see — and therefore be biased by — its meaning. Only when you have all the facts can you see which are emphasized most, which least; only when all the facts are in can you see what *is not* there.

Secondly, the reader can check on how the facts were obtained, because the method of procedure is explicit. He can check on the care with which the analysis was conducted. He can deal with the inferences separately. Thus it is possible to rely on and build upon a study which has used content analysis in a way which is not possible with an impressionistic study. For instance, I wished to know how the Romans' image of their past was changing as time went on. What I had to do was locate a succession of widely-read men, spaced out across a period of history. First I had to establish *all* of what each of them thought about a specific and emotionally significant part of that past. Then, upon these earlier case studies, I was able to build a survey.[20] Furthermore, a group can split up a major investigation and handle it between several.

Thirdly, familiarity with this technique widens the range of the questions which can be asked. Much has been written on the technique; there is to be drawn on a whole literature concerning the analytical stages and problems involved, and there is access to a mass of

20 See "The Changing Picture of Marius".

examples illustrating ingenious ways of applying it. Thus you may not only see ways of posing a question which you had not been able to pose objectively before, you may also come upon new kinds of question to pose. Moreover, when you know what can be done with this tool, you can be sure when it is not worth your while to attempt an investigation in the first place. Not only does this discovery save time; it can spare embarrassment. Check the reviews in any academic periodical to see what I mean.

Fourthly, those familiar with content analysis can be much more clear headed about drawing inferences. A fair range of possibilities for processing each step in the analysis has been explored; each person does not have to invent these processes for himself. Instead, you can put effort which would have gone into this into devising the most effective *combination* of processes. Thus it is possible to work out the consequences which each step implies for the inferences to be drawn from the investigation as a whole. For example, different kinds of sampling allow different kinds of conclusions. So do the units of analysis adopted. Conclusions can be only as good as the criteria used in deriving them from the data. Hence the stockpiling of information on the kinds of inferences derivable from various norms, standards of comparison, and theories. Also, strategies have been evolved from running cross-checks and back-checks on validity.

You can take your logic of inference into account, along with everything else, right from the time you start constructing your analysis. You simply cannot work all this out if you have to start from scratch. You will not see the range of possibilities open at each stage of the analysis. You will overtire yourself while computing the inferential consequences of such analytical measures as you can devise. Thus your capacity to calculate becomes overloaded before you arrive at the drawing of inferences, for this is typically the 'final' stage. Hence content analyses tend to appear so crisp in regard to their inferences. It is easier to think clearly about them when so much pre-thinking of technicalities has been done for you.

In more down-to-earth terms, if you can employ content analysis easily, you will produce better essays and projects, synopsize your reading more effectively and speedily, and make a more competent job of reviewing books. In the latter case, for instance, you can take what the writer claims in his preface to have done and conduct a little content analysis of the work to see whether he has done it. You will be alerted to the problems he should have dealt with in going about his study, and so will not fail to notice whether he has or has not actually dealt with them. For instance, I was once given an index of

Plutarch's quotations to review. Now Plutarch's quotations can be either at first- or at second-hand, for example 'Sulla says . . .' as opposed to 'Rutilius Rufus says that Metellus said . . . ' They can be unacknowledged *verbatim* quotations, a sign that every schoolboy was expected to know the writer concerned. Or they can be vague references ('it is said that . . . '), whose original source has been discovered by later scholars. The question was: how good was the index in these various categories? I know one of Plutarch's biographies very well, and so I listed all its quotations, assigning them, as appropriate, to each of the above categories. I then checked to see how well the index performed in each category, using the criterion: how many of these are mentioned?[21]

Consequently, instead of producing a review which says "I found misprints on pages such and such," you can state: "The book is methodologically sound/unsound because of . . . The author claims to have established so and so. What is actually there is in fact thus and such." You can review with speed and with confidence that you have the relevant facts at your finger tips. Think back to the last time you heard someone deliver a book report: could you say this of it?

Lastly, with facility in using the technique, it is far easier to assume a critical posture when reading a book or listening to a talk. You will not get bowled over so easily by a spate of words. All of which applies to this book too, of course. I had better set about delivering the goods, as you will be only too capable of checking on their specifications by the time you have read this book and had a little practice in applying the technique.

---

[21] See review of W. C. Helmbold and E. N. O'Neill, *Plutarch's Quotations*, *Journal of Hellenic Studies* 82, 1962, pp. 168-9.

2

Content Analysis: How to Make Documents Answer Your Questions Reliably

A Survey of the Evolution of the Technique and of its Current Forms

INTRODUCTION

As any literary or historical scholar will tell you, he has been analyzing content all his life. Ask him "How?" and you will probably not receive a coherent answer, however. Yet, if you define this technique, you will find that your description of each of its various parts will call· forth little cries of "But that's obvious!" or "But we *all* do that". That is the odd thing about content analysis. The more it changes, the more it is the same thing as what "we all do anyway" (but cannot define unaided).

Content analysts are much more sophisticated than this. After all, the specific and explicit definition of terms is a basic prerequisite of the technique they are using. Ask them to define what they do and they will tell you, without beating round the bush. However, you are likely to find yourself with several different versions of what this is — even on the latest and best authority.[1] Hence a whole chapter has been set aside for the purpose of making clear just what content analysis is. For, even though it is "what we all do anyway", you may be surprised when you discover what this is. It is certainly not like discovering that you have been speaking prose all your life.

It is so difficult to define content analysis because the technique can be used in so many different ways. It concerns the everyday problem of how to check source materials to see whether some theory or viewpoint is represented in them. People have all sorts of theories

---

[1] See *Communication Content*, pp. 11, 65 & 319 (five different definitions in all).

21

and viewpoints, and source materials come in every shape and size. So a framework of analysis flexible enough to work in all these circumstances has got to be a very many-sided and adaptable thing indeed. In fact, the only way of defining it fully is by saying: "This is how it came about, so that's why it's as it is." For the technique has largely grown as result of the uses to which it has been put, and these have changed considerably over the years.

Suppose there was a girdle which would fit anything, from a gnat to an elephant (and including an octopus). In one or other of its forms it would be bound to remind pretty well everyone of something or other he or she had seen. This is the kind of way in which we all 'know' what content analysis is. For we have each of us, probably, worked out various little analytical stratagems to cope with inquiries we have to make particularly frequently or for the infrequent ones that are especially important. So the technique will be far from entirely new. But the comprehensiveness of its details, and the reasoning behind the way it is put together, does make of it, in overall terms, something that moves our analytical abilities on to a new level.

This half-awareness seems to make for difficulty in explaining succinctly what a complicated procedure like content analysis 'really is.' If the writer does not give a full outline, he misleads some. If he does give a full outline, he confuses most. No one seems yet to have managed to explain the technique to general satisfaction. So let me proceed as simply as I can, and one step at a time. I will divide up the following explanation, so that readers can approach the topic each at his own pace. First I will set out conceptually what content analysis is. In this way we can at least, by grasping the general idea, have a basis to start from.

Secondly I will set out historically how the technique has come to its present form. For it 'just grew', and its current varieties represent different stages of its evolution. It can be surveyed only historically; one development cannot be deduced from another. Perhaps readers might regard this second section as a kind of appendix. It is arranged so that it can be omitted, or left till afterwards in the reading, if it is felt that the section only adds unhelpful complications to the explanation.

Thirdly I will define the technique operationally, by detailing what it is made up of. For it is really a sort of kit, out of which an analytical infrastructure can be built when there is some literary or communications problem to be investigated. So this third section will say: "These are the component parts, and here is how you put them together."

This assembly job leads to the fourth section, on how the technique works. For it can be assembled into quite different forms, as it were, and some forms perform markedly differently from others. Content analysis has weaknesses and strengths, depending on the way the components are assembled. Also, it can be linked with other analytical techniques which differ markedly from it and from each other. One combination of a content analysis plus some other analytical technique may appear quite dissimilar to another such combination. And, of course, neither may bear much resemblance to a straightforward content analysis on its own.

Finally, the fifth section will indicate what kinds of things, in particular, content analysis is good at doing. For it can be used on a variety of problems and for quite different purposes.

Sections 1, 3 and 5 by themselves will give a good general idea of what the technique is and can do. The addition of section 4, which presumes that sections 1 and 3 have been read and digested, will make this a detailed idea. However, as section 4 deals in detail with the intricacies of the technique, it makes rather difficult reading. Possibly readers may wish to omit it (and section 2) on the first reading of the chapter, returning to it (or them) when the general outline of the technique has been grasped.

Section 1: Defining Content Analysis

In the beginning (1952) there was Berelson's definition. This stated that content analysis was

> "a research technique for the objective, systematic and quantitative description of the manifest content of communication".[2]

In practice what this definition means is this. The question has to be defined in such a way that the answers to it can be counted ("quantitative"). For example 'Is Suetonius indulging in sly innuendo against Hadrian?' becomes 'How frequently does Suetonius employ the main concepts of Hadrian's coinage and to which of his characters (i.e. hero or villain emperors) are they assigned?' 'Counted' is used in rather a special way here. This presumes that counting with a zero point and a numerical scale is not the *only* way of counting. Rather, it is the final stage in a series of progressively more sophisticated ways

---

[2] See note 8 to chapter 1: the definition in the book is far crisper than in "Content Analysis" (see pp. 488-9). Incidentally, many of the later writers on content analysis assume that their readers are familiar with this article, for all later work is built upon it.

of counting which commence with the simple one of checking to see whether something is there or not.[3] Then all aspects of the question must be investigated uniformly, throughout all parts of a defined body of text ("systematic"). In process all data alike, pro and con, are impartially collected ("objective"). Communications are taken at their face meaning, not subjectively interpreted ("manifest"). Findings thus reveal trends or characteristics not otherwise observable because of the mass, complexity, or chaotic nature of the communications ("description").

Now this is a minimal definition of content analysis, and a defensive one at that.[4] It restricts the operations of the technique to those with the highest validity on the immediate face of things. It is also an unsatisfactory definition, because it does not reflect what was being done by content analysts even prior to 1952. Analysts were making inferences, and on non-quantitative evidence. In World War II, for instance, it was inferred from internal evidence that the Nazi and Fascist propaganda agencies were operating independently. This inference was later proved correct from captured documents. Finding that the Germans never lied to their domestic audience (though hints of future developments given to it might be cryptic), the British predicted the V 1 bomb six months in advance. It was also found that German newscasts gradually phased out mention of battlezones wherein their High Command was intending to mount a major operation. This finding enabled predictions of a new offensive to be made some three months in advance. [5]

Content analysis is not just a frequency count. Besides George's non-frequency analysis and (for computers) non-numerical questions (analysis via associational patterns), much 'pattern-fitting' is currently

---

[3] See especially the opening pages of P. F. Lazarsfeld and A. H. Barton, "Qualitative Measurement in the Social Sciences: Classification, Typologies and Indices", in D. Lerner and H. D. Lasswell (eds.), *The Policy Sciences*, Stanford U.P., 1951, pp. 155-92. See also *Content Analysis*, pp. 5-9.

[4] For an insider's criticisms, levelled against content analysis at this point, see I. L. Janis, "The Problem of Validating Content Analysis", chapter 4 in Lasswell's *Language of Politics*.

[5] The best discussion of non-quantitative evidence is that of A. L. George: "Quantitative and Qualitative Approaches to Content Analysis", chapter 1 in *Trends*. The type of evidence involved is that much used currently by Kremlinologists. In an official Kremlin pronouncement, much significance attaches to how a man's name is mentioned. Omission can be highly significant. Equally, cognizance by itself may reflect a major shift in official attitude. So may a shift in placement in a list of Heroes, or Enemies, of the People. Changes in the tone of associated remarks may, again, though slight, be all-important.

practised. Pattern-fitting involves comparing a complex set of inter-related words or views with various other model sets, to identify a mode of perception or reasoning.

If compared with an index, or a concordance or suchlike, the following difference will be found. A content analysis always aims to compare the data it extracts against some norm, standard or theory, so as to draw its conclusions.[6]

Hence the recent trend in defining it (1966 and 1969):   *deducciones*
> "Content analysis is any technique for making inferences by objectively and systematically identifying specified characteristics of messages".[7]

The differences are twofold. First, this definition postulates that the making of inferences is the major purpose of content analysis. Secondly, it does not limit data extraction to quantitative measurement. And, thirdly, it is prepared to attempt the assessment of what is 'written between the lines'. The "quantitative" and "manifest" restrictions have been dropped.

Now this is a maximal definition, and far from being a defensive one.[8] Expectably, it has occasioned controversy rather than consensus: as has been shown, the latest handbook provides a variety of definitions. Sections two and four will explain how this circumstance has come about. So content analysis can be defined by considering what, in the course of time and among the generality of practitioners, is the core of agreed meaning. The location of the zones of endemic disagreement can also be sought.[9]

All are agreed on what was described above as 'objectivity' and 'system'. The disagreements centre around the matters of inference and methodological rigor (quantification). There are some doubts as

[6] This point is well made by Holsti. See *Content Analysis*, pp. 5 and 28.

[7] This definition first appeared in *The General Inquirer* in 1966. It has been adopted in 1969 in *Content Analysis*: see p. 14. *Content Analysis* is the book version of the revised article on 'Content Analysis' in the second edition of the *Handbook of Social Psychology* (ed. G. Lindzey & E. Aronson, Addison-Wesley, 1968; see chapter 16, pp. 596-692 of vol. II). This article updates and replaces Berelson's article, and so must become the standard reference work. Hence this definition is now the standard definition.

[8] For an insider's criticisms levelled against this definition of content analysis, see K. Krippendorff in *Communication Content* (Introduction, pp. 3-16 & "Models of Messages: Three Prototypes", 69-106).

[9] For this way of arriving at a definition, see C. A. Valentine, *Culture and Poverty*, U. of Chicago Press, 1968, pp. 1-3 (where he is struggling to define 'culture'). Holsti employs it on 'content analysis' at pp. 2-14.

to the practicability of assessing latent meaning and using qualitative evidence (assessments of bias, use of themes as counting units). But the disagreements concern how far these things can be successfully done, not whether they should be done or not. The current strivings of practitioners reflect a concern to improve the ways of making inferences and non-quantitative assessments.[10]

The image of content analysis as a glorified frequency count is in fact a dated one. It reflects a preoccupation with, or an excessive predilection for, counting. This was evident in the early days of the technique. The first definition identifies what is currently called 'classical' content analysis. The second more truly reflects what goes on under the name of content analysis today. It has been my definition of content analysis while I have been writing this book.

What this second definition amounts to is as follows. Content analysis aims to help improve the quality of inferences made by analysis of communications. It concentrates attention on ways in which the various stages of analysis affect the inferences to be drawn from each of them. It also provides strategies for checking on the validity of the inferences finally made. As with the first definition, this one stresses that all relevant data must be extracted, uniformly and impartially, from all parts of the communication specified for analysis. But this definition does not involve just counting things to extract data, and it will deal with communications that are very complicated, disingenuous or nebulous. Moreover, it implicitly recognizes that some content analyses will, of their nature, have more immediate surface validity than others (see section 4).

Content analysis, then, is a general-purpose analytical infrastructure, elaborated for a wide range of uses. It is intended for anyone who wishes to put questions to communications (pictorial and musical, as well as oral and written) to get data that will enable him to reach certain conclusions. Some content analyses are more objective than others. All are more objective than impressionistic assessment of the same question and materials. None are perfectly objective, though some approach this goal remarkably closely.

Section 2: The History and Development of Content Analysis

The analytical infrastructure which content analysis provides meets an everyday need. Scholars have striven for centuries with this general

---

[10] This trend has been becoming evident for some time: see R. E. Mitchell, "The Use of Content Analysis for Explanatory Studies", *Public Opinion Quarterly* 31(2), 1967, pp. 230-241.

problem, in various guises. Content analysis is in fact built upon, and is a development of, such strivings. As most classicists would tell you, their German colleagues had already in the nineteenth century evolved something rather like classical content analysis. This development occurred in their researches into the sources behind their texts.[11] As most content analysts readily admit, there is evidence of sophisticated analysis, of religious texts and concepts, dating as far back as 1744.[12] In arguing about cases of disputed authorship, analyzing stylistics, or looking for the sources of a writer's ideas, literary criticism produced, at one time or another, many an analytical insight now incorporated in content analysis. Hence the feeling among some literary scholars that content analysis holds nothing new for them.

But the technique as such, in the form of a body of interrelated analytical tactics under the name content analysis, came out of studies of newspapers in schools of journalism. Newspapers are so very *countable*. They come out in series. Their pages are set out in space units. Their news is easily divisible into categories. They cover a vast range of issues, at length. Studies first employing the technique began at the beginning of the twentieth century.[13] Hence the stress on systematic, objective and quantified description of manifest content. The accurate and reliable identification of trends or biases amid such a welter of communications was an achievement in itself. But the engrossment of early researchers in counting gave the technique a bad name. (It was not helped by its origin, in the view of Literary Critics of the disciplinary Establishment.) For though descriptive studies have high and immediately apparent validity, they often establish merely what is fairly obvious or probable.

However, source materials and method combined to make nice clean crisp research projects, and the numbers of studies grew. After a slow start in the first twenty years, there was an enormous increase

[11] This is an overstatement. It ignores the faults endemic in *Quellenforschung*: flights of inferential fancy and poor judgment as to what constituted an adequate sample. Parts of some of this research were analytically shrewd, but these were not systematically separated from those which were the reverse. No overall technique was evolved. It was rather a matter of having a discontinuous variety of rule of thumb analytical stratagems available.

[12] The work always cited in this connection is that of K. Dovring. See "The Annals of Science: Troubles with Mass Communication and Semantic Differentials in 1744 and Today", *American Behavioural Scientist* 9, 1965, pp. 9-14.

[13] Our knowledge of the development of content analysis as a technique is owed primarily to the work of F. E. Barcus. See *Communications Content: Analysis of the Research, 1900-1958*, Ph.D. Thesis, University of Illinois, 1959. The best short discussion of trends in research employing content analysis occurs in *Content Analysis*, pp. 20-23.

— more than fivefold — in the twenties in studies employing content analysis. This increase continued, if at a more restrained pace of some 50% overall, in the thirties.

World War II did for content analysis what World War I did for I.Q. testing. It was pressed into service first for the analysis of propaganda, then for military intelligence purposes. The making of inferences by the technique now came to be heavily stressed. So the technique itself began to be more critically examined by its users. The work of Harold Lasswell, in this as in other respects, provided new insights and direction. His and his associates' book, *Language of Politics*, (1949) proved to be a milestone in the development of the technique. The writing of books upon the technique in fact commenced in the decade of the forties. This was to lead to a rapid increase in the sophistication of content analysts. Studies employing the technique increased massively in numbers, too, almost doubling.

Major development occurred in the fifties and sixties. Berelson's handbook on the technique brought it widespread attention, and enabled systematic, focused analysis to proceed.[14] Issues and problems became starkly apparent. To facilitate discussion, which had by now become interdisciplinary, a full scale conference was held and its findings published. This was to become a practice, every decade. The first conference took place at the University of Illinois in Monticello in 1955. The book which resulted from it was *Trends* (1959). The second conference took place at the University of Pennsylvania in 1967. The book which resulted was *Communication Content* (1969). Studies employing content analysis now began to investigate other things than the subject matter of communications, a topic which, up to now, had engrossed most attention. Moreover a significant proportion of studies, more than a tenth of them in fact, began consciously to take account of the theoretical and methodological problems involved in content analysis.

Use of the technique became common in other areas than Communications. There was much use of it in Sociology, Anthropology, Social Anthropology and Political Science. But possibly the appreciation of its potential by Psychology was to have most impact on its subsequent development. Anyway, there was an enormous increase

---

[14] The handbook was, of course, *Content Analysis in Communication Research*, (1952). This appeared, in an abridged form, in G. Lindzey's *Handbook of Social Psychology* under the title "Content Analysis" (1954). Thus a standard social science reference work had given the technique recognition and made it easily available to a wide audience. This accomplishment made the chapter *the* basic study on content analysis.

in studies employing content analysis, which more than doubled. This exponential rate of growth saw more use of the technique in the fifties than in the whole of the preceding half century.

There are all the signs that something of this rate of growth has carried over into the sixties. Precise statistics are not available, as the period postdates Barcus' invaluable study. Certainly, the rate of production of handbooks on content analysis — and good ones, too — has increased. The single most striking development of the sixties, as far as the technique of content analysis is concerned, proved to be the advent of the computer.[15] This facility forced analysts to be much more aware of the problems involved in the logic of the inferences behind their studies. It also revealed the structure of language, and brought Psycholinguistics and Sociolinguistics to the fore. The influence of semantics on content analysis has been profound. Indeed, so much do the assumptions and insights of semanticists underlie and inform the technique, that it is not fully understandable for those lacking some acquaintance with semantics. Within these special areas, content analysis flourished particularly strongly.

It was the emergence of such special areas, in fact, that brought about marked changes in the thought-world of content analysts in the fifties and sixties. In what follows a brief sketch of this thought-world is presented. A series of interlocking developments in the social science area in general brought new ways of dealing with long-standing technical problems. They also made it easier to relate a content analysis to a theoretical framework. These developments were quickly seized upon. Content analysis is not a 'discipline' in the sense that History or Classics is. Rather it is a technique of analysis used by several disciplines in common.[16] Content analysis is a skill whose leading practitioners are unusually alert men, sensitive to changes in their intellectual environment and quick to exploit the possibilities in them. Hence its current, diversified nature. What actually happened was something like the following.

First came the discovery by the behavioralists of what is now known as authoritarianism. This is a type of personality characterized

---

[15] The first handbook to describe computerized content analysis was that by R. C. North *et al*, *Content Analysis: A Handbook with Applications for the Study of International Crisis* (1963). Holsti, one of the joint authors, was the major author of the chapter on computerized content analysis. The main handbook on this variety of content analysis is, of course, *The General Inquirer* (1966). Already by the time of the 1967 conference it was evident that this variety was going to prove enormously important for the future development of the technique.

[16] See *The General Inquirer*, pp. 44-60.

by a particular set of attitudes on a particular variety of subjects. An authoritarian will tend to think in stereotypes and in a highly conventional way on subjects such as patriotism, religion and morality. This pattern will emerge strikingly in his views on art, change and deviants. His attitude to authority figures will be ambivalent, a mixture of submission before and repressed resentment against them. He will, however, be imperfectly aware of such ambivalence, as inconsistencies tend to be repressed in his thinking. This thinking will be characterized by a predilection for power and toughness, shown particularly in views on out-groups, and in a picture of the world that is rather bleak and threat-filled. Views on chance should reveal a tendency towards projection: the world 'out there' is filled with wild goings on. Other such personality types have also been identified. There is one, for instance, going with a striking 'need to achieve'.[17]

This is a psychology of a wholly different nature from that of Freudian psychoanalysis. With Freudianism, if a man said something, he meant either what he said or its opposite — and deciding which is notoriously difficult with long-dead, unpsychoanalyzable personages. With authoritarianism or need achievement or the like, either one finds the very striking and distinctive pattern of characteristics, a syndrome, or one does not. There is no need to go interpreting what a writer's words 'really' mean. And, whichever way the results turn out, there is a finding. The results also include a set of categories, namely the set of characteristics. These are derived from practical experience. They are wholly independent of the analyst. And they can easily be fitted into the content analysis.

Authoritarians perceive their own special version of reality, it was found. For perception *is* personality, as Rorschach said. Thus came the end of the 'age of immaculate perception' — the age in which it was possible to believe that a person's picture of reality is a sort of

---

[17] Arts scholars always 'knew' all of this already, of course. Actually we all 'know' (in the sense that we realize that we have hazily been aware of) the basic things about ourselves which are 'discovered' by someone providing them with a name and a set of ways for testing for them. Only after he has done this, however, do we know them with clarity and conscious awareness. Those who discovered authoritarianism were T. W. Adorno *et al*, *The Authoritarian Personality*, Harper, 1950. This book has been significantly expanded by Rokeach's *The Open and Closed Mind*. On the 'need to achieve' see D. C. McClelland, *The Achieving Society*, Van Nostrand, 1961, chapters 2 and 7. To see how well McClelland's thesis has stood the tests of time and critical review, see N. Kogan and M. A. Wallach, "Risk Taking", especially pp. 173-90, in G. Mandler *et al*, *New Directions in Psychology III*, Holt, Rinehart and Winston, 1967.

photographic copy of what is perceived. For it proved readily demonstrable that such pictures are always highly selective versions of what
is there to be perceived. It also proved readily demonstrable that the
sets of assumptions and beliefs through which we thus selectively
perceive our various 'realities' are not randomly built up and each
unique. There are uniformities in them, just as there are uniformities
in the human experience and condition. For we all go through the
same human maturation processes; and we are all alike in that we
grow up within the institutions and customs of some group or other.
Thus we tend to perceive social and other realities in the ways usual
for our group.

Now these images of reality may be conscious or unconscious. An
image that we are conscious of is generally called a 'model' nowadays.
A psychologist has a model of personality, an economist of the
economic process. A group of interrelated concepts is involved, along
with some ideas on how they mesh together. The model is used to
provide guidelines for working or experiments. Specialist groups produce such models; larger social groups are sometimes aware of them
and how to use them, sometimes not.[18] All social groups have *unconscious* images of reality, however. All sorts of things that we simply
take for granted are involved here, such as attitudes to time and
space. These are more important than one might at first think. An
aborigine can make his way through a trackless desert, an Eskimo
through an apparently featureless, horizonless white world. Put a
townee European in a similar plight, and he will be dead within hours.

These unconscious images have other components, too: views on
causation and human relationships, for instance. It is these images,
shared by those who have experienced similar upbringings, which
enable us to look into the thought-world of a people and a period.
One way of doing this is by 'psychobiography', discussed more fully
in chapter eight. That is the looking for patterns of similarities in the
pictures of this or that aspect of reality held by groups of ordinary
men. The viewpoints and values of different groups in society thus
become visible.

---

[18] It takes a set of scientific insights fifty years to become a commonplace
in the thought of an industrial society. By this time the ideas have usually
become outdated or set on one side by the scientific community which originated them. Models are abstract, summary representations of the picture of
that aspect of reality which scholars in this or that discipline are investigating.
By informing ourselves about the current state of those which relate to problems on which we are working, we can thus, to some degree, avoid the time-lag
just outlined.

Words were found, too, by the psycholinguists, to influence perception. Not as dramatically as Whorf had asserted, maybe, but significantly: what becomes conscious is what we have words for, and organization of that consciousness is further dependent on the words available in our personal vocabularies. Words make the objects they label more accessible to consciousness, and thus highlight certain aspects of the buzzing, blooming confusion outside our skins. They also, by their availability, facilitate and guide us in organizing our thinking about that outside reality.[19] To work on words, computers were brought in; to work with computers, new techniques of correlating things were evolved. All these developments aided content analysts, whose business is so largely with words.

Language suddenly revealed its structure. Do you know what percentage of your vocabulary is taken up by its ten commonest words? 10%? 25%? 50%? 25.4%, actually. A person's fifty commonest words make up 50% of his verbal output and, on the average, a writer's three hundred commonest words make up 60% of his output. All sorts of new approaches became possible with the realization of how much similarity there is in the structure of the vocabulary of a speech group. The language of a period can be taken and, after setting aside the vehicular words, the rest can be listed in order of frequency. The rest are surprisingly few, in cases involving high frequency of usage. Then the same can be done for a writer of the period. Contrast the individual with the group and all sorts of subliminal preoccupations stand out. It is rather like aerial photography of an archaeological site.[20] The range of meanings which a writer assigns to a word or the particular set of other words which he chooses to associate with it can in this way become telltale clues about his likes and dislikes.

Moreover, a computer can be asked *non*numerical questions. It will readily print out twenty words on either side of the one which is being studied. If the print-out reveals that a certain other word frequently occurs with the one in which the analyst is interested, the computer can be asked to give all cases of the co-occurrence of the

[19] See J. B. Carroll, *Language and Thought*, Prentice-Hall, 1964, chapters (6 &) 7, and also K. Postman and C. Weingartner, *Linguistics: A Revolution in Teaching*, Delta, 1966, chapters 6 & 9.

[20] For statistics concerning the structure of vocabulary see *The General Inquirer*, pp. 164-5 (& 33) and *Communication Content*, pp. 135, 163-4 & 166-7. Such patterns hold for other languages than English, and other times than those of today. See H. Delatte, "Key Words and Poetic Themes in Propertius and Tibullus", *Revue* 3, 1967, pp. 31-33; this article splendidly illustrates the text, and I owe to it the 'aerial photography' simile.

two words as a percentage of all cases involving the occurrence of the first word. This process can be extended by asking: 'Does this word or this one go along with the other two, and does this one never occur in their vicinity?'[21]

And incidentally, with a computer there are no problems of wavering, or being partial, or using too much discretion on the part of the person doing the sorting out of the words. However, there are many problems in designing a program and in preparing texts so that the computer can handle them. But, in overall terms, the use of computers has solved more problems than it has created. Scholars have simply had to invent new techniques for analyzing clusters of things, to get the genie out of the computer and put him to work.

Study of how language is actually used has shown that 'common sense' assumptions are often not very helpful. Such findings, and the computers with which they became available, have helped lead to a change in focus in the study of communications. Initially, it will be remembered, it was to the study of mass communications that content analysis owed its beginning. Newspapers, as has been seen, are so easily countable as source materials. Score can be kept of column width and size, type of headline, size of typeface, illustrations, position on page (and which page), and many such factors. And there are series, runs of data, to work with. Hence, at the outset, there was a preoccupation with the question: 'What's there, and in what proportions?' But the question changed to 'How do people use the media?' For it was becoming apparent that the way in which people actually use communicated information differs rather strikingly from the way they say they use it. For instance, people actually read car advertisements *after* they have bought their cars, to still the misgivings which are normal in the wake of any major decision taken in conditions of uncertainty. It became increasingly apparent just how complicated the whole business is.

This finding implies that it is just no good looking merely at the actual message. It has to be seen in an environment, or, as Lasswell

---

[21] On the nonnumerical question, see P. H. Goldhamer, "Toward a More General Inquirer: Convergence of Structure and Context of Meaning", *Communication Content*, p. 345. An excellent example of what is discussed in the text can be found in A. B. Ellis & F. A. Favat, "From Computer to Criticism: An Application of Automatic Content Analysis to the Study of Literature", chapter 23 of *The General Inquirer* in which it appears that, for Huck Finn, the concept "pop" was associated with the words "animal" and "death". For an impressive example of the same kind of analysis, done without a computer, see J. H. Hexter, "The Loom of Language", *American Historical Review* 69, 1964, pp. 952-58.

put it, the question is "Who says what, in which channel, to whom, with what effect?" This approach involves thinking of communications as flows set inside systems of action and reaction, and liable to particular forms of stresses and strains.[22] It thus became evident that the mere nature of the processes of communication puts pre-print man in a wholly different thought-world from his successor who is blessed with possession of the mass media. Theories on just how different have even been put to the test by the experience of the developing nations, and some generalizations have emerged which seem to hold regardless of time and locality.[23]

As a consequence of all this, attention ceased to be narrowly focused on the mere verbal communication itself. A wider view had to be taken, an attempt made to assess the total communications process and situation. Several important results followed. A wider view came to be taken of what constitutes a 'communication' for purposes of content analysis. Pictorial and musical materials thus began to be considered. Communications from different media might be studied in the one content analysis. Studies in one medium (films or television) might be employed to corroborate the findings of a content analysis of a different medium (newspapers or periodicals). For experience in analyzing communications flows showed that not one, but a battery of techniques had to be deployed. Content analysis had long been used in common by several disciplines. Now it came to be used in common with several disciplined methods of inquiry. It was no longer chauvinistically seen as a self-sufficient method of inquiry, to be used independently. Rather, it appeared as just one among many related techniques. It came to be integrated with other

[22] For the quotation, see chapter 1, note 9. For a good illustration of how this framework works when it is applied, see D. Easton, *A Systems Analysis of Political Life*, Wiley, 1965, part 2, a discussion of government in terms of the communication-flows which are involved in making decisions.

[23] A magnificent illustration of the difference between the perceptions of pre-print and of mass media man is given by M. McLuhan, *The Gutenberg Galaxy*, U. of Toronto, 1962, pp. 36-7. J. T. Dorsey tries to indicate what the differences are systematically in his study "An Information-Energy Model", in G. Heady & S. L. Stokes (eds.), *Papers in Comparative Public Administration*, U. of Michigan, 1962, pp. 37-57. F. W. Riggs does so via two 'ideal types' in his study "Agraria and Industria: Toward a Typology of Comparative Administration", in W. J. Siffin (ed.) *Toward the Comparative Study of Public Administration*, Indiana U. Press, 1957, pp. 23-116. D. Lerner looks at the actual experience of Anatolian tribesmen, moving from conditions like those of antiquity into the electronic age, in chapters 2 & 3 of *The Passing of Traditional Society*, Free Press, 1957; see also L. W. Pye (ed.), *Communications and Political Development*, Princeton, 1963, e.g. pp. 24-29.

techniques, or employed for one stage of the inquiry, within the framework of a larger investigation.

There was criticism, too, of narrowly focused content analyses. These, especially if of the 'classical' variety, might be little better than semiclerical assessment of surface phenomena in communication.[24] To interpret the mood of an age, for instance, the analyst has to be able to perceive the implicit assumptions below the threshold of mass awareness in its media. He might, for instance, investigate the kinds of human relationships that underlie the postures and social positions of personages depicted in travel advertisements. What proportions of what age-groups, races and sexes travel where, and with what expectations of service, friendliness and cultural or professional superiority, etc.? This task involves a critical awareness both of the self and of the whole perceptual process. Content analysis must be approached from a new perspective, one springing from a consciousness in depth of issues that are normally outside of awareness.

'Outside of awareness', indeed, might well describe much that has gone on in content analysis in the sixties. Few beyond a small group of specialists, almost exclusively social scientists, have any appreciation in depth of recent developments in the use of the technique. Probably as result of the tremendously increased sophistication of the technique, the content analysts are having difficulty in explaining it

---

[24] See G. Gerbner, "On Content Analysis and Critical Research in Mass Communication" in L. A. Dexter and D. M. White (eds.), *People, Society and Mass Communications*, Free Press, 1964, pp. 488-499. The work of this scholar is particularly important, because of his findings and because of the skilful and flexible ways in which he employs the technique. Gerbner expressly considers the influence which the media exercise in our complex society upon the terms in which communication proceeds. They shape our conscious thoughts and our unconscious assumptions. Hence his focus on the underlying assumptions with which the whole message system is permeated. The importance of Gerbner's work for this book will be evident in the numerous references made to it and the illustrations taken from it. No short selection of his writings can do justice to him or his thesis, but three articles are particularly insightful. One is that already cited. The others are: "Toward 'Cultural Indicators': The Analysis of Mass Mediated Public Message Systems", chapter 5 in *Communication Content*, and "Cultural Indicators: The Case of Violence in Television Drama", *The Annals of the American Academy of Political and Social Science* 388, 1970, pp. 69-81. The latter paper appeared in an earlier version which contains a more comprehensive discussion of methodological issues and so is, in this respect, not superseded by the later version: "The Case for Cultural Indicators, with Violence in the Mass Media as a Case in Point", (revised) paper to the American Political Science Association's 1969 meeting (Mimeo, Annenberg School of Communications, U. of Pennsylvania, 1969).

to outsiders.[25] Outsiders lament that it is becoming increasingly impossible to read social science publications. Though once these were intelligible, advancing specialization has led to such an increase in jargon that they are progressively becoming no longer intelligible. Outsiders may in fact be relatively less aware now than they were a decade ago of what the technique can, potentially, help them to do. Arts scholars contributed proportionately far less to the 1967 symposium on content analysis than they did to that of 1955, for instance. There was *no* historian among the contributors to the second symposium, although clearly this technique is splendidly suited for use on historical materials.[26]

Knowledge of content analysis, where it does exist among Arts scholars, tends to be dated. It is generally confined to Berelson's article. Few know of the 1955 symposium, whose importance is little appreciated. The technique is thought to have received definitive form in the Berelson study, which was largely talking about what is now termed classical content analysis. Development beyond this stage and form seems not to be considered essentially possible. The present book may rectify this situation, if it can call attention to the greatly expanded potentialities of content analysis and its steadily continuing development.

Section 3: Content Analysis as an Analytical Infrastructure: The Components and Assembling Them

A number of procedures are involved in the apparently simple matter of putting a question to a text. The question has to be carefully directed. The text must be sufficiently ample and relevant to provide an answer. Ways of extracting the data uniformly have to be found. There has to be some standard against which the data can be assessed, if their significance in answering the question is to become apparent. Grounds must be given to show that this standard really does apply to the question. And, clearly, all these considerations are interconnected. Account has to be taken of them all, together, before any

---

[25] As Barcus notes in *Communication Content*: pp. 543, 548-550 & 552-553.
[26] For the connection between historical materials and content analysis see A. V. Cicourel, *Method and Measurement in Sociology*, Free Press 1964, chapter 6, "Historical Materials and Content Analysis". In 1966 *The General Inquirer*, in a review of the use of content analysis by different disciplines, noted that historians had rather strikingly failed to exploit the potentialities of the technique (p. 51).

one of them can be proceeded with (figure 2.1 illustrates). We simply go round in circles, unless we can think clearly of this business as involving a set of distinct but related procedures. These procedures make up a structure through which analysis can be conducted. Providing this analytical infrastructure is what content analysis is all about.

To put this structure in less general terms, suppose there is a question to be put to a text. The questioner has first to decide what constitutes 'the text'. He may be interested in race relations in the mass media of the fifties, say. He cannot decide how to construct his sample of newspapers until he has defined 'race relations'. The trick is to pose the question in such a way that he can obtain an answer which can be factually documented from his sources. And

Figure 2.1: CONNECTIONS BETWEEN PROCEDURES
INVOLVED IN CONTENT ANALYSIS

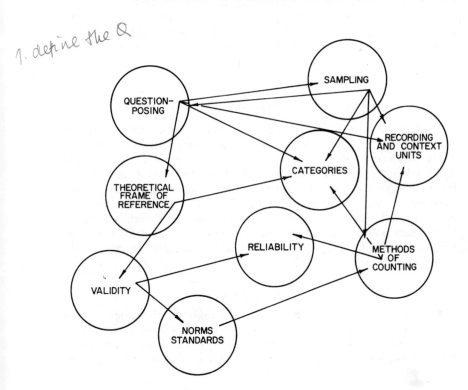

1. define the Q

this has to be an answer that someone else would obtain too. It must not involve subjectively interpreting or selecting the evidence.

Now *any* set of evidence can be 'explained' in one way or another, if findings are merely interpreted after the event rather than generated as a test for an hypothesis. But all that such a *post factum* explanation provides is a plausible but unprovable hypothesis.[27] So, from the outset, the question should embody a testable, nonidiosyncratic proposition. Otherwise the questioner will end up with mere value judgements, no matter how objectively he gathers the data. Thus he might inquire into 'aspects of race relations that are believed to have been in the public mind in the fifties.' He would also build in a check into 'aspects believed important in the sixties.' The question in this case is: 'Were these things, in fact, there?' This form of questioning enables seeing what *isn't* there, and looking for patterns. Alternatively, the question might be designed so that it bears on 'issues on which authoritarians are known to be sensitive.' The question in this case is: 'Are issues posed in *these* terms and on *these* matters indicated by theorizings on authoritarianism?' Either way, there must be some generally accepted, outside standard of comparison (such as, for the examples above, data on public opinion and on authoritarianism) against which the data of the particular analysis can be assessed, if that data is to have significance for anyone else.

CONTRIBUTIONS MADE BY THE TECHNIQUE

Content analysis as a technique has made three particularly important contributions to this business of posing questions to texts. These concern 'unitizing', standards for assessing data, and checks upon validity of findings. Before considering these contributions one by one, it should be noted that content analysis also incorporates expertise in the form of other specialist techniques: sampling, for example, and multivariate analysis. These are dealt with separately, in chapters 5 and 7. Together, this collection of stratagems makes up the technique of content analysis as it is currently practised. The collection is constituted as follows.

UNITIZING

Questions come in all sorts of forms. So do texts. How then is some uniform countability imposed on them? Sampling techniques are no help. All they do is provide guidelines so that the analyst can specify what he is going to consider, and why, and so that he can guarantee

[27] See *Content Analysis*, p. 27.

to read all of it. Uniformity is achieved by 'unitizing'. This procedure provides a standardized format in which to pose questions, and allows the most diverse literary texts to be processed in the same way. Unitizing involves counting, by recording units, context units and categories.

Recording units are the things to be counted. They may be words, themes, characters, or even interactions. An example of a word as a unit might be a study of *demokratia* in fifth-century B.C. writings; one of a theme might be 'an ikon in miracle-working action' at early, middle and late points in the Iconoclast Controversy.[28] The use of the character as a device in terms of which to conduct a count (e.g. in periodicals or novels) will be familiar to readers of literary interests. The character acts as the unit counted, and his traits or activities are categorized. In Classics a whole batch of new insights into staging matters was obtained by using this device in studies of 'the (stage-) holding role' — as well as the more conventional studies of slave roles and so on. For an example of an interaction unit, see my study "The Words *sodes* and *quaeso* in Terence"[29] where attention is focused on the way these words are used. The question is asked 'What sort of persons use them, in what ways, to what other sorts of persons? High status males peremptorily to other males of inferior status, or what?'

Any form of communication can be broken down into uniformly computable pieces, by unitizing. Context units are the passages in which the recording units are set, the contexts which define their meaning. They have to be specified, for counting purposes, and must relate in size to the size of the recording unit concerned. Thus they may comprise a sentence (for example, when a word is the recording unit), a paragraph (for a theme, for instance), a page, or a chapter. Counting need not be only a matter of quantification. There are two other forms in use. Non-frequency-counting involves *qualitative* assessment of the significance of a single, an intensive, or an attenuated mention. Contingency analysis works by contrasting the patternings of associational fields or syndromes.

Categories are the classifications, the pigeonholes if you like, into which the recording units are counted. They have to be suited to the question, the text and the recording units. A content analysis is consequently only as good as the categories, or classification system, underlying it. Now categories can be formed straightforwardly, by

---

[28] See E. Kitzinger, "The Cult of Images in the Age Before Iconoclasm," *Dumbarton Oaks Papers*, 8, 1954, pp. 103-104.

[29] *Acta Classica* 7, 1964, pp. 57-63.

taking the text at its surface meaning, or they can be formed by inference, by 'reading between the lines' when the text is disingenuous. They can, therefore, involve descriptive, factual classifications of the subject matter. Or they can involve assessments of more intangible things, such as bias.

Examples of straightforward subject matter categories are: literary figures employed/not; source cited/not; treatment full/skimpy; written early/late. 'Latent' or inferred meaning is employed to form the other kind of categories, generally in qualitative counting. The recording unit in this case is the actual word or whatever element of the text; but this unit is placed into its category by inferences drawn from its meaning in its context. Examples are: biased/not; intense/moderate emphasis.

There are no rules for forming categories, and very few standardized categories which may be used in a variety of studies. What generally happens is this. Unitizing produces an 'operational' question — one that can be put so that the answers to it can somehow be 'counted'. The sample of text is also established. Then the question is tried out on another part of the text. If it does not work very well in sorting recording units into their category-pigeonholes (the usual experience, on the first time of trying), the question, sample, categories or units are revised until a question is found which *will* work. This initial circular process is known as a 'pilot study' or 'pretest'.

STANDARDS

If the question springs from an informed awareness of related background matters, the latter should suggest a classificatory system. With questions of a biographical or psychological nature, for instance, awareness of theories on personality will suggest categories based on outside, expert findings rather than on the subjective, off-the-top-of-the-head feelings of the analyst. Here is where the second major contribution of content analysis, that concerning the assessment of data, comes in. It consists of emphasizing the necessity for such an informed background of awareness if a study is to have adequate standards by which to assess its findings.

For content analysis directs attention to the fact that, without a norm against which to compare them, individual sets of data are meaningless. Data elicited by one person's analysis gain meaning only when set against some outside criterion. Hence the care taken by content analysts to stockpile criteria — and to assess their worth. For it has to be shown that an index measures what it claims to measure, that the standard of judgement adopted is applicable.[30] At a general level, it is possible to 'make a case' by choosing categories that will single out certain types of material in a communication. The only safeguard against this partiality is to have theoretical guidelines which independently suggest categories for use. Hence, once again, stress is laid upon the analyst's background of knowledge, his framework of reference in approaching his study. For reliable, externally established criteria, some form of theory, or body of findings is essential.

In short, the reason for the development of an emphasis on having some kind of theoretical frame of reference is this. By relating the study to a theoretical background two forms of bias are avoided. First it has to be explicitly shown how the theory involved is relevant. Thus the analyst cannot unconsciously or surreptitiously adopt an approach which skews the evidence in favor of a particular case. Secondly, standards (as well as categories) are determined not by him but by *outsiders'* findings. Thus he cannot 'make a case' by skewing his analytical infrastructure so as to generate data which tell in favor of that case.

INFERENCES

Because of its emphasis on theory, the above recently evolved approach may be called 'theoretically informed' content analysis. The name will distinguish it clearly from 'classical' content analysis, from which it differs in laying much more stress on the drawing of inferences. And it is in regard to the drawing of inferences that the third major contribution of the technique has been made. There are no rules to tell anyone how to make the inferential leap. But strategies have been evolved for telling how well it has been made.

Basically, two matters are involved: reliability and validity, and primarily the latter. How reliably were the data unitized? Counting procedures and categories are concerned in this, as well as recording units. There are methods, such as panel testing (see below), of insuring against unevenness in such data extraction. How valid are the inferences that were drawn? Again, there are methods of testing. The same question can be put to an equivalent sample, or to a series of other related sets of source materials, to see if results are comparable. Data gathered by a different technique, from different but related source materials, can be contrasted, to see if the findings

---

[30] See Cicourel, *Method and Measurement in Sociology*, pp. 143 and 148-9. At the detailed level of deciding what it is that an index does measure see Holsti's discussion of readability indexes: *Content Analysis*, pp. 89-90.

of the other study and those of the content analysis converge. An 'equivalent sample' can be obtained by dividing the original sample into two at the outset. This is known as the 'test-retest' method. The 'series of source materials' approach might work like this. To investigate the psychological values of Hitler's Germany, analysts have scrutinized its plays, songbooks, handbooks for youth organizations, speeches, newspapers and even postage stamps. If this had been done as one integrated operation (as, in fact, was not the case), such a study would comprise the technique of 'multiple confirmation'. The stratagem of crosschecking on a questionnaire by content analyzing letters to the editor is an example of the third method, known as 'multiple operationism'.[31]

Without some such check on its findings, the results of a content analysis must be regarded merely as probable. Only testing against materials not considered in the original study can confirm the validity of its inferences.

RESEARCH DESIGN

Content analysis confers one other benefit, too. Detailed procedures have been worked out for the different stages identified within the analysis, and the interrelationships among these procedures have been examined (see figure 2.2). The analyst is saved a great deal of work: he does not have to invent an analytical infrastructure, starting from scratch. Instead he can start from an advanced level of sophistication in this respect. In fact, only if the details of the analytical infrastructure have already been worked out *can* anyone go on to consider the overall problem of putting them together. (This is why studies by Arts scholars tend to be so much slighter in this crucial regard than those by social scientists.) And, as shown, this whole complex of matters has to be taken into account from the very beginning in planning an analysis. Such a plan is termed a 'research design' in the Social Sciences.[32]

Basically, a research design is a strategy which takes simultaneous consideration of the following matters and their interrelationships: sampling, unitizing, standards of assessment for data analyzed, and inferential procedures. Thus the precise form assumed by any analytical infrastructure is determined by its research design. Different

---

[31] See E. Webb and M. H. Roberts, "Unconventional Uses of Content Analysis in Social Science", *Communication Content*, p. 321.

[32] There is an excellent discussion of research designs in content analyses in *Content Analysis*, chapter 2, especially pp. 24-27 and 37-41.

Figure 2.2: CONTENT ANALYSIS AS AN ANALYTICAL OPERATION

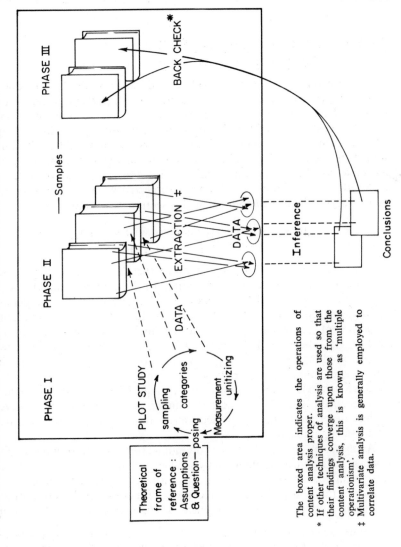

The boxed area indicates the operations of content analysis proper.

* If other techniques of analysis are used so that their findings converge upon those from the content analysis, this is known as 'multiple operationism'.

‡ Multivariate analysis is generally employed to correlate data.

problems require different research designs. Different research designs produce different analytical infrastructures, and so lead to the obtaining of quite different findings. Thus content analysis by no means imposes one stock unvarying approach, as the next section will show.

Section 4: How Content Analysis Works: Its Strengths and Weaknesses.

The research design adopted will depend partly on the kind of question proposed, and partly on the material to which the question must be put. There are precise, matter-of-fact questions, and there are general questions involving reading between the lines. Some texts involve factual, descriptive writing. Others contain subtle allusions with many levels of meaning. A content analysis can be only as objective as these constraints allow. But the technique provides a multitude of methods for keeping subjectivity and impressionism under varying degrees of control, as this section will demonstrate.

CLASSICAL AND THEORETICALLY ORIENTED CONTENT ANALYSES

A communication is only a fraction of the communications process. Communicating proceeds from the intent of the communicator through the content of what he expresses to the effect upon the person addressed (see figure 2.3). Moreover it flows through a structured environment. Language, genre, and channels of communications all exert their influences (see figure 9.2). Quite simply, analyzing the middle sections of this process — media content, say — is a far different and infinitely easier task than analyzing either of the two flanking sections. Manuals on content analysis draw a sharp distinction between these two areas of inquiry.[33] The former involves mainly description, the latter necessarily requires much use of inference (see figure 2.3).

Analysis of the content of communications is, traditionally, the domain of classical content analysis. Development of this variety of the technique marked a major advance in analytical competence. Hitherto there had been no technique for objectively establishing trends in voluminous and complicated communications, or patterns

[33] For example, the distinction is well and clearly made by Holsti in the most recent manual. See *Content Analysis*, chapters 3 and 4. As to why the second is so much more difficult, see Cicourel, *Method and Measurement in Sociology*, pp. 145-6.

of characteristics therein. Characteristics of communicators or in stylistics can also be identified, even very subtle ones, by this form of the technique. The importance of the development of content analysis resides in the fact that these are the bread-and-butter tasks of the historian and literary scholar. Yet, without the technique, they are more often than not incompetently performed.

Analysis of causes or effects of a communication involves making inferences about matters other than its content. These inferences may be direct or indirect. A direct inference might be drawn by relating a change in the content or expression of a man's writing to events otherwise known to have affected him in his private life at the time. For instance, the 'action quotient' postulates that an increase in qualitative words indicates an increase in emotional instability. So the occurrence of such an increase in a writer's work can be identified and matched to the events of his private life. The result will show whether it correlates with events there indicative of increased emotionality.[34] Indirect inferences involve a longer (and therefore less dependable) chain of inference. Basically this procedure takes the form: 'In writer x, characteristic y means the operation of factor z; hence in the like writer A, characteristic y should have the same connotation.'[35]

*Figure 2.3:*CONTENT ANALYSIS: ITS TWO ZONES OF INQUIRY

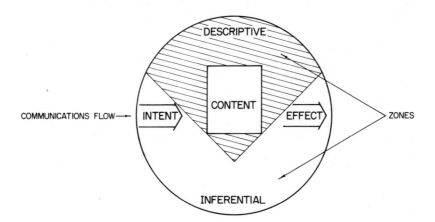

---

[34] See Garraty, "The Application of Content Analysis to Biography and History", *Trends*, pp. 176-77.

[35] See *Content Analysis*, pp. 33-35 (and cf. 69-70.)

There must be good reason for supposing that the relationship posited should hold. Hence content analyses which focus on the causes or effects of communications generally involve recourse to independent findings, of general applicability which establish the operation of such causes or effects. These findings are generally theoretical in nature. What is termed 'communications theory' involves generalizations about repeatedly demonstrated communications phenomena. Knowledge of these is invaluable in assessing the effects of communications. Take the 'embedding process' for instance. This is the process by which rumor cuts down the details of the original message, exaggerates striking features and assimilates the story to suit the preconceptions of its retailer.[36]

It is the theoretical framework of reference which suggests the standards or norms, and, in general, the logic of inference, by which to assess such data. Moreover this framework also provides impartial ideas about the categories which are so crucial in the analytical infrastructure. Thus description tends to mean classical content analysis, inference the theoretically oriented variety.

TWO DIFFERENT INFRASTRUCTURES

Just how the analytical infrastructure is in fact affected by the overall shape of the content analysis — the type of research design adopted — is next for consideration. That purpose will be accomplished by contrasting a pair of content analyses constructed on radically different lines. One will be an extreme example of a classical content analysis, the other of a theoretically oriented content analysis. The examples are meant as illustrations only, and illustrations of extreme forms of content analysis at that. In actuality most content analyses will contain a blend of items from both of these forms. On this method of illustration, by two polar ideal types, see the discussion on models in chapter 4. Contrast between the examples which follow will show how great can be the overall, cumulative effect of differences, each in itself minor, in each component of the analytical infrastructure. It will also show how great a range of 'objectivity' there can be between one content analysis and another.

Here is how the two different infrastructures might appear when put together:

[36] Maccoby, *Readings*, pp. 58-64 (cf. also 47-54). For a general model of the communications process see K. W. Deutsch, *The Nerves of Government, Models of Political Communication and Control*, Free Press, 1963, pp. 82-97.

Figure 2.4: CONTENT ANALYSIS: TWO DIFFERENT INFRA-
STRUCTURES

Details of Infrastructure	Type of Content Analysis	
	CLASSICAL	THEORETICALLY ORIENTED
Recording Unit	word	theme
Context Unit	sentence	chapter
Counting via	frequency, on computer	nonfrequency, manual content analysis
Text	ample	meagre
Sample	multistage	purposive
Aim	description of manifest content	inference from latent content
Form of comparison used to assess data ...	direct	indirect
Criteria for norms ...	inductive, from outside data	theoretical

What do these differences mean, in terms of objectivity? First, unitizing. Words are easy enough to count, but themes are difficult to define. Two people operating independently over a long period of time might not always agree in identifying the more nebulous themes or in allocating them into categories. The bigger the context unit, the greater the tendency for neutral shades of meaning to drop out.[37] Frequency counting is a mere semiclerical recording operation, whereas nonfrequency assessment requires subjective judgement. The computer ensures fast, accurate data extraction; human beings 'can't count' (in these circumstances). They tend to miss things.[38] When text is plentiful, omissions revealed by the analysis are probably significant; when it is meagre, they need not be. Purposive sampling involves subjective judgement, so may cause skewing; multistage sampling should ensure a well-drawn, representative sample. (The discussion on sampling in chapter 5 provides an explanation of the terms 'purposive' and 'multistage'.) Description of manifest content involves a straightforward, noninterpretative compounding semi-clerical operation. Inference from latent content involves compounding one act of subjective judgement with another. Indirect comparisons or inferences involve an extra, risky, inferential step. A comparison can be no better than the criterion on which it is based, and so the

[37] *Content Analysis*, p. 118.
[38] *Ibid.*, pp. 151 and 154.

factually based criterion has the advantage (in involving more immediate face validity) over the theoretical one.

THE 'SIGNIFICANCE VERSUS VALIDITY' DILEMMA

In these two cases, in every respect the classical content analysis is more objective than the theoretically oriented one. Consequently, its overall immediate validity is incomparably greater. *But this does not make it the better content analysis.* A good content analysis is one that is as objective as the constraints of question and text upon it allow it to be. It is the *question* that counts, not the count itself. It is no good producing volumes of impeccably extracted data if, in order to do so, the question has to be redefined so that it no longer asks what it was originally supposed to ask.[39] A superficial question can produce only superficial answers. Better, far, a deeply probing question. This can provide answers of comparably deep significance. But it may do so at the cost of an analysis of a qualitative nature based on gleanings from the psychologic latent within a body of writing.[40]

In content analysis, the moment of truth usually comes with the decision as to how much significance to aim for. For significance is generally obtained at the cost of some loss of validity, because qualitative analysis of latent meaning will inevitably be involved. Language is, of its nature, multidimensional. It is both instrumental (fraught with inner meanings) and representational (simply meaning what it states). Frequency-counts of straightforward, surface meaning rarely go deep enough to answer in-depth questions.

Inferring does not happen only when all the facts are in and the analyst is arguing to his conclusions.[41] For when he decides whether a text is to be 'read between the lines' — that it is instrumental, not representational — he is making an inference about it. This decision is generally made before the collecting of facts even *starts*, and it is a decision which must always be made. Hence, decisions on inference are inescapable in both forms of content analysis.

CONSTRAINTS IMPOSED BY THE SOURCES

The moment of truth involves more than a decision on the relative degrees of significance and validity in the study, however. It is also

[39] See *Content Analysis*, pp. 10 and 12. There is simply no substitute for a good question: see pp. 1 and 194.

[40] On the term 'psychologic' see R. E. Lane and D. O. Sears, *Public Opinion*, Prentice-Hall, 1964, pp. 44-53. A discussion of it occurs in chapter 3, of this book, apropos of 'cognitive dissonance'.

[41] See *Content Analysis*, pp. 12-13.

a test of the questioner's analytical skills. When faced with the same intractable question and source materials, the more skilful content analyst will produce a much more objective study than will the less skilful one. Analysis relying on impressionism would fare worse than either, of course. Impressionists are unaware of the full complexity of the analytical *problems*, let alone the variety of ways of offsetting each. In an analysis, at each stage of constructing the infrastructure, there are ways of keeping back the amount of subjectivity inescapably present. The cumulative effect of taking all the appropriate steps can be very considerable indeed.

As the text itself does so much to set limits upon the analysis, it should be considered first. Figure 2.5 sets out the main features that affect ability to perform a content analysis.

Figure 2.5: CONSTRAINTS IMPOSED ON A CONTENT ANALYSIS BY ITS SOURCE MATERIALS

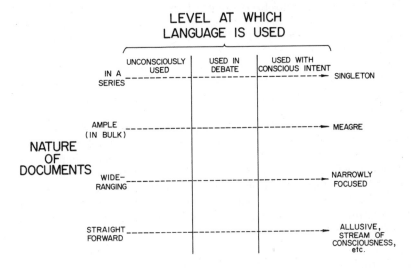

The 'good' texts — those which facilitate analysis — are in the left-hand column, the 'bad' ones in the right-hand one. The limitations imposed by the nature of a document are obvious enough. Plentiful, simple text is easier to draw conclusions from than is meagre, complicated text. But perhaps some comment on the consequences of the level of disingenuousness in writing may be in order.

The most telling linguistic give-away is that over which its producer manifestly exercised no conscious control. A thing can be so small that it is not seen, or so large that there is no awareness of it. An unconscious mannerism or verbal tic is an instance of the former; the language patterns of a speech group an instance of the latter. The most intractable level of language to analyze occurs when a sophisticated author is writing with deliberate guile. Ambiguity, multifaceted allusion and the psychologic of presentation may endow words with senses other than their surface meaning. Language presents its skilful user with boundless resources. Its major terms have layer upon layer of meaning. Skilfully combined, these become phrases resonant with halftones, undertones, overtones and echoing reminiscences. Skills in producing word magic are far better developed than those in analyzing it.[42]

Midway between these extremes comes the language of debate. The circumstances of, or sequel to, a debate make it possible to infer the intent of its participants very often, especially if there is more than one debate to consider. Language cannot pass beyond certain bounds of disingenuousness in a debate, or its producer will miscarry of his purpose. This is not to claim that such language is to be interpreted only at its surface meaning. But strategies of indirection miscarry if oversubtle. So the range of possible hidden meanings is severely restricted by the constraints of the debate, or conflict, situation. Formal constraints — of genre or of diplomatic practice — further delimit the language into levels of meaning held appropriate for debate. Pressure to produce a speedy note in reply leads to less elaboration, more simplicity. So it is simpler to analyze unconscious levels of diction, or diction used in debate, than it is to analyze words consciously used at his discretion by a skilled literary or rhetorical craftsman. Consequently a shift from conscious to unconscious levels of diction will enormously facilitate analysis, as will a redefinition of the issue so that it can be analyzed from communications of a debate-like nature.

CONTROLS ON SUBJECTIVITY

Shifting levels is where skill in question-posing and in sampling pays dividends. For instance, it may be possible to employ a psychobio-

---

[42] For systematic analysis of how the word magic of rhetoric works, see C. I. Hovland et al, *Communication and Persuasion*, Yale, 1953 and C. I. Hovland, ed., *The Order of Presentation in Persuasion*, Yale, 1957.

graphical question instead of a biographical one.[43] Psychobiography involves describing the world-picture held by a group of writers. This practice can turn what was originally destined to be a qualitative study of a single case into a descriptive study of a series of cases. Psychoanalysis involves subjective re-interpretation of data. Moreover, in literary or historical studies, it tends to concern a typical character. Hence it is difficult to find norms against which to assess the meaning of data produced by the analysis. Furthermore, almost anything can be argued from a single instance, but only as an hypothesis. It requires a series of instances to produce conclusive argument by providing the data against which the various hypotheses can be tested. Much firmer conclusions can be drawn from analysis of trends than from a 'single-shot' analysis. If there is already a trend study to deal with, the validity of the findings can be considerably increased by reviewing several streams of data along a number of dimensions simultaneously. Moreover, if the question can be reformulated so that it links up to a framework of reference based on a body of theory, that theory should suggest areas of issues into which to probe, as well as norms and categories. The theory may well enlarge the range of questions open for posing. Such enlargement will enable redefinition of the sample, for now its scope can be widened.

In regard to unitizing, a good deal of hard-won expertise is available. Themes have always been the bugbear among the recording units. There is evidence that it pays to define them very, very clearly. It may even be possible to atomize them. Atomizing involves breaking up a complex or nebulous theme into its more readily identifiable (and hence countable) component units.[44] There are various ways of checking to see how accurately themes are being identified; the simplest is the panel study. A panel of judges can independently define the themes and choose those definitions on which all, or most, agree. Alternatively a panel of coders can classify a part of the subject

---

[43] The term 'psychobiography' and its related methodology are initially owed to a paper presented by B. Glad to the 1968 meeting of the American Political Science Association: "The Role of Psychoanalytic Biography in Political Science." Briefly, psychobiography involves looking for patterns of similarities in the pictures of this or that aspect of their world held by groups of ordinary writers. It aims to make the viewpoints and values of different social classes and times visible. For further discussion, see chapter 8.

[44] See table 1.1, 'Comparative Analysis of Perceptions of Change' and discussion thereto, in *Bureaucracy in Traditional Society*. Here, the theme 'change' is broken down into the following components: Time Focus, Views on Causation, Views of Tradition, Views of Innovation, Motivation Ascribed for Changes, Beneficiaries of Change, and Effects of Change.

matter by themes into categories. The analyst's classifications are then compared with those of the panel. Agreement in classification indicates non-idiosyncratic placements and thus indicates his level of objectivity in classifying. In regard to interaction units, a great deal of work has been done by specialists bent on the analysis of interaction. Acquaintance with appropriate subfields should lead to the discovery of an appropriate formula for economically coding a set of interactions. (See the discussion of interaction analysis in the next section.)

In regard to context units, it is as well to know the price which must be paid for using big ones. Then they can be avoided if there is need to reflect midmost as well as extreme positions taken in the source material. With categories, oddly enough, the reverse is the case. If subcategories proliferate, these minor distinctions may obscure major trends latent amid the data.[45] But, if it is necessary to use an elaborate system of classification, the risk of misclassification can be lessened by going about classifying thus. First classify into major areas (on the first pass through the source material). Then, *in each major area*, classify into minor areas (second pass). Next, in each of these, classify into fields; and so on, down to sub-sub-fields. Thus in any instance only one sharp yes/no distinction has to be drawn rather than finding it necessary to make a whole string of interrelated decisions. For the latter is a complex procedure, known to induce misclassification.[46]

Counting is another matter concerning which expertise has been built up. If it is a matter of quantitative assessment, in authorship problems or stylistics say, the trick is to look for the little things too small for a writer to be conscious of: use of 'whilst' instead of 'while', for example. Alternatively, a complex pattern (even a thought-pattern) can be used as a yardstick. The 'minor encoding habit' is an example of the 'little thing', and the weighted index is an example of the complex pattern. A variety of such indexes has been evolved. Possibly the best example is the 'attention score'. This lists the ways in which a newspaper can give prominence to an item in presenting it: size of headline and typeface; illustration by some form of picture; position on page, and on front or near-front page, and so on. Each mode of presentation is then given a set of numerical weightings to correspond to the range of degrees of emphasis possible within it. Items are then uniformly scored on all such counts. Converging emphases, which indicate in-

[45] See *Content Analysis*, pp. 97-98.
[46] *Ibid.*, pp. 138-9. For discussion in this book, see figure 8.6 and discussion thereto in text.

tensity, are thus revealed by the total scores gained.[47] With qualitative assessment, of bias, say, it is sometimes possible to establish that the taking of this or that position involves a value-judgement, *pro* or *con*. By defining such positions so that each typifies a particular form of value-judgement, it becomes possible to use them as subject-matter categories. Thus what had been a subjective assessment can be made into a mere clerical matter of listing facts. If subjective assessments must be made, various scales have been evolved to limit the play of the analyst's subjectivity, or to facilitate the making of judgements which involve using several criteria simultaneously. Devices like the 7-point judgemental scale and the Semantic Differential are employed in such cases. The latter is based on findings which show that people tend to judge things in terms of whether they are good or bad, strong or weak, and active or passive. So a writer's diction can be scored in these respects by employing a special framework.

Then again, *both* quantitative and qualitative assessments can be used together, to complement one another (by assessing in terms of frequency and intensity combined, for instance). The long-standing controversy over the propriety of employing qualitative measures has been judged a non-issue. Qualitative and quantitative measures are now seen to be complementary, not opposed. They reach into different aspects of the subject matter. So studies are nowadays designed to allow use of more than one measure.[48] Similarly, contingency analysis can be used to complement one or both of these other methods of assessment. By now well established as a third method (it first came to prominence with the publication of *Trends*), contingency analysis operates by establishing a pattern against which patterns in the communications can themselves be matched. This pattern may be the syndrome of some personality theory. Or it can be constructed in a 'thought experiment' (see below). Or it may be created by plotting into a matrix constructed by using the appropriate technique.

MULTIVARIATE ANALYSIS

Multivariate analysis is a technique in its own right, and a sophisticated one at that. (Applications are described in chapters 7 and 8.) The idea behind multivariate analysis is that of showing how one thing is related to one or more others. This is often done by setting out their relationships in tabular form. A simple example will show what is

[47] For other such indexes, see Garraty in *Trends*, pp. 176-8, and *Content Analysis*, pp. 75-77, 89-90 & 155.
[48] See *Content Analysis*, pp. 5-12.

meant. Suppose I suspect that Suetonius's writings contain derogatory innuendoes aimed at Hadrian's personality and habits. I can list the mannerisms and foibles attributed to Hadrian and then examine each of Suetonius's *Lives* to see whether such traits are commented upon as characteristics of the emperor in question. I can also inquire whether Suetonius's language gives any hint as to his attitude to this or that trait. This enquiry produces a matrix: across the top are twelve divisions, one for each of the *Lives*. Down the side are twenty or so divisions, one for each mannerism. In each square of the matrix I can record Suetonius's attitude to the mnnerism concerned. For Suetonius, some of the emperors concerned are heroes and some are villains. If the mannerisms are negatively presented, and attributed only to villain emperors — as in fact very largely is the case[49] — I have established very strong factual evidence for my thesis. In this case the matrix and the signs indicating negatively presented data constitute the patterning process.

This pattern matching can be a complicated business, as so many things have simultaneously to be considered. Use of a computer confers major advantages in this situation. It is fast, and free from error in retrieval and correlation even when many items are involved all at the one time. Manual analysis definitely is not. So if the task is to explore a pattern of verbal associations or a semantic field, it can be done best by directing non-numerical questions to a computer. These questions involve a program which prints out set numbers of words before and after key words. The program also retrieves all passages containing words in clusters specified in the light of the analyst's assessment of the first print-out.[50] Computerized content analysis has a unique advantage: it does not 'box you in'. If, after analysis is started, another question is to be asked, it is easily possible to do so. Once the text is on the computer tape, a new set of questions can be asked of it in a matter of minutes. In the case of a manual content analysis, on the other hand, a new question means a new study — or re-doing the first one from the beginning. This disparity is due to the fact that this process of extracting the data, which is the longest and most laborious part of a manual content analysis, is the speediest part of a computerized one.

To offset this advantage, use of computers exacts a price. Preparation of text for taping can involve subjective judgements in categoriz-

[49] See "How Suetonius' *Lives* reflect on Hadrian", *Proceedings of the African Classical Associations*, 11, 1968, pp. 7-21.

[50] A good example of this can be found in the study of Mark Twain by Ellis and Favat, chapter 23 of *The General Inquirer*.

ing words or concepts. Moreover the computer is not nearly as good as a human reader at spotting themes. Consequently, decision to use the computer involves the 'significance versus validity' dilemma all over again.

VALIDITY

In regard to norms, content analysis is less remarkable for its ingenuity in providing them than for its focusing of attention upon them. The need to establish what is normal for the communicator's group has been clearly demonstrated by studies which failed through not doing so. Norms (for word- or concept-use) can be established for others of the group of which the writer being studied forms part. His can then be compared with theirs. This can even be done within the work of one man: usage norms found in one part of his work (where stress may be unusual, say) can be compared with norms established for the whole of his work. Alternatively, some theory may indicate normal behavior or what have you. Or normal practice in the outside world can be compared with the norms assumed in the writings under review. These general guidelines can be adapted to fit a wide range of situations.

It is in regard to validation of inference that the technique has shown ingenuity. There is the stratagem of switching levels, to probe into the unconscious rather than the conscious writing of an author. Thus, a theoretical framework to select an area for probing (such as, say, 'attitudes to change') can be adopted. Personality syndromes can now be revealed merely by describing what the writer 'sees'. Similarly, frequencies for (other than basic) words within his speech group can be established and then compared with the writer's own ranking of these words by frequency. This comparison allows the quirks in his subconscious to stand out.

Languages have structure. If at the start, words which all relate to one major concept are grouped, cross-linkages will be discovered. For these major concepts themselves group together by association into larger themes. (There are some 114 in English.) This gives access to the basic themes which are important within the ways in which the people of a period talk about their 'reality'. It also provides a yardstick against which to measure individual writers of the period. A writer may have striking omissions, or additions, in the word group which he associates with a particular concept, or the conceptual group which he associates with a particular theme. Hence, by approaching his diction at this level, access can be gained to characteristics in the individual's writing and personality of which he may himself be unconscious.[51]

The other major strategy in regard to inference is that of running a check on the conclusions. This check can be managed by splitting the sample into two at the outset, and redoing the investigation on the second part to see if similar findings result. Or several different but related sets of source materials can all have the same question(s) put to them, to see if findings confirm one another. Or a different type of analysis can be conducted into related material in the hope of producing converging findings.

THE SYSTEMS APPROACH TO CONTENT ANALYSIS

Finally, the technique enables looking at this complex of operations as an ensemble. Indeed, in some ways it compels doing so. Using a computer, for instance, forces an analyst to specify the logic behind each step of his inquiry in the most rigorous terms.[52] Setting out a research design for a manual content analysis involves a clear statement of how all parts of the infrastructure relate and contribute to the overall goal of the inquiry. From this vantage point, surveying the study as a whole, it is sometimes possible to see a way of linking a content analysis to other studies. Or a way may be seen of incorporating another technique — such as a sociogram — within it, or even of incorporating *it* within another technique. For instance, considering the effects of a communication involves considering the overall communications process. That process is commonly thought of as a flow. To analyze flows, some form of systems approach is generally used. Such approaches are likely to be increasingly used in conjunction with content analyses, and so it is as well to have an outline idea of what is involved.

Content analysis is, to my understanding, clarity itself in comparison to systems analysis. However, in general terms, the latter technique works like this. It identifies the crucial actors or factors in the area of activity in which it is interested, thus isolating one aspect of a complex overall problem for consideration. So as to make analysis of their interaction possible, it defines these actors as constituting a 'system of action'. The actors are a system in the sense that they are seen, for purposes of analysis, as a set of parts, interrelated in some

---

[51] This matter is further discussed in chapter 3; see also the comments of S. Y. Sedelow and W. A. Sedelow Jr. "Categories and Procedures for Content Analysis in the Humanities" in *Communication Content*, p. 493.

[52] See *Communication Content*, pp. 118-20 (& 537) and *Content Analysis*, pp. 191-2.

specific way, in combination with a framework within which the action goes on. Such systems can be viewed as operating at various levels. For the overall system contains subsystems. This systems framework enables moving from in-the-big analysis to analysis of detail, and back, without confusion. The "ocean of words" which envelops the people of any particular period, affecting and affected by them, can be viewed in such a way.[53] Within the language of a given people at a period, that of a specific speech-group constitutes a subsystem and that of an individual a sub-subsystem.

Thus a systems approach provides an overarching framework within which smaller-scale analyses can be conducted or interrelated. So a content analysis can be employed within a systems frame without exaggerating the significance or proportions of that content analysis. Also, its relationships to other techniques or studies can be kept clear all the while. The applicability of such a framework to the study of the effects of communication is obvious.[54] After all, content analysis can consider only *part* of the overall process. It may take its standards from outside and back-check on its inferences by converging studies which do not employ content analysis. A very, very simple example will show what is meant.

I had been listening to a paper on "Propertius, the Parthians and Propaganda". This paper collected all Propertius's indexed references to Parthians and drew conclusions therefrom to Propertius's aims as a propagandist. As this is a common procedure in Arts investigations into 'propaganda' in literature, I wished to convey, to a large general audience, some misgivings about the approach. A great deal of work has been done by content analysts on propaganda. The findings are clear. Analysis of propaganda is a complicated business. To focus discussion I used Lasswell's communications flow framework (see figure 9.2): "Who says what, in which channel, to whom, with what effect?" For to demonstrate propagandistic intent or effect (this distinction was not made), there is need to consider more than the message on its own. The personality and circumstances of the alleged propagandist must be known. (Very little indeed is known about Propertius.) The limitations imposed by the genre and the language of the day must be considered (not done in the paper). The *totality* of the alleged propaganda itself, as contrasted with other comparable topics in Propertius's work, must be examined (also not done). There should

---

[53] See A. Rapoport, "A System-Theoretic View of Content Analysis" in *Communication Content*, pp. 17-38, especially 31 and 36.

[54] For an example which illustrates this point splendidly, see Gerbner's study "Cultural Indicators: The Case of Violence in Television Drama".

also be knowledge of the audience to whom Propertius is addressing himself, their reactions, and, finally, if possible, how Propertius himself reacted to this in the later stages of his 'propagandizing.' (None of these things are known.)

MAJOR FORMS OF CONTENT ANALYSIS

Discussion of this topic has brought us to the end of the list of controls on subjectivity which a skilled analyst can call upon. It is, as has been seen, quite a lengthy and complicated list. For content analysis does not provide just a series of components from which an analytical infrastructure can be built up. Rather, it provides a range of variants for each component in the series, and a variety of wholly different ways of putting that series together. This ample choice is what enables the infrastructure to be adapted flexibly to the peculiarities of the problem being dealt with. Thus, as has been shown, there are two major varieties of content analysis, classical and theoretically oriented. Both can be used in conjunction with other powerful tools or techniques: computers and systems analysis, for example. If the decision is to use some such combination, the analyst will find in drawing up his research design that a distinctive form is produced in each case. Figure 2.6 indicates the major combinations involved. Figure 2.6 assumes that a content analysis is manual unless it is expressly stated that a computer has been used. The figure is not exhaustive; its prime aim is clarity. It sets out common and distinctive forms of content analysis so that illustrative examples can be easily found and overall differences clearly demonstrated. Hence it does not go into computerized content analysis cast in systems terms, or other elaborations of basic major forms of the technique. The best way to see what results is to consider some examples. The systems forms can be taken first, as they have just been discussed. The following is a very simple example of a classical content analysis cast in systems terms.

This analysis deals with the problem of trying to establish which ruler was responsible for a specific administrative reform. Contemporary sources were not interested in the detail of administrative history. Also, they record events year by year, thus obscuring chains of events related to long-range planning. This comment goes for subsequent sources too, by and large. So a systems diagram — one of those pagefuls of little boxes all interconnected by lines — was created by a 'thought experiment' mentioned above. Taking account of what I knew of the technology and administrative practices of the time, I

Figure 2.6: MAJOR FORMS OF CONTENT ANALYSIS

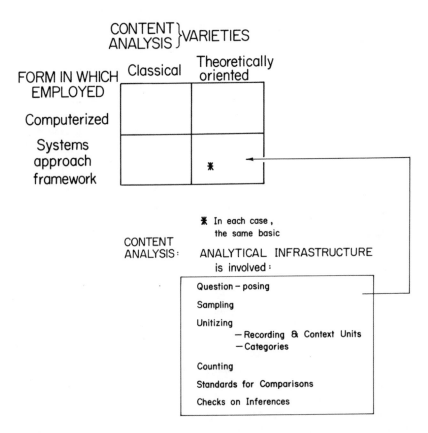

drew up a diagram to indicate the consequences which must have followed from the major changes that the reform necessitated. All the ramifications — side effects, complexes of interdependent adjustments, etc. — were plotted in as 'boxes' in the diagram. Each box then became a category in the subsequent content analysis. For at this point all the source materials were analyzed to see whether this combination of changes was recorded for the reign, as opposed to the periods before and after.[55]

[55] See my paper "The Emperor Claudius and the Grain Trade", delivered to the Northern Great Plains History Conference, 1969, mimeo, Department of History, University of Manitoba.

Contrast this with the theoretically oriented content analysis employed within a systems framework which is outlined in chapter 8. The difference between theoretical and classical content analysis in their systems approach forms should then become clear.

Now contrast the difference between classical and theoretically oriented content analysis in their computerized forms. Basically, computerized content analyses fall into two main classes.[56] One employs some variant of a straightforward frequency count. Examples of this form in the guise of pieces of literary detection and of non-numerical questions have already been discussed. The former involves comparing the frequencies of 'minor encoding habits' in a text of disputed authorship with their frequencies in the writings of various claimants to authorship. The latter form involves analysis of a word's associational field. Comparing the rank order of word frequencies in a given author with that of a speech group would come under this heading,[57] too. All these forms involve classical content analysis. The theoretically oriented forms are all based on some variety of 'dictionary' and work as follows.[58]

What is involved is a conceptual dictionary, a kind of thesaurus. This consists of a number of key words, each representing a conceptual category. These categories are specified by the theoretical framework on which the dictionary is based. Thus there are anthropological, political and psychosocial dictionaries. There are also special purpose dictionaries, created for testing specific hypotheses — about the use of alcohol, for instance, or the 'Icarus complex'. The theory sets out the relationship between its subject matter and the conceptual categories it employs. Words which relate to each conceptual category or 'tag' are then listed under each tag. Typically, this results in grouping some 4,000 words into fewer than one hundred categories. Vocabulary is structured. The ten commonest English words account for more than 25% of a person's verbal output. The 3,000 commonest account for 92.5% of it.[59] Consequently a dictionary listing 4,000 words in the form of word-roots (though not 'and', 'but', 'the' and the other commonest words, for these are irrelevant to the inquiry) provides

---

[56] See *Content Analysis*, p. 153. For further discussion of computerized content analysis in this book see chapter 6.

[57] See *Content Analysis*, pp. 154-5.

[58] The handbook on computerized content analysis is *The General Inquirer*, which discusses these 'dictionaries' in chapters 3 to 5. There are also some subsequent comments in *Content Analysis* pp. 156-64 (Holsti is a leading authority in this field) and *Communication Content* pp. 343, 360 and 163-4.

[59] *The General Inquirer* p. 164.

a fairly full coverage of most texts. A 'left over list' enables seeing words which do not fit into the dictionary's categories. So the words listed under any category can be added to if necessary.

However, such dictionaries can, as things stand, be used only on English-language writings. The limitation applies because it is necessary to cut down on the variety of verbal forms in order to classify economically. Prefixes and suffixes have to be lopped off words, to cut them down to their basic word roots. Procedures for such automatic truncation of words have been evolved only for English as yet, in connection with these dictionary programs.

By using such a dictionary, writings can be compared to see how they stand, in relation to one another, in regard to the issues on which the theory behind the dictionary centres. Thus there can be tests for a 'need for achievement' or an 'urge to power'. Or the value systems of different political parties can be investigated. Or the folk tales of different societies can be compared for their latent assumptions and strivings. Presumably this kind of comparison could be made with detective stories, too. It can also be seen how persons with different characteristics (for examples, popular/unpopular students, successful/ unsuccessful writers) compare in regard to some of the above theoretical criteria. In this way latent characteristics or unconsciously held assumptions can be established by using written data on a scale, and with a complexity, hitherto impossible. Such is theoretically oriented content analysis when computerized.

THE ART OF USING CONTENT ANALYSIS

In the detail of its analytical infrastructure, then, content analysis is almost infinitely adjustable. But it also varies extensively in its overall general appearance, as seen in the case of the four major forms just considered. This varying means that a great deal of judgement and skill is required to use it. It is an art, not a science. As seen, its use involves, at the outset, a fine sense of judgement. A balance has to be struck between the nature of the question to be asked and the counting to be done. Also, the skill with which the infrastructure is assembled makes an enormous difference to the findings that come out of it and to their validity. Demonstrably, it is possible to get better at content analysis with practice: more reliable, more objective, more ingenious.

This is no routine experimental technique which automatically produces results simply by being applied to any text at randon. The contrary. Content analysis cannot be used to 'go fishing' — to explore a text in the hope of making a discovery.[60] It *must* be used clinically. That is to say, the analyst has first to be thoroughly conversant with the subject under inquiry and with the writer(s) involved and his (or their) background. It is from this familiarity with the subject and writings that the initial question comes. Also, familiarity enables him to see more deeply into the implications of his findings. The more familiar he is, the more questions he will have at the end, as he looks his findings over. The technique can provide only an answer to a question; it cannot supply the question.

But there has to be familiarity with the technique, too. It is this familarity which makes it possible to pose the question once it has been thought up. For skill is required to turn a fuzzy question into an operational one. And further skill is required in constructing an infrastructure which will maximize both the validity and the significance of the findings produced in answer to that question. Moreover, there is no all-purpose variety of content analysis, and very little in the way of standardized categories. Certain standard types of *problem* do recur (comparisons of textbooks or of biographical depictions, for instance). Consequently, an infrastructure evolved to deal with one problem of this type can be easily adapted to deal with another similar problem. See the discussion of standardized categories in chapter 8. But the essence of the technique, and the reason why it is so complicated, consists precisely in the fact that each instance of its use is unique. Every study involves its own individual peculiarities, and a form of the technique has to be evolved to meet these, word perfect. The work necessitates a craftsman's skill, not routine odd-jobbing.

But if content analysis is an art, it is an art that involves determinate, practical skills known to give results. These have been (and are still being) carefully elaborated. The care that has been put into their construction and exposition means that they can be quickly taught. By learning them, a beginner can be made master of a complex of analytical skills which represent years of cumulative, ingenious labor. Anyone who aims to be a craftsman with words should possess these skills, for they are designed to deal with some very common problems. To show why, this section concludes by considering how an intuitivist who is not aware of the tools deals with the problems.

Suppose he has to contrast Victorian views on the place of women in society, as exemplified by various Victorian novelists. Do not be misled by the fact that he can provide a devastatingly sophisticated

---

[60] A point repeatedly made in *Content Analysis*: see pp. 27, 41, 67 & 94 (and cf. 151-2).

criticism of the detail of someone else's reconstruction of such views. Ask him how he would go about doing the job himself, and he will be most unlikely to display an equal sophistication in constructive analytical technique. In practice, answers tend to stress sage cautions about 'exercising due care' and 'using discernment' while not stating how one does. The importance of intuition is emphasized, as is reading to get a 'feel' for the period. (Content analysis too requires these steps, of course. But it does so as preliminary to, not a substitute for, methodical inquiry.) But intuitivism and impressionistic reading are not methods.[61] Nor is sitting in a room full of Victorian furniture while writing.[62]

In the Arts area in general, impressionistic studies abound. They contain arguments from the 'striking' or 'extreme' case, the 'typical' instance, or the 'illustrative' example without specifying samples or norms. Unsystematic inductions, based on reflections upon personal experience, abound. This is to ignore the problems which content analysis has been created to deal with. But ignoring them does not make them vanish. It is true that, by ignoring them, the intuitivist can contrive to make his reconstruction or interpretation appear sophisticated, because the cramping restrictions imposed by methodical analysis have not been observed. However such impressionistic approaches generally produce insights fit only for armchair or coffee-shop debate, not systematic research which can be tested and built upon.

Section 5: Where Best to Use Content Analysis

Use of content analysis must be discriminating. It involves too much labor to be used if equivalent results can be obtained by another, less toilsome process. Besides, it is not an all-purpose tool, nor is it equally suited for use on all types of source materials. However, certain types of *source materials* almost cry out for use of content analysis. Moreover there are *purposes* for which it is particularly useful. And a great deal of work has gone into adapting it for use in certain specific *problem areas*. Consequently it pays to know what the circumstances are in which this technique can be used most gainfully or with particular appropriateness. These circumstances are reviewed in this concluding section under the headings: source materials, purposes and problem areas.

[61]See *Content Analysis*, p. 19.
[62] On the inadequacies of traditional historical approaches, see the historian Lee Benson, "An Approach to the Scientific Study of Past Public Opinion", *Public Opinion Quarterly* 32, 1968, pp. 526-529.

SOURCE MATERIALS

To start, consider the source materials which call for the use of content analysis. The most obvious case occurs when source materials are voluminous and complicated, and when they contain all sorts of different kinds of subject matters. Especially if detailed investigation or a complicated question is involved, such a case is the exact predicament that content analysis was originally invented to deal with. Impressionistic reading is notorious for producing misleading results here. If anybody is to be able to rely on the data extracted, content analysis must be used.

Another type of source material which calls for the use of content analysis is the language of a writer or a group, when this has to be studied intensively. No matter whether it is structure or thought-patterns which have to be investigated, this material invariably turns out to involve complicated analysis. Content analysts have elaborated various techniques (such as Evaluative Assertion Analysis), and incorporated others (such as semantic field analysis), for use in similar circumstances. Used in conjunction with a computer, these techniques facilitate the processing and correlating of vast amounts of data. Consequently, before launching into an investigation in this particular problem area, it is wise to become informed about the technical expertise cumulatively acquired by content analysts.

Content analysis is also indicated when source material is used to complement some other kind of data during an inquiry into attitudes. For instance, after a questionnaire has been put out, letters to the editor on the topic involved might be subjected to content analysis. Or after how a certain decision was made has been analyzed, departmental memoranda on the subject might be content analyzed. In both cases the aim is to see whether findings from the two separate analyses converge. Looking at this process from a content analyst's viewpoint, it is termed multiple operationism: the using of other techniques to produce findings to confirm those of a content analysis. Alternatively, it may be desired to ask the same question uniformly of several radically different types of source materials, ranging from songs to stamps for instance. In such cases, the ability to conduct a content analysis may enable the use of source materials which otherwise could not have been put to use in such inquiries. And, unlike a questionnaire or 'participant observer' technique, content analysis cannot influence the data as they are being produced. It operates on the finished product.[63]

63 In general on this topic see *Content Analysis*, pp. 14-20.

PURPOSES

As to purposes, there are three for which in the main, content analysis is used. The commonest and most basic purpose is that of describing some aspect of those source materials which are so complex and voluminous (for example, newspapers) that only content analysis can cope with them. This was in fact the primary purpose for which classical content analysis was evolved. It is surprisingly difficult to describe masses of complicated source materials accurately. Disparaging remarks about 'mere' description presuppose a high standard of performance in this regard which often the disparager cannot manage. For content analysis alone guarantees *total* extraction of relevant data (*con* as well as *pro*) and unfalteringly focused attention. It alone enables researchers to look for very complicated things, and, by employing patterned questions, even for the *absence* of things or patterns. Hence the 'serendipity effect', much talked of in connection with the technique: it turns up quite unanticipated findings. This luck happens because it compels the analyst to investigate all aspects of his question uniformly. Consequently, he inquires into matters which are not normally considered significant. Also, unexpected finds occur because this approach reveals otherwise undetectable patternings and gaps in the data.

Thus the technique aims to change the data-gatherer's quest from that of seeking proof of his own views to that of simply conducting an investigation. Generally, the 'views' being tested are not his, but come from outside opinion or from his theoretical background. They are guidelines. He has a finding, whether they stand or fall. Moreover, the data extracted are, in themselves, individually so insignificant that their overall implications are not readily apparent. Hence there is little emotional involvement however the data appear to be turning out. So, typically, the outlook which goes with content analysis is: "I wonder what actually *is* in the text?" and not: "I'm sure that such and such is there, and I'll find a passage or two to show I'm right."

This posture aims to move debate to more sophisticated levels, from mere plausibility of hypothesizing to argument demonstrable by proof. For it makes an end of the all-too-familiar situation wherein two schools of thought argue inconclusively past one another. Typically, in such cases, one school bases its viewpoint on fifteen passages from the source materials. Its rival supports its different viewpoint by citing a somewhat different selection of thirteen passages from the same materials, and arguing away the implications in two or three other passages.

This posture also makes it possible to argue *from evidence* against the oracular position: "My view on the matter is such and such."

Merely to counterpose another such Pronouncement, though this is often done, cannot advance discussion when source materials are complex and voluminous. For the sorry fact is that impressionism or intuitivism on its own makes very wasteful use of such source materials. It simply cannot garner data from them at all fully, if complicated questions are involved and there has to be movement back and forth between levels of analysis. Methodical investigation is required if inquiry is to be exhaustive as well as detailed and planned.

For methodical investigation, the other two major purposes of content analysis are, likewise, most important. For they are these: to test hypotheses, and to facilitate the making of inferences. The thought experiment described in section 4 ('Which ruler was responsible for a specific administrative reform?') is a good example of the use of content analysis for hypothesis-testing. The advantages conferred by the technique in such testing are owed to the following facts. Content analysis makes the analyst aware of, and able to manage, a whole complex of related analytical problems. Furthermore, it does so without involving him in an emotional proof/disproof commitment likely to bias his judgement. Consequently it gives him the ability to turn an hypothesis into a set of questions, be they ever so complicated, and put them to a text, dispassionately.

'Facilitating inference', the third and last major purpose, generally involves some form of multistage content analysis. That process works like this. A content analysis of one set of materials (writings of individuals exhibiting characteristics of a certain type of personality make-up) establishes a body of findings (the characteristics shared in common by persons of this personality type). These findings are then used to distinguish between cultures, by looking to see whether their writings contain a lot or a little of these characteristics. This distinction at last enables doing what was intended from the outset: to compare the characteristics (not by content analysis) of the communities which had the high and the low scores. For example, a sociologist was investigating a personality syndrome which he termed "Icarianism", a cluster of traits prominently featuring fantasies of flying. First he studied a series of individuals each exhibiting 'Icarian' traits. This study gave him a specific pattern of traits which all such individuals shared in real life. He then examined the folk tales of various societies to see how much notice was paid in each to the traits from this pattern. He was thus able to identify societies where ideas related to Icarianism occurred frequently, and societies where the reverse was the case. Once he had examples of either extreme he was able to look for the characteristics shared by the societies of one extreme and contrast them with those shared by the society at the other.[64] An investigation of this kind necessitates the ability to plan a series of analyses in overall terms, to distinguish between levels of analysis, and to relate the whole to a theoretical background. Content analysis provides the infrastructure without which it is not possible to evolve a research design that will enable reaching the final set of conclusions in this process.

PROBLEM AREAS

Finally, there is the matter of the development of the technique in its application to certain problem areas. Much has been done to improve the efficacy of the technique in certain areas which are naturally suited to its operations. Here, building from strength has resulted in impressive accumulations of expertise. One such area has already been mentioned: intensive study of idiolect and linguistic sub-groups. But content analysis can be applied with maximum suitability in analyzing the images which people have of this or that aspect of reality. This is the kind of thing which it does best, in fact. Certain regularities seem discernible in applications of content analysis to this particular problem area. For in analyzing images there is a tendency to assume a particular view of personality. According to this, the person who knows most about the writer is held to be the writer himself. Also, a writer's world-view is taken as telling a lot about the writer himself: what it tells of 'the World' is another matter altogether. Thus, by 'merely describing' that world-view according to various theoretical frameworks which indicate psychologically telling issue-areas, a personality syndrome can be laid bare. There is consequently no need for psychoanalytic depth-interpretation. This straightforward approach avoids many problems concerning latent inference.

This view, that perception is personality (Rorschach), is outlined in more detail in chapter 4. That chapter goes into such matters as perceptual filters and cognitive maps in an attempt to outline what the 'new look' in Psychology has discovered about how people 'see' things.

A particularly good way of effecting entry into a man's thought-world is by examining his geographical and topographical impressions of it — if his works allow of such examination. For much of his image of such things occurs in forms unconsciously dating to his childhood days, and even in pictorial images. Approach at this level is revealing.

---

[64] See D. M. Ogilvie, "Individual and Cultural Patterns of Fantasized Flight" in *Communication Content*, pp. 243-59, especially 246 and 256.

It admits a searching look into aspects of the personality as a set of perceptions which function in a fashion formed before self-consciousness begins. These aspects underlie and shape all later and more sophisticated modes of relating to reality.[65] So in looking into "John's Picture of the World around him,"[66] it is possible to identify features of his 'cognitive style' — patterned ways in which he associates things. Such probing is the more effective because it is conducted upon an aspect of the writer's thought-world of which he is normally unconscious, but to which he will normally make frequent (if inadvertent) references. A good deal of sensitive and intuitive work has been methodically done in this area.[67]

Analyzing the images held by decision makers has proved a particularly helpful complement to study of the decision-making process by other techniques than content analysis.[68] What content analysis aims to do in such studies is to establish what a given decision maker thought the situation facing him to be, or who his informants were. His 'definition of the situation' cannot be simply presumed to be what any modern, with perfect 20-20 historical hindsight, now sees as an 'objective' definition. One very elaborate framework of inquiry has been evolved which can relate the logic (or illogic) of a speaker's presentation of his case to a range of various world-views, and hence to perceptual (and thus to personality) types.[69]

Inquiries of this sort link the analysis of images to that of inter-actions, the next great area specially suited to the strengths of content analysis. The advantage here is that source materials produced by people interacting with one another tend to be readily responsive to content analysis. Debates or conflicts tend to lay bare the purposes of those participating in them, because the circumstances attendant upon and consequent to them expose the courses open to the participants, along with their manoeuvres and intent. This is especially true if things can be arranged so that it becomes possible to study, not one, but a series of such conflicts. A multitude of interpretations

[65] The basic psychological mechanism involved is the 'orienting reflex', mentioned by Carroll (*Language and Thought*, p. 80). See in general R. Lynn, *Attention, Arousal and the Orientation Reaction*, Pergamon (Oxford), 1966.

[66] Chapter 6 of *Bureaucracy in Traditional Society*.

[67] Further discussion occurs in chapter 8. For a splendid example of what can be done starting from such a base, see H. R. Isaacs, *Scratches on Our Minds: American Images of China and India*, Day, 1958.

[68] See *Content Analysis*, pp. 79-80.

[69] E. S. Shneidman has done much to develop this approach. See "Logical Content Analysis: An Explication of Styles of 'Concludifying' " in *Communication Content*, pp. 261-279.

is always possible when dealing with a single case. When a series is being studied, however, the abundance of the data enables the testing of hypotheses and thus those that do not work can be whittled away.

Skills in analyzing debates or conflicts have been much developed as the result of practical experience. Games theorists have been asked this kind of question: "In such and such a situation, if we back down, will they become more aggressive or will they back down too?" Investigation of series of crises has resulted in the evolution of general guidelines for the analysis of conflict situations.[70] These can be adapted to help in designing a content analysis.

A theoretical background framework of reference is also available. For this is the general area to which studies of group dynamics relate. This is not to claim that findings on the dynamics of small groups can be presumed to be automatically applicable to those of big groups. They are not. Findings have to be chosen based on work on interactions which is at a level appropriate to the interactions being dealt with. As already stated, the standards selected must be shown to be applicable. Again, certain assumptions about personality, those of the transactionalists, tend to underlie analyses of interaction. Some form of 'field theory' framework is often adopted to investigate a subject's 'life space'.[71] By using this framework, inquiries into a personality, the environment, and interactions between that personality and environment can be interrelated. Meanwhile, account can also be taken of a specific set of background forces playing upon them.

[70] See C. A. McClelland, *Theory and the International System*, Collier Macmillan, 1966, pp. 105-106. On 'interaction analysis' (shortly to be mentioned in the text) see 103-107. This is a delightful little book, always enjoyed by Arts students. It talks with great clarity about models and systems analysis, and so could well be read with profit in conjunction with the present book. The main work specifically relating content analysis to the study of conflict situations is North *et al*, *Content Analysis*: *A Handbook with Applications for the Study of International Crisis*. For a more recent commentary on such work see J. E. Mueller, "The Use of Content Analysis in International Relations", *Communication Content*, pp. 187-97.

[71] For a discussion of 'field theory' as applied to personality see I. G. Sarason, *Personality*: *An Objective Approach*, Wiley, 1966, chapter 6. The concept "life space" is discussed on pp. 106-108. It is "the total configuration of psychological reality at any given moment," "determined by the environment and the person." It has an interior boundary (psychological 'reality'). Outside is the physical world. But the boundary is permeable. Contrast this with a Freudian psychoanalytic world in which there is no 'you', only 'I' (super-ego, ego and id). Yet, obviously, our sense of identity is formed by seeing ourselves as others see us. So we need a form of analysis that will make it possible to focus on interactions, and see our subject as a person-in-relationship-with-an-environment (one inseparable complex). This field theory aims to do.

By now a little special field termed 'interaction analysis' has built up.[72] A striking feature of work in this area is that different approaches come together and complement one another. Content analysis has benefited enormously from this. Dream analysts have evolved economical ways of coding very complex or nebulous chains of interactions.[73] This coding is most helpful in dealing with recording units. Sociograms or genealogies can be employed to provide categories, and even to reshape questions, in an analytic infrastructure. There is also some general work on social networks which can help a content analyst in constructing his research design.[74] Marriage guidance counsellors have evolved ways of establishing whether 'her picture of him' resembles 'his picture of her picture of him.'[75] Such work is of enormous assistance in the difficult business of establishing standards for comparing data produced in the analysis. The result of all this work amounts to a stockpile of analytical procedures for the investigation of human interrelationships. This stockpile can be of great assistance to anyone who is investigating the history of the family or of a family. It can also be of help to someone who is inquiring into personal interactions at different points in the evolution of the novel or in a particular novelist's writing, and so on and so forth.

Finally, content analysis is increasingly used in the analysis of cultural differences.[76] It is assigned this task because it can process vast amounts of writing of different kinds while looking for complicated patterns. Also, it can shift levels of analysis and build upon itself. Typically, this is where cumulative content analysis comes into its own. The "Icarianism" study noted above can be an example. Various problems relating to the tactics and strategy of analysis have been resolved, and much expertise has been built up in process. In regard to sampling, for instance, it appears that popular works or those used in the teaching of youngsters are most likely to give access to major underlying assumptions prevalent within a community. In regard to unitizing and related matters, there is specialist work on the analysis

---

[72] The main handbook is R. F. Bales, *Interaction Process Analysis*, Addison-Wesley, 1950.

[73] For a good example of this work see C. S. Hall, "Content Analysis of Dreams: Categories, Units and Norms", in *Communication Content*, p. 152.

[74] See J. C. Mitchell, "The Concept and Use of Social Networks" in J. C. Mitchell (ed.), *Social Networks in Urban Situations*, Manchester U.P., 1969, pp. 1-50.

[75] See R. D. Laing *et al*, *Interpersonal Perception: A Theory and Method of Research*, Tavistock, 1966. Chapter 5, "The Interpersonal Perception Method," contains a lucid exposition of a most complicated series of ideas.

[76] See *Content Analysis*, pp. 80-83.

of values which outlines problems and some solutions.[77] In regard to standards of comparison for data produced by the analysis, two general lines of strategy have evolved. One is that of examining the changing image of one or more culture-heroes to see what qualities different epochs in their culture saw fit to value or depreciate.[78] Alternatively, some form of personality syndrome — need for power or for achievement, for instance — can be used to see how different epochs or cultures rate in its terms. As a check on inferences, some form of multiple operationism can be used in an attempt to establish converging findings by using different techniques on different kinds of source materials. Usually cited in illustration is a two-phase study. This first employed a questionnaire to discover what were the topics of concern to the public. It then content analyzed the 'letters to the editor' of various news media to see whether similar concerns appeared therein.[79] W. J. Paisley speaks of the strategy as deploying several measures to bear in from different angles on ("triangulate") the central core of overlapping findings.[80]

Assessment of 'the spirit of an era' — 'The Victorian Mind', '*Romanitas*' are examples — is a common and generally poorly handled topic in literary or historical studies. Without some form of analytical infrastructure to direct inquiries, the fuzziness of the concept combines with the chaotic mass of the source materials to overwhelm the assessor. Hence studies result which reveal more about the writer's own values than about their alleged subject.[81] As the analytical problems involved in studies of this type are so great, it is clearly advisable to be informed as to the expertise available for conducting them.

SUMMING UP

Perhaps the following table will sum the foregoing discussion up most concisely. It attempts to indicate the purposes and areas best

[77] The main handbook is R. K. White, *Value-analysis*: *The Nature and Use of the Method*, Libertarian Press, New Jersey, 1951.

[78] For an illustrative example, see "The Changing Picture of Marius".

[79] Seee E. Webb and M. H. Roberts, "Unconventional Uses of Content Analysis in Social Science" in *Communication Content*, p. 321.

[80] See his introduction to Part III, "The Recording and Notation of Data," *ibid.*, pp. 285-6.

[81] A point that is explicitly made by the Classicist M. I. Finley in "The Ancient Greeks and their Nation: The Sociological Problem," *The British Journal of Sociology* 5(3), 1954, p. 258.

Figure 2.7: SCOPE AND LIMITATIONS OF CONTENT ANALYSIS AS A TECHNIQUE

Purposes of Technique	Areas Suited For Use	Modes of Operation	Technical Problems	Controls on Subjectivity
DESCRIPTIVE: Identifying characteristics within communications	Analysis of IMAGES of reality	Frequency counts (quantitative)	Inference as to representational or instrumental use of diction by source	Theoretical framework of inquiry and switch to unconscious level of diction
	INTERACTION analysis	Non-frequency counts: assessing bias of intensity (qualitative)	Reliability of coders	Panel tests
INFERENTIAL: Testing hypotheses	Intensive study of IDIOLECTS or LANGUAGE GROUPS	Pattern matching (contingency analysis)	Objectivity in assessing bias and intensity	Redefinition of categories into subject-matter variety
Producing data from communications so that inferences may be drawn (via multi-stage analysis)	Comparing CULTURES		Validity of criteria of evidence	Externally validated criteria.
				Checks via converging analyses

served by the technique, together with its main modes of operating, problems therein, and ways of limiting the subjectivity inherent in all such analysis.

The best conditions for content analysis involve two things. One is abundant data. The other is some form of theory which relates textual indexes or categories to behaviors or characteristics in the originator of the text.[82]

WHEN TO USE COMPUTERS

This section would not be complete without a note on when to use computers (and when *not* to use them) in conducting a content analysis. Computers confer such special benefits in analyzing content that, as seen, a special variety of content analysis has developed, rapidly and vigorously, in connection with their use. There is even a specialist literature on the application of computers to the analysis of literature. This field is serviced by journals of its own.[83] Hence there is a constant flow of new ideas, many relevant to computerized content analysis, from this related field. But, as has also been shown, the costs of using computers are high. Preparing text for computer use is a tedious business and may inject unsuspected subjectivity into the subsequent analysis. Computerized thesauruses are not as flexible as those produced by more fallible humans. The use of computer logic restricts the range of questions currently posable. So general guidelines as to when use of computers is advisable and when it is inadvisable will help analysts reach a decision more speedily in each special case.

Circumstances which call for use of a computer are as follows. A huge volume of data for detailed analysis or data involving complicated correlations or many crosscheckings are best handled with a computer. Its speed and accuracy and total recall cannot be matched by human clerical skills. Sometimes other investigators have related texts on computer tapes. Then an analyst who puts his text on tape may well be able to run his questions quickly through their materials as well, thus generating complementary findings. He may wish to make a further inquiry into his text employing a set of questions generated by his first set of findings from that text. If so, it pays to use a

---

[82] See Paisley, Introduction to Part III of *Communication Content,* p. 283.

[83] There are, for instance, general purpose journals such as *Computers and the Humanities* (a quarterly, from Queen's College of the City University of New York), *Computer studies in the Humanities and Verbal Behavior* (a quarterly from Liège, Belgium) or the monthly newsletter *Calculi* (published by the Department of Classics, Dartmouth College, Hanover, New Hampshire, U.S.A.).

computer. For, with computerized content analysis, extracting data is the quick part of the content analysis — the very opposite of a manual content analysis. Alternatively, if it is wished to expand the set of categories in the light of the findings (impossible with a manual content analysis), a computer 'dictionary' with a left-over-list will have to be used.[84]

Circumstances where use of a computer is inadvisable are as follows. Complicated or nebulous themes which cannot be atomized are difficult to write a computer program for and are best analyzed by hand. It may be prohibitively expensive to reduce a complex text into computer-readable form, if all that is intended is a single study of the text. If the data which are to be extracted are easy to identify or quantify — as with straightforward word counts or space-time measures (inches of newspaper space) — again, it is not worth the trouble of reducing the text to computer-readable form and having a special program written. Finally, it is not worth using a computer if only a limited amount of information is desired from even a vast quantity of material. This would be the case, for instance, in non-frequency counting, where an analyst wishes merely to establish whether a given feature occurs.[85]

The realities of the situation are that it takes money, time and organization to execute a computerized content analysis. It may well be necessary to secure a grant-in-aid from somewhere, persuade a programmer to write a special program, and await the availability of a special typist and of running time. The mere organization of the practical details of all of this activity will add measurably to the overall difficulty of the study. It is worth the effort only for a major study. But most of the projects upon which content analysis is used are small-scale, routine matters: book reviews, surveys to be done in limited time and on limited funds. Many content analyses can be done with punch cards, by employing multivariate analysis. In such a case the analyst is probably able to process the cards himself, for the card-sorting machines are generally standing idle while people queue to use the computers (or computer programmers). Manual content analysis is, in fact, likely to remain the workhorse of those using the technique.

CONCLUSION

This then is what is currently going on under the name of content analysis. In a sense, it is like having ready-made a collection of sieves

---

[84] See *Content Analysis*, pp. 151-2 and 191-4.
[85] *Ibid.*, pp. 152-3.

of different shapes and sizes. You select the one (or ones) you want to use. You can even use them one after, or inside, another. The possession of such sieves will not necessarily make anybody a good miller. But it will be very difficult indeed to do a good job of milling without them. Suppose that you are confronted with an outpouring of details and have to sift them this way and that, to find in what proportions certain specific types of details are represented in them. The findings you produce will be directly related to your skill at doing the sifting. And this skill, in turn, will be enormously increased if you acquire some formal training in sifting. We are all familiar with work in the Arts which concludes with guesstimates or with bald hypotheses and conjectures, out of sheer incompetence in handling the details it has surveyed or amassed. This practice, after all, is "only what we're all doing."

3

Content Analysis And General Semantics:

What The Words You Use Tell About You

INTRODUCTION

Content analysis is largely a matter of studying words. If words are the tools of your trade, the more you know about them the better. This chapter should serve to increase readers' awareness of what is currently going on in the study of words. Words, and the language they constitute, are an integral part of our thought processes. So any increase in language skills or sophistication means improved thinking ability. The relationship of this chapter to the rest of the book follows from that premise.

More specifically, the relationship between content analysis and general semantics is exceedingly close yet far-reaching. Content analysis presumes a semanticist's approach to word meaning. It incorporates semanticists' findings on ways in which words are in fact used in the psychological economy of an individual style or in the shaping influence of speech communities. The language of a speech community may have characteristics which no one individual member displays in full. These can become evident only when communications are studied in overall terms. An individual's writings, when studied as a 'universe' of data, tell a lot about him. But they can do so only if they can be compared to the linguistic patterns normal for his group. Moreover, the mass media constitute channels through which communications flow, and in so doing they influence the contents and directions of the flow. Often this influence works in unexpected ways, as studies of communications flows have revealed. Consequently, there are established findings related to individual and communal communications behavior. It is best to be aware of what these are, when they concern the type of behavior being studied.

The aim, then, is to provide an overall orientation to work in the general area of semantics, wherever it concerns content analysis. This orientation is concerned primarily with two things. One is to outline the ways in which content analysis assumes that words 'work'. The other is to indicate background findings which set limits on the operations, or which direct the course, of a content analysis. My experience is that much of what is in this chapter tends to be rather novel to Arts students. Various aspects of it invariably fascinate different members of any study group working on content analysis. It appears that an overall survey provides a foundation which gives a different quality of awareness to subsequent work in content analysis. Such a survey also engenders a much greater realization of the significance of current work in the Social Sciences, about ways in which words, and communication in general, are being studied in a wide variety of disciplines as we enter the 1970s.

For nowadays students of history and literature tend to be asking new sorts of questions of their source materials. Increasingly they want to investigate social issues, climates of opinion, or states of mind. The old ways of analyzing documents were not intended for these new questions, by and large.[1] Asking the new style of questions without knowing the new style of techniques which enable getting answers to them is rather futile. It is rather common, though. There follows an outline of what these new techniques are, so far as they relate to the study of words — and relate in ways which can be used in content analysis. The books mentioned in the course of the outline should enable the reader to explore on his own any of the points which particularly interest him.

There is a variety of ways of studying words.[2] Readers will be all too familiar with grammars. They may, however, underestimate dictionaries. It was from the latter that the movement known as 'descriptive linguistics' originated. This movement involves views such as: "Dictionaries are history books, not law books," and "the spoken language *is* the language." It leads to histories of the language — studies of key words across the centuries. And it leads to dialect study, and to the study of usage (which stands in relation to grammar as behavior does to etiquette). Out of all this came semantics, the study

---

[1] L. Benson, "An Approach to the Scientific Study of Past Public Opinion", *Public Opinion Quarterly* 32, 1968, pp. 527-9.

[2] A highly readable account can be found in Postman and Weingartner, *Linguistics: A Revolution in Teaching*. The table at pp. 204-205 is particularly helpful. For a survey of approaches relevant to this chapter, see D. Hymes (ed.), *Language in Culture and Society: A reader in Linguistics and Anthropology*, Harper International, 1966.

of the relationship of language, thought and behavior.[3] The semanticists' discovery that "the language user is the source of whatever meanings the language has" has been described as a linguistic discovery on a par with the discovery of the concept of zero in mathematics. Out of semantics has come psycholinguistics, or the study of language by psychologists,[4] and, most recently, sociolinguistics, or the study of language by sociological means.[5] Work in all these fields is currently going at a great rate. And they are all interrelated, as figures 3.1 A, B and C indicate.

The first figure attempts to outline the main assumptions of a semanticist in producing different kinds of definitions, be they historical, operational or what have you. He has two major preoccupations, with meaning and with the flux of linguistic usage. For, in the first place, a semanticist tends to have some very clear assumptions about word meaning. Words may be seen as tools for conceptualizing or as pawns in some strategy of word play. But, basically, usage is seen to determine meaning, a view which involves an empiricist's, experimenter's view about meaning in general. This attitude underlies all content analysis. Meaning or practice is taken as something to be established, not assumed. In the second place, a semanticist is likely to be preoccupied with the development of a word's significance, over time, in the stream of language. An abstract word in practice has many facets of meaning. The precise variety of facets which a man chooses to employ has psychological significance for his thought-world — a line of thought which leads off into Psycholinguistics.

[3] The semanticists do tend to be difficult to read, because they are writing about a very difficult subject. However, in my experience, students have found the following books helpful and readable: S. Ullmann, *Semantics: An Introduction to the Science of Meaning*, Blackwell, 1962 (particularly chapters 3 to 5 and 9), and, at a more general level, S. I. Hayakawa, *Language in Thought and Action*, Harcourt, Brace & World, 1963 (second ed.)

[4] For a general survey of such work see Carroll, *Language and Thought*, particularly chapters 3, and 5 to 7. In general on psycholinguistics see N. N. Markel, *Psycholinguistics: An Introduction to the Study of Speech and Personality*, Dorsey, 1969. The close relationship between this field of study and the technique of content analysis is indicated by the fact that three chapters (8 to 10) are devoted to content analysis.

[5] For a particularly readable (and highly significant) instance of sociolinguistics at work, see Lawton, *Social Class, Language and Education*. Pages 156-161 provide an outline of the overall import of the book's findings. On the significance of the techniques of analysis forged in linguistics for anyone bent on studying social phenomena, see Cicourel, *Method and Measurement in Sociology*, p. 179.

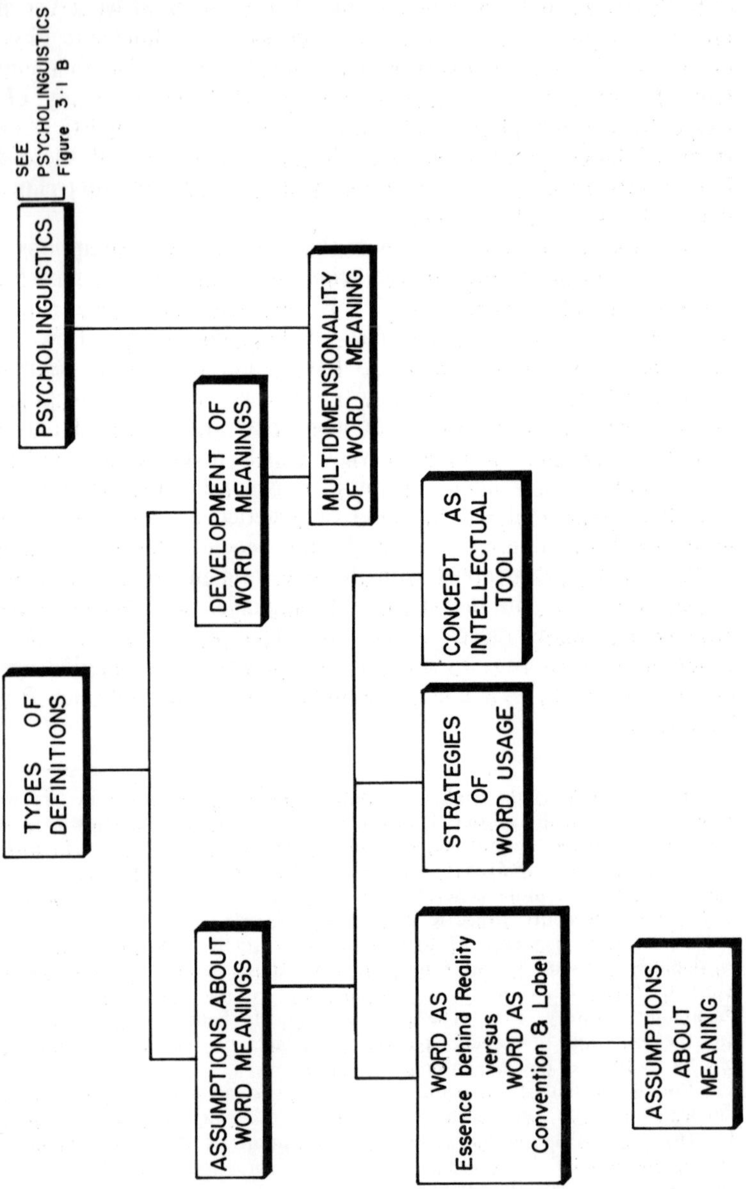

Figure 3.1A: MAJOR ASPECTS OF A SEMANTICIST'S VIEW OF WORD MEANING

Figure 3.1B: PSYCHOLINGUISTICS AND SOCIOLINGUISTICS FROM A SEMANTICIST'S VIEWPOINT

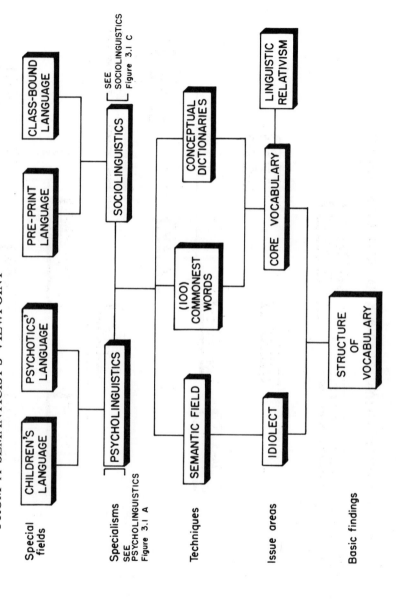

Figure 3.1C: COMMUNICATIONS FLOWS AND MESSAGE MEANING

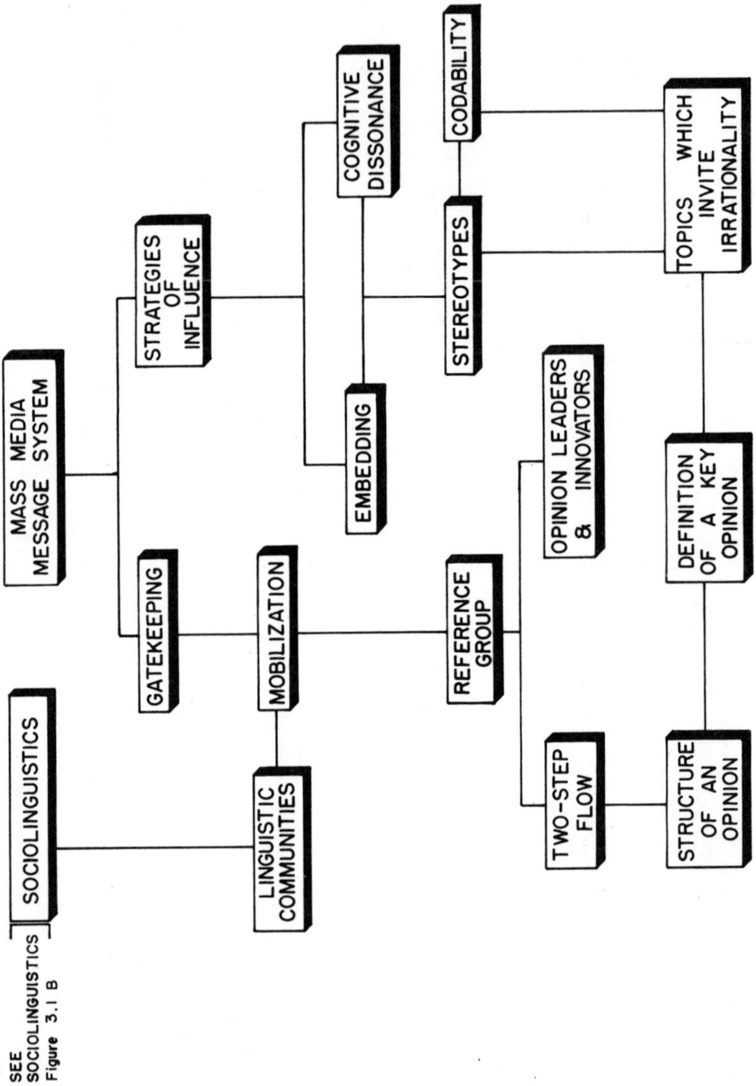

SEE
SOCIOLINGUISTICS
Figure 3.1 B

Psycholinguistics is the connecting link between figures 3.1A and 3.1B. The latter figure attempts to show the consequences of the discovery of how structured vocabulary is. Again, there are two main lines of development. There can be examination of the language of an individual (his idiolect) or that of a speech community. One theory, linguistic relativism, even holds that the 'reality' which is perceived is determined by the language the perceiver's community uses. Investigating an individual's language is generally done by examining the association of his ideas with crucial psychosocial issues, which requires examination of verbal associational fields. This interest leads to psycholinguistics: the study of a man's personality through the words he chooses to use. Well developed areas of study within this specialism involve the language of children and that of the mentally ill.

In investigating *group* use of language, on the other hand, an analyst will probably make comparisons of differences in vocabulary structure or in the availability of concepts. (All techniques at this level can be used on *either* individual or group analysis, however.) Group use of language is the idea studied by sociolinguistics; it has well developed fields of study concerning pre-print languages and class speech patterns.

Sociolinguistics is the connecting link between figures 3.1B and 3.1C. The latter shifts attention to another level. It involves cybernetics and communications theory, and tries to outline how communications procedures affect perceptions of what is being communicated. Again such procedures can be approached from two viewpoints: the effect of the channels of communication, or the effect of the dynamics of communicating. To take the effect of the communications channels first, the channels constituted by the mass media involve corporate policy. In editorial and financial decision-making, key men control the gates, setting policy and shaping communications flows. The media mobilize the public, by circulating information and providing the terminology and ideology underlying public debate. But some groups participate in public debate in a less well integrated fashion than do others. (Study of who they are and how this comes to be is a matter for sociolinguistics.) For the public confronts the media in informally structured groups rather than as individuals. All these are facts which impose certain uniform patternings upon the opinions held.

But the dynamics of communicating also play a similar role, as new messages struggle to impinge on our overpopulated consciousnesses. Advertisers, in particular, have evolved some most ingenious strategies to cause their messages to slip through. Word-of-mouth transmission distorts what is transmitted in certain quite regular ways. So do our prejudices when confronted by unacceptable material. Some issues are easier to think clearly about than are others. So it is that the process of communicating shapes a person's opinions in certain set ways. Hence a man's opinion is capable of being depicted with a fair degree of objectivity, and compared with what it was before or with what the next man's is now.

It is hard to decide where to start on the job of setting out the relevance of all these findings. For they concern content analysis in so many, and such interlinking, ways. There is no one clear and obvious sequence of narration. We are not dealing with a series of causes and effects, but with a 'ball of snakes' type of interrelationship. To make the best of a bad job, start by taking a look at our assumptions about words, and then at how language influences thought. Then consider the significance of the findings that vocabulary has 'structure' or relatively fixed patterns of usage. End up by assessing how it helps to know what the characteristics of communications flows are. Figure 3.1 A, B and C may be found helpful as frameworks, respectively covering the three areas outlined in the last three sentences. Each figure, as already outlined, sets out the skeletal infrastructure of the narrative. This is not a unilinear progression, but a branching out with some intertwining. So it may help to have an overview of the branches in stark outline. The diagrams provide that overview.

WORD MEANING

First then, consider how to go about defining a word. One possibility is: "It used to be used to mean such and such; then it came to mean so and so; but now it seems to mean this and that" (consider the word 'gentleman', for instance). This is an historical-social definition. Another possibility: "When so and so uses it, he means the following things . . . " ('democracy' for a major political figure). This is a semanticist's definition, stressing the necessity of looking for a writer's actual practice, and not presuming that 'we all know what he (or it) means.' A further possibility: "For that other person the word always has the following emotional overtones" ('law and order' for some other politician). This is a definition which faces up to the facts that most words both refer to things and also have an emotional significance for their user (think of 'hippies'). The fact is that a word *always* carries a number of messages simultaneously. It is multidimensional. There are shades of meaning and levels of applicability. Intonation helps define these; so does context. Pronunciation indicates class and regional background. These too can endow a word with a special significance.[6] Another kind of definition: "An example of this ('soul', for instance) is as follows." This is definition by illustration. Or: "Let us call it 'stress' when the pituitary gland is shrunken, the endocrine gland swollen and there's some disturbance of the tissue of the wall of the stomach." This is an operational definition; that is to say, it can actually be tested, by doing something, whether the state of affairs referred to by the definition exists. Or the definer can say: "Democracy is government of the people, by the people, for the people." This is definition by *pre*scription rather than description: by asserting the definition fervently enough, it is hoped to make things as it says they are. The same one word — think of 'democracy', 'bureaucracy', 'capitalism' — can be defined in all these ways.

Words, then, are 'slippery' things. They shift, sometimes almost imperceptibly, sometimes more dramatically, in the course of time. 'Time' here can be a century in the life of the language, or twenty years in the career of a writer. Take a word like 'democracy'. It has a nuclear core of meaning, something to do with 'power for and in the hands of the people.' It also has a varying mixture of other, more peripheral, connotations. At the moment, and in the West, these are: representative government, regular free elections, due process, majoritarianism, etc., etc. Also, it has an overall 'feel' about it, that is sometimes good, sometimes bad.[7] It is a multifaceted amalgam of shades of meaning. And it is, typically, a word with blurred edges. Anybody will 'know what it means' if he knows how to use it and respond to others' use of it. That is if he is a contemporary, *using* it. To 'know what it means' for someone in the past, an historian must know how *he* used it. Words, that is, do not have 'meanings' in the sort of way that children have parents. They have *uses*, identifiable in particular places and periods.[8]

There is no 'ideal reality', no 'basic essence', no 'inner picture' of which the word is a label. As a person matures, word 'meanings' shift and change for him. They are readinesses to respond to others' use of

[6] See Cicourel, *Method and Measurement in Sociology*, pp. 175 and 188.

[7] The classic among content analyses of the concept 'democracy' is I. de S. Pool *et al*, *Symbols of Democracy* (Hoover Institute Studies; Series C, Symbols: No. 4; Stanford U.P., 1952). It is impressive methodologically and in its findings, and makes easy and interesting reading.

[8] These points are cogently argued by T. D. Weldon, *The Vocabulary of Politics*, Penguin, 1953. See chapters 1 and (especially) 2 for a vigorous statement of the contentions in my text.

the label or instances of the phenomena it labels. But they are also readinesses to summon the label up, independently (and often correctly), at will. These readinesses are like those at work in our attitudes and in the ways in which we go about perceiving things. Indeed, they are part of those attitudes and ways of perceiving things. If a man's brain-tissue is damaged in a car crash, he not only loses his memory and the use of certain words, but his relationships with others become less flexible, and there are certain types of 'perceivings' — such as categorizing things — that he cannot do. Never one of these deficiencies alone; always the whole set. If a man is 'brainwashed' and his *usages* of certain key terms changed, his attitudes to, and perceptions of, the phenomena involved also change. When a hypnotist's word becomes law, his subject gets blisters from the 'burns' which the hypnotist tells him he is experiencing.[9] One experimenter took a pair of retarded twins and, by giving one more exposure to words than the other, produced permanent differences in their attitudes and perceptions.[10] Language is not just a tool which we use. It is part of our apparatus for relating to the world around us. It interacts upon, and develops along with, our perceptions. To a very large degree, what becomes conscious is what we have words for.

This thesis does not mean that words are 'only conventions' which anyone is free to reinterpret, at his pleasure, for the purposes of discussion. To argue thus is to say: "These are only the rules; therefore I'm free to break them — but of course we're still playing the same game." Nor does it mean that, "as there are no basic essences behind words, therefore words don't really mean anything." Language is social: group consensus gives words their meanings. These meanings are added to in the course of the group's experience. A person responds to them in the way that is normal for his group. Nobody can arbitrarily change word meanings and still expect to be understood.

Consider the following two strategies for winning a verbal argument. The first involves preempting the 'hero words'. 'Democracy' is only a variously interpretable label, you say; so let *your* version be called 'democracy'. The other man can find some other label for his, and so on for the other key terms. Now, whatever you *claim* about the meanings of these words, the audience is going to respond with the normal

---

[9] See *Meaning and Mind*, chapters 8 to 10.

[10] See *Social Class*, pp. 45-47. The whole of this chapter (4: "Language and Thought") well repays reading. It complements and substantiates Terwilliger's findings.

reactions which the terms evoke within the group. Specially defined meanings soon are lost from their memories. Your opponent is thus encumbered with either negatively-charged or meaningless terms. Guess who loses. The second strategy involves the use of *portmanteau* words, that is words which have an unusually wide-ranging and nebulous penumbra of associations. They allow your audience the maximum possible range of 'interpretation' of what you are saying. Skill with words can often be precisely a matter of misleading ambiguity.

It follows that this viewpoint does not lead to a morass of relativism. It does not support arguments such as "the assertion that autocratic rule is a bad thing is a value judgement and therefore empirically undemonstrable." It says that reactions to verbal labels embody the consolidated experience of a society, and so they had better be taken seriously. If values are 'merely what people think' (i.e. the concept 'autocratic rule' has a predominantly negative 'feel' about it for most people), then the question is "what in fact do people think about values?" Assuming that one 'knows', and then playing with the terms as though they are algebraic symbols (and according to axiomatic logic), merely removes the whole operation from the world of social realities to which the terms are relevant. Induction (argument from the consequences of data which have been amassed) rather than deduction (argument by deductive logic from first principles) is required. Take all the people who have experienced autocratic rule and some other form of rule against which they can meaningfully compare it, and find out how many prefer one to the other, and why. This operation gives the factual, historical basis for the value-laden associations which the term has.[11]

LANGUAGE AND THOUGHT

Clearly, the way in which a particular man uses a word may not tell very much about the word. But it can tell a lot about the man. In fact, one way of probing into a man's basic assumptions involves a detailed study of a strategically chosen group of the words he uses. The ways in which he uses a set of key concepts is compared with the ways in which others of his group use them. The inquiry proceeds as follows. A word cannot be used independently of other words. Along with a word's mixture of shades of meaning, there is an associational field consisting of the word company it keeps, and the

[11] These two paragraphs are much influenced by the work of the transempiricist G. Sartori; see *Democratic Theory*, Wayne State U.P., 1960, especially chapters 4 and 6.

sorts of contexts in which it tends to crop up. Thus a word will have a wide range of nuances, company and contexts. So will the other major words with which it is linked. The question is: which does our man choose to stress, to notice, and to ignore? Do his preferences and overlookings indicate a particular position on issues to which the terms relate? How does this all compare with the general usage of his speech community? What others in that community exhibit verbal patterns like his? What characteristics do he and they share?

There is another way in which the words a person uses can be employed to tell things about him. The total range of words and concepts available in his usage can tell what age he is, and what age his society is in. Here is how such an approach works. Consider first the maturing stages through which the individual, rather than the society, goes.

A child spends his first two years acquiring the ability to form and express concepts — in becoming able, let us say, to categorize a variety of variously sized, colored and shaped animate objects as 'dogs'. Until he is about seven, he is still going through a stage of preoperational intuitive thinking, and acquiring the concepts of space, time and causality. Thereafter, to the age of eleven or so, he acquires the ability to think operationally — to check his perceptions or conclusions by experiment. Formal thinking in abstract propositions (by hypothesis) comes after this.

One theory is that expression consists of two forms of speech, 'inner' and 'outer'. 'Inner' speech starts as the child's talking to himself for self-guidance. It is increasingly internalized, becoming the verbal level of the interior stream of consciousness. 'Outer' speech is the child's attempts to communicate with others. This waxes in vocalization as 'inner' speech wanes therein.[12]

Children's vocabularies differ at these various stages. Suppose someone were to give a group of children, then a group of adults, a series of words and ask them to tell what other words spring to mind — or a series of little drawings, asking in this case for stories 'telling' about the drawings. He would find that something like 20 percent of the adults' words would involve a visual contour, as opposed to about 70 percent of the children's words. About 40 percent of the adults' nouns would have implications of size, as opposed to about 85 percent of the children's. The children's nouns would be

---

[12] See L. S. Vygotsky, *Thought and Language*, M.I.T. Press, 1962, pp. 44-51 (and see the summary of his findings in chapter 7 there).

far more concrete than those of the adults. They would contain no superordinate terms.

Examples of levels of terminology are:

ABSTRACT	SUBORDINATE	SUPERORDINATE
Fish	Stickleback	Vertebrate

Word associations tend to fall into the following patterns:

STIMULUS WORD	CHILD'S RESPONSE	ADULT'S RESPONSE
Dog	Tail	Cat; Poodle; Animal

The children's verbs would name actions, not states (which would be frequently mentioned by the adults).

A child cannot perform the conceptual activities of one of these stages unless he has the concepts available in his vocabulary. Children from large families, who acquire their verbal skills largely from their fellow siblings, are 'retarded' in comparison with children whose skills are acquired in association with adults. Something like 70 percent of British scientists, for instance, are *first* children.

The world which the child perceives is not just a smaller version of the adult's world. It is a different *sort* of world. For, initially, a child experiences reality directly, through the senses; taste and touch play a far larger part than with adults. Later, the words foisted upon him by adults 'help' him experience his reality. Consequently there is a radical break in the way reality is perceived as the child learns to speak.[13] Our ideas, it has been said, are our spectacles. With literacy comes a major reorientation. First of all literacy opens a door to a limitless number of new ideas. Secondly the word — there it is, on the paper — can no longer be identified with the thing it labels. The pupil must leave the primitive tribes of children with their special world of games and rituals, dating back for hundreds of years in many cases. No wonder many baulk.[14]

LANGUAGE AND TECHNOLOGY

Some claim that the child, as his verbal and conceptual skills successively mature, passes through a series of stages akin to those

[13] See E. G. Schachtel, "On Memory and Childhood Amnesia" in T. Talbot (ed.), *The World of the Child*, Doubleday Anchor, 1968, Chapter 2.

[14] See McLuhan, *Gutenberg Galaxy*, pp. 90-92 (citing I. & P. Opie, *Lore and Language of Schoolchildren*, Oxford U.P., 1959, pp. 1-2).

through which human society has, historically, evolved. Consider briefly what there is to be said for such a view. If we consider human societies as groups within which communications flow, then, clearly, there are successive stages of development.[15] There are pre-literate societies, and pre-print societies, for instance. Furthermore, with the coming of telecommunications, society's ability to handle messages changed radically. Computers have recently brought about another such change. Each of these stages has certain quite distinctive characteristics. For the way a person can handle communications, which means information, affects his perceptions.

A pre-literate society is still at the word-magic stage. The word *is* the thing: hence spells and curses. Hence also no fiction. It is unthinkable.[16] Men think in terms of myths. And mythical thinking differs from logical thinking rather as pre-operational thinking differs from operational thinking.

Pre-print society, then, is characterized by logical thought. Aristotle, who came relatively shortly after the discovery of the alphabet (which made widespread literacy possible), had made mankind analytically aware of thought processes.[17] But pre-print man differs from the man of a print culture. Pre-print man reads audibly. He savors every word. For every word in the relatively small range of books available to him has many layers of meaning. He 'sees' things as his pictures show them, in a mosaic field of forces, not with the unilinear, perspective viewpoint of man of the print culture who 'sees' in 'single chain of consequences' fashion. Men in a print culture read silently. They skim through part of the vast range of books available to them. They think more in statistical terms.[18]

Telecommunications are produced only by scientifically advanced societies. The scientific viewpoint is dominant and pervasive in such societies. It involves a very special view of words, which are seen

15 In his study "Agraria and Industria" F. W. Riggs outlines the systematic ways in which communications in a traditional society differ from those in an industrial society. He then proceeds to show the linguistic and conceptual consequences. See pp. 73-81 and 53-61 (& 64-67).

16 See *Meaning and Mind*, p. 90, and McLuhan, *The Gutenberg Galaxy*, p. 20 (cf. also pp. 18-19; 25; 37; 65 & 71-2).

17 Even in the case of the ancient Greeks, however, the limitations imposed by the stage of development of their language restricted their intellectual activities: see B. Snell, *The Discovery of the Mind: The Greek Origins of European Thought*, Blackwell, 1953, p. 244 (and chapter 10 in general).

18 See McLuhan, *The Gutenberg Galaxy*, pp. 85-104 and 111; cf. also 16, 28, 43, 77-9, 124, 130-33 and 136. On the viewpoint expressed in the text, see J. S. Bruner, *Toward a Theory of Instruction*, Norton, 1968, pp. 24-29, where it is termed 'evolutionary instrumentalism'.

as conceptual tools with which to perform explorations in under-standing. Highly abstract ways of thinking come to be practised. A pre-print society simply does not have the volume, or complexities, of abstractions characteristic of the language of these telecommunications societies. Thus there are currently some languages which simply do not have adequate verbal and conceptual resources to translate the scientific textbooks of the advanced communities.[19] Telecommunica-tions also involve a much greater amount of communicating, and much greater awareness of other cultures. So this is the stage where seman-tics appears. Language now comes to be viewed as a product imbued with the characteristics of its culture, to be studied dispassionately and scientifically. This stage, then, matches the stage of formal thinking, in terms of abstract propositions. This was the culminating stage in the development of the individual human's thought processes, it will be remembered.

But from the computer has come yet a further technological devel-opment affecting our communications behavior. It can process data at a speed, and in quantities, hitherto unimaginable. And it has brought a new attitude to language, which is now seen as a flow of information among transmitters and receptors such that losses in information carried in the network can be counted. This attitude goes by the name of the cybernetics approach. 'Cybernetics' means 'steering' in the sense of 'directing' or 'governing' (it originates in the Greek word for 'helmsman'). The *rationale* behind the name is something like this. A government can be compared, say, to a racehorse. How it works can be studied by looking at its political institutions, which is like an explanation in terms of the racehorse's skeletal structure. Or centres of power can be studied, which is like looking at its muscles. But before either of these can work, it must have information: the nerve-centres must be activated. So if how information is fed in and round about inside is looked at, how governing or directing occurs can best be understood.[20] Hence psycholinguistics, which looks at the characteristics of the transmitters and receptors, and sociolinguistics, which looks for patterns in the information flowing through what is seen as a 'system'. Possibly it *might* be said that this stage represents the stage of psychological insight achieved by the mature person.

CONCEPTUALIZATION

The major turning point, however, in this growing sophistication about the language we use came with the idea of treating words as

19 See *Social Class*, pp. 75-76.
20 See Deutsch, *The Nerves of Government*, pp. 76-97.

conceptual tools. Look at what this implies. Hans Selye is the discoverer of the General Adaptation Syndrome and a researcher whose work has led to the discovery of ways of coping with a number of diseases for which, prior to him, there was no counter. He starts his book on stress by recounting how, until he had formed his basic new concepts, he just was not able to see the wood for the trees amid his data. Only when he had formulated the concept of 'the non-specific syndrome' (the bodily conditions present in all cases no matter what the disease), could he start to put those data into order so as to see what was correlated with what. He was able to delimit the area for investigation by defining it. He could see what *wasn't* there.[21]

Now his is a very special sort of definition, an operational one — the one on stress, already cited. It says "When you do certain things and get such and such results, then you've got what I call stress." It goes along with a number of other such definitions. This kind of language is called by outsiders 'scientific jargon'. It is a language of great precision, used with care and deliberation by a group whose members all have special knowledge of, and experience in working with the equally carefully limited subject matter involved. No science can advance without some such foundation. It is a special way of intellectually equipping oneself to perform certain special types of perceptual activity.

Look at this another way. Sigmund Freud equipped mankind with a battery of new concepts for the discussion of subconscious mental states and activities. His work did two things. First, it led to the 'discovery' of those states and activities; it turned them into public events. Poets and novelists had known of them intuitively, of course, long before Freud. But Freud's terminology, with its operational definitions, enabled *anyone* to see, and to see forever, what was involved. Secondly, Freud's concepts acted to open the floodgates of public debate. For they enabled discussion on the previously tabu subject matters of sex and sensuality to proceed in unemotional, reasonable terms. The whole nature and direction of social perception of the matters involved was altered. This achievement was so great because it involved the formulation of concepts of a type which are not easy for our cognitive facilities to cope with, apparently.

Basically, there are three kinds of concepts: conjunctive, disjunctive and relational. A conjunctive concept is one which involves the joint presence of the appropriate values of several attributes. A dis-

---

[21] See *The Stress of Life*, Longman, 1957, chapter 7; chapters 4 and 5 also contain a very interesting discussion of the semantics of inquiry.

junctive concept involves their joint presence or any combination of their presence. A relational concept involves the specific relationships between defining attributes. Disjunctive concepts are confusing to the human mind. Yet many psychological concepts are of this nature.[22]

Typically, Freud uses the stuff of which concepts that attempt to ensnare for us the shifting patterns of psychological traits have perforce to be made. And so it is in other fields of scientific endeavor. Those who are expanding the frontiers of human understanding are grappling with adversaries whom the layman cannot see, by the use of conceptual skills which he cannot, often, comprehend. But, whether the layman comprehends what psychologists are doing or not, they are currently at work on the psychology of cognition, reshaping our ideas on how we think, perceive and learn. And they do this reshaping partly by providing concepts which enable us too to identify for the future the various phenomena which they have 'discovered' by replacing preconscious half-awareness with operational definitions.

Consider one of their concepts: codability.[23] This concept concerns the way in which we go about the business of recognizing something that we see. Recognition turns out to involve both the stimulus which that something provides and certain qualities in the label that we have for it. For the existence of a name facilitates our ability both to recognize and to remember the object it labels. Show children little symbols with names alongside them — 0-0 for instance. Two weeks later ask them what it was they were shown. They will remember it as 0~0 if it was initially described as 'eye-glasses', 0=0 if it was called 'a dumbbell'. Some colors just are not seen if the people in question do not have a name for them: the Iakuti, for instance, have only one name for the colors blue and green.

Two things are involved, the stimulus and the concept. Certain stimuli are more codable than others; this factor is termed 'stimulus codability'. Some colors, for instance, are much more readily identifiable if people are asked to tell what they are. The concepts involved are right at the centre (rather than at the outer edges) of people's awareness — they can be easily located within the color categories involved ('category centrality'). These concepts always turn out to be coded with a short name ('category codability') which springs

---

[22] See Bruner, *A Study of Thinking*, pp. 41-3. On the difficulties experienced by the human mind in coping with certain types of concept, see *Communication Content*, pp. 51-54. For the concept 'public event', see Sarason, *Personality*, p. 12.

[23] On this concept see Carroll, *Language and Thought*, pp. 95-8. On the influence of verbal labels on thought, see *Social Class*, pp. 59-61.

readily to mind without misgivings ('category availability'). When an individual hesitates over identifying a color and is inconsistent in his placements, some haziness over the labelling involved within the speech community at large will be found. 'Codability' involves all these four concepts. Psychologists can test a concept's codability. Stimuli become more striking, then, if there is a name for them. And ways of investigating them can be stated and tested better, if there is a name to do it with.

Demonstrably, the labels with which thinking is done affect the nature of that thinking.

This effect is perhaps nowhere more strikingly apparent than with the phenomenon known as stereotyping. In our thinking, it would appear, we have the ability to deal simultaneously with only a rather limited number of bits of information: about seven or so. The mind cannot increase the number of bits, but it can increase the size and complexity of each individual bit.[24] So, without the human habit of lumping things together into categories, we just could not put order into the thousands of stimuli with which we are continually bombarded. Classification enormously simplifies the making of discriminations among them. It brings vast economies in the efforts expended in doing so. Children overeasily form large abstract categories. The primitive mind also tends to do so, apparently. We gradually attain habits of greater specificity, as cultural groups and as individuals. But it is very often a rough-and-ready business. A concept consists of a bundle of associations clustering around one or two key verbal labels. It should be able to be revised if its holder comes upon experience that expands or corrects it. Sometimes it cannot be revised like this. It (or rather, the readinesses to perceive which make up the attitude set in which it is embedded) resists the implications of new information, for they would necessitate extensive realignments internally. In such a case we are dealing with what is termed a stereotype. A person with a negative stereotype consisting of the concept 'Jews' or 'Negroes' reacts to the label in his mind rather than to the actual people whom he meets, for instance. Alas, prejudice, which so largely results from stereotypes, is so much a part of all our experiences that readers will not need any further discussion of this point.[25]

[24] See G. Miller, "The Magical Number 7, Plus or Minus 2: Some Limits on Our Capacity for Processing Information", *Psychological Review* 63, 1956, pp. 81-97.

[25] On stereotyping see *Meaning and Mind*, pp. 268-74. The classic in this field is G. W. Allport's *The Nature of Prejudice*, Doubleday Anchor, 1958; see chapter 11. Chapter 11 of Hayakawa's *Language in Thought and Action* gives a semanticist's view.

LINGUISTIC RELATIVISM

All these ideas of conceptualizing and stereotyping have considerable bearing on the theory that our native tongue imposes a special orientation upon our perceptions, through the concepts it contains and the ways of handling them which it allows.[26] This is the well-known Whorf hypothesis, sometimes termed linguistic determinism. Now in fact the core vocabularies of our major languages seem to code much the same set of things in the ten thousand or so words involved in each. Where these languages actually differ is the relative ease with which different things can be said in them. It is easier, apparently, to say or think some things in certain languages than in others. This discrepancy can have serious consequences for a speaker of a language, if the 'things' which are hard to code in his language are important. Concepts which enable us to think about the way we think are clearly of the utmost importance, for instance. Consider the implications of the fact that the French word *'conscience'* is the equivalent of *both* the English words 'conscience' and 'consciousness'.[27] The codability of some things differ from one language to another. Also, as the sorry business of stereotyping shows, some people handle the resources of their language differently from others *in the same language group*. Figure 3.2 shows what this difference could mean.

Let's examine the implications of this carefully.

Figure 3.2: SPEECH COMMUNITIES AND CORE VOCABU-
        LARIES

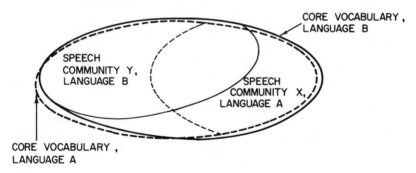

[26] B. L. Whorf, *Language, Thought and Reality*, M.I.T. Press, 1956. For the qualified acceptance of this hypothesis expressed in the text, see Bruner, *Towards a Theory of Instruction*, pp. 19-20, *Social Class*, pp. 64-76 (an important critique of the hypothesis), and *Meaning and Mind*, pp. 286-94 & 310.

[27] *Social Class*, p. 66.

In the first place, two people can both speak the same language while using it quite differently. The wry description of the English and Americans as 'two great peoples sundered by a common language' springs readily to mind. There always are, observably, regional dialects and class speech mannerisms within any language. The full significance of the latter is just beginning to become apparent. The British have given their working-class children equality with their middle-class children in access to secondary schools *without materially affecting the failure and drop-out rates of the former.* Inquiry (employing content analyses, incidentally) has shown that the speech patterns typical of the working class underemploy the resources of the language.[28] Comparisons of the speech and writing of boys in either group shows a slight difference in the actual structure of the vocabulary but a considerable difference in the ease of handling complex syntax. In both cases the middle-class children have the advantage. They can handle their words *and their thinking* with more flexibility and precision. And a cumulative deficit is involved: there is more disparity between the older than the younger groups of children. The working-class schoolchildren thus have a narrower view of life's potentialities — and their own.

This means that it simply cannot be *assumed* that a particular speaker of a language has at his command the full resources of his native tongue. He will tend to have those of his speech community. These will not necessarily overlap with the speech communities of other classes or status groups speaking that language. Nor will they necessarily cover the whole range of resources available within the language. How a speech community uses the linguistic resources of its language is a matter which must be inquired into, not taken for granted. Upon its use of those linguistic resources will depend the group's picture of its social — and other — 'realities'. Thus the changing content of the linguistic resources of a dominant speech group will reveal its changing preoccupations and definitions of reality. And what a man defines as reality *is* real in its consequences for him, remember. As such, it is a fit subject for historical or literary inquiry. Moreover, just because the English and French languages — for the sake of an example — provide 'pretty much' the same facilities for expressing perceptions, this similarity does not mean that the parts of those languages used by members of their dominant speech communities necessarily overlap. In Canada, for instance, this is so far from being the case that attempts to communicate between the two have been termed the 'two

[28] See *Social Class*, chapter 6 and especially pp. 140-43 (cf. also 157-60).

solitudes'. The contrast between what 'history' means to a French-Canadian and what it means to his English-speaking counterpart is striking. So, unfortunately, are the consequences.[29]

SOCIOLINGUISTICS

"All very well," the reader is no doubt thinking, "but just how do we go about assessing what the linguistic resources of an individual or a speech community are?"

Well, that job can be done by a psychobiographical study. This might, for instance, inquire into the views, as expressed in their correspondence, of union leaders (as opposed to politicians, writers, etc.) in regard to a range of socially strategic issues. Or there could be a content analysis of essays, written by middle-class and working-class schoolchildren, respectively, on a topic such as 'social change'. Probably, there would be a tendency to use a computer, in spite of its inadequacies and limitations, because it would enable the processing of such a huge quantity of written data. With its aid a conceptual inventory of a language for a given period can be made by grouping words under the concepts with which they are associated. The concepts are then grouped under the themes around which the concepts are found clustering. These themes tend not to be too numerous to handle. One such study, for example, found 114 themes adequate to deal with the resources of the English language.[30] The overall pattern of themes can now be used as a yardstick by asking: 'Which of these themes (and which concepts within each) does this author (or speech community) in fact use?' The sum total of a writer's work is treated for such purposes as a universe of data. It is called his 'idiolect' when so used. The version of the themes which is found there can be compared with those common in this or that speech community in his language group. Overlapping will then indicate the community whose frame of reference was closest to his.

In these inquiries, a look out must be kept for 'semantic fields'. Imagine a mosaic: masses of tiny pebbles fitted exactly together so as to form a complex pattern. A semantic field is the same thing, made out of words. Kinship terms in an African language and military

---

[29] Hodgetts, *What Culture? What Heritage?* pp. 33 and 80-84.

[30] Computer programs have been developed which construct a dictionary that maps out the vocabulary structure of an individual patient in psychiatric care. On this general topic, see *Content Analysis*, p. 154, and J. Laffa, "Contextual Similarities as a Basis for Inference" in *Communication Content*, pp. 159-74, especially 162-64. For further discussion in this book, see figure 8.12 and text thereto.

ranking systems in a European one are examples of semantic fields. When a speech group elaborates part of the structure of its vocabulary so as to form a semantic field, it is a sure sign that the cluster of related activities are highly important to it. Anyone studying pre-industrial society, for example, will simply not find the plethora of terms familiar to moderns for describing economic activities. A maximization of profit economy involves a completely different life style from that of a redistributive system, so much so that the basic value systems of the two cultures differ radically and, with them, so does the structure of the vocabulary.[31]

COMMUNICATIONS FLOWS

But, it may be countered, people *aren't* computers. They just do not think about their languages like this. Right. But analyzing language usage is a different thing from using the language. How, in fact, do people 'use' language, at this level — that is, when we are considering it as massive flowings of communications within a speech group?[32] Clearly, their usage practices are partly determined by the level of technology. For technology provides the channels through which communications flow.[33] Many of the new states which have emerged since World War Two have exchanged, almost overnight, the largely pre-industrial methods of communication of a tribal community for industrial telecommunications networks.[34] So it is now known from practical experience how the means of communication available to it affect a society.[35] It is a complex business, and so the best way of showing what is involved is to depict traditional and

[31] See K. Polanyi, *Trade and Market in the Early Empires: Economies in History and Theory*, Free Press, 1957, pp. 239-57. On the lack of conceptual clarity involved in the discussion of economic activity in antiquity (one of the joint authors, H. W. Pearson, speaks of a "conceptual twilight"), see pp. xvii-xviii and 3-11. A more easily readable discussion of these matters will be found in chapters 1 and 2 of R. L. Heilbroner's *The Making of Economic Society* (Prentice-Hall, 1962). Heilbroner makes much the same case.

[32] The findings of current research into communications are conveniently gathered together in survey form in W. Schramm (ed.), *The Science of Human Communication*, Basic Books, 1963.

[33] See note 18. The classical work on this topic is H. A. Innis' *The Bias of Communication*, U. of Toronto Press, 1951; see pp. 3-60.

[34] This is the subject of Lerner's book, *The Passing of Traditional Society*; see chapters 1 to 3. Chapter 1 — "The Grocer and the Chief: A Parable" — is particularly readable.

[35] See Pye, *Communications and Political Development*, chapters 1 to 3, 9, 14 and 18. For a general survey of the findings in this area see R. R. Fagen, *Politics and Communication*, Little, Brown, 1966, chapter 7.

industrial society as two contrasted *systems* of communications.[36]

Illiteracy tends to be high — about 90 percent — in a traditional community. Communications are largely oral. They spread sparsely and unevenly through the community. Closeness to an influential person, wherever he may be, means high levels of information. Failing this, an individual can be located in the neighborhood of important events without necessarily being well informed about them.

An industrial society, on the other hand, requires a literate labor force. So most of its people are literate. Communications are mainly through the mass media of newspapers, radio and television. There tends to be an overabundance of news everywhere within the community, and the news 'breaks' as it happens.

As result of their wholly different exposures to information, the peoples of such societies tend to have quite different ways of handling it. A traditional society will tend to have a Great Tradition within which the gentlemen of its numerically small elite are all alike at home. This elite will comprise all the highly educated, all the experts — in law, religion, commerce and military matters — and all the intellectuals. Local 'little traditions' will flourish among the masses, along with marked regional diversity of dialects and so on. Such people may have considerable spectator expertise in the ways of government and The Great, but their orientation to them will be that of rather passive subjects, by and large.

In an industrial society, the population is what is termed 'mobilized'. It expects, and is expected, to have opinions.[37] This is not just a matter of polls and the availability of various kinds of census statistics (though the existence and availability of such things makes a qualitative difference in the self-awareness of the population involved). Public opinion — which appears only in societies with telecommunication facilities, incidentally — requires a public language for debate. There cannot be issues unless there are the terms with which to discuss them. The media spawn people whose aim it is to facilitate 'objective' discussion of public phenomena. Increase the conceptual resources of public debate and the quality of such debate is altered.[38] Not only do many more people than in a traditional society have an opinion

[36] As in Riggs' "Agraria and Industria". This work has been developed by some of Riggs' later writings. See, for instance, *Administration in Developing Countries: The Theory of Prismatic Society*, Houghton Mifflin, 1964, chapter 6.

[37] Contrast the shepherd's reaction, typical of the lower orders in traditional society, in Lerner, *The Passing of Traditional Society*, pp. 21 and 24.

[38] See R. Inglehart and R. Schoenberger, "Communications and Political Mobilization", (mimeo) paper to the 1968 meeting of the American Political Science Association on "cognitive mobilization" (pp. 6-10).

(and on many more matters), but they expect it to be taken into account. A participant orientation is common. This is a much more turbulent society in matters of opinion. There is no one small *elite* monopolizing all the advantages of education and expertise. Such things are scattered around amongst all kinds of professional and specialist groups. There is no one Great Tradition any more, either. It and the regional diversification have been bypassed by the emergence of the jargons, or specialist languages, of the various scientific or specialist subcultures.

COMMUNICATIONS THEORY

What happens to the 'overpopulated consciousness' of man in mass society? Getting a message across to him in this babel of overcommunication has been described (by an advertiser) as like trying to reach a man on a burro at the bottom of the Grand Canyon by throwing a bagful of confetti at him from a mountain at the side. But advertisers keep trying, and we have gradually acquired some practical knowledge of how people 'use' these facilities.

Initially a kind of state of psychological nudity was thought to prevail. The public was thought to consist of many individuals, with radio messages or whatever striking directly home to each. In fact, however, people tend to be plugged in to a communications network consisting of social groups. Anyone who wants to get the latest on films, clothes or even on newscasting on a particular topic tends to go to someone he expects will 'know' about such things, and ask him or her. There is simply too much information available for any one person to deal with it all. So individuals set themselves up, informally, as 'experts' on this or that topic. Such individuals handle the flow of information related to their special interests appearing in the media quite differently from the way the rest of their group does. They invest much more time in gathering it. They tend to specialize in particular topics. And this habit becomes known within their circle of acquaintance. So the messages from the media reach the individual in two steps, as it were. They proceed from the mass medium to the group expert, and then to the group member.[39]

It is in fact the *group* which, to a very large extent, governs what messages shall be perceived as trustworthy, important or relevant.

[39] The classical work on the 'two-step flow' is that of Katz and Lazarsfield, *Personal Influence: The Part played by People in the Flow of Mass Communications*. For a short survey see Katz, "The Two-Step Flow of Communication: An Up-to-date Report on an Hypothesis", *Public Opinion Quarterly* 21, 1957, pp. 61-78.

News is 'discovered' (becomes truly meaningful) largely as result of its being discussed. Now people tend to mix with people 'like themselves'. The resultant group, the reference group, is the means whereby an individual can establish a meaningful identity amid the uncertainties and ever-pressing changes of our impersonal, pluralistic industrial society. Within the group there tends to be an overall opinion leader. There are innovators, too, or 'early adopters' of novelties. Such people tend to have very different characteristics. The opinion leader represents, as it were, the quintessence of group feelings. The innovator is typically a marginal man, on the periphery of the group — even 'in step with a different drummer' (that is, he is half-way to having another reference group). It is only when the opinion leader gives his sanction to a change that the group switches to it.[40] I do not wish to imply that this process happens formally, or even very consciously. But these are the often unconscious trends which research on the dynamics of social groups has shown to be operating.[41]

GATEKEEPING

It follows from all this that not every message can get a hearing. The social groups, the communications networks, and the media set up a kind of field of forces through which only certain messages can proceed; and they must travel by specific routes. A message has to be meaningful to a group before that group will start to act upon it. Messages can be tied up only in certain particular bundles (that is, they have to be significant for specific groups of vested interests) so as to form 'issues' which will attract public support. And then it is no certainty that attention will be paid by the persons to whom outcry, in the form of issues, is addressed. After all, there are so many voices clamoring for their attention. A crucial role is consequently played by the 'gatekeepers'. These are the people who decide what shall be heard, what information shall be brought to the attention of the great man or men who must decide.[42]

If you think about it, this is how things happen in real life. Only

[40] The classical work in this area is E. M. Rogers, *The Diffusion of Innovations*, Free Press, 1962.

[41] For instance see H. Menzel & E. Katz, "Social Relations and Innovation in the Medical Profession: The Epidemiology of a New Drug" in Maccoby *et al*, *Readings in Social Psychology*, pp. 532-45.

[42] For a discussion of the significance of 'gatekeepers' see Easton, *A Systems Analysis of Political Life*, pp. 87-92; 133-40 & 424; for a case study, see D. M. White, "The Gatekeeper: A Case Study in the Selection of News" in Dexter and White, *People, Society and Mass Communications*, pp. 160-71 (a content analysis).

the historian with his perfect 20-20 hindsight ever sees a situation in all its clarity. And, in fact, if a crisis is examined by looking at the streams of information which overwhelmed the capacities of the men who made decisions therein, it is possible to get something of a shock. 'Plots', very often, appear traceable rather to an historian's paranoid style than to the chaotic facts. The attack on Pearl Harbor, for instance, has been much illuminated by this kind of treatment.[43] Moreover, the decision-maker acts on *his* opinion of the public opinion of the seriousness of the issue. It cannot just be assumed that these are identical.[44] If people have assumed identity, it has been, I suspect, more because they did not know how to establish what these opinions were than for any good reason.[45] Opinion is a difficult thing to measure objectively.

PUBLIC OPINION

This difficulty has not prevented diverse people from trying, however. So, once again, we have some knowledge based on practical experience. Equally important, we now have the conceptual tools with which to paint a portait of an opinion. And, once again, the study of children and their opinions has provided basic understanding.[46] For it appears that opinionation *precedes* knowledge. We imbibe class and party identifications in all sorts of roundabout ways when we are quite small, then proceed to notice facts, and mix with people, in ways which bear out those prior opinions. This is known as the 'socialization process'.

[43] See R. Wohlstetter, *Pearl Harbor: Warning and Decision*, Stanford U.P., 1962.

[44] A classic for its demonstration of how limited can sometimes be the picture of the situation held in the room at the top is R. A. Bauer *et al*, *American Business and Public Policy*, Atherton, 1963. For a brief outline of some of its major findings, by one of the joint editors, see L. A. Dexter, "Communications — Pressure, Influence or Education?" in Dexter and White, *op. cit.* pp. 395-407 (see especially p. 402).

[45] Ways of assessing the accuracy of one person's view of another person's view have been explored by Laing *et al*, in *Interpersonal Perception* (see chapter 2, note 39). A beautifully executed assessment of such a "meta-metaperspective", involving students' views of their parents, occurs at F. Barron, *Creativity and Personal Freedom*, Van Nostrand, 1968, chapter 22, especially pp. 276ff. For a discussion of the analytical problems involved in this business of assessing aspects of interactions, see G. J. McCall and J. L. Simmons, *Identities and Interactions*, Free Press, 1966, pp. 255-72.

[46] For a good brief survey, see F. I. Greenstein, *Children and Politics*, Yale U.P., 1965, or, in more general terms, P. Mussen, "Early Socialization: Learning and Identification" in G. Mandler *et al*, *New Directions in Psychology III*, pp. 51-110.

But opinions alter as people mature.[47] The adolescent rebellion against parents combines with a high valuation of the teen-age peer-group. If this group and the high school are both exercising similar influences, there can be a break with parents' and past opinions. Such a break is particularly likely if, in the new world that an individual has to move into as an adult in his early twenties, he has to live amongst workmates or neighbors whose opinions differ from those of his own earlier experience. But there is every likelihood that school and early maturity will provide influences which reinforce those of that early experience. It is, in fact, only in the case of movement from one class to another within society that they will fail to reinforce one another, as a general rule.

In the later twenties and in the thirties a person tends to be established in his adult roles and to have discovered a social group which suits his tastes. This is the supportive social environment which defines each person's 'life space', a term which here means the social and geographic areas within which people tend to make friendships, and from which they derive support for their social identity and definitions of social reality. From this point on, only the growing conservatism of the ageing process will tend to influence his opinions, given a fairly stable situation in the community at large.

It is necessary to be able to examine a number of opinions during several years to find out such a kind of thing; but then this is a perfectly legitimate way of using opinion polls. And, once a number of opinions can be looked at, other things about them will be found out too. Suppose there was to be an examination of the results of a questionnaire survey of opinions on pollution. It would be found that opinions vary in the amount of information which they contain. They also vary in the way in which their component parts are put together: some are more organized and coherent than others. They vary, too, in the degree to which really significant issues are salient within them, and in the degree to which action can be seen as a logical consequence of the views maintained. A varying amount of moralizing, mystification (belief in God, chance, etc.) and personalization (belief in Great Men rather than Social Forces) goes into them. Opinions tend to be pro or con a given issue and to be held with varying degrees of fervor or indifference. When compared, one can be average for its social group, another extreme. An opinion can be 'scored' on each of these aspects: they are called 'dimensions', and each visualized as a continuum running from high to low. The overall set of ratings is called a 'profile'; and profiles, once established, can be compared.[48]

[47] See Lane and Sears, *Public Opinion*, chapter 3.
[48] *Ibid.*, chapter 2.

Moreover, once a start is made at looking into lots of opinions, it soon becomes apparent that there are topics and circumstances which give rise to a disproportionate amount of irrationality. 'Foreign policy' (as opposed to 'a minimum wage') is a good example. Debate is conducted in abstract terms. Information levels are low and inaccurate. Consequences of proposed courses of action are difficult to estimate. Tabu materials (sex, violence) and out-groups likewise bring out more repressions than common sense. And opinions will not be judiciously formed if the individual is under stress, whether that stress is caused by poverty, low status, social isolation, war, or crime in the streets.[49] This is the *rationale* which lies behind the 'judo theory' of propaganda. That consists of a strategy involving the use of an initial claim by one side of such a provocative and/or misleading nature that the other side, in responding to it, will appear in an invidious light; typically, the public in general begins to take notice only in time to observe the reply. The judo theory is exemplified currently in the form of Kropotkin's "propaganda of the deed" as employed in activist or anarchist strategy. This strategy involves aiming a blow at a vital person or institution, in the hope that those who identify with him or it will react violently. The chances are that this situation will win the sympathy of outside groups ("the resonant mass") for those reacted against, or outside groups tend to give primacy to the reaction as it was this which drew their attention.[50] Word magic seems to be as alive as ever when it comes to terms which are difficult to define crisply or by some practical test: think of 'liberalism'.[51]

We know a little more, nowadays, than we did in the past about the ways of the bitch-goddess Rumor. And much good it seems to be doing us. Someone can be shown a highly emotionally charged picture and asked to describe it. Ten persons, or weeks, later it will be found that certain things have happened. Together they go by the name of "the embedding process", and they represent one of the ways in which the transmission of information works among humans.[52] The quantity of detail drops sharply away, until only a truncated but easily

[49] *Ibid.*, chapter 7, especially pp. 75 ff.

[50] See T. P. Thornton, "Terror as a Weapon of political Agitation" in H. Eckstein (ed.), *Internal War: Problems and Approaches*, Free Press, 1964, pp. 82-88.

[51] Even stronger, suggests Terwilliger, because moderns refuse to admit the power of words: see note to p. 320 of *Meaning and Mind*.

[52] In the study cited, a drawing of a violent little incident in the compartment of a passenger train was involved. On this and the "embedding process" see G. W. Allport and L. J. Postman, "The Basic Psychology of Rumor", in Maccoby, *Readings in Social Psychology*, pp. 54-65.

remembered residue remains. Striking details are exaggerated, hum-drum matters forgotten. The motivation and causation supplied become those which seem most 'natural' to the group among which the rumor is circulating. I found the same phenomenon to be operating when I examined the picture of a hero-figure of their culture held by a succession of *litterati*. The latter were renowned as well-read men for each of the centuries involved, and so represented the group memory of that hero-figure. The test thus replicated that involving memory described in the text, but covered seven hundred years, not ten weeks.[53]

To think about it, the amount of garbling that is bound to happen when someone tells someone else about something is very considerable at the best of times. Consider the simple little diagram figure 3.3.

Suppose someone writes an account of an incident in French. Then along comes an historian who incorporates that account into his history of the incident written for an English-reading audience. The individual's selective filter can be faulty or inadequate. His attitude sets can be biased or insensitive. The channel may distort: novels tell things differently from history books. The languages may not make for easy literal translation, especially if the writings occurs at widely different periods. And the message may be poorly or inaccurately arranged. Each telling or hearing of the tale can *only* introduce garbling.

COGNITIVE DISSONANCE

One form of garbling in particular has been receiving much attention recently. It is variously known as 'cognitive dissonance' or 'the strain towards congruence'.[54] These terms refer to the fact that our minds tend to baulk at simultaneously holding opinions which are mutually irreconcilable. Consequently they work on the matters involved so as to bring about harmony and alignment. Suppose that I have a high opinion of a particular person and no very high opinion of a particular policy (racial discrimination, say). Clearly, I expect that person to *dis*like that policy. If he does not, I will 'turn it over in my mind' until I have 'it all straightened out'. I can do this by changing my mind about the person or the policy, *or* by misperceiving his position (blank incredulity, etc.). The 'weakest link hypothesis' suggests that

[53] See "The Changing Picture of Marius", p. 15.
[54] For an outline statement, see Lane and Sears, *Public Opinion*, pp. 44-53; for a more detailed exposition, see R. Brown, "Models of Attitude Change" in R. Brown, *New Directions in Psychology*, Holt, Rinehart & Winston, 1962, pp. 1-85.

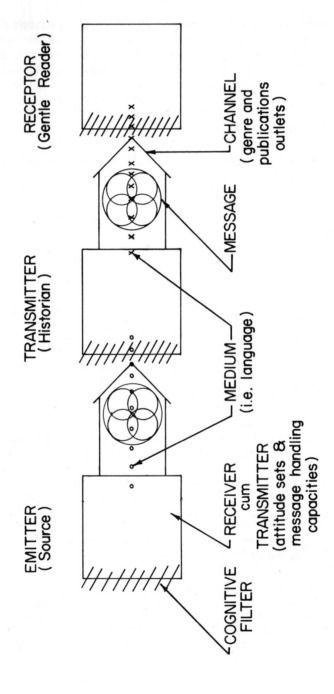

Figure 3.3: THE TRANSMISSION OF INFORMATION AS A PROCESS

the opinion changed will be whichever is less important to me. And there is every probability that I will react *psycho*logically rather than logically: that is, I will economize on psychic costs, because a total review of my opinions and value-system may involve emotional disturbances, or time, which I cannot afford. This difficulty may well lead me to reinterpret the person's statement on the policy: 'he was misquoted', 'joking', 'quoted out of context', and so on. We have all seen this kind of thing happening. For example, think of the ways intelligent people so ably misinterpret campaigns on cigarette smoking. The "worse peril" technique (dwelling on the infinitely greater perils of motor car driving, for instance) features prominently among such red herrings.[55] Or think of the ways in which other intelligent people successfully urge one to do or buy things![56]

It is this type of psychologic which causes the 'boomerang effect'.[57] A civil liberties group, say, is arguing for fair play in a civil rights issue. It thus draws the attention of the majority to that issue. Now, if that majority was previously markedly illiberal, the arguments will make a difference. The majority may become merely illiberal. This represents quite a shift of attitude. But it still leaves that majority on the wrong side of centre on a continuum extending from 'the extremely illiberal' to 'extreme liberalism'. The majority has now been goaded into activity, however. The activity, in consequence, tends to be the reverse of that which was anticipated by those who precipitated it when pleading the civil rights cause.

CONSENSUS AND DISSENSUS

These findings on attitudes and opinions have indicated a way of assessing a society's solidarity. It can be done by studying how a controversial issue is treated among the language communities which

[55] See Brown, *op. cit.*, pp. 51-52.

[56] Apparently, a dramatic fear-inducing communication has a much smaller long-run effect than does a low-keyed one which appeals to rationality. The former appeal may even produce the opposite effect to that intended. See I. L. Janis and S. Feshbach, "Effects of Fear-Arousing Communications" in *Journal of Abnormal and Social Psychology* 48, 1953, pp. 78-92. For a survey of advertisers' strategies, based on psychological research, see D. F. Cox, "Clues for Advertising Strategists", in Dexter and White, *People, Society and Mass Communications*, pp. 358-93.

[57] When the result of an appeal is the exact opposite of what was intended, such a result is termed a 'boomerang effect': see Hovland, *Communication and Persuasion*, pp. 63 and 141-3. See also previous note.

are the sub-groups of that society. Suppose one sub-group injects an issue into the public debate and the others can take it up and discuss it while keeping the main outlines of that issue rationally (if critically) at the centre of their discussion. Clearly, in such a case, there is a shared set of concepts available for public debate and considerable similarity among the various value-systems involved. But suppose the issue becomes grossly distorted as it passes from one sub-group to another. In this case, equally clearly, these conditions do not hold for some or all of the groups. The point is, however, that by using what are objectively the main points of the issue as a yardstick, the extent and the direction of the divergence can be measured within each language community individually, and within the community as a whole. In this way, an assessment can be made of the solidarity of the community as a whole, and of the extent to which any group feels itself to be a member of that community.[58]

Such debate can be 'measured' in the sense that its content can be quantitatively analyzed (by content analysis: that is what this book is all about). And the reason why it can be measured is because certain types of words and ways of handling them are *necessarily* involved.[59] Take the debate on the abolition of the death sentence in England, for instance. There was ample information available, and so people's ways of handling it were put clearly on display. Participants to such a debate need to have 'conceptual clarity' — a clear idea of the basic concepts involved. (This debate also necessitates clearheadedness in the analyst about *his* moral values and the extent to which the concepts involved can be applied in actual practice.) They also need concept attainment: that is, the ability to place facts into the appropriate category with ease. And they need ideas on social causation (normally indicated by the influence assigned to chance, social forces and so on), and some form of belief system to provide an overall framework of reference. Observably, most people were far from perfect on all these counts. But the point is that they can be rated for their showing on each, and the overall profile calculated in this way can be used for drawing comparisons.

---

[58] For a discussion of some cases in point, see Fagen, *Politics and Communication*, pp. 102-106 and 126-8.
[59] See Lane and Sears, *Public Opinion*, pp. 66-69.

OPINION CHANGE

Furthermore the possibility exists of measuring the 'sleeper effect'.[60] By this the following phenomenon is meant. People tend, in time, to forget the specific details of an important but complicated message, film, debate or what have you. But an awareness of its overall implications slowly crystallizes with time. Alternatively, a message which was initially rejected because of the personality of the speaker urging it will come to be accepted, in time, for the reasonableness of its content, its speaker being forgotten. In the case just mentioned, Parliament claimed to be 'educating' the public on the death penalty issue, for instance, and the movement of opinion since the previous debate showed such a sleeper effect to have in fact operated.

CONCLUSION

For anyone interested in content analysis, the significance of the work which has been briefly outlined in this chapter is enormous. It provides a framework within which to set up an analysis. For it tells about words and ways of perception, about attitudes and public opinion phenomena, about writers and language communities. It indicates what is to be gained by switching levels of inquiry, going from the individual to the group, from the case study to the survey. It outlines possible courses for investigations, for ways have been evolved of assessing *any* climate of opinion, *any* writer's thought-world. It provides clues both to strategy and to tactics. There are guidelines on how to divide a major issue up so as to enable a series of content analyses to be conducted on its various parts in such a way that their findings will converge. There are other guidelines which provide, ready made, a set of categories for this or that type of content analysis. In short, knowledge of the work done in this general area is a prerequisite for anyone who wishes to move from 'classical' content analysis to any of the theoretically-oriented, systems related, or computerized varieties.

[60] On the 'sleeper effect' see Hovland, *Communication and Persuasion*, pp. 244, 254-9 and 280.

4

Content Analysis and The 'New Look'
In Psychology

Selective Perception and Models

INTRODUCTION

For many a person with a liberal Arts background 'psychology' is tantamount to Freudian psychoanalysis. I once even heard this put, by a classicist, as "We're ahead of the Social Sciences: *we* know about Freud." There is little indication of awareness of the decades old 'New Look' in Psychology, of the work, that is, on the psychology of cognition, perception or interaction. Views such as "I don't know what authoritarianism is, but I *do* know that it can have no connection with Classical Antiquity" are not uncommon.

For psychologists involved in this 'new' movement in psychology, awareness and assessment of selectivity in perception are of central importance. There is much preoccupation with objectively establishing how people perceive their various versions of reality. This work concerns a content analyst in two ways. It provides him with techniques which he can incorporate in analyzing a writer's picture of reality. Also, it improves his self-awareness of how he goes about creating his picture of reality.

Consequently content analysis is closely and fundamentally connected with this new movement in psychology. The analysis of images

---

This chapter is based upon a talk which was originally given for the Canadian Broadcasting Corporation FM Network program, IDEAS. The talk was called "Models and the Historical Method." Correspondence and the general reaction to the talk was favorable. Much of the format and style of presentation has been retained, as this is not a topic on which it is easy to talk lucidly.

of reality, for instance, involves the identification and description of someone's selectivity in perception. Analysis of idiolect assumes a psycholinguistic viewpoint. Classical content analysis is concerned with imposing constraints on our selectivity in perception when we read. Theoretically oriented content analysis aims primarily at exploiting the insights or techniques furnished by this new movement. It may use them to improve the infrastructure (recording units, categories and norms) or the inferences of a content analysis. Or they may be brought in to provide a theoretical frame of reference.

Where the preoccupations of content analysts and those of scholars involved in the New Look come together is in regard to the use of models. For models constitute one of the main methods of keeping selectivity of perception under observation and control. The term 'model' is relatively freely used among people with a liberal Arts background. But there seems to be little clear agreement among them as to what the term means, or how one of the things so described is used. In particular, there does not seem, generally speaking, to be any overall picture of the variety among models, and their diverse purposes, nor of the advantages and disadvantages involved in using them. It is useful, therefore, to set out that overall picture of these things, for partial knowledge of models needlessly limits the appreciation and exploitation of their full range of potential uses.

This chapter, then, constitutes an attempt to bring together psychological theory, models and content analysis. This gathering is made to show how the two former can be put to use to improve a study involving the latter. Such an attempt is in line with the major aims of the book. For this, above all others, is the interface area, the area wherein are situated so many of the interconnections between content analysis and other techniques and theories. The better anybody's background knowledge of this area, the better will his content analysis be.

Section 1: Selective Perception

STIMULUS — FILTER — RESPONSE

"To a mouse, cheese is cheese — that's why mousetraps work."[1] The stimulus — aromatic, tasty cheese — produces the inevitable response: nibbling. But to a young lady a smack on the bottom can

---

[1] Wendell Johnson, quoted by S. I. Hayakawa, *Symbol, Status and Personality*, Harcourt, Brace & World, 1953, p. 17 (rather an uneven book, but containing some good chapters).

mean an unpredictable number of things, to judge by the variety of responses observable. There is no one-to-one reaction of stimulus: response. The same piece of behavior can result in quite different reactions even from the same young lady. For between stimulus and response, in human reaction, there exists an intervening stage of interpretation. We receive so many sense impressions, in a constant stream, that there has to be some kind of filtering process to sort them all out. This filtering is done fairly automatically because, by adulthood, we have all gone through a long process of socialization consisting of various forms of instruction in interpreting things.[2] Our various 'realities' are thus socially defined. We see what we have been conditioned to see, very largely.

There is an affliction of the eye which is remediable by surgery. A person blind from birth can thus suddenly be given normal vision. Some have. It takes years before they 'see' (that is, recognize) identifiable objects in the confusing welter of visual impressions that are man's lot. They have to *learn* what there is to be seen.

COGNITIVE FILTERS AND MAPS

Even without having the psychologists who work on perception to tell us so, it is obvious from everyday experience that people tend to see things in a highly selective fashion. Try making a pass at a pretty girl in a situation where others too are competing for her attention and you'll get the general idea. This selectiveness involves two different kinds of seeing. One is seeing what is there; the other is seeing what it means.[3] 'Seeing what's there' involves selecting, from the myriad stimuli with which our senses are bombarded, objects few enough and significant enough for us to be able to cope. What is known as the 'cognitive filter' performs this screening service for us. We have all met the sort of person who just does not see something or other which is crying out for attention, as we see things. 'Seeing what it means' involves arranging the things which come through that filter into meaningful patterns. It is statistically likely that most readers of this book will be acquainted with one or two persons suffering paranoid tenden-

[2] For a brief outline of what is involved in the 'new look' in psychology in regard to such 'filters' and so on, see McClelland, *Theory and the International System*, pp. 7-15. This account is without parallel for lucidity and succinctness. It may prevent confusion to know that the process here termed 'socialization' is called 'enculturation' in anthropological jargon.

[3] There is an excellent discussion of this in O. R. Young's *Systems of Political Science* (Prentice-Hall, 1968): see pp. 10-11 & 97-99.

cies. Such people can see 'plots' galore in the chaos of frustrated intentions and garbled communications which constitutes the daily business of living.

At the filtering stage, it is the ideas and assumptions that we have picked up as children or in school or at work which operate, fairly unconsciously by and large. We tend to take rather a lot for granted concerning where we are, who we are, what our past has been, how one gets along with other people, and how things work. This process involves a complex of ideas about geography and cosmology, personality, time and history, value judgements and physical causation.[4] An aboriginal from Alice Springs, an Eskimo from Inuvik and a European from Paris would all have quite different complexes of such ideas.

At the arranging stage, some order has to be created out of a welter of sense impressions. A word is only *part* of its total body of communications: it comes along with a host of other signals, such as class or regional accent, facial expression or intonation, emanating from its sender.[5] Filtering merely reduces superabundance to abundance. Here the difference between chaos and clarity is organization. Basically, what has to be done is establish frameworks of reference, so that impressions can be sorted into *this* subject area rather than *that* one. It has also to be decided what are the really important matters within each area, so that the others can be related to them and the details put in order of relative importance. Finally, it is necessary to have a range of ideas available on how things relate to one another within any given field of forces constituting one of these subject areas. Some kind of conceptual map is needed for this sort of thing. These are often quite conscious. Check with any friendly neighborhood Maoist.[6]

Taken together, filter and map can constitute a definite way of seeing things, called a 'cognitive style'. There is such a thing as an

---

[4] Boulding's book *The Image* makes this point in an unforgettable fashion: see his introduction. For Arts students, incidentally, coming upon this book seems invariably to be remembered with great pleasure, much like the pleasure associated with discovering *The Lord of the Rings*.

[5] See E. T. Hall, *The Silent Language*, Doubleday, 1959.

[6] Clearly, in dealing with a matter as complex as politics, it considerably expedites thinking to have several frameworks of reference and sets of concepts available. See R. E. Ians, *Political Ideology: Why the American Common Man believes What he does*, (Free Press, 1962) for example pp. 346 ff. Cast in terms similar to the present discussion is chapter 2, "Tools for Thinking: A Few Basic Concepts", of K. W. Deutsch's *The Analysis of International Relations* (Prentice-Hall, 1968).

'Arts mind', for instance, and it operates quite differently from a 'Science mind'.[7] Given the same ambiguous little drawings, Arts people will reconstruct quite different stories interpreting them than will scientists. They make different sorts of drawings, too, for that matter.

DEFINITIONS OF REALITY

"What a man defines as reality is real in its consequences for him." Such 'defining' goes on at both stages: we define something out there as significant enough to pass through the filter, and we define items that have passed through the filter as being related to one another. Clearly, this defining business is crucial. Equally clearly, a person can be either consciously aware or quite unconscious that such defining is in fact going on, and that there are various ways of going about it. The person who *is* aware is, quite simply, open to ranges of experience which are not available to the person who is unconscious of this defining business and its consequences. In fact, studies of highly creative people indicate that awareness of how their own perceptions are working on external reality is, strikingly, a common characteristic.

SPAN OF JUDGEMENT

Defining is not a completely random process. We all tend to go about it under certain similar constraints. Apparently our span of absolute judgement is limited.[8] Get someone to classify tones of sound, taste-intensities, or distances along a scale and he will tend to do so accurately only while operating with six or seven classes or categories. If distinctions have to be made within a more diverse range of classes, error increases rapidly as that range increases. And this constraint also affects the span of immediate memory, apparently. Again, about seven items in a string seem to constitute all that can be retained in the memory. These limitations of our ability to cope with incoming sense impressions severely restrict the number and quality of impressions that we can assess. They in this way limit our conscious awareness.

There are two main ways of coping with these limitations. If the

---

[7] See L. Hudson, *Contrary Imaginations*, Pelican, 1966, pp. 57-67; the following chapter (4) traces the personality correlates that go along with these differing mental sets. This is a British study; for an American one see C. Bereiter and M. B. Freedman, "Fields of Study and the People in Them" in N. Sanford (ed.), *The American College*, Wiley, 1962.

[8] See Miller, "The Magic Number 7", *op. cit.* n. 24 of chapter 3.

number of items that can be held within the span of memory cannot be increased much, the size of the individual 'item' can — by making it a string of things rather than just one of them. Apparently a man learning radio-telegraphic code initially takes in each separate dot and dash as just so many 'dits' and 'dahs'. Next he hears groups of 'dits' and 'dahs' as letters, then even bigger groups as words, and finally still larger groups as whole phrases. Our Morse man thus organizes the bits of incoming sound into linked chains, rather than into series of individual noises, each on its own. Consequently, he can hold many more details within his awareness, span of memory, or consciousness.

There is a second way of coping. Instead of making an absolute judgement (e.g., "it's a little bigger"), the number of aspects of the thing on which judgement is being passed can be increased: it can be assessed simultaneously on a number of dimensions. Thus, instead of position being assessed on a single line (scale), it can be assessed relative to two crossed lines (axes). Judgement can be made in terms both of volume of sound and of stress, or of sourness and of spiciness of flavor. In this way more aspects of a complex phenomenon can be assessed, if at the cost of losing some fineness of discrimination on each individual aspect.

This is what we actually do in real life. We make sense out of complex happenings by seeing them in patterned ways. In cybernetic terms, we recode the incoming bits of information into large blocs or concatenations. This recoding is generally done by a verbal process: we put labels on whole masses of items, which thus become seen as unified, if complex, wholes (e.g., "He's an introvert"). The step from using labels to stereotyping ('the departmental Fascist') is an easy one. A metaphor or simile can be used for the same purpose. Or, if we are conscious of what we are doing, we can use models.

MODELS: DEFINITIONS

The word 'model' has become so fashionable and overused that it has become all blurry round the edges. There remains some hazy central core of meaning and all sorts of outer shades of meaning. Defining it tells more about the person doing the defining than about the word, very often. Anthropologists, for instance, seem wedded to structural-functional models. A scholar with mathematical skills thinks primarily in terms of mathematical models. (This field of model building is not discussed here at all.) So it is instructive to engage the gentle reader in this business of defining it. What does the word 'university' mean? What is your image of a university? Picture it in your mind's eye. How many leaves of ivy are on the topmost story of the ivory tower in the centre of the picture? It is not that kind of picture? Probably not. For thinking about a complicated thing like this or others like it ('democracy', say, or 'bureaucracy') is done in terms of a cluster of abstractions and their interrelationships. 'Democracy' as a concept will probably feature, in a North American mind, concepts such as majority rule through political parties and elections with safeguards for minorities.[9] It will also involve representative government and an independent press and judiciary, with bureaucratic appendages as public service instrumentalities, all within some form of bargaining system of relationships.

A concept which is as well articulated as this is known as a 'model'. Its purpose is to organize the data which have filtered through the sieving process. It is an outline of some major phenomenon which includes leading ideas on the nature of the entities involved and the pattern of their relations. In any discussion of abstractions, theoretical backgrounds are forced out into the open sooner or later. Models force them out *sooner*. They are consciously-used frameworks of reference based upon collections of findings and related theorizings.

MODELS: INEVITABILITY

Any historian will tell you that this is "only what we all do anyway," and so there is no need for such formal and elaborate shennanigans. Now it is true that nobody can think about abstractions like the above without *some* form of mental shorthand. But, as any couturier can tell you, there are models and models. As a help in processing data — as a help with those vital statistics, some do more than others. When models are used unconsciously, how can the one that will do most be selected on the particular occasion involved? Discerning use of models involves being highly aware of what is being done. And, notice, some such frame of reference, or model, must be used. For using models is not a form of intellectual masturbation which can be abstained from by the intellectually pure who see reality 'as it really is,' with immaculate perception. No two people ever see the same reality when psychosocial matters are involved. Reality is too complex. Besides, psychologists can show that the picture inside the head is no 1:1 representation of the goings on outside the head. Have you, as a motorist, ever been involved in a minor front end collision involving some panel beating? Well, utter objectivity of social (or any other) judgement is just as common among historians and literary scholars

[9] This is not to say that this is what democracy 'means'. See *Meaning and Mind*, pp. 307-308, for a commentary on this (and the Soviet) definition.

as it is among drivers of the other car in such circumstances. There is no such thing as immaculate perception.

This is where models come in. They help to keep a check upon at least some of the idiosyncrasies with which our perceptions abound. Consider what actually happens. Suppose an historian is writing a biography or assessing a situation wherein some great man's inspired lunacy has been particularly in evidence. Whether he will or not, the historian is involved in assessments concerning personality. But there is no such thing as personality.[10] It is 'only' a construct or model. It is a model which defines what sorts of things to look for and in what sort of patterns of co-occurrences. The 'things' being looked for are so nebulous that, accordingly as they are grouped into *these* rather than *those* blocs, so different overall behavior patterns are obtained. According to the view of personality, then, different aspects of behavioral activity are emphasized, and so the same person can appear in a different light. For a striking illustration, compare the Alexander the Great depicted by a psychoanalyst with the Alexander depicted by a territorialist (ethologist). Interpretation is really seen at its best in such cases of demonic culture-heroes about whom precious little is known.[11] The various conceptual frameworks or models of personality are thus in a way like so many different sets of eyeglasses. They enable picking out different things amongst 'what's out there'. This is what models are for.

Now the vagaries of so-called 'common sense' views of personality have been amply demonstrated. Nowadays it is simply not possible to avoid using some form of psychological frame of reference when writing about an historical or literary figure. Given the plethora of confusing data involved, a model of some sort is needed before order can be put into such data. But there is more to it. For the fact is that his knowing a few psychological concepts, or even knowing about one model of personality, does *not* mean that a scholar is 'using models'. Using models involves knowing of the existence and potentialities of several models, and deliberately selecting one rather than another because it fits the inquiry and subject matter best.

Thus, if a literary scholar knows about the psychoanalytic model of personality, he has indeed moved to a position in which he is consciously using a model of psychological reality. But his options

10 See Sarason, *Personality*, p. 15; actually the whole of Sarason's introduction (pp. 1-19) will amply repay reading by anyone interested in this present chapter and in chapter 3.

11 See Carney, "Commentary on a Psychoanalytical Study of Alexander the Great", in *Proceedings of the Second Annual Northern Great Plains History Conference*, U. of Manitoba, 1967, pp. 88-95.

consist of subscribing to, modifying, or rejecting that *one* model. He is encapsulated within its terms of reference: even in rejecting it, he will still be thinking, and organizing his data, largely in terms of its concepts and boundaries. Only when he is aware that there are other, wholly different schools of psychological thought available to him (self-in-personality theory and field theory — involving transaction-alism — for instance),[12] is he free to select a framework that is suited to his problems and to his available data. If these models are the spectacles through which we see, as it were, it may well be helpful to have other than dark glasses — when moving around inside a darkened room for instance.

Freudianism overrepresents the negative aspects of the functioning of personality as result of its very selective focus. Hence the disappearance of heroes from the literary world of writers, for whom psychology, by and large, means only Freudian psychoanalysis. This is not altogether a blessing, because Freudianism appears to be culture-bound, that is, linked to a certain culture rather than of universal application.[13] It should be noted, however, that the Neo-Freudians and Ego-psychologists have to some degree abated the full severity of the Freudian view on the predestination wrought by infancy. Indeed they have relocated psychologically significant happenings as late as the identity crisis of the teens.[14] This new awareness has brought historical personages back within the purview of analysis. *Something*, after all, is generally (mis-) remembered about the teens of a Great Man.

Try thinking about economics in other than maximization of profit terms to experience personally the constraits which a model, or powerful frame of reference, imposes.

Section 2: Different Types of Models and their Uses

So far, then, we have an operational definition of what a model is, and some indications of why we use these models. What causes confusion is the fact that models are of different types. They come in different sizes — mini, midi and maxi — and are used for different purposes: one for what it reveals, another for its powers of suggestion, yet another as an experiment, to see if it gets certain specific results. It is wise to look first at these different purposes.

[12] For a survey of the different schools of thought see Sarason, *Personality*, Part I.

[13] See M. Duverger, *The Idea of Politics*, Methuen, 1966, pp. 26-27.

[14] On the maturing stages of the human psyche, see E. H. Erickson, *Childhood and Society*, Norton, 1950, pp. 72-108 and 247-74.

CROSS-CULTURAL MODELS

A very obvious use of models is as a form of assistance in human data processing, that is, their use to suggest ideas and connections and thus to expand and refine the user's frame of reference. What is known as the 'cross-cultural' model is involved here.[15] Consider an example to see how this particular variety of model works in practice. Suppose you had to analyze Byzantine bureaucracy, as I did.[16] Now how you go about doing this depends on your views on what bureaucracy was all about and how it operated at this particular point in history. Meeting with assurances that "we all know what it is," you ask half a dozen of 'all of us'. Two things emerge. First, six different pictures of what Byzantine bureaucracy was all about emerge. Secondly, in each man's picture there are features to which he idiosyncratically attaches a far higher significance than does anyone else. Clearly, if you were to rely on any one picture, a product of one person's viewpoint, you would introduce serious skewing into your findings.

Like most abstractions, this one is tricky to handle: it can mean red tape (bureau pathology), the power of the bureaucrats (bureaucratism) or even, I suppose, efficiently organized impersonal management (bureau rationality). These are all definitions of the way it functions. It can also mean an hierarchical structure of offices governed by rules operating across time. This last is a different sort of definition: it is a definition in terms of structure.[17] Now these slippery words have a sort of central core of meaning and all sorts of nuances on their periphery. They have an emotional charge from such traumatic experiences as filling in tax forms. So we are all, as individuals, likely to have our own special idiosyncratic overall combination of emphases and associations in the picture that the word conjures up for us. And our pictures will have blind spots.

What the cross-cultural model does is to examine what is known about bureaucracy. It does so in two ways. First, it reviews different points in time in the evolution of bureaucracy. Secondly, it reviews the range of forms of bureaucracy occurring in various cultures at each of those points in the evolution of those cultures. The model also

[15] See, for example, W. Delany, "The Development and Decline of Patrimonial and Bureaucratic Administrations", *Administrative Science Quarterly* 7(4), 1963, pp. 458-501, or S. N. Eisenstadt, "Bureaucracy and Bureaucratization", *Current Sociology*, 7, 1958, pp. 99-165.

[16] See chapter 1 ("Problems involved in Studying Bureaucracy in Antiquity") of *Bureaucracy in Traditional Society* for what follows.

[17] See F. W. Riggs, "Bureaucratic Politics in Comparative Perspective", *Journal of Comparative Administration* 1(1), 1969, pp. 5-11.

incorporates the various theorists' interpretations of all this information. It can thus say that, at such and such a stage (e.g., in a pre-industrial society with an agriculturally-based economy and extended family systems in the Mediterranean area), bureaucrats are likely to be found preoccupied with overlapping spheres of competence imposed by the ruler as a check on the growth of the powers of bureaucratic chiefs. And there may be surprises, for bureaucracy does not *have* to be rationality — and efficiency — oriented. In this way the cross-cultural model can make historians sensitive to *others'* views of the relative emphases of diverse issues and pressures, and direct their attention to things they had not thought of. As one ripe historical sage put it to me: "It just reminds you of things." Yes, but it 'just reminds' you of things you didn't know about.

The model in this way serves as a sort of gigantic check-off list — like the sort of list that families who go camping gradually build up over the years to remind them what to take along. It provides a frame-work of reference when there is a very elaborate and complicated comparison to do.[18] Suppose the task is to look for a lot of items, and for a particular *arrangement* of those items, in a situation where mention of them is scattered higgledy-piggledy far and wide in the source materials. It is very difficult to keep in mind, amid all the distractions of those materials, *all* the things being looked for. A model facilitates the search. It groups the things together, with their interrelationships all depicted, in a condensed and simplified format. With a model, it is easy to keep in mind what are being sought.

IDEAL (DEDUCTIVE) TYPES

There are various ways of setting up such models. One of them, the cross-cultural model, has already been considered. Possibly the most famous, however, is Max Weber's 'Ideal Type'.[19] There is some con-fusion as to precisely what Weber meant by this term, but two main usages are plain. The first, and most obvious, is as follows. The cross-cultural model informs a frame of reference by reminding an analyst to look out for this and not that, etc. The ideal type *forms* a frame of reference. Suppose a particular bureaucracy is to be investigated and the value-system underlying its ethics, or operational code should be known Suppose there is reason to suspect it to be oriented towards rationality

[18] See Meehan, *Theory and Method of Political Analysis*, pp. 149-50 and 162-3.

[19] See for example M. Weber, "The Essentials of Bureaucratic Organization: An Ideal-Type Construction" in R. K. Merton *et al*, eds., *Reader in Bureau-cracy*, Free Press, 1952, pp. 18-27.

and efficiency. If rationality and efficiency are the underlying principles of organization, it will follow that its institutions will have to include certain types of bureaucratic machinery and its practices will have to work in certain very specific ways. So how such a bureaucracy would ideally function is worked out. This is the ideal type. There is no suggestion that such an ideal bureaucracy ever existed. But it is possible to work out logically, from first principles, all the details of the whole complex configuration which should be present in the extreme or ideal case that exemplifies what is being looked for. There now exists a complex check-off list against which can be compared the particular bureaucracy under investigation. The question, therefore, now becomes: is this actual bureaucracy like the ideal one? Is it at least enough like it to establish beyond reasonable doubt the influence of rationality and efficiency as dominant in its operational code? To find out, it may well be necessary to turn parts of the model into the categories of a content analysis. For only with a content analysis can the source material be systematically explored in a really complicated investigation.

POLAR EXTREMES

A natural outgrowth of this 'ideal type' model is that involving 'polar extremes'. In this case a second ideal type is established, detailing how things would be if exactly the opposite set of first principles were operating. The two antithetical models are conceived to be extreme points on a scale running from one ideal type to reach its opposite extreme of development in the other. Both polar extremes are ideal types in the sense that they are logical abstractions, not specific type-examples from the real world. The object being examined can now be contrasted with each polar extreme, to see which it resembles more. This is generally done with very complicated 'objects'. In such cases, unless there exists an equally complex yardstick to judge them by, the multifariousness of the data leads to not seeing the wood for the trees. An example which springs readily to mind is that of the polar types of traditional and modern societies much used in comparative politics.[20]

There can be, of course, other arrangements than that of two polar extremes; for instance, a triple distinction of traditional, transitional and modern societies. Incidentally, it was only because it was possible to view such amorphous masses of details as whole (if complex) entities that it came to be realized that another distinct type existed. Scholars were able to see that, in reality, a number of societies

[20] As in Riggs' study "Agraria and Industria".

resembled an intermediary (but, as a complex, wholly different) type far more closely than they resembled either extreme.[21]

IDEAL (INDUCTIVE) TYPES

This point leads to the second variety of 'ideal type'. This involves the most basic use of models, that of simply describing things. A model can be a simplified framework which acts as a set of inter-related guidelines to impose some kind of conceptual order upon a complicated mass of details. In such a case an ideal type is a model which builds on data from a wide variety of sources to give a general picture. Think of Sjoberg's book on the preindustrial city, for example.[22] It is like the concepts of 'the average reader' or 'the normal individual'. Nobody will ever meet one. But the concept of 'the normal' is needed to draw comparisons. So it is with this type of 'ideal model'. It gives an overview of the commonest salient characteristics in capsule form that will never be met in reality, but in so doing, it gives the general idea of what is involved and why. Arts scholars will say such models are mere pretentiousness, because "we all know this (what such a city was like) anyway." Ask such a belittler of this approach just what it is that 'we all know' about life in the preindustrial city. But read Sjoberg first. Then you can 'remind' the skeptic of all the other things he 'knows' but he has failed to mention.

ANALOGICAL MODELS

The most familiar form of model, however, is that involving its use as a kind of extended analogy. Such models are often unconsciously used. They involve basic, unspoken assumptions about causation and so on. In the past, people unthinkingly adopted them because they were assumed by the writers whom they read. Of late, however, some scholars have become concerned about the limitations imposed on our thinking by the acceptance of such analogies. There is currently much debate about their implications. For, in real life, people tend to have some such analogy, whether consciously or not, as a basic working hypothesis.

I suppose we are all very familiar with this use of analogy.[23] At one

[21] See Riggs' *Administration in Developing Countries*, chapter 1.

[22] G. Sjoberg, *The Preindustrial City Past and Present*, Free Press, 1960; for a summary outline of the book's findings, see chapter 11.

[23] Particularly good on this matter is chapter 3 of A. Inkeles, *What is Sociology? An Introduction to the Discipline and Profession*, Prentice-Hall, 1964.

time, for instance, society was seen in terms of a *mechanical* model. The terms 'balance of power', 'countervailing forces', 'checks and balances' and 'equilibrium' still survive, left over from this period. At another time, society was likened to an organismic system or entity. This view produced concepts of 'maturing stages', functional and teleological activities, homeostasis, and so on. A later way of viewing society was in terms of ecological adaptation. This model allows for changing interactions between (equally changing) organisms and environment. It allows us to conceive of society as a sort of gene pool, constantly throwing up changed individual combinations, which flourish or perish accordingly as they are successful in adapting to environmental conditions. The advantage of this kind of model is that it is 'open-ended': that is, it allows for change.[24] Which, observably, happens. Ask any campus anti-radical.

POSTULATIONAL MODELS

Finally, models can be used analytically. Take a simple illustration, that of the postulational model or thought experiment. Supposing an analysis has to be performed to discover whether some complex, ramifying causal relationship in fact exists. This investigation involves not a single connected causal chain but *sets* of interacting variables and relationships. It is not possible to make the examination by pulling out one strand of causality at a time for analysis, any more than one bit of clockwork can be pulled out at a time to see how a watch works. It is a case of all together or not at all. So a model is made of how things *should* interrelate if they are as suspected. This model is a much simplified form of the external reality, isolating just those aspects of it with which the problem is concerned. But it enables a check to be made on an interrelated complex of events all together rather than piece by piece. The original bit of reality can be tried out to see if it fits the model. Either answer, yes or no, gives a finding.

Possibly readers will remember the thought experiment already described in several parts of chapter 2, including the text on the pages following figure 2.6. It sought to establish, from very intransigent source materials, whether in fact a vast administrative change, involving all kinds of side- and after-effects, took place at a particular time. What an analyst is really doing, in such cases, is establishing a form of master pattern, then seeing whether, within predetermined

[24] For an excellent (and highly significant) discussion, see chapter 2 of W. J. Buckley, *Sociology and Modern Systems Theory*, Prentice-Hall, 1967 (to whom I am indebted for the concept 'immaculate perception', incidentally).

tolerated limits of variation, anything like it exists in the data.

This 'pattern-fitting' type of approach is much used in analytical models. Here is an example. "Have no fear," says my wife of our small son. "Oedipus is here." Now consider: if iddy dislikes daddy, he can be said to have an Oedipus complex; if he *likes* daddy, he can be said to be *suppressing* an Oedipus complex. Either way, he loses and the theory is safe from proof, disproof, or whatever. But supposing a model says authoritarianism — or need achievement or what have you — is present if the following syndrome of reactions to the following issues can be found in this subject's case. If this fairly specific set of criteria is met, the case is made; if it is not, then the case is shown to be invalid. This kind of model provides some form of testability. With an untestable theory, a good verbal symbol-manipulator can 'shadowbox with reality' for ever. With this type of approach which tests for 'goodness of fit', however, the self-cleansing properties in the material can operate upon the analyst, restricting his gifts for verbal hallucination. He has to show how the facts square with some quite specific claims contained in his verbiage.

This type of model, often loosely called a theory, is the stuff of which many advanced models in the Social Sciences are built. In the beginning a postulational model is produced which explains most known data. Then scholars test it by experiment, or new data come in. It is, in consequence, 'refined' — by being emended (or replaced!) as findings indicate. It thus develops over time. Its current status is thus seen as merely one more phase in its ongoing development. The model is as good as the results it provides, and is valued solely for its utility as an instrument of inquiry.

Now many historians or literary scholars will say that this is all very obvious. Psychologic rather than logic is presumably behind this belittling view. Try the experiment of reading the literature on models and then decide for yourself how 'obvious' the current practices in model-building are. All sorts of concepts have had to be evolved in the course of elaborating such models, and these have given us an improved intellectual tool kit for coming to grips with psychosocial reality. Observably, we are producing better social history or literary criticism now than we were ten years ago. It is more sensitive and self-aware. Sophisticated use of models has contributed to this development.

One feature of this belittling approach is worth bearing in mind. The facts are that the techniques available for analyzing social phenomena are relatively few and imprecise, and the data on which they have to be deployed are difficult to deal with. Hence it is much easier to criticize how someone else has gone about analyzing a complex social phenomenon than it is actually to perform that analysis oneself. Any history textbook will provide a supply of illustrations. But if it is intended to weigh all the evidence, as scholars in the Arts claim to do, then the task will be made much easier by having a wide range of models available. With their help, it is easier to decide how, what, and why to weigh, and to implement the final decision. Having the latest, or a suitable, model is thus not a mere matter of being fashion-conscious.

Section 3: Advantages and Disadvantages in Using Models

Models give their users certain advantages, if at a certain cost. As mini-skirts go with chubby thighs, for instance. Consider the advantages first. The cross-cultural model facilitates interdisciplinary work. Take the one mentioned above. By using it, an historian can draw upon the resources and insights generated within the fields of Political Science and Sociology, for these will be paraded before him in easily usable forms. Presumably few teachers will make so bold as to tell students that communicating across disciplinary boundaries is "what we're all doing." Moreover, the model can reveal omissions in a scholar's own picture of the 'reality' it concerns. It may also reveal that the actual case being studied has some very unusual features about it. For this is a thing which cannot be seen, ordinarily, in studying a single case, as there is no yardstick against which to measure findings. The model provides an overall framework of reference, in detail, cast in comparative terms, and bringing together the insights of a number of disciplines. So analogies, connections, or omissions, matters which would not normally have been thought of, are often unexpectedly suggested — the so-called serendipity effect.

ADVANTAGES

Awareness of the presuppositions behind the type of model that serves as an analogy gives some degree of conscious control over basic assumptions. Levels of thought where normally unconsciousness prevails are influenced — for instance, as to the full range of implications of a frame of reference. With the ideal and polar types, and especially with the postulational type, complicated analytical operations can be performed upon material which could not have been so analyzed without these models. There is more to this than has so far been indicated, and so this point is worth developing.

Models come in various sizes: mini, medium and maxi. An example of the small scale one is the Pavlovian model of progressive mental breakdown under extreme stress. According to this model, the mind goes through three stages. In the first, or equivalent stage, it responds equally to a major or a minor stimulus. One dollar is as welcome as a hundred. In the second, or paradoxical, stage, its normal reactions are reversed. Weak stimuli elicit more response than do stronger ones. One dollar is *preferred* to a hundred. In the third or ultraparadoxical stage, it becomes so confused as to love its tormentor.[26] An example of a middle-sized model is the cross-cultural model of bureaucracy, already discussed. It covers a bigger topic, over a longer period, from a wider range of viewpoints. The large scale models are normally termed systems approaches.[27] They stand, in relation to the others, as a master plan does to its component strategies and their tactics. They are intended to enable focusing on the whole picture, frame and all, not just a particular corner of it. They provide a gigantic framework of reference, a structured space within which other lesser-scale models can be deployed.[28]

Such models are proposed to deal with at least some of the problems involved in the mental activities attendant upon conducting any inquiry. People are normally oblivious to the distorting influence of the eyeglasses through which they look. These models should create awareness of the influence of such glasses: lenses, framework, the whole combination. They enable being conscious of, and thus moving easily between, levels of analysis. They enable the testing of alternative models in coping with part of the overall investigatory framework, or even the testing of alternative overall frameworks.[29] In this way the framework bit by bit, yet still as a complex, can be brought into line with the needs of the situation. There is no commitment to any one

[26] See J. A. C. Brown, *Techniques of Persuasion: From Propaganda to Brainwashing*, Pelican, 1963, pp. 217 ff.

[27] See Meehan, *Theory and Method of Political Analysis*, pp. 161-2.

[28] On the relationship of the systems approach to lesser models see Young, *Systems of Political Science*, pp. 8-10 and 93-102. Easton brings out the notion of providing a framework, within which smaller-scale models can be deployed, in chapter 1 of *A Systems Analysis of Political Life*. As to the need for such a device, see Duverger, *The Idea of Politics*, Preface. Here the abundant information available on a whole range of issues is contrasted with the "almost complete absence of a general view which alone would make it possible to understand the importance and significance" of the various individual issues. An example of such a large-scale approach occurs in chapter 8.

[29] On shifting levels see McClelland (beautifully clear, as ever) *Theory and the International System*, pp. 93-95; the whole of chapter 4 merits reading. On testing alternative models (in regard to the various models of bureaucratic systems), see J. D. Thompson, *Organizations in Action*, McGraw-Hill, 1967, chapter 1.

tactic, set of tactics, strategy, strategies, or even master plan. Thus the whole framework of investigation can be pretested in a series of pilot studies — an improvement over discovering its inadequacies two-thirds of the way through the project when irretrievably committed to it.

There is another problem with which such models aim to cope. Normally, to examine a complex phenomenon, it is frozen into in-activity as it were, and a cross-section of it investigated while it is stationary. Some of these models are intended to make it possible to examine a flow of action, to observe the pattern of the actions them-selves, disembedding these from their environment. This observing is accomplished by visualizing the phenomena under consideration as a set of working relations among parts. These are then set up as a system relevant to the problem which it is desired to analyze.[30] My inquiry into current trends in Classical scholarship was cast in the form of an analysis of a communications-flow, a very simple version of one of these flow analyses. However, this is not the place to become involved in the subject of systems analysis; it is not the subject of this book. I wish merely to draw readers' attention to its existence and potential significance for their inquiries.

One last benefit conferred by the use of models is that they save an enormous amount of very difficult mental work. In any inquiry, it is necessary first to work out how to go about investigating. Only then can the job of actually going through the materials be begun. These models provide a range of tactics and strategies, of master plans even, for coping with the first stage of an inquiry. The volume and variety of ideas they provide at the very least stimulates the investigator's own flow of ideas. Sometimes, indeed, it solves his problems without more ado. But models can help in another way, too. In practice, when decid-ing the best way of tackling a complicated major problem, the total range of possibilities is likely to be considerable. So it is never possible, as it inevitably turns out, to test them one by one to find which is best. In fact there is no search for the very best way of conducting the inquiry. The first thing to do is try to devise a good (not the best) strategy for searching for the best way of conducting the inquiry that circumstances will allow. Now the maxi-models mentioned above have been designed to help do just this. So, all in all, knowing about models and how to use them enables considering more, and more diverse, ways of handling problems.

[30] See A. Kuhn, *The Study of Society: A Unified Approach*, Irwin-Dorsey, 1963, pp. 36-54, especially 37-9 & 48-54.

DISADVANTAGES

But models also involve disadvantages,[31] prominent among which is one sometimes described as 'the iron law of perspective'. Certain things are focused *on* only by turning the focus of attention *away* from others. Proportionately as the model rivets attention upon an issue from this angle or that, *other* angles, or things extraneous to the issue, go unheeded. Given only our human faculties of cognition, however, this inattention happens model or no model — in fact, only when using a model is there awareness that it is happening. The snag is that our perceptions, and thus our findings, can be distorted by the pattern of sensitivities which the model imposes. Hence the price of using models is eternal vigilance.

Models are ways of viewing things. They may lead us to an overemphasis on precision, a search for a perfection of interrelations which is not there in the real world. We may become attached to a particular model and use it in and out of season, as it were.[32] Think of Freudian analysis of ancient world personalities, for instance. A variant of this kind of overattachment to a model is the so-called 'drunkard's search'. Here the data to be passed under review is simplified either so that the model is easier to work with, or so that a more elegant model can be used.

Overemphasis on model-building in itself is not an unknown failing, incidentally. It is possible to get overengrossed in the technicalities and apportion an undue amount of attention to the finding, or setting up, of an analytical infrastructure. The model is a tool. What is important is its efficiency and cost. Elegance or fashionableness are only secondary considerations. When a building is being erected, what is wanted is not the most elegant scaffolding, but rather the most efficient at the lowest cost. And the scaffolding is not left in front of the building after the latter is completed. To do either is badly to reverse priorities. The aim is to solve problems by dint of using *any* technique; to reach the goal by stopping at nothing intellectually. Parading analytical skills is a luxury for which a well-planned inquiry will not allow time.

Another problem is scale. What may work one way in the small scale of the model may work quite differently in the larger scale of reality.

[31] Chapter 7 in A. Kaplan's *The Conduct of Inquiry: Methodology for Behavioral Science*, (Chandler, 1964) includes some very good criticism of models, and has much influenced this part of the chapter.

[32] Young has a special little subsection, highly relevant to this part of the discussion, on "The Theology of Models": see *Systems of Political Science*, pp. 103-106.

A change of scale may actually involve a change of relationships. The dynamics of small groups are quite different from the ways in which large groups work, for instance. Super-kiddy's antics in his play-group merely increase the tempo of, or area covered by, play. A demagogue working through organized groups can shape the lives of many peoples over a wide area of space and time.

Models are, or can be, non-cumulative. Thus when an oculist tries out his series of individual lenses in his empty eye-glass frame contraption as he tests for the strength his client needs, he is presenting a sequence of lenses such that, by adjustments, he eventually hits on a pair which gives the client 20-20 vision. But one model may give a version of reality that is so totally different from that given by the previous model as to leave us at a loss how to evaluate the two sets of results (even with the advantage of perfect 20-20 historical hindsight).

We use models, then, without entirely believing in them. Converging results, however, after the application of diverse models, show that findings are something more than mere subjective impressionism. Care is needed, obviously. Consider the rapid rate at which different models (of society, say, or of personality) have been altered, and the consequences of new ways of thinking about models (systematics and the systems approach, for instance). It would be rash to assume that this process is complete or will slow down. Today's sophistication is tomorrow's shortsightedness. Traditionally minded critics, before rushing in here, might do well to tread warily round the question of where this leaves *yesterday's* sophistication, however.

Great claims for a technique or approach tend to lead to undue depreciation of it by reaction. This is the case with the historical method and, I suspect, with similar claims on behalf of literary criticism. The historical method seems mostly to consist of impressionistic and rule-of-thumb procedures, and has been known to yield quite partisan findings. There are historians who are very interested indeed in methodological rigor, as the existence of the *Historical Methods Newsletter* (*Quantitative Analysis of Social, Economic and Political Development*) and other work already cited in this book testify. They are as yet, however, hardly in the majority in their profession. So, though some historians make great claims for their method, others and outsiders in general react with some scepticism.[33] Let me not cause a similar reaction by overclaiming for models. Better to conclude with a minimal claim for what they can do. The essence of

[33] As evidenced by such books as Dance's *History the Betrayer* or Hodgetts' *What Culture? What Heritage?*

what is involved, then, is simply this: a strategy for bringing more of our own — or someone else's — assumptions under conscious control than is normally possible.

Basically the case for models is as follows. Apparently we tend to 'make sense' out of the stimuli that unceasingly bombard us by organizing them in various simplified forms. If you want to call this process 'the objective reporting of fact,' no one can physically stop you. Part of this objective reporting or simplification or whatever is this business of recoding the stimuli we choose to perceive. When such recoding is done consciously, with some attempt at rigor, it is called using models. It is rather like using eye-glasses to offset an astigmatic condition. How can it be known that they won't, until they have been tried?

5

Sampling: Selecting A Representative Cross-Section Of A Body Of Writings

INTRODUCTION

Sampling is a topic to which a great deal of attention has been paid by statisticians. A considerable amount of expertise has built up in consequence. General surveys are available, setting out the major insights and procedures discovered, and written in terms which non-specialists can understand.[1] Reliance on common sense or native ingenuity simply means neglecting information of such fundamental general importance that it is everywhere available in handbooks. Nobody would dream of failing to acquaint himself with this type of information if it had to do with the background of the topic or writer he was studying. Yet failure to construct a proper sample is every bit as ruinous to a study as is failure to become acquainted with background knowledge. For the sample is the foundation upon which any study rests. Everything depends on it. The study can be only as good as the sample on which it is based. Hence this chapter is aimed at outlining what is involved in drawing a sample for a study employing content analysis.

---

[1] There is an excellent explanation of sampling, in general overall terms, in R. B. Miller, *Statistical Concepts and Applications: A Non mathematical Explanation*, Science Research Associates, 1968, pp. 101-113. *C.A.C.* is the handbook which deals with the employment of content analysis in studying the mass media. Consequently sampling is a particularly salient issue for it. As result the book contains an excellent treatment of the subject (chapter 4). The section on sampling in the current handbook, *Content Analysis* (pp. 127-35), is also well worth reading.

BASIC CONCEPTS

First, then, a pair of definitions concerning the notions of population and of sample. A 'population' consists of those characteristics of all the persons, objects, actions or conditions to which conclusions are going to apply. So defining the population is really the same thing as stating what the inquiry is going to be all about. It involves defining the ways in which the persons, objects, or whatever are going to be measured, as well as defining all of those persons, objects, and so on that are going to be considered. So a precise definition of the aims of a content analysis will necessarily include a precise definition of the population to which it refers.

A 'sample' consists of one or more measurements or observations taken ('drawn') from a selection of persons, objects, etc. This sample is drawn from within the population with the aim of reaching some general conclusions about that population. The sample thus can provide answers only to the questions implicit in the definition of its population. The danger attendant upon all sampling is that of drawing a biased sample. This is a sample which for some reason selectively over- or under-represents some sections (subsets) within the population. Avoiding bias is best accomplished by random selection, because with random selection everything within the population has an equal chance of being chosen for the sample.

The sample is the body of documents which is actually analyzed in the study. The full range of documents relevant to the study has to be discovered first before they can be 'sampled'. Sampling is done by extracting from them a selection representative of the body as a whole. If he is not careful in forming his selection, the sampler can himself create in the documents which he is analyzing patterns or emphases not in the overall body of documents. For instance, if he is examining a novelist and considers only passages on themes *he* finds interesting, he may end up with an overrepresentation of passages of a psychological, a humorous, or of an analytical nature, or whatever the case may be. His selection thus exaggerates these features in the writer's work and simultaneously ignores other features which may be more prominent in actual bulk, dramatic economy, or verbal intensity. Distorted or grotesque findings can follow, and the study may well be completely unbelievable.

PRIORITIES

Oddly enough, sampling is often the aspect of a content analysis to which least attention is paid. What happens is that the person who is to do the study has a particular question which he wants to ask, or he may have worked out an ingenious framework of inquiry. He has often spent so much time evolving question or/and framework that he finds himself without adequate time to assemble all the relevant documents — so he confines his study to those which are available. It is of crucial importance to know what documents are in fact available to examine *before* investing time and energy in elaborating questions or analytical framework. In my experience, time after time students put off doing a project until the last minute because they 'know just how to handle it.' Then some key document or text turns out not to be available; so they cannot perform the inquiry intended (and no other may be possible in the time remaining). It is not unusual for faculty, amid the preoccupations of term-time, simply to put off a study to the vacation, assuming the availability of source materials — only to have to waste weeks of vacation time assembling the necessary documents by university library inter-loans, and so on.

Or the person conducting the study may pick out the documents which suit *his* question or framework. However well he does the rest of the study, however, if the documents on which it is based are imperfectly chosen, it will be valueless. So if anybody catches himself putting this matter of sampling *last* on his list of things to attend to, he must remember that the *first* thing any reader will do is check on his sample: the reader can spare himself the trouble of reading that study at all if there is anything wrong with the way the sampling is done.

THE VICIOUS CIRCLE

The exact nature of the question to be asked cannot finally be decided without considering the documents. And the documents cannot be considered without having the framework of analysis in mind. All three — question, documents, framework — have to be borne in mind together. Each depends on the next in a sort of little circle. To enable questions to come to grips with a representative selection of the documents to be considered, it may be necessary to make alterations to the framework of analysis. This need, in turn, may well require altering the question slightly so that it becomes capable of being put to the documents. So a start can be made only with that body of documents in mind, and the questions and framework evolved only by constant reference to those documents.

This procedure is known as the pilot study or pretest. In practice, it is most unusual not to have to run at least one of these before producing an analytical infrastructure which will fit the data. This is yet another indication that content analysis is a clinical procedure.

Normal practice in Arts seems to be spending 5 per cent of the researcher's time evolving the questions and methods for his investigation, 90 per cent of the time working through the documents, and 5 per cent working out conclusions. In the Social Sciences, these proportions seem to be more like 60 per cent, 30 per cent, and 10 per cent respectively. A wholly different attitude to question-posing (or research design, as it is known in the Social Sciences) is involved. The better the foundations, the sturdier and the more speedily erected the building.

EXPLORATORY ILLUSTRATION: A CLEAR-CUT PROBLEM

These are general considerations. A better idea of what is actually involved in sampling can be obtained by considering a couple of examples of the process itself. First, a neat, clear-cut case. Suppose you are considering the climate of opinion in the fifties in regard to some major issue of domestic policy. You will review what the newspapers say about it.

Practical questions of the availability of back runs of a range of newspapers always bedevil studies employing content analysis. If the project permits, preplanning should involve an application for a travel grant; in the usual nature of things, interlibrary loans are out of the question. Failing a grant, one has to cut the coat according to the cloth. This process takes time.

Sampling involves deciding upon what parts of which newspapers to consider, and at which periods. Are you going to consider the front page or the editorial page? How big does a mention have to be to make it worth considering? The character of the parts of the paper considered will affect the volume of data to be processed and thus the number of papers that you will be able to process.

As to numbers of papers: what chains, what regions and what political viewpoints are to be considered; and how many papers from each? What size of readership is necessary before you consider analyzing a paper? Decisions in regard to numbers (and times, the next point to be considered) crucially affect the representativeness of any selection.

Finally, which years are you going to consider, and, inside them, which months? How are you going to get a balanced selection of days? A Saturday edition is a different paper from a Tuesday edition; you will need to randomize your dates and to choose a similar pattern of weekdays for all papers sampled. Randomizing cannot be accomplished without a formal procedure, which will be described further later. The more days and the longer the period you choose to consider, the greater the pressure on you to consider fewer parts of the paper because of the sheer bulk of the data processing you are giving yourself to do — unless you can computerize your study, of course.

And it is not the case that newspapers pose more problems in regard to sampling than do other documents. It is simply that, given their easily quantifiable make-up, it is easier to spot the sampling problems, and harder to fudge the resultant issues.

Figure 5.1 indicates, in simple outline, what is involved. There is a further discussion of this figure in chapter 7. You have to decide on the variety of source materials to be used; is it to be newspapers or broadcasts? Then you must decide what range of examples you will select within the variety chosen. If you decide on newspapers, for instance, will you opt for big city papers or small town ones? Then you have to decide what aspects of their contents should be considered, perhaps big issues only, or prespecified themes? You will then have to decide, although this is not shown in figure 5.1, how much detail you will go into: emphasized items only, or full coverage of everything relevant? Also, you will have to decide what time period should be investigated. One year? Several years? You may well have to restrict this larger time period by selecting subperiods within it; Saturday editions only? Perhaps a 'constructed week' — a Monday here, a Tuesday there . . . ? All these decisions are, clearly, interrelated. Whatever documents you choose, you will have to face these problems of parts, numbers, representativeness and time periods for consideration. To bury your head, ostrich-like, and ignore the problem will not remove it.

SAMPLING TECHNICALITIES

Now that the actual problems with which anyone would have to deal if he were conducting this sort of investigation have been reviewed, it is time to consider the tools available for coping with them. A set of measures has been evolved to deal with these varied and interlocking problems. Fundamental to this set is the technique of multistage sampling. In fact a series of sampling problems must be resolved one after the other (here considered as 'stages') before a decision can be made about what combination of things will constitute the sample: which newspapers to look at? On what dates? For what types of news item and presentation of that item?

Such matters are sometimes referred to as 'universes'; however, the term is confusingly used, frequently being interchangeable with 'popu-

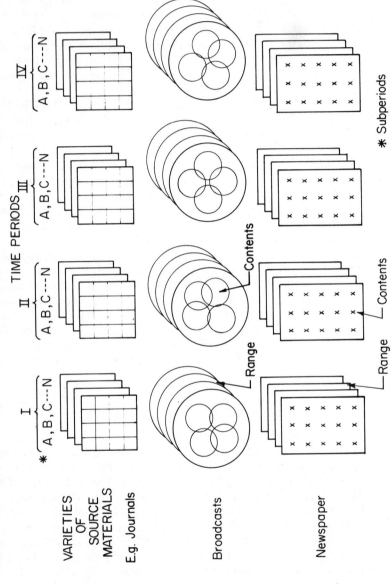

Figure 5.1: THE INTERRELATED DECISIONS INVOLVED IN SAMPLING

lations'.[2] A 'universe' is all the possible *conditions* in which the objects being considered as a population may be found. Each universe involves its own distinctive sampling problems. Take those of the above three stages or populations, for instance. They form an irreversible, if interlocking, sequence. For, when the *final* decision is being made, the sample to be drawn from the universe of one stage cannot be decided without first a decision being made on the sample to be drawn from the one which came before it. So several different sampling procedures must be used, one for each stage, before the final sample can be obtained. This is the process of multistage sampling.

SAMPLE SIZE

Two basic questions have to be considered at each stage: the size of the sample and the randomness of its selection. The size of the sample depends on the amount of uniformity or variation in the behavior of the object being studied. The more uniform this is, the smaller the sample necessary to include a representative selection of behaviors; the more variable, the larger. A small sample can give only a rough measure of a general phenomenon. For a large number of items, or for a complex set of relationships, a large sample is needed to make sure that they are all represented in it. Generally speaking, the larger the sample, the more thoroughgoing the analysis. With small samples can come large sampling errors. But different sizes of sample may well be necessary for the different universes to be dealt with at the successive stages of the multistage sample.

RANDOMNESS

The other basic question, as stated, involves randomness of selection. Randomness does not mean arbitrary selection by whim, for whim is not random: it is psychologically (not logically) determined. Nor does it mean allowing what's available to act as a chance assembly. If 'what's available' has been retained, it will have been retained for a purpose. So it will have been selectively, not randomly, assembled. If pure chance is wanted, a *procedure* to get it must be devised. Tables of random numbers are available, with instructions as to how to use them.[3]

Homespun methods are available. One is to flip a telephone directo-

---

[2] They are so called in *C.A.C.* (p. 23). Miller defines the term as here, but comments expressly on the inconsistency with which it is used: see *Statistical Concepts*, p. 101.

[3] See *C.A.C.* pp. 17-18.

ry open at random and take the fifth number of the series of numbers constituting the phone number nearest to the finger or pencil with which you opened the directory. You then repeat this process, choosing the seventh, third or fourth number or whatever in the series, until you have a list of numbers of the length required.

MULTISTAGE SAMPLING

The normal stages involved in the multistage samples are those of titles, dates, and content.[4] At the 'titles' stage comes selecting which newspapers, magazines, etc. to sample; this stage generally involves stratified sampling. In this procedure, the population is classified into strata according to certain criteria, which are, generally, size of readership, ownership of newspaper chain, political slant, regional origin and so on. There are reference works which will provide such details uniformly: for Britain, Willing's *Press Guide*; and for North America, *The Editor and Publisher Yearbook*. Once the strata have been determined in this way, a random sample is drawn from each. No individual item or group can feature in more than one stratum, and all such items or groups must appear somewhere, in one stratum. The total of objects drawn constitutes a sample for this stage.

'Dates' involve interval sampling. Each weekday tends to have a distinctive character about it, as far as concerns the type of news materials which its newspapers carry. A series of days chosen one after the other will overrepresent a particular set of issues or distort a trend by exaggerating the significance of part of it. Some combinations of times can be a-typical: a group of days might happen to be chosen all of which saw major news items 'break' or, alternatively, which fell in times of unusual quietude. To deal with this type of problem, a 'constructed time period' has been evolved. This is an artificial week (or month, or year) drawn at random from the universe of days or weeks represented by stratifying the population into days or weeks (or months or years).[5] The analyst can then check back on the representativeness of the time-units involved.

'Content' will involve the problem of what to choose. This matter is generally dealt with by purposive sampling: the analyst, from his knowledge of the press, selects the material which best represents the item or issue involved. This is not a random sampling process; subjective judgement is involved. Alternatively he may simply analyze everything in the parts of the papers in which relevant items appear. More

4 *C.A.C.*, p. 23.
5 *C.A.C.* pp. 25-6.

usually, however, the categories determined by the theory behind the form of content analysis adopted will suggest what choices are to be made at this stage. It is, however, worth noting that this is the least developed of the three stages in terms of sampling techniques available for use therein.

RECAPITULATORY ILLUSTRATION:
A BLURRY PROBLEM

However, in the majority of cases it will be less clear-cut sampling problems which must be dealt with. Take the case of a comparison among some textbooks. Recent criticism has urged that students are ill-prepared for such studies,[6] and so the example should prove doubly helpful. It is useful also to examine just how questions, analytical framework, and documents for analysis all influence one another as the analyst goes about selecting his sample.

First the question. One researcher may want to ask how French-Canadian history textbooks differ from their English-Canadian counterparts in presenting Canadian history. Another may want to ask how American textbooks differ from Canadian ones in depicting the war of 1812 between their two countries. Someone may want to ask to what extent textbooks are moving with the times: what is the difference between the British history portrayed in the English textbooks of the late forties and that presented in those of the late sixties? How soon are new insights produced by research work apparent in the textbooks?

Now consider the analytical framework. Either one or several sensitive issues are picked in order to compare the treatment given them in the various textbooks to be considered. Further, it is necessary to decide the total range of viewpoints, or aspects, to be considered from either point of view (or point in time). It can now be asked how much print is allocated to this issue (or these issues) in each textbook — both in relation to the amount of print in the textbook as a whole and in relation to other equally important issues. This problem will involve some form of matrix and multivariate analysis. See figure 8.8, and, in general, chapter 7. How much space is given to the various viewpoints or aspects of each side in each textbook? How are these matters presented: are they explained in terms of social forces, great men or chance/deity? With clarity and understanding, or confusedly and inaccurately? How colorful or emotional is the language used in depicting them? Do such words occur frequently or

[6] See Hodgetts, *What Culture? What Heritage?* pp. 25-26.

apropos of comparable issues elsewhere in the textbook? What are the other issues which such words are used to describe, and what is the author's attitude to those issues? Are value judgements passed? If so, the same types of question as for words will have to be asked.

It now remains to find a selection, a sample of the textbooks which will permit these questions to be answered. One textbook cannot be used as an illustration of either side of the case because any one book is likely to have all sorts of little oddities in it which merely reflect its author's idiosyncrasies. The book may well have been adopted as a textbook in spite, rather than because of, such features. Several books are wanted on either side in order to distinguish generally accepted trends from views peculiar to an individual author. And it will have to be decided what is to be the minimum period of use, and what the minimum number of users, that will make a textbook fit to be considered. It is wise also to be sure that all books are intended for the same age-groups of pupils, and that the dates within which they were used were contemporaneous. An obvious precaution which should be taken very early in this process is to check whether the textbooks in question are in fact available. It is very surprising indeed to find how often such books are simply dispensed with and copies not kept in any form of archive.

Suppose that there is a range of textbooks which can actually be consulted, representing either side (or both periods, depending on the question being asked). Another set of problems, at a different level, are now to be coped with. Just how sensitive and how central is or are the issue or issues? This factor can be assessed by securing the opinions of a panel of people who have some expertise in the area concerned. Or a group of specialist works on the area can be surveyed to see whether they agree with the analyst in assigning such emphasis to the issue or issues. There can be a check on the total range of viewpoints or aspects by this kind of test, to ensure that it really is full and contains only significant items. Finally, it will be necessary to decide whether the issue or issues chosen are clear-cut enough to allow counting operations to be performed on descriptions of them. Is it possible always to tell when the author begins his approach to them in his text or terminates his observations, asides, and references relating to them?

Suppose that a good choice has been made, and that, with some alterations, the selected issues and aspects can be used. Now comes the third and final level of sampling problems. The task is to check how much space was allocated to the issue (issues) in question in relation to other equally important issues. It requires testing the sample of 'equally important' issues to ensure that they really are equally important. The panel test or check against specialist studies will determine this. Analysis of bias involves qualitative assessments. 'Measuring' the direction and intensity of bias is considered in chapter 6. But the matter of presentation always confronts an analyst with difficulties. He has a sample within a sample on his hands. What does 'frequently' mean, for instance? How can he test for it? He can take any twenty, thirty, forty or even fifty pages of text and check them through to see if the words involved recur. Or he can check the issues which the author has singled out for emphasis and see whether the words occur there. Or he can see if they recur apropos of the other issues selected as being equally important, or — if he does not find them there — in a random sample of other major issues. The same holds for the inquiry into value-judgements. At this point, the practical question of whether there is enough time to budget for these operations can begin to be realistically posed. By now it should be known what the whole sampling operation and related analytical processes are going to cost in time. Is there enough time? What must be cut? Can it be cut without ruining the study?

PARALLELS BETWEEN THE ILLUSTRATIONS

This less clear-cut case can be reviewed quickly in terms of the methods and problems considered in the previous, more sharply defined one. Both involve trend studies, that is to say studies based on series or runs of data. But this second study resembles in some ways the kind of situation involved in a case study where the population is all drawn from a single source, the writings of one man. The 'population' comprised by the total body of writings of any one man is known as his 'idiolect'. Study of the language of any textbook will involve study of its writer's idiolect. The total output of a writer can be used as a means of checking upon the emphasis involved in any one passage by establishing his normal practice, and then contrasting the passage in question with this norm.[7]

Now, first of all, it is obvious that here is once again a multistage sampling operation to be performed. Choice of textbooks (or 'titles') will require construction of a stratified sample of textbooks. Dates will not come in unless, of course, the views of different periods are to be considered. In this case representative dates must be established. 'Content' will clearly involve a series of major decisions. Choosing

---

[7] Already discussed in chapter 3. See also Hall in *Communication Content*, p. 156.

issues will probably entail purposive sampling. The variety of terms of presentation to be considered may well be predetermined by the categories of the content analysis. But it may equally well be possible to random-sample pages or issues as a means of selecting a sample of vocabulary structure.

MINIMIZING COUNTING

The aim in content analysis is to do the *minimum* amount of counting possible while still reaching valid conclusions. This aim involves two different aspects of counting, as indicated by the following two questions: first, how much detail is required? And, secondly, how much material is to be considered? Consider the matter of detail first, for the units in which the counting is done largely determine how much counting is needed. The smaller the units that are used for counting, the greater the amount of counting that will have to be done. The crucial question in this regard thus becomes: what are the units which will produce valid findings at the minimum cost in labor? It has been found that large units (that is, themes) can give quite as reliable results when carefully used as can small ones. The large units are, of course, much more economical to use.

But there is also evidence that the kind of units chosen can influence the findings reached through them. Experiments have shown that use of large recording units (for example 'a monograph' or 'article', as opposed to 'a word') tends to emphasize striking features. Similarly, large context units (for example 'the article', rather than 'the sentence') tend to cause neutral passages to receive less attention than striking ones. However, the most well-known difficulties concern the best size for context units in contingency analysis — analysis of 'what goes with what?' If a small span of context is chosen as the unit, then many possible co-occurrences are ruled out of consideration. But if a large span is chosen as context unit, then almost anything may be said to co-occur with just about anything else. The experts advise a context unit in the range of 120 to 200 words.[8]

Clearly, then, units have to be very carefully chosen, with an eye to the overall economy of the analysis. This is a matter for decision at the level of detailed analysis. But, at the second level outlined above, when it comes to the overall problem of final sample size, the crucial question is: how small can the inquiry be and yet remain meaningful and valid? The smaller the sample, the greater the possibility of sampling error, and hence the greater the skill required to draw it.

[8] See *Content Analysis*, p. 118.

The thing to remember is that the larger the sample, the less the risk of sampling errors — if the sample is well drawn.

SAMPLING DESIGN

The drawing of the sample is a matter of sampling design. Decisions as to size play a major part in this. What is involved becomes apparent in a review of all concerned in designing the sample. Different sizes of sample are, clearly, involved at the different levels of this inquiry. A decision must be made on the number of textbooks to be considered, the number and nature of time-periods, and whether or not to probe vocabulary structure. At this last detailed level, decisions as to the size of counting units will have to be made, too. As sampling design thus involves a series of decisions, it can significantly affect results.[9] Choice between designs thus is essentially a choice between different strategies, each with a different end-result or pay-off. There is a device, the so-called 'pay-off matrix', which helps in deciding such matters.[10]

This is an occasion to return to the series of decisions involved in the sample under discussion. The number of books considered governs the number of issues which can be analyzed, again unless a computer is used. The more books, the more data to be processed, and so the fewer the issues which can be surveyed. The number of issues governs the detail which can be explored. If a number of issues are considered there will be a better chance of establishing trends than if only one issue were considered. But a number of issues may involve either having to cut back on the number of *aspects* of each which can be analyzed, or having to limit the detail which can be examined in the *presentation* of the issues. In particular, the feasibility of performing a word-study — always costly in time, but often dramatic in its findings — becomes less as the number of issues is increased, and with it the mass of words to be checked. Also, some issues are more clear-cut than others. Consequently they can be handled more quickly and easily. The analyst is lucky, however, when the clear-cut issues are also the ones which give the best findings. Sensitive issues are generally the controversial ones, and these have fuzzy edges; that is, much has been said and done to complicate them. The nature of the issues involved may thus involve laborious, detailed analysis. This consideration in

[9] *Ibid.*, p. 132. Holsti's comments on sampling designs are well worth reading, too: see pp. 128 and 132.

[10] Possibly the most dramatic illustration of how this device works involves the 'sentry matrix', which always seems to intrigue newcomers to this approach. See, in general, Bruner, Goodnow, and Austin, *A Study of Thinking*, pp. 75-77.

turn affects the amount of ground which, in practice, a study will be able to cover.

SAMPLING AS STRATEGY

Sampling thus resolves itself into the taking of strategical decisions. Figure 5.2 is an attempt to illustrate this concept in simple outline.

Figure 5.2: SAMPLING DESIGN: A MULTISTAGE SAMPLE

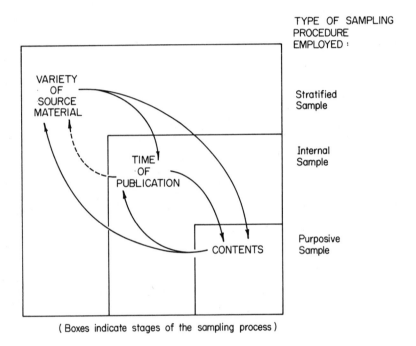

(Boxes indicate stages of the sampling process)

Selecting a sample involves deciding on three things. What variety of communications is to be considered? From what period is the variety decided upon to be selected? And what parts of the communications so selected are to be considered? These are the three stages of a multistage sample. Each affects the other two, as follows. A decision on the variety of document, which is where a start is generally made, affects decisions on the periods of issue and the content to be considered. The availability or lack of the documents at various periods may cause reconsideration of the range of choice within the variety of communications chosen. The period when they were produced will almost certainly influence the contents of any documents. The numbers and kinds of issues considered within the documents, together with the detail in which they are considered, will control the numbers of time-periods and of documents sampled. All these interconnected decisions are, moreover, affected by overall decisions taken in designing the sample. A decision on sample size or on what constitutes 'representativeness' will have a thoroughgoing influence at every stage. A slight change of question may be decided upon, either to maximize the potential in the materials to be sampled or to permit a better sample to be drawn. These overall decisions invoke matters of judgement, or strategical considerations.

There must be a weighing of the advantages and disadvantages which result from widening or narrowing the focus of inquiry at each of these levels. The analyst will also have to decide what items must be included to make his analysis both relevant to the question(s) and representative of the documents. Of the combinations of issues, aspects and details which fulfil the latter requirement, there may be one which does so either much more economically than the others or with the promise of much more significant findings. A good sample is one which does whichever of these things is more important under the circumstances. Not many of these are seen, but when one is, it is found that the study which is based on it is an obvious success right from its opening pages. In sampling, it pays dramatic dividends to be clear headed and to think the problem through like a general marshalling his battle plans and resources. A failure in intelligence is likely to be disastrous in both cases.

6

Content Analysis: Component Techniques

Unitizing, Classifications, Assessments and Inferences.

INTRODUCTION

This chapter discusses the actual procedures involved in carrying out a content analysis: extracting data; classifying and weighing those data; criteria used in assessing them; reliability measures, and checks on inference. For convenience of reference, this rather long chapter has been divided into four sections. This division is to enable a reader to locate discussion of any particular issue or procedure more easily. (The Index of Matters should help in locating minor matters.)

Section one contains a discussion of counting, and includes a note on various types of scales and properties (relational, structural, etc.). It also discusses question-posing, and recording and context units.

Section two deals with categories, including a note on theoretical and standardized categories. It discusses the creation and application of systems of categorization. There is also comment on criteria (norms, standards, etc.) for evaluation of data so classified.

Section three deals with quantification (frequency counting, indexes, etc.), qualitative measures (the semantic differential, evaluative assertion analysis, and so on), and contingency analysis (e.g., analysis of topic groups). There is discussion of the significance of frequency, of assessing bias and intensity, and of critical content analysis. The practical need for a maturing phase is illustrated by a discussion of cumulative content analysis.

Section four deals with reliability and validity. There is comment on the constraints imposed upon a content analysis by the nature of its leading question and its source materials. Types of inferential activity are contrasted. Methods for checking on the inferential stages in content analysis are considered. Involved are the initial decision on whether to read between the lines, and the final leaping to conclusions. Various backchecks or converging analyses are considered as a means of checking on conclusions. Checks on reliability of coding data are reviewed, as are the pros and cons of using computers.

Section 1: Counting and Unitizing

Essentially, content analysis is the knack of reformulating the kinds of questions ordinarily put to literary texts so that it becomes possible to count the answers. This means that a flexible definition of what constitutes 'counting' is needed. To say that "Either you have a zero point and a numerical scale (0,1,2,3,4, ...) or counting is impossible" is too restricting. It is also incorrect. It is more accurate to regard this type of counting as the *best* sort of counting, coming at the far end of a range of computational practices. These commence with very simple operations and go on to more sophisticated ones, ending with the numerical scale and zero point which springs immediately to mind when we ordinarily think of counting.

The very simplest kind of counting involves a mere check to see whether something is there or not. (I have heard this check termed 'the virginity principle'.) The next simplest is: "Is there a lot or a little of this 'something'?" Then comes: "Here's a yardstick — in comparison with it, is our 'something' high, medium or low?" This 'yardstick' could well be an 'ideal type', either the logically deduced model of what ideally ought to be, or the descriptive type which represents a composite general picture, both discussed in chapter 4. Then comes "In relation to this yardstick, in aspects A, B and C, how does our 'something' compare with theirs?" It can be seen how rapidly quite a sophisticated form of counting can be reached (the last question involves multivariate analysis), even without a zero point and a numerical scale.

How can these forms of counting be put to use? The first, and simplest, can be a telling question when shrewdly aimed. It is a non-frequency question: it simply establishes whether a thing is, or is not, so. The most obvious use is in inquiring whether a word or idea occurs in such and such a writer or period. The question is simply: "Did they have this concept at this time or didn't they?" The inquiry stops as soon as one instance turns up. Let me give you an amusing instance. The Conventional Wisdom on the Roman general Marius has been much influenced by Plutarch's biography, and builds massively on his contention that, although Marius was brave when facing an enemy battle-line, he was a coward when facing a citizen assembly. The question was quite simple: does this contention occur in any other source? The answer was: No.

The question, though simple in itself, can be asked in sophisticated, involved, or roundabout ways. What may be asked is: "Does he *not* mention this?" — that is to say, the analyst may be looking specifically for what *is not* there. Or he may break a complicated topic down into a sequence of interrelated things. The first 'things' in this break-down are zones. The next things are different areas within these zones. The next things are fields within the areas; the next subfields, and so on. There is an example of this type of cumulative question-posing in chapter 8, including figures 8.5 and 8.6. In such a case, the question is simply: "Is it this or not?" That is, "Does it go into this zone or that?" Then, "Does it go into this area or that?" In this way, with considerable objectivity, speed, and uniformity of judgement, a mass of things can be classified into a very complex set of pigeon holes.

The 'it' in "Is it there?" can on occasion be a complex pattern. In such a case, it is simply a matter of recording the first meeting with an instance of the first item involved in the pattern, then commencing a search for an instance of the second. The idea is to see whether *the pattern* is there or not; and this task is accomplished by checking on its individual pieces. For instance, if the analyst has a conceptual dictionary for a speech community, as described in chapter 8, he may want to establish what themes, or even words, a writer avoids.

Here is a simple example of looking for a complex pattern. Roman aristocrats' tomb inscriptions sing the praises of their occupants in a formalized way. A speech of a non-aristocrat, Marius, was particularly infamous, according to contemporaries, for its criticism of the performance and qualities of contemporary aristocrats. It elaborates on each of the topics which constitute the formal pattern of aristocratic tomb inscriptions. Each topic is discussed in the frame of reference of those inscriptions, but from exactly the contrary viewpoint. Thus, without a word of reference to those hallowed inscriptions, they are tacitly parodied with savage humour.[1]

The second kind of question involved frequency. It was, remember, "Is there a lot or a little of a certain 'something'?" Here is an example of the sort of thing which can be done with this type of question. The above-mentioned Roman general, Marius, was infamously associated with a putsch occurring during a counter-coup and known as the 'Marian Massacre'. My suspicion was that his contemporaries had not realized this. My question went like this: "Here are a number of

---

[1] See Carney, "Once again Marius' Speech after Election," *Symbolae Osloenses* 35, 1969, pp. 63-70. On conceptual dictionaries, see figure 8.12 and discussion thereto in text.

contemporary sources. Let's try this fellow. Now, does he mention a lot or a little about the 'massacre'?" If there is a yardstick — and they are easy to acquire: see discussion on themes, below — more interesting questions can be asked. For example: "Here are a string of authors arranged in chronological sequence. Now is it true that the 'massacre' grows in horror, blood spilt, etc., the further away from contemporary times you progress?" The check is simply whether writer No. 5 is scoring higher, in comparison with the yardstick, than writer No. 1, and writer No. 9 higher again than No. 5.

But the most rewarding of these quantitative questions tend to be the last type initially mentioned. Thus, it can be asked: "In regard to emoluments, legal privileges and promotions, does the middle-level bureaucrat (John the Lydian) have more or less to say than the top-level one (Cassiodorus)?"[2] Think of this type of question in the following form: "In regard to the following aspects of living conditions, does the U.S. press of the early sixties have more or less to say about urban blacks than the press in the late sixties?" Clearly, questions such as these are the bread-and-butter type questions which the ordinary everyday reader of literary or mass media materials is always having to ask.

These different ways of counting what is in the source material each reveal a different aspect of its contents. Holsti has a brilliant illustration of this.[3] Suppose there is a pair of candidates running on a law and order issue. Now that issue can be decomposed into a number of themes, each consisting of treatment of one aspect of the overall issue. It can now be asked: "Of this list of themes, how many occur in the speeches of each candidate?" This is a simple 'is it there or isn't it?' type of question. Next comes a 'more or less' type of question. "What is the major theme in each speech by each candidate?" Or it can be asked: "When X mentions any aspect of law and order, what other ideas or symbols does he use in connection with it?" This is like the 'what goes with what?' type of question. The straightforward numerical question is, of course, simply: "How many times is each theme mentioned in each speech by either candidate?" As Holsti shows, these different ways of assessing the speeches produce markedly different results. Consequently it is wise not to rely wholly on any one — especially the last, even though that is, numerically speaking, the 'best'.

---

[2] For a detailed exposition, see section 2 of chapter 10 of *Bureaucracy in a Traditional Society*.

[3] *Content Analysis*, pp. 6-8.

In many cases, however, the main difficulty consists of thinking up a way of putting the question so that it *can* be counted, in whichever way. This business of making a question 'operational' is of such fundamental importance that every analyst had better consider carefully what ways there are of doing it. Obviously crucial to the ways of counting just described is the business of estimating what constitutes 'more' or 'less'. This decision is made by means of 'scales'. It is just as well to have an outline idea of what scales there are and what they can do. The more ways an analyst knows of performing counting operations, the wider the range of questions he will be able to think up.

There are four scales: the nominal, the ordinal, the interval, and the ratio. The nominal is the most rudimentary. It classifies merely by assigning an identifying term or number, as with subject-matter categories (pro, con; early, late; etc.). This operation establishes the mode, or classification which occurs most frequently. The analyst looks for the identifying term(s) which acts as a sort of lowest common denominator by being common to the largest number of writings classified.

Next comes the ordinal scale. When one item has more of a certain thing than another item has, it is, relative to that certain thing, higher on this scale. This scale may involve the sex appeal of beauty queens; or it may be that Smith's writings have more on hippies than do Jones's, or Brown's. It is possible to rank items on an ordinal scale and thus establish the median, the one in the middle relative to the others.

With the ratio scale, the full range of mathematical operations is possible, and many of them can be performed on interval scales. The interval scale not only ranks items in a series but also quantifies the distance between them by marking out that series into a succession of stages. Think of the income distribution chart that our helpful income-tax collector is kind enough to give us: that is an interval scale. An interval scale may be arbitrary, but it uniformly demarcates a series into quantified segments so that items can be put into their appropriate segments. It is the yardstick we were considering earlier.

The ratio scale involves a zero point and numbering, as in a system of weights and measures, for instance. With either of these scales, the mean, or average, score for the whole group of things so classified can be established.

The usefulness of the last two scales is obvious, that of the other two less so. A couple of illustrations, however, will show that the former pair, too, can be of use. Look at the mode first. Plutarch has written a biography of Marius. It is a pastiche of snippets of information. These snippets have one thing in common. Plutarch has information on Marius's actions *only* when Marius participates in an incident in which one of the following is involved: Catullus, Metellus, Rutilius Rufus, and Sulla. Now these men all wrote autobiographies, except Metellus, for whom Rutilius wrote a biography. The discovery of this modal characteristic of each little action-filled scenario inspired me to take a similar look at the related *Life of Sulla*. To cut a long story short, what I found there was this. Depiction of Sulla was almost uniformly favorable. When it was not, Plutarch was either introducing a piece of information from a named source, or Sulla's career path was crossing that of someone else who had left a literary record. Plutarch says that he used Sulla's own *Memoirs*; in fact, content analysis of Hembold & O'Neil's *Plutarch's Quotations* indicates that these *Memoirs* are among the small group of sources which Plutarch cites very frequently indeed. The other works in this group are nearly all literary. Clearly Plutarch fed in what other material he could gather, to offset Sulla's patent self-glorification. Note what the concept of the mode allows us to do in a case like this. It enables us to see a pattern of common characteristics in a very odd assortment of things which were made into a nominal scale of content categories by being called scenarios on this or that. It also made it possible to obtain a quite different pattern from another document, and to compare the *dis*similarities in these two patterns.

When *the median* can be established, the extremes can be eliminated, and groups cross-compared in terms of that complex of characteristics which is associated with this, the midmost position in each group (better done with mean scores). Or the analyst may wish to select the median position in each of a range of aspects of something when he is trying to build up a composite picture of that something, as an ideal type, say.

Obviously, once involved in this business of counting, it is preferable to start classing things into groups, as well as treating them as individual items. It will help to know how groups differ from individuals for purposes of counting. For collectives have properties (characteristics) which individuals do not. Thus an individual has *absolute* properties, characteristics which are peculiar to himself, no matter what group he may be in (age, say, or place of origin, or sex). But he possesses other properties only in his capacity as a number of a group. These are discovered only by examining group characteristics. Characteristics like these are termed *relational* properties. They are exemplified by the 'stars' who are revealed by a sociogram as overchosen by their peer group — or by wallflowers at a dance.

Individuals also have *comparative* properties in their capacities as members of groups. A comparative property is determined by comparing one member of a group to others in terms of some absolute or relational property. Thus his position among the siblings of a family group is such a property. Over 70 percent of British scientists, it was noted, were first children: this is an example of a comparative property and its use in inquiry. Here is another. The chances of anyone who comes fourth or later in a sibling group of possessing fluent linguistic skills (and all that goes with them) are far lower than if he had come first, second or third.[4]

Sometimes, however, it is the properties a person has simply as being a member of a group which are all important. Think of 'Oxbridge/Ivy League graduates'. These are *contextual* properties. They differ from comparative properties because they are the same for all members of the group, whereas it is precisely the different aspects of individuals' relationship to the group which determine comparative properties.

Once it is known how to classify individuals in relation to the group, a start can be made at classifying groups in terms of the relationships existing within them. A collective — a kin-group, say, or a clique — can be identified by performing some kind of analytical operation to determine its membership. This analysis is generally done by performing some mathematical operation on some property of each individual. In the case of a clique, for instance, the search might be for a certain pattern of votes cast on a certain cluster of issues spread over several months of meetings. Groups are formed from the classes which are discovered in the course of this analytical operation. Thus McClelland, by examining writers for the amount of imagery related to strivings to achieve contained in their work, was able to establish groups which had high scores for achievement imagery, and others whose scores were low.[5] These scores are *analytical* properties of the groups concerned.

A collective has *structural* properties, too. What these are is established by analyzing the relationship of one member of a collective to some or all of the others. The *gentes maiores* (greater family groups) of the Roman Republic are an instance. They are those senatorial families whose members habitually gained more consulships than did members of other family groups within the Senate. And finally, a collective has *global* properties. These are characteristics of the group itself as such, not of its individual members. Thus countries can be compared by contrasting their global properties: the amount allocated to defence, for instance, or to education.

This review can end with an illustration of how a content analyst could use such knowledge. In his investigation of fantasies relating to flying, Ogilvie first analyzed a series of individuals exemplifying such fantasies.[6] He in this way established the cluster of traits which went with these fantasies. This cluster is an analytical property of a behavior pattern. He then compared folk tales to see which scored highly, and which scored low, in terms of mention of such traits. The two groups thus identified are another instance of an analytical property of a collective. Then he compared the societies whose folk tales had high scores with those whose scores were low, to see what structural or global properties distinguished such groups. This study is not only a model of cumulative content analysis, it also has a splendid clarity in the design of its analytical infrastructure. It is based on the drawing of clear distinctions between the various group characteristics which we have been considering.

But, if the foregoing discussion has revealed anything, it should be the value of the shrewdly put question. Without clear-headedness in regard to what questions to pose, nobody can ever become a good content analyst. Fortunately, I have never met anyone who was not clear-headed in this regard. However, it may be worthwhile drawing attention to the fact that, as far as content analysis is concerned, there are three kinds of questions, but it can cope with only one of them.

The first kind of question is one that semanticists term mere 'noise'. Such questions cannot be 'operationalized' — made capable of being tested by some process which enables them to be refuted or confirmed. This difficulty is very often because they contain highly abstract notions which befuddle thought: "Is liberty promoted or restricted by the rule of law?"[7] Oddly enough, however, this kind of question can be produced by applying rigorous techniques of investigation — if they are applied to materials which do not admit of the use of such techniques. Readers acquainted with literary criticism will be familiar with this variety of question. They meet it, typically, in the form of questions aiming to establish the dependence of one writer, whose works survive, upon one or more others, none (or very

---

[6] See chapter 13 in *Communication Content*.

[7] Well discussed in Weldon, *The Vocabulary of Politics* (this is one of his illustrative questions): see pp. 36-45, and cf. pp. 10 & 26-7.

little) of whose works survive. Questions of this first type are generally, however, the result of tangles of verbiage.

The second type of question involves questions which can be operationalized. The third involves questions which cannot, at least as yet. But these are obviously meaningful and not just conjuring with words. The great questions of religion and philosophy, on the value of freedom or human dignity and the like, come into this category. New ways of posing or testing questions are continually being evolved, with the result that what were once questions of type three have become questions of the second type. Whether this happens or not, however, some of these questions remain, confronting us in all their stark significance. The realities of existence keep bringing them to the fore.

Content analysis is concerned only with the second type of questions, those capable of being posed in such a way that some form of quantification or pattern-matching can assess their results. But it is almost incredible what sorts of questions can be made operational in this sense. Lynch, for instance, has evolved a form of analysis which makes the concept of the imageability of a city into a sharply defined, readily identifiable and assessable entity.[8] He can thus ask all kinds of operational questions about the image of a city. In fact, the questions in this second category are the ones we employ in everyday use. Try asking nothing but the other two kinds for a week and see where you end up.

Content analysis has the merit of forcing us to examine the nature of the question we ask. It requires that we try to make our assumptions, definitions, and models as explicit as possible. It suggests a variety of ways of making questions operational. But all this means is that we are made conscious of problems, and of approaches, which we might not otherwise have thought of. Some ways of posing a question are much more economical of effort and productive of findings than others, and certain aspects of a question are likely to be more productive of insights than others. Content analysis will not tell us which ways, or aspects, to choose. It will merely force us to consider these things. The greater resources and abilities of the technique will indeed encourage us to think more critically about background matters of tactics and strategy in question-posing. But there is a danger: that they may also encourage us to ask fashionable or easily answerable

[8] See *The Image of the City*, pp. 9-10; 46-48, & 155-6. This little book, incidentally, is a joy to read. It will provide its reader with a flood of highly diverting illustrations of points made (much less joyfully) in the present chapter.

questions. Comments in chapter 4 on 'the drunkard's search' are relevant here.

Which is all very well, you may be thinking, but we have to have something to count. The principal contribution of the technique is precisely that it has explored the whole business of breaking up a text into distinct, countable items (sometimes termed 'unitizing'), of classifying these items, and of weighing them against one another. Consider in detail what it has to say about each of these three steps.

Basically, four forms of counting unit are in use. There is the unit which involves a single entity, generally a word or phrase. Then there is the theme. The character can also be used as a unit. Finally, a set of interactions can be regarded as a complex little whole and termed an interaction unit. Each of these units is given its precise shade of meaning by its context. So, along with the counting or coding or recording unit, it is necessary to specify what setting is considered adequate to establish the precise meaning of that unit. This is known as the context unit. For a word, this unit will probably be its sentence. A theme may require a paragraph, or a page, or even a chapter as context unit. So may an interaction unit. The larger the counting unit employed, the more likely it is that nuances will drop out, because an increasingly complicated item is being counted under a single heading. Typically, the more striking aspects become those for which the item is counted, and neutral aspects recede from prominence, becoming underrepresented in the count.[9]

The word or phrase is an obvious type of counting unit and requires no explanations. Analysis is easy when its counting units come in easily identifiable wholes. Thus my study "Problems and Prejudices in the Humanities" employed the titles of books or of journal articles as counting units. Others may, however, find that they need more eleborate 'single entities' for counting units to bring out contrasts with greater sharpness. Lawton, who used a weighted index, states that "recent studies of children's language and environment have moved away from simple linguistic counts in order to investigate kinds of thinking."[10] This 'weighted index' is really a battery of single-entity counting units used together for scoring a text. They are: a subordinate clause dependent on the main clause; a subordinate clause within or modifying another subordinate clause; a verbal construction (gerund, infinitive or participle) within a subordinate clause; and a subordinate clause within a subordinate clause which is itself within a subordinate

9 *Content Analysis*, pp. 118 and 165.
10 See *Social Class*, pp. 156-7 (& 108-109).

clause. The total of the last three types, expressed as a proportion of all four (an analytical property), is employed to compare the essays written by working-class schoolboys with those of middle-class schoolboys. It is thus fairly easily possible to build up a sophisticated counting instrument by clearly specifying a number of individually simple single-entity counting units and then using them together in a preconcerted way.[11]

By a theme is meant a *conceptual* entity: an incident, thought-process, or viewpoint which can be seen as a coherent whole. It is easier to define a theme by giving illustrations than by defining it in generalized, abstract terms. An illustration which seems generally to be liked is the following. The theme is 'an-icon-in-divine-action.' It was employed in an exploration of how the Iconodules ('Slaves of Images') reacted in the Iconoclast ('image breaking') controversy.[12] There are differing Iconodule accounts of how the icon comported itself during a Saracen attack on its city. Early in the controversy it features in stories merely as the passive recipient of prayers. At the midpoint of the controversy come accounts depicting it as having glowed with a wondrous light during the attack. In the final stages of the controversy, when the Iconodules were winning, it began to be said that the icon got down from its niche in the town's walls and ran around dealing death and destruction to the Saracens.

Using themes as counting units often enables constructing ingenious analyses, producing very dramatic findings. Moreover themes can sometimes reach into aspects of a communication which cannot be dealt with by frequency counts or even contingency analysis: where two or more passages contain almost identical words but mean wholly different things, for example.[13] The trouble is, however, that they are not clear-cut, self-evident wholes as words are. Indeed, they can sometimes be quite fuzzy. Consequently there tend to be problems of reliability in coding them. One analyst may, for example, not always be sure whether what he is dealing with is an instance of the theme he is investigating, or, if so, how much of 'it' should be classed as 'theme'. Someone else might have different views in such a case. These problem cases may lead to over- or under-including instances during counting.

[11] *Ibid.*, pp. 109-111 and 118-20.

[12] Kitzinger, "The Cult of Images"; see for example pp. 103-104. There is an interesting brief discussion on themes in *C.A.C.*, pp. 47-9; see also *The General Inquirer*, pp. 35-9.

[13] See *Content Analysis*, p. 160.

It is known what makes for error in this process.[14] Above all else, it is necessary to have the clearest possible definition of what constitutes the theme. And the person identifying it must not have to make a series of different sorts of judgements in doing so. This difficulty can be avoided by atomizing the theme and using a 'decision tree' type of identification routine. Atomizing consists of breaking the theme down into its component elements in such a way that these can be clearly specified, and therefore easily counted (see maximal theme, below). This procedure, incidentally, sometimes enables the analyst to see other, larger themes underlying the one which he initially set out to consider, for the elements often group together in other ways, once decomposed. Contingency analysis can be employed to resynthesize themes, if reconstituting them involves difficulties because so many elements are involved.[15] The decision tree approach involves organizing the sorting out of data into classes in such a way that any one decison involves only the question "Does it go here or there?" This function is illustrated in figure 8.5. But sometimes it may not be possible to atomize a theme. It may be the interrelationship that is all important rather than the elements, for instance. The whole point of the analysis of a 'stream of consciousness' style may be precisely the advantage conferred by using a rather generalized theme. This is an area in which we are likely to be confronted with the significance-versus-validity dilemma.

However it is simply amazing what ingenuity can do when it comes to making quantifiable entities out of fuzzy themes. Some examples are cited below. The most brilliant illustration I know is Lynch's treatment of the theme of the 'imageability of a city', already mentioned above. Although *The Image of the City* is not a formal content analysis, it employs, here and there, content analytic procedures. Another advantage to the use of the theme as a unit of analysis is that it permits analysis of non-verbal materials. A theme can just as easily be used in the analysis of the pictorial treatment of a subject by a painter or weaver.[16] Content analysis, in fact, has been constructed so that it can analyze *any* form of communication. It is not a technique for

---

[14] *Ibid.*, p. 136.

[15] See Hall, *Communication Content*, pp. 151-152.

[16] See *Centuries of Childhood*, Chapters 2 and 3, and *The Achieving Society*, pp. 124-7 and 304 (and, in this connection, E. Aronson, "The Need for Achievement as Measured by Graphic Expression" in J. W. Atkinson, ed., *Motives in Fantasy, Action & Society*, Van Nostrand, 1958, pp. 249-65).

use merely on texts. Indeed it is being increasingly used on non-verbal materials.[17]

But consider some specific examples of the use of the theme as the unit of analysis of communications. In his analysis of the symbols associated with the concept of democracy in the world press, Pool treated democracy as a theme.[18] He defined it by evolving an extensive list of symbols which tend to be used in discussing democracy. These came from three main areas: the institutions associated with representative government, concepts related to the idea of freedom (and its opposite), and concepts related to mass orientation of institutions. Other items were added as result of pilot studies, which indicated areas in which the initial list was not sufficiently inclusive. The theme 'democracy' thus comprises any combination of the above list of component subunits which appeared in any given passage. It turned out that the theme involved significantly differing constellations of concepts at different points in time and according to the nationality of the press being considered. This is a good example of a theme which can be readily identified. Two different analysts using it to score the same documents independently will produce the same scores.

This type of listing operation is a procedure which obviously necessitates elaborate pretesting. Computerized search programmes have met this difficulty by the device of the 'left over list', which is explained in the discussion of conceptual dictionaries in chapter 8.

Consider an example of a theme connected with the less easily countable world of literature. In the discussion on the Marian Massacre, I mentioned that it was easy to measure whether one writer had written 'more' or 'less' on this topic than had another. This measurement would be made by using a yardstick, which I undertook to describe in my discussion of themes. Here is how such a yardstick is constructed. The Marian Massacre is regarded as a theme. A maximal version of this theme is constructed by searching through modern

---

[17] See *Content Analysis*, p. 22 and Paisley in *Communication Content*, pp. 283-5. Readers might be interested in the following studies, which give some idea of the range of applications to which the technique can be put: A. W. Burks, "Icon, Index and Symbol", *Philosophy and Phenomenological Research*, 9, 1949, pp. 673-89; C. S. Hall and R. L. Van de Castle, *The Content Analysis of Dreams*, Appleton-Century-Crofts, 1966; W. J. Paisley, "Identifying the Unknown Communicator in Painting, Literature and Music: The Significance of Minor Encoding Habits", *Journal of Communication* 14, 1964, pp. 219-37; and N. Schidt and B. Sveygaard, "Application of Computer Techniques to the Analysis of Byzantine Stickerarion Melodies" in H. Heckmann, ed., *Elektronische Datenverarbeitung in der Musikwissenschaft*, Regensburg, 1967.

[18] See *Symbols of Democracy*.

specialist treatments, which give the fullest accounts of the massacre available. This search builds up a long list of all the things which anyone has ever accused Marius and company of being responsible for in connection with this massacre: so many murders and assaults; various acts of rapine; diverse consequent suicides; and so on and so forth. This is the yardstick, or check-off list. Now the sources are arranged in chronological sequence, and in each case just what combination of the above is imputed to Marius is established. For the purposes of the analysis, whatever each writer mentions *is* the Marian Massacre, as far as he is concerned.

The context unit can be defined as one paragraph per item and symbols prearranged to indicate when allowance had to be made for a greater or a lesser span of context than this. In this way the context unit itself can be used to provide additional data (as to volume) on the extent of an individual author's coverage of the theme (which is checking for content).

Basically, the idea is to ignore what a writer says a theme means, and instead to focus on what it is that he mentions when he talks about it. The maximal version is a necessity. It lists the widest possible range of things which he *could* mention. Thus, exactly what he *isn't* mentioning can be seen. By including all items cited by all the experts, the analyst eliminates his own idiosyncrasies: he established his criteria by using the combined wisdom of a panel of independent experts. He is not making elaborate and subjective judgements about the author's presentation. He simply establishes whether an item is there or not, and, if so, whether it gets more or less than a specified amount of coverage. He then simply tots up his overall findings in each case. By grouping the authors into the time-periods of the outside, independent experts, he can even state what the general picture was at each of those periods and precisely how it differed from those around it. It is childishly simple. But just try doing it impressionistically!

When dealing with themes, then, some kind of operational definition of what constitutes the theme will be wanted. Some variety of the question "Who does what, how, to whom and according to whom?" will produce such a definition. It will be necessary to decide what are the kinds of parts, the sub-units, into which to split the theme. This division may vary with a case study involving provision for unique features and allowance for change in the course of time, or with a general survey involving comparisons of individuals and groups. If the job entails simply noting where and when a theme crops up, large undifferentiated amounts of text can be used as context units. But if there is to be a cross-comparison of the treatment of sub-units, allowances for differences in the background texts may have to be made. Comparison of full and skimpy accounts may be possible only by expressing the occurrence of the sub-unit as a fraction. For instance, suppose there are ten aspects — sub-units — of an issue. One text may mention only three of these aspects and very briefly at that, in a line or two each. The other may mention nine of them, all quite fully, giving none less than several paragraphs, some several pages. In one case, a particular aspect is one out of three (out of a possible ten) sub-units mentioned, and in the other it is one out of nine. The former constitutes a skimpy text, the latter a full text.

When putting the pieces together again, it is generally worthwhile to see what goes with what, in case other more fundamental themes lurk unnoticed behind the one which is being reconstructed. One way is by linking the component units together into various interaction chains, to see whether they lead anywhere.[19]

All the handbooks on content analysis cite the character as a recording unit.[20] This concept may cause beginners some confusion, because the character is also used, even more commonly, as a framework for providing categories. Essentially, the character is used in three ways: as a unit for plotting data in with; as a matrix for mapping data in to; and as a standard of comparison. In both of the latter cases it is providing a system of categories. Some examples will illustrate. First of all, the analyst may want to plot into the category of 'being in possession of some kind of attitude, skill or trait' various fictional characters or professional characters or what have you. He might want to ask the following kind of questions, for instance: "Which professional groups are seen as having any of the traits A through F? Does this differ in print as opposed to on film, and in 1970 as opposed to 1960?" Or he might ask: "Which characters sometimes/always/never appear on stage simultaneously with character X?" This is the sort of question that has enabled classicists to show that classical plays were designed to be acted by three or four actors, who doubled up on roles. These questions use the character as a recording unit proper.

The other two ways of using the character differ from this. To use it as a device for mapping into, an analyst might ask: "How many references — and of what kinds — are there to character X in documents A through E?" Or, when checking on stereotypes, he might ask: "How many and what sorts of characteristics are attributed to 'Social

---

[19] See Hall, pp. 153-5 and 151-2, respectively, of *Communication Content*.
[20] For good, if brief, discussion of the character as recording unit, see *C.A.C.* p. 34 and *Content Analysis* p. 117.

Scientists' or 'Englishmen' (or whatever) in these documents?" This question produces such things as the image of the Englishmen in French-Canadian novels. But the character can also be used as a framework of reference for comparative purposes. Thus: "The culture-hero Y as a character is well known for the following major characteristics and achievements. Here's a list. Let these constitute his 'character'. Now let's see which of these characteristics the following writers mention and how they 'mention' them." Or: "The character of the hero/anti-hero/villain/etc. in this novelist's works is made up repeatedly of the following characteristics. Let's assemble them as a composite list. Now let's look at what we know of the novelist's personal characteristics, to see how autobiographical his character depiction is." In these two uses of the character, it serves as a way of classifying data, and so is a way of categorizing. As a concept, 'the character' is too gross, generally, to use as a recording unit. Almost certainly a unit of smaller scale will be wanted to analyze interrelationships, for instance.

This point leads to the interaction unit. This type of unit has been evolved to enable the analyst to focus on the flow of interactions between people, rather than on actual objects (such as words), or blocs of thought (such as themes). In this case the context unit is that length of text which contains enough exchanges for the interaction to be completed. Consider an example. I had a suspicion that a particular Latin word was used in a restricted way, that it was in fact a 'male' word, used only in male company.[21] The interaction unit was defined in the following way: "When *sodes* is used, who is using it, to whom, and in what circumstances?" This question involves the following sets of interactions:

		USER				STATUS OF USER		
		Male	Female			Superior	Equal	Inferior
	Male				STATUS Superior			
ADDRESSEE					OF Equal			
	Female				ADDRESSEE Inferior			

Discussion could be amicable, dispassionate or hostile. This factor was indicated by plotting the letter A, D or H into the appropriate cell while recording each interaction. The context unit was two sentences, to allow for statement (or question) and reply.

---

[21] See "The Words *sodes* and *quaeso* in Terence".

This kind of analysis will quickly identify what patterns there are of the above type in the source material. With it, a rather nebulous thing — an action and reaction, occurring in all kinds of situations and with all kinds of words — can be turned into just so many countable interchanges. For each of these interchanges now becomes capable of being described in a small number of standardized ways and terms. The types of interaction analyzable by this particular framework are not very complicated, it is true. But it is a framework that can be developed to perform more complicated tasks. Moreover, it is connected with a body of work produced by scholars who have been studying interactions. So it provides access to ideas which can save much perplexity for those who have to perform some such assessment of literary texts. A review of the possibilities is in order.

In the first place, an interaction can be viewed as a chain of events and coded as such, in a special abbreviated fashion. This shorthand notation cuts down the amount of descriptive detail enormously. It thus enables seeing various complex interactions in terms simple enough for patterns within them to stand out. The dream analysts have done some path-breaking here. Here is a formula of theirs which describes such an interaction chain:

$$1 \; F \; S \; C \; 7 \; \rangle \; D$$

This formula means one person — a female, a stranger and a child — made an attack upon the dreamer (in the reported dream). The initials are obvious enough: they are related to a key list of abbreviations and various positions in the formula. The arrow shows the direction of the action. Various types of action are listed under numbers: visual, cognitive, expressive, verbal, locomotive, physical, and so on.[22] This kind of formula is obviously capable of being adapted to all sorts of circumstances.

If several interchanges are available for study, and they can be examined in context (so that the analyst can search for content in messages by considering their antecedents and consequences), then the procedure known as black-boxing can be used.[23] In that procedure, the analyst sets aside all attempts to probe the motivations or whatever of the parties actually in dispute. They are 'black-boxed'. He treats all threats, cajolery, pleas as inputs into the interaction situation. All decisions, stallings, and so on are treated as outputs. A series of situa-

---

[22] See Hall, *Communication Content*, p. 152.
[23] See McClelland, *Theory and the International System*, pp. 104-105, and Meehan, *Theory and Method of Political Analysis*, pp. 198-206.

tions can be taken and the nature of the outputs which a given participant produces examined, pairing the outputs with the inputs directed at him. Again, these can all be coded by some formula indicative of types of content, nature and intensity.[24]

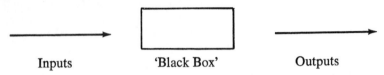

Inputs	'Black Box'	Outputs

Generally speaking, if there is information on *any* two of the three parts of this input-black box-output formulation, it should be possible to make inferences as to the remaining one. However, if there is no evidence on the black box, and if the activities inside it are *very* complex, this inferring may not be possible. In such a case further evidence on its workings must be sought to assist the analysis. To help anyone confronted by this type of problem, there is much literature on it available, including some computerized studies.[25] Once again, the general formula for handling this type of situation is capable of a variety of uses.

Thirdly, a framework (and accompanying terminology) has been evolved for investigating the accuracy of a person's picture of someone else. It is called the Interpersonal Perception Method.[26] Suppose the problem is to establish the accuracy of a given student leader's view of a given university administrator's view of that student's view of that administrator. There is a relatively simple formula:

$$(1) \qquad UA \rightarrow SL:\ UA \quad \left\{ \begin{array}{l} \rightarrow\ =\ \text{view of} \\ :\ =\ \text{position on} \end{array} \right.$$
$$(2)\ SL \rightarrow UA \rightarrow SL:\ UA$$

A maximal version of the (variously described) student leader's view of the administrator is devised. Just which parts of this view actually feature in the administrator's view is then established (1). What parts of it the student in question is imputing to the administrator is determined next (2). (1) and (2) can now be compared. Actually, only a limited number of outcomes (of accuracy, inaccuracy, misperception and appreciation) are possible in these so-called dyadic situations. These have been explored, and there are various formulae,

---

[24] For a good discussion of such *formulae*, see North, *Content Analysis*, chapter 3.

[25] See G. Psathas, "Analyzing Dyadic Interaction", chapter 24 of *Communication Content*.

[26] See Laing, *Interpersonal Perception*, chapter 5.

like the above, available for investigating them. If it is necessary to analyze such things, the sensible thing to do is to consult the experts and the body of work which has been built up. One person's unaided efforts over a weekend or two are unlikely to produce quite the same amount of inspiration in regard to the conduct of such an inquiry.

Fourthly, there is even a diagrammatic device for plotting patterns of interaction. It is called a sociogram and is discussed in chapter 8. Once these patterns have been established, the characteristics of the various interaction units which make them up can be analyzed. Or, the analyst can watch how they individually react to something as it flows through the system of interactions.

The interaction unit in this way links content analysis to interaction analysis and transactionalism. Consequently it can make available methods of investigation used in these adjacent fields. Some very ingenious and flexible techniques of analysis will thus be found linked to it.[27]

Section 2: Categories

Actually, breaking a text up into countable units is not a difficult thing to do. The real difficulties lie in classifying and weighing these units. Consider the business of classification first. The classifications sort out the things being counted into classes or compartments (termed categories) relevant to the questions being asked. So a content analysis can be only as good as its categories.[28] Selecting categories is no easy matter. They have to suit both questions and subject matter. To suit questions, the categories have to set out clearly what sort of thing has to go into each of them, and how that 'thing' is to be recognized. To suit the subject matter, categories have to do two things. They must each be inclusive enough to hold all appropriate items, and together they must cover the whole range of issues pertinent to the inquiry. Everything has to be fitted in. The main pitfall in fact is likely to be the category for left-over matters. Headed 'other', 'etc.', this is known to social scientists as a 'rag-bag category'. If a lot of material is accumulating here, the analyst has not thought out his overall system

[27] See the concluding discussion in McCall and Simmons, *Identities and Interactions*, pp. 255 ff.

[28] So *C.A.C.*, p. 39; actually, this chapter (6) contains an excellent discussion on categories. So does *Content Analysis*, pp. 95-116 (*c.f.* also 48, 63 and 154) which is, as ever, very clear. The article by Lazarsfeld and Barton on "Qualitative Measurement" is a classic as a discussion of methods of categorization.

of categories very well. This situation may result in his having to begin all over again from the beginning. The device of the pretest or pilot study, described below, is intended to detect such poor categorization right away.

Furthermore, the categories have to be such that an item can be classified under only one of them, not under several. Also, all categories have to be related to one uniform system of classification. If the analysis involves more than one level of approach, a separate set of categories will be needed for each level, and the levels will have to be kept quite distinct.

Various types of issue have been repeatedly investigated and so there has been an accumulation of ideas and experience related to categories which are generally suitable for use with each. Consequently, some guidelines are available to those who are inquiring into matters like stylistics, propaganda, or general subject matter classification. Much work has been done on fictional populations (the characters or characteristics of people written about in journals, etc.) and on traits and goals, values, attitudes and relationships.[29] Such guidelines must be adapted to suit any particular problem, of course. In fact, as already indicated, a pretest of the categories intended for use is highly advisable. Known as a pilot study, it tries out the initial choice of categories on a portion of the source material. If they do not work, it may be necessary to change them or the recording unit, or change the way the question has been posed, or even sample the source material in a different way. This is a circular process. The analyst keeps making adaptations to one, then another of these four things until he has a combination that works. He can see whether the categories are adequate only by putting them to use. It is infinitely less costly of effort to discover their flaws straight-away through a pilot study. If the discovery is made halfway through the content analysis itself, the whole will have to be scrapped.

In classical content analysis, in fact, the only guidance available as to how to form categories consisted of the advice to run a pilot study. The analyst simply worked away at questions, units, categories, and subject matter, in a series of little pretests, until he hit upon a working arrangement. For, until the advent of theoretically oriented content analysis, there were no rules for forming categories. Nor were there any standardized or 'pre-cut' categories.[30] This was a critical weakness

[29] There is a series of lists of different classification systems in *Content Analysis*, pp. 104-115.

[30] The advent of the computer has led to much greater pressure for the construction of standardized categories: see *The General Inquirer*, pp. 42-3.

within the technique. It was possible to make a case, unconsciously, by subjectively preferring one combination of categories or classes to another: this preference could create in the analysis a pattern of sensitivities biased to select data relating to that case.

The development of theoretically informed content analysis is of much importance. The theory now suggests what the categories should be. If the search is for authoritarianism, for instance, it says: "These are the issue areas to look at, and those are the modes of thinking to look for." Categories can be developed, based on such instructions. Then categories can be set up using unbiased outside expert opinion, based on well-documented research. For in fact, if inferences are to be made by using content analysis, some guidelines are needed indicating why the things being unearthed in the text relate to other things, behaviors or attitudes, beyond or behind that text. To establish that case, such guidelines have to be based on evidence validated by studies of *other* cases or materials.[31]

The above-mentioned inferences may be either direct or indirect. Suppose they are direct. Readers may remember the previous discussion of direct inference and the illustrative example used in chapter 2. The 'action quotient' index relates increase in use of adjectives to an increase in emotion in the user. So biographical data on the user's career were to be examined to see if there was evidence of increased emotionality at the time when the rate of use of adjectives went up. But it is not possible to tell when the use of adjectives 'goes up' until it is known what it normally is. This point leads to a basic issue: content analysis data are useless unless there is some standard against which to compare them.

Hence the establishing of norms is vital to a content analysis. How can anyone know what constitutes emphasis in a writer's presentation, or intensity in his diction (to take two very commonly investigated subjects), until he establishes the writer's normal performance in these respects? Until 'the normal' is known, the *ab*normal cannot be detected. A writer's normal procedure can be established on internal evidence.[32] It is a matter of averaging out incidence of the phenomenon

[31] 'Theory' means quite different things to, for example, an historian and a sociologist. To the former it merely indicates some kind of generalizations. To the latter it means an analytical framework, based on actual findings: see Cicourel, *Method and Measurement in Sociology*, p. 146. It is here employed in the latter sense. Thus it is that it can provide guidance in setting up the infrastructure of a content analysis: *ibid.*, pp. 142-4. As to external validation of the relevance of the guidelines adopted, see Paisley, in *Communication Content*, p. 283.

[32] See Hall, *Communication Content*, pp. 155-57.

in relation to quantity of text. But it is not possible to establish what is special about his style except in relation to what is normal in style for his speech community.[33] There must be external evidence, outside norms, against which to appraise his unusualness.[34] Whether a journal is under-representing an ethnic group in its fictional population cannot be determined unless it is known how well that ethnic group is represented in comparable roles in real life, for instance.

Unless norms are known, interpretation of data may give most misleading results. The illustration generally given involves dream interpretation. Elderly people were concerned in one case and inhabitants of New Guinea in the other. It was assumed by the analysts that certain features of these dreams were unique to each group and hence specially significant. Actually, these features are common in the dreams of the generality of mankind, and so had no special significance.[35] The validity of inferences depends on the analyst having good norms, as well as good data, to help in reaching them.

In fact inferences cannot be better than the criteria used in arguing to them, and any content analysis will inevitably involve at least one comparing of its data against some form of standard.[36] Take the indirect inference mentioned above, for instance. This inference involves a line of reasoning that, in broad, general outline, goes something like this: "This man (situation, etc.) under study is like that one. So such and such an action should mean such and such an intent, as it did in that man's case."[37] Here it is necessary to establish two things, not one as in direct inference. One is that 'this man' *is* like 'that man'. The other is that action and intent are necessarily (rather than accidentally) related. The norms or standards involved here are those of psychological, communications, or other theory. For the relationship just mentioned has to be demonstrated, not assumed. Outside evidence is required for this.

Thus it is that content analysis involves the use of theories from the Social Sciences for the construction of its categories.[38] This requirement explains why the present book has to be so broadly based. There are

---

[33] Paisley's chapter "Studying 'style' as a Deviation from Encoding Norms" makes this point well. See *Communication Content*, pp. 133-46.

[34] See *Content Analysis*, p. 31 for some examples.

[35] See Hall, "Content Analysis of Dreams: Categories, Units and Norms", p. 155 of *Communication Content*.

[36] Holsti, Introduction to Part II, "Aspects of Inference from Content Data", *Communication Content*, pp. 116-7. Holsti makes the latter point at greater length in *Content Analysis*, pp. 5 and 28.

[37] *Ibid.*, pp. 33-35.

[38] Krippendorff, *Communication Content*, p. 12.

two major difficulties in this reliance on the theoretical frameworks evolved by others. The first is that the well-established theories tend to concern only minor matters which can be investigated under carefully controlled laboratory conditions. The 'big theories' of wide significance tend to be more in the nature of hypothetical formulations of a probable case.[39] The second is that, if the job is to interpret what someone else meant by his theory, that theory is likely to be distorted in the process by the introducing of mistaken emphases, irrelevancies or misrepresentation.[40] Nonetheless, there is an abundance of such theories and of studies employing them. So help is available in the formation of categories, for those who know where to look for it. Chapters 3, 4 and 8 try to indicate where this might be.

Actually, there are not a great many types of categories available for use. There are class structures. These are the kinds of categories found in Roget's *Thesaurus* or in Linnaeus's biological classifications. Things can be grouped together because they are similar in some aspect or aspects. Or things can be grouped by positioning them along a continuum, a scale or dimension. Things can also be grouped together because it can be seen they are located in proximity on some form of map or diagrammatic representation. The various systems approaches alluded to in this book group things together in some form of abstract relationship. In fact one content analyst focuses precisely upon 'cognitive style', or the way a person reasons. His categories of analysis comprise 'idio-logic' (aspects of reasoning), 'contra-logic' (private epistemologies), 'psycho-logic' (personality characteristics which accompany the foregoing) and 'pedagogologic' (the logic of that presentation which will communicate to the foregoing).[41] Some things group most naturally with their opposites: hot and cold, short and long. These ways of classifying things are imposed on us by the way our minds work, not by outer reality. It is difficult to think outside of their terms of reference.[42]

Computers seem to be thought by some content analysts to promise a way of getting round many of the difficulties of subjectivity in categorization. Alas, this hope is as yet far from being the case, for subjectivity creeps in during the long and wearisome business of reducing a text to a form which can be read by a computer.

[39] Rapoport, *ibid.*, p. 38.
[40] Hall, *ibid.*, pp. 150-51.
[41] "Logical Content Analysis: An Explication of Styles of Concludifying", chapter 14 of *Communication Content*.
[42] See J. Deese, "Conceptual Categories in the Study of Content", pp. 45-54 of *Communication Content*.

To find the 'proper' synonym for a given word often involves a subjective judgement. The meaning of a sentence can be more than just the sum of the words which compose it. In fact, classifying language into a set of categorized meanings may not be altogether possible in strict logic. Quite simply, humans are better at noticing things about language meaning than are computerized dictionaries or search procedures. As clerks, recording frequency of occurrence or searching for things, computers leave humans standing. They are faster, more reliable, more clear-headed in their reasons for choosing this rather than that. But the awkward fact is that computer-produced word-groupings are not nearly as good as the faultily human, regular thesaurus.[43]

As already stated, content analysis is an art. It is used clinically. A great deal has to be known about both disease and patient. What is intended is to bring a particular problem to a solution by using this technique. There are various ways for the analyst to exercise control over his own subjectivity when evolving categories. One has been considered, that of employing classifications suggested by the findings of outside experts' studies bearing on related matters. Consider what others there are.

There is no one ideal or best way of carrying out a content analysis. Nor is there any set of categories which will work in all circumstances. The technique involves various components and various ways of putting them together. The analyst picks that combination which suits his particular problem. But similar types of problem do in fact occur as do similar types of issues (already discussed). So a basic set of categories, evolved to deal with a specific type of problem, comes to be, in effect, a set of standardized or pre-cut categories; some are discussed below in chapter 8. They have to be altered here and there in their detail, of course, to deal with the differences which are inevitable between a generalized statement of any problem and a specific instance of that problem. Consider a very simple problem and set of categories which illustrate all this. Doing so will get us away from these abstract and generalized observations and into the hard practical realities of this problem.

Suppose the job is to compare two or more biographies concerning the same subject. Figure 6.1 will illustrate the steps involved. This is not to suggest that the analytical format illustrated exhausts the possibilities for this kind of analysis. In fact, all that is involved in

---

[43] See Goldhamer at *Communication Content*, pp. 352-3 (cf. p. 351) and also Holsti, *ibid.* pp. 118-20 and P. J. Stone, *ibid.*, "Confrontation of Issues. Excerpts from the Discussion Session at the Conference," p. 154.

Figure 6.1: A FRAMEWORK FOR COMPARING BIOGRAPHIES

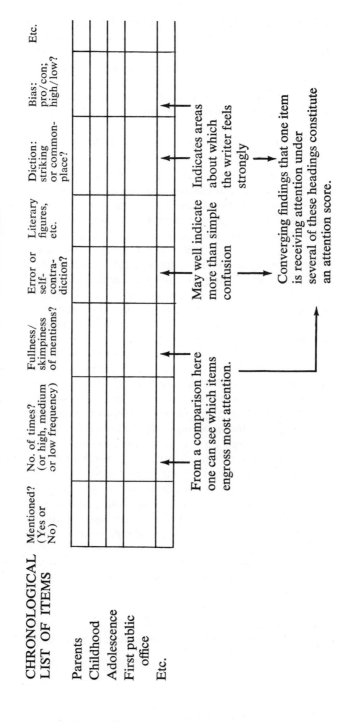

WAYS IN WHICH ITEMS ARE HANDLED

CHRONOLOGICAL LIST OF ITEMS	Mentioned? (Yes or No)	No. of times? (or high, medium or low frequency)	Fullness/ skimpiness of mentions?	Error or self-contra-diction?	Literary figures, etc.	Diction: striking or common-place?	Bias: pro/con; high/low?	Etc.
Parents								
Childhood								
Adolescence								
First public office								
Etc.								

From a comparison here one can see which items engross most attention.

May well indicate more than simple confusion

Indicates areas about which the writer feels strongly

Converging findings that one item is receiving attention under several of these headings constitute an attention score.

it is micro-analysis — analysis of fine detail. It needs to be supplement-
ed by a second framework which looks at aspects of the picture in
the writer's mind 'in the big' (macro-analysis). This technique asks
about the friends and enemies, successes and failures, and virtues and
vices ascribed to, or associated with, the subject. It sorts data into
categories, such as: value-judgements passed upon him; persons to
whom he was compared; statements of what was believed about him,
and so on.[44]

The subject's career is treated as a theme. A maximal version of
major issues is obtained and listed chronologically, giving womb-to-
tomb coverage. These items now become a list of categories, reading
down. Another series is created reading across. First comes a simple
non-frequency question: is this item there or not? Then another simple
question, but this time involving frequency: if so, how often? Then a
more complicated question: is the treatment full or skimpy? This
business of cutting a scale or continuum or dimension into two and
saying 'anything in this part is high (good, pro) and anything in
this is low (bad, con)' is known as 'dichotomizing'. 'Fullness' may be
defined arbitrarily from the analyst's knowledge of the writer, preferably having his judgement checked by securing the estimate, independently made, of someone else who is familiar with the writer. Or
the biographer's practice in this matter may be compared with the
general economy of treatment throughout his work and fullness defined relative to that. The next category is again simple and factual:
does the biographer make any mistakes or contradict himself in dealing with this issue? The next category commences analysis of the
writer's diction in a simple, factual way. It merely asks: "Are literary
figures, etc., found in his treatment of this subject?"

From this point on the categories are more difficult to deal with.
To establish whether the biographer's words in discussing the issue are
striking or commonplace involves making a judgement not of fact
but of values. Did the writer himself consider such diction striking?
It is not in all cases possible simply to presume knowledge. In some
cases, of course, it is obvious — to another native speaker of the
language involved. But, if the language is not our own, or if the usage
involved is not contemporary, it is as well not to rely on 'common
sense'. In the course of a study cited above, for instance, I inadvertently discovered that the innocuous-looking word *quaeso* had the
meaning 'Do you mind?' It was in fact a highly aggressive, male word,

---

[44] See Carney, "Content Analysis for High School Students", *Quarterly of
the Manitoba History Teachers' Association*, 1, 1969, pp. (12-) 13.

used to social inferiors. When studying a language or a culture that is not our own, we tend to be much more alert to this problem.[45] So it is not possible to presume knowledge with the last category. Sometimes it is quite obvious that a biographer is biased for or against his subject. But sometimes it is difficult to be quite sure. Ways of dealing with this problem are indicated below, in the discussion on qualitative assessment.

This practical discussion of how to categorize has identified a number of practical difficulties. It will be noticed that the series of categories (reading across) ranges progressively from categories involving very little subjectivity to those involving more. This placement is deliberate. Familiarity with a writer grows upon the analyst. So the first steps in analysis, occurring while he is also acquiring detailed familiarity with the work, must be simple ones. It is suggested that the steps be performed separately. First go right through the writer's work searching for any mention of each item. Merely put a tick in column one if it is mentioned. Probably the analyst will be operating with a 5 x 3" card index; he would be well advised simultaneously to record where the mention occurs on the appropriate card. On the second run through, he can count numbers of mentions and then be in a position to decide whether any one aggregate number is high, medium or low — for this can be established only in relation to the author's general practice and emphases. But more is involved. By taking each category separately, only *one* judgement has to be made at a time on each issue. If all six must be made at once, the analyst's powers of discrimination will be overloaded, for many of the decisions involve cross-comparisons based on all the foregoing materials.[46] One person can shift a bookcase full of books from one side of a room to another if he works in stages, to a plan, taking half a dozen books at a time. He will never manage if he tries to shift the whole thing all in one.

An analyst can check on the reliability of his assessment of items and categories by having someone else redo a part of the categorization independently. Overlapping placements mean that the procedure is free from hidden assumptions and idiosyncrasies. Very clear and detailed description of categories is essential before such a test can be staged, which is partly why it is a good idea to have one. Accurate definition will force the analyst to become clear in his own mind about exactly

[45] See Cicourel, *Method and Measurement in Sociology*, pp. 155, 145, 149-50.
[46] See the discussion of the advantages and disadvantages of the four 'selection strategies' which people were found to employ in making discriminations of assessment, in Bruner, *A Study of Thinking*, pp. 83 ff.

how his categories relate to what he is doing. Once he has a collection
of items all allocated to categories, as in figure 6.1, he can bring out
trends within them more clearly if he disregards categories which are
uniformly used either very little or very much.[47] Similarly, if he has
such findings on several writers, in two groups say, he can obtain a
very marked contrast by taking the writers who constitute extreme
examples of the different tendencies in either group.

But the main finding which came out of the practical problem just
discussed was undoubtedly that there are two sorts of categories. One
is descriptive or factual. The other involves assessing bias in, or intensity of, expression. Actually, besides these modes of assessment,
termed quantitative and qualitative, there is a third one. This involves
looking at contingency: looking to see "what goes with what and how?"

Section 3: Measurement

Quantification is the least complicated of these three modes of assessment. It involves factual categories, such as: Was this written early or
late in the writer's career? What is the source of this idea? What type
of publication do such depictions occur in? On what page and in
what size of typeface do these newspapers run this story? What literary
tropes, figures, or mannerisms occur in such depictions? Items such as
these can be assigned to their categories on objective grounds. This
mode of assessment, then, involves frequency counts as its basis from
which conclusions are drawn. Some expertise has built up. For instance, if the task is to decide who produced a work whose authorship
is disputed, the thing to look for is the 'minor encoding habit'. Things
an artist has no control over are very minor things indeed, occurring
at the subconscious level. In a painter, it is likely to be the way he
depicts ear lobes or fingernails. In a composer, it is matters like simple
transitions of pitch. In a writer, it is a choice of one form of a conjunction rather than another. The statistical frequencies of such things
are established in each of the artists who is a candidate for authorship
and then his statistics are compared to those in the disputed text.[48]

[47] See Laffal, *Communication Content*, p. 170.

[48] The study which is always cited in discussions of the 'minor encoding
habit' is F. Mosteller and D. L. Wallace, *Inference and Disputed Authorship:
the Federalist*, Addison-Wesley, 1964; the words 'while' and 'whilst' turn out
to be crucial. For an excellent survey of the problems involved in this variety
of literary detection, see Paisley, "Studying Style as a Deviation from Encoding
Norms", *Communication Content*, especially pp. 138 and 143-44. For observations on non-verbal material, see Paisley's study "Identifying the Unknown
Communicator."

Work of this type has discovered some odd features of language. These involve patterns of frequency which yield telltale clues about a writer. For instance, the vocabulary of a language is structured. Its ten commonest words will make up more than 25 per cent of its bulk, the hundred commonest well over 50 per cent. But apart from these common words, the others are used more sparingly.[49] Once an uncommon word (in this sense) has appeared, however, there is every probability that it will recur — a few times. If a particular writer repeatedly uses a word which is statistically infrequent in his speech community, he is either preoccupied with a topic, or has some form of predilection for the word. This fact is likely to be psychologically significant: very high frequency use of such words is a feature of delusional languages.[50]

It would appear that a writer has a certain proportion of adjectival (qualitative) to verbal (action) forms in his work. This proportion has been termed the 'action quotient' (Aq). An increase of the ratio of the former in proportion to the latter indicates increased emotion in that writer. A way of inferring the amount of tension that a writer is laboring under involves the 'discomfort-relief quotient'. This is established by expressing these words in any way indicative of discomfort as a proportion of all words in any way indicative of relief or reward plus all words indicative of discomfort. The writer's vocabulary is examined for fluctuations in such proportions. Periods when he is suspected of being under tension are contrasted with non-crisis periods, to establish evidence of fluctuation.[51]

Increasingly, it is becoming apparent that complex forms of counting are necessary to explore mental states or activities, as these are reflected in language. Lawton's 'weighted index' for comparing the language patterns of two social classes has already been cited.[52] However, a basic word list has been evolved for English, detailing the commonest words in use. It can be a very useful yardstick in appraising diction. Removing such very common words from the count

---

[49] See *The General Inquirer*, pp. 164-5 for statistics of word frequency in the overall structure of the vocabulary. For a list of common words see J. McNally and W. Murray, *Key Words to Literacy: A Basic Word List*, London, 1962.

[50] *The General Inquirer*, p. 33.

[51] See *Trends*, pp. 176-8, where a formula is given: $DRQ = \dfrac{D}{D+R}$.

(For other such indexes, see *Content Analysis* pp. 75-77.)

[52] See *Social Class*, pp. 108-109; see also 116-20.

can uncomplicate calculations and make for crisper comparisons of writer's idiosyncrasies.

But beyond doubt the most significant development concerning this mode of inquiry has come as result of a new strategy for deploying it. Gerbner is probably the ablest exponent of this strategy. He poses a sharp distinction between 'form-oriented' and 'meaning-oriented' (or 'critical') content analysis.[53] The counting of forms (of expression or content) or of conventional meanings (of words, items or themes) has high validity, but is a semiclerical operation. Inferences of any depth and critical meaning can be drawn only by consciously shifting the level of attention towards subconscious trends. These have to be chosen so that they are represented by items which can be quantitatively assessed. The focus of questioning can thus be shifted so that it bears on implicit underlying trends which, once detailed, make assumptions stand out. Here are some illustrations of what is meant. Who in fact is the hero figure in pop culture? Statistically what sorts of characteristics are attributed to him, most often? (He is an 'idol of consumption'.) How in fact is organized labor presented in films? Statistically, how often are unions cast in hero roles? (An unsavory image appears.) Statistically, what do romance magazines in fact advise young female lovers to do? (Adjust.) Who kills whom in TV drama? (Young All-American Whites fare best.) How many TV dramas set in the past, present or future feature violence? (*All* dramas set in the future.)[54]

Such work hovers at the borderline between quantitative and qualitative assessment, to which we now turn. Qualitative assessment often involves non-frequency content analysis, already mentioned as the Virginity Principle. For the all-important thing about a statement may simply be that it occurs (or does not occur).[55] A leading Soviet figure may fail to mention Stalin in a major anniversary speech or may — just once — honor some borderline political figure with a fleeting, but favorable, notice. Kremlinologists take due note; for it is upon such things that official recognition, or the opposite, depends.

Here is another way of looking at all this. By the Emperor Trajan's day, the Roman imperial coinage had lost so much in weight and purity that it proved worthwhile to call in all coins in circulation and

---

[53] See "On Content Analysis and Critical Research", pp. 488-97.

[54] "Cultural Indicators: The Case of Violence in Television", pp. 18-20.

[55] The best description of what is involved in non-frequency content analysis is still that of A. L. George, "Quantitative and Qualitative Approaches to Content Analysis", chapter 1 in *Trends*. See especially pp. 10; 11; 12-13; 24, and 27-8 (-32).

strike afresh at the most recent, and lowest, standards. There were commemorative reissues of the older coins so replaced, out of respect for ancestral custom and the deified emperors of the past. Certain of them, however, were tacitly omitted from these restrikings. And, when an emperor was so represented, only a few of the many coin designs originally struck depicting him were resuscitated. Sometimes these involved singular combinations of heads and tails. Demonstrably, then, in some cases simple frequency counts can miss important facts.

After all, while frequent mention makes it possible for the thing mentioned to be noticed, it is emphasis that *compels* notice. And centrality within the focus of attention may be a matter of salience, strikingness, emphasis, or what have you, not a frequency of mention.[56] As result of investigations of this subject, there is now considerable agreement as to the significance to be attached to frequency of mention. For Pool, writing in 1959, frequency was the most basic and direct, if crude, measure of significance.[57] But this viewpoint rests on two assumptions: that frequency indicates concern or preoccupation, and that every mention has the same emphasis or intensity. Clearly this situation may sometimes be the case, but it need not necessarily be so.[58] Indeed it can be shown that different ways of counting the same source materials bring out different facets of significance, none of which is uniquely correct.[59] These different methods of counting are, in practice, complementary. It is general practice to use first one, then another in the course of a content analysis.[60] For, in fact, to establish the significance of a statement for its author, there is need not just for one measure, a frequency count or quantitative assessment, but for several — non-frequency or associational emphasis, qualitative or contingency assessment. Applied to the same data, these measures will corroborate one another if they turn up converging findings.[61]

In the business of assessing bias, two things rapidly become evident. In the first place, bias has many aspects; it is multidimensional. Still, two of these aspects are overwhelmingly important. One is the direction of bias: is the writer pro or con? The other is its intensity: is he very much so, or just a little? Secondly, means of measuring or weighing

[56] Gerbner ("Cultural Indicators", pp. 20-22) puts this strikingly. He defines 'centrality' as "essential to the plot: even the barest of outline synopses must mention it."

[57] *Trends*, p. 194.

[58] See *Content Analysis*, pp. 45 (note 2), 79 and 122-3.

[59] See the discussion, *ibid.*, pp. 5-9.

[60] *Ibid.*, p. 11.

[61] Holsti, in *Communication Content*, p. 113.

these degrees of bias are necessary. And in fact this area of content analysis has spawned a host of mini-techniques for coping with its special problems. They do not really come in any logical sequence, but it makes sense to start with the simplest ones and follow to where discussion of them leads.

Now the first technique is a very simple one which can be highly effective when used with discernment. It involves a shift, from evaluative categories to descriptive (factual) ones. The question is redefined to permit employment of a series of descriptive categories, which, when taken together, will indicate trends displaying bias. Items whose mention must tell for or against the presumed target of the bias must be found and listed. Then the analyst sees who is assigned which, and how. In the case of Plutarch's *Life of Marius*, for instance, Marius and the autobiographers were all variously involved in a series of battles. The result is that the responsibility for victory in each battle is disputed. A simple check on who it is to whom Plutarch assigns responsibility in each case may well indicate bias. (It does, actually: Marius, to contemporaries Rome's greatest military man, is credited with responsibility for *none* of the victories.) It is surprising how often a question can be redefined in this way, with a little ingenuity. Here is a rather neat little example. It concerns Thucydides' objectivity. Factual categories were employed by posing the question somewhat like this:[62]

Figure 6.2: A REDEFINITION OF BIAS IN FACTUAL TERMS

TARGET OF POSSIBLE BIAS	GOSSIP RECORDED		SPEECHES		INCIDENTS BEFALLING	
	Favorable	Unfavorable	Initiating	Responding	Auspicious	Not
Pericles	4	—	2	1	5	? 1
Cleon	—	5	1	—	—	3

Pericles and Cleon were chosen because they both featured prominently as formative influences on Thucydides' life. Hence emotional reaction, if it were to appear anywhere, would be likely to appear in connection with mention of them.

Great care is needed in the choice of items meant to discriminate. It is necessary to be clear why they do, and to define them very precisely. Often themes are involved. A variant of this technique involves

[62] See A. G. Woodhead, "Thucydides' Portrait of Cleon", *Mnemosyne* 13, 1960, pp. 289-318. This writer is not consciously using content analysis (and I have simplified his findings somewhat, to produce the illustration).

shifting levels from a writer's conscious to his unconscious use of verbiage. Again the object is to discover trends which can be quantitatively assessed.

Bias is never a matter involving only one aspect of a writer's expression. But a mosaic pattern will not be produced by proceeding deductively along one line of analysis, as McLuhan keeps telling us. It helps to look at the overall picture. The device known as the 'attention score' does this job.[63] It was evolved for analysis of newspapers, but figure 6.1 shows that it can be adapted to other literary media. This is how it works. The analyst adopts quantitative categories, such as the following: type of headline; position on page; column width and length; size of typeface; number of illustrations; frequency of occurrence. The amount of attention given to each issue or item being considered is counted under *each* of these categories. In counting, each item can be compared to all the others in respect of each category and scored high, medium or low in relation to the other items, in regard to that category. Or, from his knowledge of the newspapers in question, the analyst can define a graduated scale for each category, and rate each item relative to it. He can then tot up how each item scores on all the categories put together, and rank all the items in relation to one another. Or he can establish those to which prominence is given on all or most of the above counts. The point is that a writer has only a limited number of formal means of indicating emphasis, when it comes to the physical presentation of his material. So his use of them can be checked, and in quantitative terms at that.

And, when you think about it, a writer generally has only a limited number of avenues open to him when it comes to biased presentation. Bias can be directly or indirectly expressed, and it can be indicated in words or attitudes. The following diagram may help focus discussion:

	PRESENTATION	
LEVEL	DIRECT	INDIRECT
VERBAL	Value-judgement laden terminology.	Justification for action; consequences dilated upon.
ATTITUDINAL	Approach adopted.	Motivation ascribed to characters regarded with favor/disfavor.

[63] See *C.A.C.*, pp. 35 and 60 (and 95-6 for comments on the merits of the computerized version).

These four modes of presentation thus comprise areas to be automatically searched by anyone suspecting bias in presentation.

A writer's actual words — adjectives, for instance — often directly yield telltale clues to his evaluative, ideological or moral viewpoint. Indirectly, the justifications which he provides in explaining action or the consequences of that action upon which he chooses to dwell can do the same thing. Several attitudes to a biography or a social issue are generally possible. Each tells something directly about the person who espouses it. Any approach that a writer frequently adopts is thus directed by psychologic rather than logic. Moreover, an approach may involve defining a situation in such a way that one of the actors must show up badly. In a tense and prickly situation, a commentator can focus on disputes or on pacificatory overtures, for instance. So we can check on the ways in which a writer habitually defines situations in which a given character appears. At the indirect level, an abundance of choice is open to a writer when it comes to ascribing motives. When you think about it, a complex situation is rather like a Rorschach test: it is a confused tangle. So what we choose to identify in it springs, to a considerable degree, from our own inner promptings, not from the external dictates of the situation. Consequently, investigation of the motivations and personalities ascribed to an author's 'goodies' and 'badies' will again tell the investigator a lot about the values and biases of their author.[64]

One method, value analysis, directly concerns these search areas. This method involves taking note of every goal and every value judgement mentioned in a writer. The count then proceeds. The count does not just involve frequencies. It also inquires what goals are represented and which are not; what objects are favorably or unfavorably depicted, and how intense is the degree of feeling expressed. This method reveals preoccupations within a writer's thought-world at a level more subtle and, simultaneously, more extensive than impressionistic reading can.[65]

In measuring degrees of partiality or of intensity, it has been found useful to have some form of scale as a yardstick. A writer has only three options in those cases: he can be neutral, moderately biased or extremely biased. This observation gives the following five-stage scale (a seven-stage scale is often adopted):

---

[64] Gerbner, "Cultural Indicators: The Case of Violence in Television Drama", pp. 24-25.

[65] See *Trends*, pp. 178-80; cf. *Content Analysis*, pp. 60 and 108-110.

Very pro	Moderately pro	Neutral	Moderately con	Extremely con
+ +	+	0	—	— —
Very high	Moderately high	Middle	Moderately low	Extremely low

The finer the distinctions the investigator can draw, the greater will be his ability to place things. And in fact difficulties in placing examples of direction or intensity generally involve only certain ranges of the scale. Extreme and neutral positions, for instance, are fairly clearly recognizable, usually. Ways of controlling judgements in the hazy areas are discussed below. Here it should be added that these scales need to be used with a little common sense. If engaged in a detailed study of one item or individual, the analyst may well need a seven-stage scale. But if he is engaged in finding the general direction of the prevailing bias from a trend-study involving many cases, a wide range of fine distinctions may merely obscure the general picture. In general, it pays to use the least complicated scale that the investigation will allow.

The snag with these scales is that a word is not just favorable or unfavorable (or varieties thereof) in meaning. There are many other possibilities besides. *Several* scales are needed, in fact. And this is just what the 'semantic differential' is: see figure 6.3.[66] Apparently, when we pass general judgements on things, we do so not only in terms of whether they are 'good' or 'bad', but also in terms of their strength or weakness, and also their activity or passivity. We use other dimensions too, of course. But these are the three which people everywhere use, whatever their culture or period in history. The 'differential' involves three scales, to locate a word in 'semantic space' — its position on these three ratings combined, here represented as plotted in a field. Each scale, of course, allows the three options already discussed. Hence the zones: intensity increases outwards. The objective is to circumvent the following problem: if merely plus and minus scores are assigned, a highly opinionated writer may appear with a total score indistinguishable from that of a determined fence-sitter. After using the present device to assess a total score, a writer can be rated as + or — as the majority of his analyzed words fall toward the good, strong and active or the bad, weak and passive ends of the continua respectively. You can yourself plot a writer's words into such a semantic space.

As this is a fairly subjective process, it will be wise to run a panel test upon all placements, to see how reliable they are. The panel test

[66] In general, see Carroll, *Language and Thought*, pp. 102-105. For its application to content analysis in particular, see *The General Inquirer*, pp. 48-9; 61 (& 152) and 188.

Figure 6.3: THE SEMANTIC DIFFERENTIAL

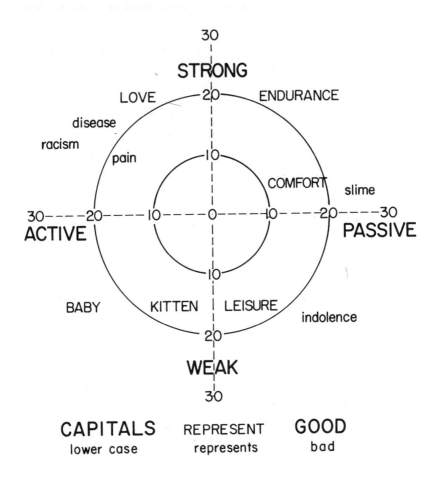

involves having one or more competent judges independently place a string of the words involved. General agreement upon placement will be indicated by overlaps, and the differential will enable seeing quickly and clearly whether there is agreement. Disagreements may decide an analyst to reclassify. They will certainly draw his attention to imperfections in his own criteria of assessment. He will also, of course, have to decide carefully which passages are to be studied by this process. Indeed, the semantic differential is most often used as a means of seeing whether members of a language group agree upon the feeling-tone of a word. It can also be used to explore another person's stereotypes or perceptions, by content analysis of such items as questionnaire responses or solicited essays. Thus a teacher might explore professional stereotypes by asking students to rate such 'typical figures' as 'a Classicist' or 'a Chemist' in terms of its battery of antithetically paired adjectives, each at either end of a seven-point scale. It can then be seen whether any figures tend to receive similar depictions, or whether any virtues and vices tend repeatedly to cluster together. It can then be seen which respondents have chosen to link the figures or virtues in that way — or the clusters of adjectives which are used to describe a typical figure can be compared with those used to describe a good/bad man, friend, husband, etc.[67]

Moreover, there is another way of assessing a given word's meaning for a writer. This way consists of examining the associational field in which that word occurs. First a check is made to see which other words tend to be used along with the one (or ones) in which the investigator is interested. He must also be on the alert for words which are remarkable by their absence. How frequent are the words associated in this way with the key word? What issues are used in connection with these words elsewhere? What are the common characteristics of passages in which these words are used, or of issues apropos of which they are used? How do they relate to the overall economy of the work, and to issues which independent judges would deem comparable? Between them, the cluster of words and the series of issues associated with the key word and its closely associated terms should reveal the writer's biases. Sooner or later these two lines of inquiry will converge upon evidence that will indicate the writer's values or attitudes.

It is unsafe to assume ability to decide upon the writer's meaning of a word over whose placement the panel has disagreed. Indeed, even a common sense agreement is not overly trustworthy, for the common sense of one social group and period can seem uncommonly odd to another such group or period. In the sense of its psychological associations, rather than what it factually denotes, a word's meaning

---

[67] In regard to analysis of a word's feeling-tone, see *The General Inquirer*, pp. 61 and 152. For analysis of stereotypes and perceptions, see L. Hudson, *Frames of Mind; Ability, Perception and Self-perception in the Arts and Sciences*, Pelican, 1970, pp. 46-52, 63-66 and 73-74.

can be assessed only by examining it in relation to the writer's overall, or normal, usage.

Now, unless a computer is available or the writer's works are well indexed, inquiry into his use of words is going to be prohibitively expensive in terms of time. A computer will give a print-out of all passages in which the word is used, or it can be asked non-numerical questions pertaining to the word's associational field.[68] Without a computer or an index, there will be some very demanding work to do: close examination of the diction of comparable issues for one thing, and a search of at least a representative sample of text to check on the frequency and patterns of the word's usage for another. So such word studies will normally be justified only in detailed case-studies involving an individual author.

For other types of problem there are other techniques. One is termed 'evaluative assertion analysis'.[69] This technique seeks to do with assertions what atomizing does with themes, namely to make them uniformly assessable. This it does by a standard format and scoring system. As to the format, each sentence is broken up into three parts, so that it can be easily 'counted'. The parts consist of:

object under study/connecting verbal link/term of commonly agreed meaning.

This formula is intended to encompass all statements making qualitative remarks about the object: "Henry/is/a spoiled brat" or "Henry/sometimes *may* be/a little assertive." A variant to the formula deals with statements about performance:

First object under study/connecting verbal link/second object under study.

"Henry/hates/sissies" or "Henry/does seem occasionally to behave a little boisterously towards/quiet little boys." Sometimes the first object under study may even be 'masked' before scoring commences, by being designated with a symbol or generalized description.

A sentence may constitute one assertion or may have to be split up into several. It all depends on the number of contentions it makes

---

[68] On the non-numerical question see chapter 2; *cf.* Goldhamer, in *Communication Content*, p. 345. For an illustration, see chapter 23 of *The General Inquirer* where, for Huck Finn, the concept 'pop' is shown to co-occur with 'animal' and 'death'.

[69] The scholar most prominently associated with this technique is C. E. Osgood. The best description of it is that of Osgood, S. Saporta and J. C. Nunnally, "Evaluative Assertion Analysis", *Litera* 3, 1956, pp. 47-102. For short surveys see *C.A.C.* pp. 62-3, and especially *Content Analysis*, pp. 124-6.

about the object under study. "Henry is a spoiled/brat" contains two, for instance. Each contention is set out as in the formula by recasting the initial sentence as a series of assertions according to the format: "Henry/is/spoiled"; "Henry/is/a brat."

The 'object under study' is something or someone in regard to which attitudes vary. The idea is to see *what* in fact these attitudes are. The term of commonly agreed meaning is a term of expression which can be easily rated. Cases where agreement is less sure are rated by a panel of judges. This possibility means that the technique may in some cases measure the effect of the statement on others rather than the intent of its originator.

A seven-point scale is used, running from very strong/positive/etc. ($+3$) through neutral to the reverse (-3). Both the verbal link and the 'term of commonly agreed meaning' or 'second object under study' are rated on this scale. These ratings are then multiplied. The product for *each* statement is then added up, to give a total plus or minus score for the document. "X — is that really Henry? — gets -72." This total is then divided by the number of contentions involved (say 11) to give the average score per thematic contention.

Now it is a most laborious business rewriting a text to this format, and it is most time consuming establishing uniform panel ratings on scores for terms that are not immediately and self-evidently placeable on the 7-point scale. Consequently the technique is meant for use when precise data is wanted on a small number of things. This limitation tends to indicate a key decision-maker's implicit attitude towards an issue or policy — a university president's attitude to some mooted complex reforms, for instance. Some less cumbersome method would be used if the task were merely to establish bias in general and so on.

However, a modified version has been evolved for speedier assessments. In this case the format is simpler:

object under study — evaluative (good/bad) assessment
          . . . . dimension 1;
       — dynamic assessment (in terms of activity
       or potency) . . . . . . dimension 2.

Each sentence, or contention, is first assigned to the appropriate dimension. The dimension is scored either positively (+, for connotations of 'good', 'strong', etc.) or negatively (-, for connotations of 'bad', 'weak', 'inactive'), or given a mixed score (+/-) where raters disagree. In this way large numbers of quite lengthy passages can be scored relatively quickly on the basis of placements whose validity is ensured by the fact that several judges have independently agreed on them.

Elaborations of this general formula have also been evolved, though not necessarily for use solely in evaluative assertion analysis. It may, for instance, be necessary to make yet finer distinctions — of intent, for instance, in interaction analysis. This task involves a refinement in the method. Thus, this link may itself be scored on two criteria: the nature of the action involved ('hates', 'is boisterous'), and its intensity or level of commitment or intent ('is', 'may be'). So the *nature* of the action can be rated on a seven-point scale, and its *intensity* level can be rated on another type of scale which tabulates scores assigned to expressions of potentiality ('would', 'could'), wish ('wants to') and also statements ('does'), normative ideas ('ought to') and commands, etc. The scale involved runs from 0.4 to 1.0. The rating on one criterion is multiplied by that on the other to give the overall score for the verbal link in the format. Called the 'intensity reduction measure' and intended for computer studies,[70] the idea is applicable to manual studies. It certainly calls attention to a form of assessment likely to be of considerable general utility in the analysis of interactions.

In practice the tendency is to use several of these techniques together. In the first place, as mentioned, if several different assessments are made of the same data, findings common to them all produce more convincing conclusions. Secondly, these mini-techniques complement one another and go naturally together. Some go with intensive case-studies involving a writer's verbal habits. Others suit surveys of trends. For instance, if serious bias and high emotionality on the part of a writer is suspected, the Aq or DRQ tests will serve as a cross-checking device. In studying a series, fluctuations in the degree of favoritism shown by a writer can be investigated to see if they coincide with passages thought for other reasons to show bias. If favorable attitudes are expressed as a proportion of all attitudes, favorable, neutral, and unfavorable, normal practice can be contrasted with that exhibited in a specific quantity of text. Trend studies in fact rapidly lead to the evolution of formulae for expressing this kind of thing.[71]

It is possible even to shift levels, and look at the total situation, the whole flow of communications (as indicated by figure 9.2). In this way it is possible to consider outside evidence, unconnected with the immediate content analysis. This evidence could be the reaction of the

[70] See Holsti, "A Computer Content-Analysis Program for Analysing Attitudes: The Measurement of Qualities and Performance", *Communication Content*, p. 374.

[71] See Gerbner, "Cultural Indicators", p. 21, note 18 for a simple illustration. Chapter 9 of *C.A.C.* lists a series of mathematical approaches, not of such a simple nature.

target audience to the author's writings, for instance. In fact, as such shifting of levels is much practised in content analysis, the technique has come to be regarded as itself essentially one of a battery of tools to be used to complement the others.

We tend to see things in complexes; so it makes sense to analyze them as configurations, or in a patterned way. And this realization leads to the third mode of assessment, that involving contingency or "what goes with what?" Actually, it has already been twice foreshadowed. The weighted index, discussed in the survey of frequency counting procedures, is a form of patterning device. So is the associational field, just mentioned in our discussion of qualitative methods of assessment. As already stated, these three modes of assessment are interconnected. However, contingency analysis is the most complicated and sophisticated form of the three. What is involved is not just counting frequencies, but questions such as: "Do you find X (and Z) when Y is there?" It is a matter of establishing the co-occurrence of two or more items or characteristics within a given span of text, speech, painting, etc. Now this may not be an easy thing to do. There may be some three or four things which tend to go together; sometimes they do, sometimes they do not, but rarely do all four co-occur. The problem thus becomes one of creating some kind of patterned framework into which to plot series of co-occurrences so as to allow irregularly appearing patterns to show up. This job is normally done by using the matrices of multivariate analysis, if not the advanced mathematics of factor analysis or cluster analysis. To add a digression on the first of these to this chapter would insupportably overload it. In fact multivariate analysis has a chapter to itself in this book, and there is another on analyzing clusters. Detailed discussion of contingency analysis will keep till then.

For there are other complications involved as well. Analysis of "what goes with what?" very naturally shades over into "and how?" One great service that contingency analysis renders, for instance, is that it can put themes together again after they have been 'atomized' for more accurate identification. When an analyst has broken dreams into their basic elemental images, contingency analysis will enable him to see which of these elements co-occur in dream after dream. He may thus be able to see the deeper, basic themes implicitly underlying the surface themes. But seeing how these co-occur may very well involve working out a 'logic of association'. The psychologic behind the traits of a personality syndrome involves such a logic, for example. The pattern may be so complex or irregular in appearance that the investigator has to have an inkling that it may be there before he can spot it. Consequently possession of a variety of theoretical frameworks tends to go hand in hand with the conducting of a contingency analysis.

Alternatively, it may be necessary to work out a 'logic of contiguity' to perform a contingency analysis. For example, to decide whether 'the sun' is, for a particular writer, a male or a female symbol, may well involve the following steps. First the concepts which the writer uses in writing about father figures on the one hand, and women on the other, are established. Then the concepts used in writing about the sun are likewise established. Finally the analyst checks to see whether there are more overlaps in the associational fields of 'father figures' and 'sun', or in those of 'female figures' and 'sun'. Here deciding what kinds of contingencies to look for and in what sequence involves working out a 'logic of contiguity'.[72] There is a method for dealing with this type of problem: the Venn diagram. It is discussed in chapter 8. This business of pattern making and matching is too complex to be relegated to a side discussion.

The main discussion of contingency analysis, then, will be found in the next two chapters. Only one application will be touched on here. This is the analysis of topic groups.[73] This technique is used in the analysis of non-fiction, and in analyzing series of communications at that. Each individual communication is broken up into subject-areas or topics. An investigation follows into how these are patterned: what subject areas occur most frequently and how are the various subject areas associated with one another? This is done, at my level of mathematics, by diagrams, rather like the sociogram discussed in chapter 8. Each subject area is represented by a circle. The size of its circle denotes the amount of attention given to it, relative to the other subject areas. Arrows indicate proximity or association. Unbroken arrows show the main or strongest associations or connections; broken arrows show indirect or secondary associations. Clusters indicate the topics which in practice group together. Violence, for instance, in studies of U.S. newscasts relating to educational matters, appeared in association with school-community and race relations. In Britain, where it appeared, it was mentioned in connection with health (injuries to teachers). In West Germany it appeared mostly in the context of student private life or family affairs.

[72] For a good short definition of contingency analysis, see *Content Analysis*, p. 7. Hall discusses the matter of resynthesis of themes by contingency analysis at *Communication Content*, pp. 151-2. Krippendorff discusses the logic of association there too, at pp. 73-75. On the logic of contiguity, see Laffal, *ibid.*, pp. 167-70.

[73] See Gerbner, "Cultural Indicators", p. 32 and figures 6-8.

It pays to allow a maturing phase between activities in assessing or measuring and the drawing of conclusions from such activities. It is not mentioned in the textbooks on content analysis, but, in practice, after anyone has had his nose to the grindstone doing an analysis in fine detail, his vision loses its focus. He may simply not see the really big things that are staring him in the face. It may not strike him, for instance, that some major aspect was not touched on by the writer. What tends to happen is that, after he puts things back into perspective and proportion, major insights simply erupt unbidden out of the preconscious. But it often takes a week or so for this to happen. And it has a habit of happening when he is not concentrating on teasing conclusions out of the heap of facts piled up by his analysis.

Scoring and assessment can be mere clerical work. It is not necessary to be fresh to do it. Thinking about the overall implications of a study, however, involves reflection. Time should be budgeted so that findings have a little time to sink in before the point of making inferences from them is reached. Such scheduling will be particularly necessary if the task requires shifting levels in a quantitative analysis to look for the basic implications in underlying trends. It will also be necessary in a cumulative content analysis.

Cumulative content analysis seems particularly suited for exploring differences between cultures or epochs. But it need not be restricted to such uses. For instance, after establishing an idiologic (mode of thinking and arguing), Shneidman *infers* a contralogic (picture of the world, causation, etc. necessitated by the premises of the idiologic).[74] Now it might be possible to turn the findings of the first stage into questions concerned with the world-view hypothesized by the analyst. These questions could then be put to the subject's writings, where these existed and allowed of it, in the form of a content analysis. This procedure would enable the analyst to *demonstrate* the existence of the inferred contralogic. Other applications of this form of content analysis will no doubt occur to the reader.

Two kinds of cumulative content analysis are discussed elsewhere in this book. The first is straightforward. An example cited in chapter 8 requires evolving a series of biographical reconstructions of an historical character, Marius (stage 1). The character is then used as a theme for comparative purposes: major aspects are listed and the manner in which each is mentioned by contemporaries is established. The component facets of each segment in this series of reconstructions are now compared. What items are added, dropped, de-emphasized,

[74] See *Communication Content*, pp. 262-3 and 272-5.

re-emphasized or distorted in each reconstruction? This procedure (stage 2) gives the picture of that character which different periods held, and thus reveals something of the world-view held in those periods.

The second kind of cumulative content analysis is more elaborate. The example cited in section 5 of chapter 2, Ogilvie's study of Icarianism, starts by employing content analysis to establish, from a group of biographies, a syndrome of characteristics going with a given psychological syndrome or whatever (stage 1). Then folk tales or other communications are examined to see to what extent that syndrome appears in the communications of each of a number of societies. Then the societies whose folk tales score high are compared with those whose folk tales score low, to see how the characteristics of the high-scoring groups differ from those of the low scorers (stage 3, but not part of the content analysis).

In another instance of this type of cumulative analysis, McClelland first works out (partly by content analyzing Thematic Apperception Tests) the kinds of fantasy produced by persons with a high need to achieve. He then content analyzes folk tales and children's reading books from different societies, to discover which societies rate high and which low on such a measure. He then (and this is outside the content analysis) examines the characteristics common to high-scoring societies and contrasts them with those common to the low scorers.[75]

Thus, in cumulative content analysis the first stage produces hitherto unavailable findings, on which the second stage proceeds to build.

Now a pause between the first and second stages (and, indeed, between the second and third) in such cumulative content analyses is highly advisable. Stage one involves analysis of details. But overall implications must be derived from the details before the questions which inform the second stage can be established. This step forward requires switching to analysis at a general level, which requires adopting a wholly different framework of reference. If he passes immediately from stage one to stage two, the investigator will risk producing a superficial rather than an in-depth assessment of the findings of stage one. Countable items will engross attention. Latent patternings, subtle emphases and significant tacit omissions may pass unnoticed.

Section 4: Reliability and Validity

Pause for a moment, too, and contrast the foregoing with an impressionistic approach. Remember that impressionists have no monopoly

---

[75] McClelland, *The Achieving Society*, pp. 39-46 and 57.

on sensitivity or on bright ideas. But, after having had the bright idea, at the stage when the impressionist is already beginning to write, the content analyst is just beginning to sift the data. Yet both, necessarily, confront the same analytical difficulties. A string of hit or miss 'common sense' snap decisions, one for each link of this chain of interconnected analytical stages, can produce imperfections in the analytical infrastructure. Not that the above is perfect. Far from it. But it *is* formed in awareness of areas where skewing is likely. Content analysis consciously weighs the pros and cons inherent in using one mode or technique of assessment rather than another. It tries to alleviate the compounding of the load on the analyst's discriminatory capacities. For the new look in psychology shows that these capacities set bounds to a person's interpretation of outside reality. What virtue or justification is there in ignoring this situation?

But, if we are all going to be virtuously methodical, we had better also pause to look at the limits of the possible involved in these assessments of ours, performed in the course of a content analysis. Awareness of such limitations should at least cause us to waste less time in trying to do the impossible! And no discussion of techniques of assessment would be complete without a review of their reliability and validity. This chapter will, accordingly, close by considering this matter. It will also consider how best to use these techniques as a help in drawing conclusions, and in checking on conclusions once they have been drawn.

Consider first the limitations imposed by the data. Figure 2.5 may help. The nature of the data and the questions to be posed both set limits on the kinds of analysis possible. If there is only one passage or one document to work on, the number of conclusions which can be drawn from it may be very large. But the number of ways open for substantiating them will be proportionately small. A series of passages or documents, on the other hand, allows the testing of hypotheses, and thus permits more convincing arguments for the conclusions. Content analysis is a technique designed for processing abundant data. It requires a certain minimum amount of documentation before it will work properly. So it cannot always be used — when source materials are very skimpy, for instance. Full rather than skimpy documents, similarly, make for better content analysis. Likewise, an encyclopaedic writer yields more clues about himself than does the writer of a specialist treatise. If all of a writer's output is available, there exists a total population, his idiolect. From this all kinds of evidence and inferences can be drawn. See the discussions of speech communities in chapter 3, and of the conceptual dictionary in chapter 8. If only a few scattered fragments remain, the analyst's case is desperate, because he cannot obtain a representative sample of the author's writings.

But there is more to it. A 'full' document may contain all sorts of autobiographical asides, or psychologically significant value judgements. A writer who abides closely by the impersonality proper to his genre is less revealing. In such cases the analyst will have to shift levels, to probe the writer's language at the level of unconscious usage. Straightforward writing is, in some ways, much easier to dissect than is abstruse, allusive or highly abstract writing. It is easy to break up a policeman's report of a traffic accident into its component parts. Words or phrases can be lifted out. But try pulling a word out of its texture of associations in a T. S. Eliot poem!

There are ways of coping, of course. Themes can be analyzed in such allusive writing, and analysis shifted to the level of the unconscious in the writer's verbal expression. For, at the level of unconsciously used diction, verbal tics, or avoidance of patterns of emphases elsewhere common in the writer's speech community, stand out very clearly. It is much more difficult to examine words which a writer employed with sophisticated disingenuousness. The question as to when to read between the lines is always difficult to decide in such cases (see further below). But if a dialogue, argument or debate is being examined — or, better still, a series of them — the task is easier. The protagonists cannot be too duplicit, or they will fail to communicate. And the background to the discussion helps to identify what it is that each side is really after, as in the technique of 'black-boxing'.

Consider the differences between a study using analysis and that based on a questionnaire. The questionnaire creates a set of responses elicited so as to cover all aspects of the matter in which the questioner is interested. Failure to respond is significant. Emphasis must be meaningful. How deeply meaningful the answers to a questionnaire are, is, fortunately, a matter into which we need not go. About the meaningfulness to a man of his life's literary work, however, there can be less doubt. But, in analyzing it, the content analyst has to devise ways of teasing answers out of documents written with other things than his questions in mind. Failure to 'respond' need not be significant. The significance of emphases needs to be carefully established, for they need not be relevant to the analyst's questions or interests.

Then again, if themes are being used as units in conducting the analysis, findings will be more open to debate than if words are the units. The latter are easier to count, and different analysts can be relied upon to produce the same count. Classical content analysis produces more immediately acceptable results, generally, than does theoretically oriented content analysis. But its findings are more superficial, and so are the inferences to be drawn from it. Yet, for the theoretically oriented variety to be usable, abundant data is needed as well as a 'theory' which tells why the features being identified in the text should be related to the phenomena to which it is inferred that they are related in the content analysis.

As seen in the discussion of posing questions, to apply rigorous methods of inquiry when the documents are not suited to them is mere pretentiousness. The 'best' form of content analysis is the most rigorous that questions and documents between them allow. Hence studies employing content analysis can differ from one another along the dimension running from subjectivity to objectivity, some being more objective than others. It is as well to recognize this fact. Questions involving words as recording units put to a series of communications will produce findings of superior validity, on the face of things, than will questions involving themes put to one document. Questions might be asked involving subliminal patterns in a writer of encyclopaedic range, voluminous bulk and pedestrian style who was much given to personal reminiscences. As opposed to this situation, key words might be analyzed in a writer on a specialized topic, of slim bulk, subtle irony and an impersonal style. Again, the former set of questions will produce findings that are the more immediately valid. Validity in such cases is determined by the nature of the questions and of the source materials. These are matters outside the control of the content analyst.

Secondly, there are limitations of a rather different nature on the applicability of these methods of assessment. They involve the restrictions imposed by the kinds of inferences possible to draw from content analysis. At the most obvious level, all that a man's writings can do is present his picture (not 'the reality') of a period or subject. By using content analysis his image of this or that aspect of the period or subject involved can be described. Indeed, content analysis is *the* technique to use if the task is to assess someone's image of reality.[76] Hence it is obviously highly suitable for biographical studies.[77] But it

---

[76] This point is strikingly demonstrated by the very great numbers of studies of this nature which employ content analysis; see the bibliographies to *The General Inquirer* or *Communication Content*. It is difficult to know which to single out for special mention, as there is so much excellent work to choose from. However, possibly Gerbner's "Images across Cultures: Teachers in Mass Media Fiction and Drama", *The School Review* 74, 1964, pp. 212-29, may not seem an inappropriate choice for readers of this book.

[77] This was recognized as early as the first conference on content analysis. See the historian Garraty's comments in chapter 6 (pp. 171 ff.) of *Trends*, the book which resulted from that conference. Alas, historians do not seem to have followed up this early lead: see *The General Inquirer*, pp. 51-53.

is one thing to assess the image of reality held by a man or, even better, a group of men,[78] and quite another to psychoanalyze someone by using the tool. In the latter case more may be demanded from the tool than it can possibly give.

As seen in chapter 3, in some ways all men are alike — in that they go through the same maturing phases, for instance. In other ways, certain groups of men are alike in that they shared the same processes of socialization. But in some ways we are each of us as unique as our fingerprints. No one has had precisely *your* experiences, for instance. Yet it is through the awareness and sensitivities created by your unique blend of genetic inheritance and life experiences that you interpret events. You do not simply respond blindly to a stimulus. Your response is conditioned by your interpretation of what that stimulus means, as it is perceived by your cognitive filter, a matter discussed in chapter 4. Now this interpretation is not a directly observable phenomenon. It goes on inside your head. It has to be inferred, by others, from what you do.

Now suppose you are analyzing some great man. You are necessarily dealing with the exceptional, the unique. You may well be able to describe his image of some aspect of his long-since-defunct society. But you will have to *guess* his motives for perceiving it as he did. If you are lucky, his perceptions may reveal some recognizable personality syndrome. If you are not, you are caught in an impenetrable thicket of possible motivations. Try naming three great men on each of whom a definitive biography exists which everyone accepts. Ever thought why this does not happen? So, if you employ the technique to analyze the personalities of defunct men who are also a-typical literary or political supermen, you will produce highly subjective results. It makes no difference how good are the tools you use in such inquiries. The nature of the enquiries themselves is such that only subjective results are possible.

Moreover, there is a third limitation. Content analysis bears only on the content (or message) link in the chain which extends from the communicator's intent through that message to its effect on some target audience.[79] To make inferences from message to *intent* will require one (or more) of three things. Either several different content analyses, all converging upon some common group of findings. Or some

[78] See the discussion on psychobiography in chapters 2 and 8. For work illustrative of this general approach, see H. R. Isaacs, *Scratches on Our Minds: American Images of China and India,* and *The New World of Negro Americans,* Viking, 1963.

[79] See *Content Analysis,* pp. 35-37 and 87-93.

type of theory, relating modes of perception to personality characteristics. Or external data, and a study, on the communicator. To infer what the *effect* of the message was, one needs some evidence of 'feedback' — the reactions of the target audience. Hence the stress laid by the scholars who work on communications upon seeing communications as a flow process, and upon analyzing not just the message but as much of the total context as possible.[80] This scope may involve using content analysis as one of a battery of techniques of analysis. It probably will mean some form of systems approach to content analysis, a point discussed further in chapter 8. The longer a chain of inference stretches, the more numerous and the stronger its links will need to be. 'More numerous' may mean the use of several varieties of content analysis or other analytical techniques. 'Stronger' means that there must be ample data to draw upon. These constraints are inescapable.

The pilot of a jet 'uses a different piece of sky' from that which he uses when flying a propeller-driven aeroplane. Correspondingly, if a fairly rigorous method of inquiry is used, the range of activity will be limited to certain types of question and material. Intuitivists, like historical novelists, are freer. But then, they do something quite different. This is not to imply that this method grants freedom from subjectivity. But with it, anyone will be operating far more objectively than is possible without it.

The reason why subjectivity is inevitable is very basic. There is no such thing as the 'content' of a document — 'content' that is independent of the person examining the document.[81] The same document can mean wholly different things to different users. 'Content' is produced by the interaction between reader and document. The reader is in a particular situation and frame of mind. He wishes to use the document for his own special purposes of inquiry. Consequently any content analysis involves its own conception of the content of the documents on which it bears. So does an impressionistic study, of course. But the latter is generally oblivious to the consequences that follow from this selectivity.

It is important to be aware of how the investigator's frame of reference can affect what the 'content' of a document is. Hence the earlier discussions of cognitive filters, definitions of the situation, models, and so on. Theoretically oriented content analysis is so impor-

---

[80] See *C.A.C.*, pp. 2-11. On the concept of 'feedback' see Deutsch, *The Nerves of Government*, pp. 88-91, 128-30 and 182-99; or, more fully, part 5 of Easton's *A Systems Analysis of Political Life*.

[81] See Krippendorff in *Communication Content*, p. 7, and Gerbner in "Cultural Indicators", p. 13.

tant because it relentlessly forces the investigator to examine his own background assumptions. But the material, too, exercises an influence, according to what the analyst defines 'the material' to be. Hence the entire chapter on sampling. However, there is still another way in which the analyst influences what 'the content' of a passage is. For he sometimes must decide at the outset of his study whether the writer means what he says, or must be read between the lines. It is not always easy. Yet, when this question is important, the consequences of faulty inference will be disastrous. Hence the final question in the chapter: What techniques for checking on the validity of inferences are involved in content analysis?

This is a matter on which content analysts are very sensitive and, consequently, quite a battery of techniques has been evolved. Consider the above issue, that of representational versus instrumental diction, to see what is involved. Now it may be arguable that, although on the face of things the writing should mean such and such, it cannot be taken at its face value because the writer's biases or values are incompatible with such an interpretation of his meaning. Such an argument requires ability to demonstrate that such biases or values exist. To demonstrate bias, the whole battery of techniques just mentioned apropos of qualitative assessment can be brought in. To identify a writer's values, all the measures which were discussed in relation to the analysis of an associational field can similarly be drawn upon.

Alternatively, it may be shown that the writer has personality characteristics which cannot harmonize with a reading of his writing at its face value. These are discovered by shifting the level of analysis to reach into mannerisms in that writer's work of which he is unconscious and which constitute such personality characteristics. There are various ways of doing this. Some form of conceptual dictionary can be used. It will enable contrasting the writer's subliminal preoccupations with those of his speech community, so as to isolate values or emphases of peculiar importance to him. Or some form of theoretically oriented content analysis can be employed. This will enable identifying some personality syndrome whose consequences for its possessor's view of 'reality' are known.

It may even be advisable to shift levels by overpassing the individual and looking for subliminal trends within a message system of which his writings form part.[82] In a way, this is an operation equivalent to comparing an individual idiolect to a speech community, but executed

[82] See Gerbner in *Communication Content*, p. 128.

at a more complex level. No one communicator may present all of these trends, but they permeate that system as a whole in a special pattern and create distinctive emphases. In the light of the assumptions indicated by such trends, the meaning of the specific writer is thus shown for what it is. Yet another way consists in going outside a writer's focus of attention to matters and areas incidental to his main concerns. These might comprise background detail unthinkingly filled in, in a novel — or peripheral matters where correspondence is concerned. A writer's picture of reality and, indeed, his value system can thus be revealed, as Isaac's work has shown.[83] The searcher looks to see what kind of assumptions underlie the sorts of things which occur in this out-of-focus zone: how are they handled; what kinds of relationships repeatedly occur?

Thus, when confronted with the problem of deciding whether or not to read between the lines, there are a number of ways open for establishing whether it is proper to do so. One of them may even provide justification for the decision. Certainly a group of them, used in combination, ought to do so.

In fact, this technique of using a combination of measures has been evolved as a means of checking on the validity of inferences. It has already been mentioned in chapter 2, so only an outline sketch is provided here. Conclusions can be tested by a check aimed at disproving them. The test involves taking the conclusions based on one set of documents and seeing whether a second comparable set of documents yields the same conclusions when the same questions are put to it. One way of doing this is by the 'test: re-test' method. The population is split in two at the outset and from the beginning a check on the findings produced from the first half is planned to operate by repeating the content analysis on the second half. Or some variety of convergence analysis may be employed, perhaps by content analyzing several related bodies of documents, posing the same question and looking for overlaps in the findings (multiple confirmation). Better still, test another related body of documents by some technique other than content analysis (multiple operationism). The objective is either to take only those findings common to all studies as constituting the conclusions, or to demonstrate the validity of the inferences by producing the same or similar findings under independent inquiry. Some illustrative examples will be found in chapter 8.

The basic assumption behind this technique is that, if conclusions

[83] See above, note 78 for bibliography; the second work is especially relevant.

have not been tried against some testing process independent of that which initially produced them, they are still unproven. Inferences are only as good as the quality of both the data and the criteria used in arguing to conclusions.

Unfortunately, there is no technique for drawing conclusions or making inferences, and this inferring process is not part of the content analysis. But some form of backchecking on conclusions or inferences, or of generating converging data so as to validate them, is nowadays regularly included in a content analysis.

Mention of the quality of the data produced by a content analysis brings up another problem involved in inference to conclusions. This one concerns the reliability of the data from which inference proceeds.[84] Would someone else doing the counting come up with a different number, or differing proportions, of units? Would another judge have assigned the same things to the same categories? Basically, two ways have been evolved for dealing with this problem. One is the panel test, of which there has been repeated mention. Someone else tests the counting or assignments by redoing them, independently. Alternatively, the overlapping placements produced by a body of independent judges are counted for purposes of the analysis.[85] A variant of the panel test is the so-called 'paired comparison', which works as follows.[86] The text is sampled to obtain a small but representative range of statements. These are then arranged in pairs. A panel of judges then rates each pair, establishing which member is more intense, emphatic, biased or whatever. Then the pairs are all compared with one another and ranged in descending order of intensity, etc. This range or scale then becomes a set of categories for classifying intensity.

The second method of improving reliability in extracting data requires use of a computer, thus ridding the process of the bogey of human clerical or judgemental error. A computer will unfailingly extract all relevant data at incredible speed, and perform complicated correlations of those data without error. There is no risk of subjectivity in allocating recording units into categories. There is even a side benefit: using a computer demands absolute clarity as to the logic behind inferences and hence behind the content analysis as a whole.[87]

---

[84] Well discussed in chapter 8 of *C.A.C.*, and at pp. 135-142 of *Content Analysis*.

[85] See *Content Analysis*, pp. 32 and 130, and Paisley in *Communication Content*, p. 136.

[86] See discussion in *Content Analysis*, pp. 123-24.

[87] *Ibid.*, pp. 151 and 191-192.

However, the success of the computers in doing what they can do well should not blind us to the costs involved in using them. Their use may only push the vagaries of human assessment one stage further into the background, not remove them entirely. For, in the preparation of the documents for the computers, a great deal of judgement is involved in placing items into their 'proper' equivalence classes.[88] Humans are better at noticing things about word meanings than are computerized search procedures.[89] Humans are not as fast, maybe, nor as infallible. But they are much more sensitive to meaning-in-context. Words of identical spelling but radically different meanings, which cause computers so much trouble, are no problem. Themes, which are so difficult to define to a computer's satisfaction, likewise cause a human analyst far fewer problems. It is often very difficult to write a program which can do what a quite unremarkable human scorer can do. And there is the additional practical problem of finding a computer programmer with the inclination and time to write one (supposing there exists the money to pay for his time).[90] In short, rigorous mathematical procedures for analysis of verbiage lag far behind the advanced front where the manual content analysts are skirmishing in their more rough and ready way. So, in using a computer, an investigator purchases reliability at the cost of flexibility and sensitivity.

The grim fact is that, in this matter, flexibility and sensitivity are generally purchased at the cost of rigor. Deciding when that cost is too high invariably involves the analyst in an agonizing moment of truth at some point in the setting up of his study.[91] Mention of moments of agony undergone in the course of preparing for a content analysis study may have moved readers to wonder whether this chapter is ever going to come to an end. Well, it has.

[88] See H. P. Iker and N. I. Harway, "A Computer Systems Approach towards the Recognition and Analysis of Content", *Communication Content*, p. 384.

[89] *Ibid.*, pp. 351-2 and P. J. Stone at p. 524. Much still remains to be done in improving computer programs. For an illustration of the thesis that allusion is what gets lost in computerization, see Raben, chapter 9: "Content Analysis and the Study of Poetry" in *Communication Content* — for instance p. 179.

[90] See L. T. Milic, "Making Haste Slowly in Literary Computation", pp. 149-50 in E. A. Bowles (ed.), *Computers in Humanistic Research*, Prentice-Hall, 1967.

[91] As Holsti comments in *Content Analysis*, p. 142.

7

What Goes With What?

An Elementary Introduction to Simple Multivariate Analysis

SETTING OUT INTERRELATIONSHIPS WITHIN DATA

When there are many details to handle and the questions to be put are not simple straightforward ones, it is not always easy to see how best to go about the job. Yet scholars often want to ask questions like: "How does this writer contrast with that one, in respect to the following points, in regard to such and such issues?" Such questions require setting the facts out on display, so that it can be seen how one thing relates to several others. It may be the aim to contrast several things all at once. The task might, for instance, be to see how a writer handles gossip when it pertains to some of the characters about whom he is writing. Figure 7.1 depicts Suetonius' reporting of rumor in the biographies of (and about) the emperors involved.

Figure 7.1: "THEY" SAY - - - - - -

about	FRIENDLY THINGS		NEUTRAL THINGS			UNFRIENDLY THINGS	
	Refuted	Confirmed	Neutral to favorable	Neutral	Neutral to hostile	Re-futed	Con-firmed
VESPASIAN	1	1	—	1	1	4	2
(Titus)	—	4	—	—	—	3	—
DOMITIAN	—	1	1	—	1	—	7

Or there may be need for a framework enabling the setting out of a mass of details to see what goes with what. The Emperor Hadrian's reign saw some 1,100 different issues of coins. Some were gold, some silver, some orichalcum (a mixture of bronze and zinc), some copper. They bore various messages (legends) and pictures (types). Suppose the object is to see what were the emphases in Hadrian's public relations (and remember that the only way to discover what is *most* emphasized is to uncover the whole range of emphases). It will be necessary to ask (at least): what were the numbers of different legends on single metals (i.e. just on the silver), as opposed to those on combinations of metals, at various periods in the reign? How in fact would *you* go about posing such a question? As you will see, upon reading on, it is really very easy.

Or then again, the aim may be to investigate a series of hunches to see whether combinations of facts that would substantiate them can be found within a mass of details. This is one way of reconstituting the policy decisions taken by someone in authority, for instance. Take the last question. If a way can be devised for setting out the various proportions of messages (legends) run at different periods on the different metals and combinations of metals, it then becomes possible to check into the following matters. Which legends were run on several metals, and when? What target audiences does this imply? (Different status groups handled different metals, to a considerable degree.) How coordinated (in the various provinces) were public relations attempts? Where and when did most changes in messages occur? Alternatively, if it is possible to establish how the various provinces feature in the issues of the various metals, it can then be asked: how does all this relate to the Emperor's travels in the provinces? Is a different group of provinces to those emphasized on the coinage of the previous reign picked out for attention? How does all this relate to the various theories on trading areas, or important outlets for precious metals, within the Empire?

There is quite a simple difference between a lame hypothesis ('it may be that such and such is the case') and a finding in a case such as the above. It resides in knowing how to pose the questions involved. And these questions are quite common, everyday kinds of questions. Time and again researchers find themselves having to rummage in a mass of details to see if, or how, one thing goes with several others. But there is no need for them to wrack their brains each time trying to create, especially for each occasion, a custom-tailored kit for doing the rummaging. There is a method of sifting heaps of details so as to find out what goes with what. It is a method that will work whatever the 'things' are that must be sifted out, and however they 'go' with one another. If there is a mass of details and the questions are like those above, this method is in fact the only known way. It is called multivariate analysis. It is such a basic, elementary technique, in its simpler applications anyway, that knowledge of it tends to be assumed by most social scientists. Here is an example of a simple application, to show what it is and how it works.

ILLUSTRATION OF A 2 x 2

Imagine a big bag containing well over 1,000 marbles. Some are big, some are small. Some are smooth and shiny, some have a dull, matte finish. All are green, but some have blue on them, others yellow. In some cases the blue or yellow is in streaks, in others it is in blotches. How many kinds of marbles there are and how many there are of each kind must be established.

It is done with a thing — a little analytical device — called a 'two-by-two': see below. This handy little ready-reckoner can be extended indefinitely, to cover all sorts of complicated cases. Here is how it works. Take the colors on the marbles. They are blue and yellow, in blotches and streaks. Four combinations are possible:

	Blue	Yellow
Blotches		
Streaks		

You may say: "This is all very well; but what if there just don't happen to be two nice convenient sets of characteristics to be correlated?" All right, make it difficult. Suppose there are half a dozen or so colors arranged in a range of patches or specks of color. The two-by-two is simply expanded to fit the range of particulars to be dealt with.

Figure 7.2:

	Black	Blue	Brown	Green	Orange	Pink	Red	Yellow
Bands (wavy)								
Bands (straight)								
Blotches								
Spots (big)								
Spots (small)								
Streaks								

Here is an 8 x 6 matrix. It is only an expansion of the 2 x 2, and it is easy to see how to go about expanding it. The 2 x 2, then, is the basic idea, the simplest case. It is easy to think in terms of these 2 x 2s, and through them to get the overall larger idea of multivariate analysis.

"How about the other characteristics?" may be asked. "How do they fit into the 2 x 2?" Well, it is expanded again, only a different way this time — like this:

Figure 7.3:

Matte			Shiny		
	Blue	Yellow		Blue	Yellow
Blotches			Blotches		
Streaks			Streaks		

That is to say, a marble can be any *combination* of colors and patches, and it can also be glossy or dull in texture. So the classifier simply makes two lots of 2 x 2s, one for glossy marbles, one for dull ones. And, you've guessed it, he then continues with this type of expansion to bring the other characteristics in. The whole collection of boxes is simply treated as one box, and another one put beside it.

A marble can be any combination of colors, patches and glossiness (or lack thereof); it can also be big or small. So one set of compartments containing all the combinations of color, patches and glossiness is needed for the big marbles, and another set of similar compartments for the small ones.

Figure 7.4:

	Matte			Shiny		
		Blue	Yellow		Blue	Yellow
Big	Blotches			Blotches		
	Streaks			Streaks		
		Blue	Yellow		Blue	Yellow
Small	Blotches			Blotches		
	Streaks			Streaks		

That is to say, the number of initial matrices (2 x 2 'boxes') is doubled to cope with each new characteristic. This process can go on indefinitely, with one 2 x 2 nesting inside another as indicated by the heavy crossed lines in figure 7.4. Here is an illustration of a further expansion (you can think of others):

Figure 7.5:

	Heavy		Light	
	Matte	Shiny	Matte	Shiny
Big (Radioactive)	B. Y. Bl. Str.	B. Y. Bl. Str. **Big**	B. Y. Bl. Str.	B. Y. Bl. Str.
Small	B. Y. Bl. Str.	B. Y. Bl. Str. **Small**	B. Y. Bl. Str.	B. Y. Bl. Str.

	Heavy		Light	
	Matte	Shiny	Matte	Shiny
Big (Nonradioactive)	B. Y. Bl. Str.	B. Y. Bl. Str. **Big**	B. Y. Bl. Str.	B. Y. Bl. Str.
Small	B. Y. Bl. Str.	B. Y. Bl. Str. **Small**	B. Y. Bl. Str.	B. Y. Bl. Str.

"But", you say, "supposing the characteristics just don't conveniently come in pairs?" Well, the 2 x 2 is only the *simplest* form in which to do this type of analysis. As before, it can easily be expanded, if a more complicated framework is needed:

Figure 7.6:

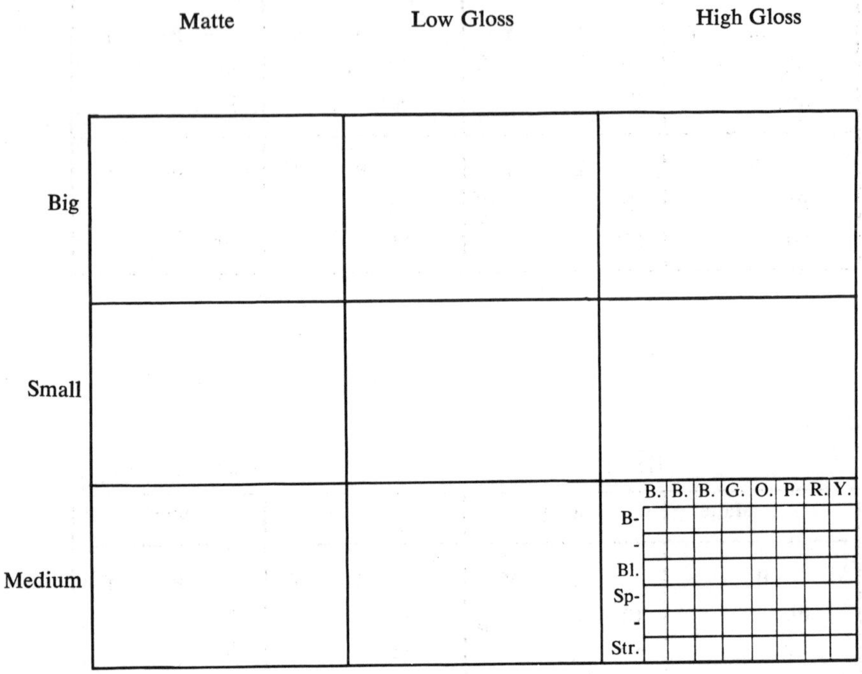

	Matte	Low Gloss	High Gloss
Big			
Small			
Medium			

(High Gloss / Medium cell detail:)

	B.	B.	B.	G.	O.	P.	R.	Y.
B-								
-								
Bl.								
Sp-								
-								
Str.								

Figure 7.5 is capable of handling 64 combinations of details/characteristics, and figure 7.6 432. But the general idea should have been grasped by now.

"All right," you think, "the next time a mass of detail is presented to me like marbles in a bag, I'll know just what to do with it." Think back to the discussion on counting. Content analysis can very easily produce facts in the form:

Mr. Smith's editorials fall into three distinct periods, early, middle, and late. When he discusses state aid to private schools, he sometimes presents favorable, sometimes unfavorable views. And he either writes at length or quite briefly whenever he deals with this topic. Figure 7.7 shows how to set the data out for analysis.

Figure 7.7:

PERIOD OF WRITING

DISCUSSIONS OF THE ISSUE:	early . . .		. . . middle . . .		. . . late	
presented . . .	at length	skimp-ily	at length	skimp-ily	at length	skimp-ily
— favorably						
— unfavorably						

It can also produce the more complex matrix of figure 6.1, where an attempt is made to put the details of a writer's image of an historical personage in terms which can be counted.

The 2 x 2 heightens awareness of shifting levels of analysis and therefore gives greater control over the level of analysis at which the operations are proceeding. The 'nesting' effect was discussed above. One group of 2 x 2s can fit inside the four 'cells' of the next. For instance, there were four possible combinations of arrangements of colors for each of the two types, matte and shiny (figure 7.3), and so on. It is in fact possible to move from one level of analysis to another for purposes of following an inquiry through. Scholars can actually take *part* of a matrix and, by shifting to a more detailed level of analysis, make that part itself into a matrix. Compare figures 7.8 and 7.9. In this way the investigator can, at will, go more deeply into any part of the subject under discussion. Look at an illustration of this shift in levels of analysis.

Readers are asked to note that the actual facts involved in this illustration are quite peripheral to my exposition of the process involved. My central purpose is to show how the business of moving from one level to another is done better than discussion in the abstract can. Naturally, I tend to cite examples dealing with matters with which I am familiar. Moreover, I can use the following one illustration to exemplify one feature after another of multivariate analysis, thus avoiding repeated digressions which would be inevitable if I had to employ a fresh illustration for each feature. This choice of illustrative material is merely for convenience, however. It does not mean that the technique deals only with such matters. You will no doubt readily be able to think of applications to matters central to your own inquiries and concerns. Anyone who can, do so: it will supply another illustration, all the better for its being particularly meaningful to you. The specific details are the husk, as it were. The kernel is the technique of shifting levels of analysis.

Let me interpolate an illustrative example to give you some idea of the flexibility of the technique. In examining "The Social History of English Writers", Raymond Williams reviews some 350 writers born between 1480 and 1930.[1] He categorizes the writers by their social origins under an eightfold system of family classification; by their educational background, considering four types of schooling; and by their method of living under three headings: independent, employed, and vocational. The period considered is broken up into 50-year subperiods for purposes of cross comparison. Readers should, by now, be able to recognize the set of nesting 2 x 2s which is involved in an inquiry organized in this way.

However, for the purposes of my exposition here, take an easily countable illustration, so as to obscure the outlines of (or within) the shift as little as possible. Roman coins, with their ever-changing depictions and catch-phrases, were the one mass medium of Classical antiquity. They give the official, governmental view. For example, *concordia exercituum* means that, in spite of all the evidence before everybody's eyes that different army units are fighting, your emperor wishes to assure you that there is 'Concord between the armies.' Now emperors tended to direct their public relations activities where these would do them most good. Supposing I want to find out whether an emperor directs his public relations activities towards the senate (to win it over) or towards the lower orders in his society (to consolidate support from this element when he is having a spat with the senatorial order). Thousands of issues of coins are involved, and so I decide to run the following quick check. I take a series of emperors who form an historical epoch and look at the numbers of issues of coins which they put out in various metals. Precious metal currency would be handled mostly by the higher orders of the society of the time, and so this will give some idea of where an emperor was concentrating his attention. The following matrix results:

[1] R. Williams, *The Long Revolution*, Pelican 1965, chapter 5, pp. 254-70. A series of multivariate matrices, occurring apropos of use of content analysis of mass media content, will be found in Williams's book *Britain in the Sixties: Communications*, Penguin, 1962, chapter 3, pp. 27-62.

Figure 7.8:

	Nerva	Trajan	Hadrian*	Antoninus	Aurelius	Commodus*
Gold						
Silver						
Orichalcum+						
Copper						

*These emperors' relations with the senate were not good. Relations between the other emperors and the senate were generally good.
+The second two are the base metal currencies.

I have not in fact done this — nor has anyone else, surprisingly enough (maybe because you need familiarity with this tool before you can cope with the superabundant data involved). Hence I cannot put any figures into this matrix. However, in the case of the previous dynasty, that of the Julio-Claudians, emperors like Caligula and Nero (whose relations with the senate were bad) do seem to have issued more coins in the base metals, with themes aimed at the lower orders. For instance, issues of non-precious metal coins bearing themes to do with services rendered the people of the city of Rome occur in the following frequencies:

	(Julio-Claudians)		(Flavians)	
	Augustus	Claudius	Nero	Vespasian	Domitian
	6	3	114	50	110

Nero and Domitian were on terms of bitter enmity with the senate, whereas the other emperors enjoyed good (or, in Claudius' case, fair) relations with that body.

This is analysis at a very gross, general level. It may produce a quick finding if it throws up marked disparities in the overall patterning of issues struck in the various metals. This result would occur if the two emperors whose relations with the senate were bad put out radically different proportions of issues in the various metals from those put out by the other emperors. But no discernible patterning may result from an analysis conducted at such a general level. This lack of result may mean merely that analysis in such broad general terms has only obscured things. An emperor whose relationships with the senate were, in overall terms, good may have had periods when relations were bad. If he operated one policy in the former case and the reverse of that policy in the latter and I simply lump both kinds of policy together, the opposite trends may simply cancel one another out. One overall set of figures for the reign will in this case merely confuse the issue.

So, if no discernible patternings result, I will have to deal with the matter at a more detailed level. I will have to look at the individual reigns. This is known as switching from macro- (or 'in the big') analysis to micro-analysis (analysis at a detailed level). What happens is that I take each 'column' (the four 'boxes' running downwards) and make it into a matrix. I will do this by dividing each reign up into periods, according to the emperor's relations with the senate, and seeing what happens to the various metals in each period. Here is an example of what this might look like:

Figure 7.9:

Hadrian's reign

	117-22	125-8	132-4	134-8	138-9
Gold	15	—	1	21	4
Silver	23	—	4	23	15
Orichalcum	27	8	5	37	13
Copper	3	2	—	1	7

Actually, the figures in this matrix represent not *issues* of coins but non-stock *themes* appearing on the coinage. What are involved are cases in which the Emperor dropped the formal, official conventions to put a specific message over. I have cited these figures for two reasons. First, I can re-use this particular matrix to illustrate other points later. Secondly I thought that readers might be interested in an actual application of the technique to a specific historical problem in a published study.[2] The periods taken for analysis involve times in which this Emperor was faced with clear-cut public relations issues, which make it easier to pose questions to the materials. Readers should therefore note that the matrix of figure 7.9 is thus not a simple straightforward shift of analytical levels. It involves the importation of some further categories of analysis as well. This complexity proved unavoidable if I was to secure an illustration taken from an actual study.

The dates really ought to cover the entire reign, chopping it up into periods when relations were more or less good and others when they were bad. The study cited in the previous paragraph, however, was examining periods of crisis, and these were not, initially anyway, continuous. (The period 138-9, that is the year after Hadrian's death, was included because Hadrian's successor had immediately to promote

[2] See "Political Legends on Hadrian's Coinage", *The Turtle* 6(5), 1967, pp. 291-303.

a vigorous public relations campaign to refurbish Hadrian's image, thus making the coinage of this period almost indistinguishable from Hadrian's.)

It is, of course, possible to move to a yet more detailed level of analysis. I might have taken from figure 7.8 the individual boxes — they are known as cells — and made a matrix out of each. In this case I would first break down a reign into periods in which emperor-senate relations were good and bad respectively (date line running across top, as in figure 7.9). I would then list all the themes which appeared on each metal (the list of themes would run down the side, in place of Gold, Silver, etc. of figure 7.9). This step would require a matrix for *each* cell of the matrix of figure 7.8.

SUMMING ROUND THE EDGES

The aim in moving from one level of analysis to another is, of course, that of securing more, or more relevant, findings. But it is easy to get so involved in the business of making the move as to not take full advantage of the mass of new findings produced in the process. This is rather like cracking a walnut and then taking only the first piece of broken nut found in the resulting debris. There might have been found five times this amount of walnut by sifting carefully through that debris.

The commonest failing is that of forgetting to 'sum round the edges' of the new matrix. Thus figure 7.9 could also be represented like this:

Figure 7.10:

Hadrian's reign

	117-22	125-8	132-4	134-8	138-9	
Gold	15	—	1	21	4	41
Silver	23	—	4	23	15	65
Orichalcum	27	8	5	37	13	90
Copper	3	2	—	1	7	13
	68	10	10	82	39	209

It is possible to work out how many issues of each kind of coin the Emperor had struck (figures down the right-hand side of the matrix) or how many issues came out in each period (figures along the bottom). The figure at the bottom right hand corner is the total of all the issues involved. It is obtained by adding up the numbers running down the right-hand edge *or* those along the bottom. These two sets of figures have to come to the same total, as they are merely the same set of coins counted in two different ways.

SUBSTRUCTURING

These 'sums round the edge' permit generalizing about the figures in the cells of the matrix. Perhaps it is because this step involves moving back up again to an intermediate and higher level of generality that beginners in particular fail to do it as a matter of course. But there is a more common lack of awareness about a different kind of gain which accrues from this shifting of levels of analysis. A process known as 'substructuring'[3] results from the use of these matrices. By substructuring is meant the fact that the matrix automatically sets out all the combinations which are logically possible between the two things involved. Thus attention is automatically directed towards possibilities which would not otherwise have been thought of.

Substructuring, then, does not concern how data is set out. Rather, it involves the way in which a matrix can lead analysts to see all the potentialities inherent in the questions they are posing. As will be seen later on, too, in the discussion of reduction (which is the inverse of substructuring), the matrix can set the analyst's *thoughts* out, as well as his data by showing that combining one thing with one or more others results in just so many specific combinations (see discussion of figure 7.22). Consequently, the implications of an initial question can be explored by the use of such a matrix. That question can thus be expanded or refined. It is precisely this business of sharpening up questions that is involved in substructuring.

The usual illustration goes as follows. Supposing the task is to work out the kinds of interaction possible in a staff-student relationship.

---

[3] See A. H. Barton's comments on "Substruction of the Property Space of a Typology," in his brilliant article "The Concept of Property Space in Social Research", pp. 40-53 in P. F. Lazarsfeld and M. Rosenberg, eds., *The Language of Social Research*, Free Press, 1955. The article by Lazarsfeld and Barton on "Qualitative Measurement" will also be found most helpful for the above, and following, discussion.

Here is how it might look on a matrix:

Figure 7.11:

STUDENT

FACULTY MEMBER	Desirous of guidance	Accepts guidance	Wishes to reject guidance
Desirous of providing guidance	1	2	3
Accepts the principle of guidance	4	5	6
Wishes to reject any claims to guidance	7	8	9

Now some of these types of interaction fall into categories which are obvious. Cells 1 and 2, for instance, comprise the situation which might be described as traditional, strong leadership; cells 3 and 6, its opposite, revolt. Cells 4 and 5 represent a situation which might be described as moderate direction and cell 8 remissiveness in providing direction. But what of cells 7 and 9? Both are real possibilities, once you think about it for a moment. But they are not ones that readily spring to mind. Seven involves faculty refusal to perform a duty in spite of calls to that duty. Nine involves mutual antipathy, and is likely to engender serious trouble. Our various academic hells have few furies like a student scorned: though he wants guidance, so that he can reject it, faculty do not care enough about him to want to give it in this hypothetical case.

PICTORIAL REPRESENTATION

Failures to realize the full potential of the facts gathered are due to the complications which arise once what was originally one act of analysis is expanded into a series of such acts. Attention can become overloaded with things of which account must be taken. This problem can sometimes be avoided simply by improving the presentation, by laying out the facts differently. The 2 x 2 (and still more the 10 x 6) matrix does not present its data in a self-evident fashion. Sometimes, moreover, the mere proliferation of 2 x 2s makes for difficulties in putting the resultant findings together again. There are a number of ways of coping with both the problem of presentation and that of sorting into appropriate piles the boxes which spring out of nowhere when levels are shifted. Look at both these matters, taking presentation first.

The snag about the 2 x 2 is that there often has to be quite hard thinking before the significance of the figures in the cells becomes clear. A real danger exists, in consequence, that, if there are too many boxes, or if they are individually too complicated, it may simply not be possible to see the wood for the trees. This kind of difficulty can be made much less by the way in which findings are presented. For instance, pictorial representation shows findings up in a much more self-evident way than does representation in mathematical terms.

For a clear illustration, consider figure 5.1, whose relationship to a 2 x 2 is patent. The figure consists, essentially, of drawings instead of numbers, fitted into a 2 x 2 pattern instead of a formal framework of squares. The intent is to show all the different factors which have to be taken into account in drawing a sample. In fact six variables are involved, of which five are represented pictorially in figure 5.1, as is indicated in the discussion of the figure. To set out that discussion in 2 x 2 form would require a minimum of three sets of nesting 2 x 2s in a 64-cell matrix. The figure represents this in a much less complicated way. It sets out boldly the two basic decisions, as to varieties of source materials and choice of time-periods. This represents the largest 2 x 2, enclosing all the others. Less boldly, it depicts the choices at the next level: what range of material within each variety, and what subperiods within each time-period are to be selected? This level represents the medium-sized 2 x 2s nesting within each cell of the largest one. It also depicts a further, yet more detailed, choice: what parts of the contents of these materials are to be considered and in what detail? (The latter point is not shown.) This further depiction represents the smallest 2 x 2s nesting inside each cell of the medium-sized ones.

Pictorial representation is in fact so much more intelligible that certain set ways of going about it have been evolved. These are in frequent use, and will be quite familiar from everyday reading. One is the bar graph. Here is an example of an imaginary nature to illustrate:

Figure 7.12:

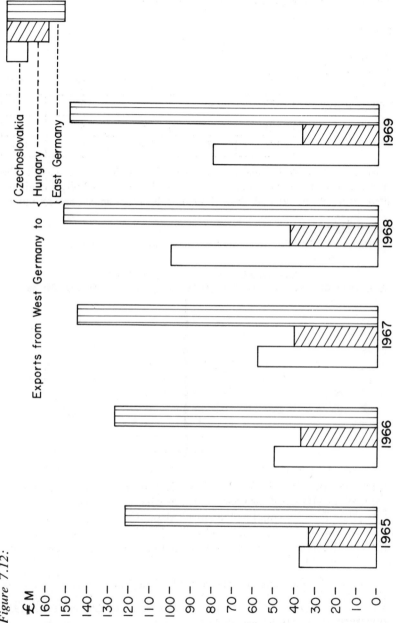

This bar graph represents the following matrix:

Figure 7.13:

In years

Exports in £ millions to	65	66	67	68	69
Czechoslovakia	37	49	57	101	77
Hungary	31	36	40	43	37
East Germany	121	125	146	153	148

Most often correlations are displayed in the following way in the presentation of voting studies and so on. Here is a wholly imaginary illustration of the sort of thing I mean.[4] Readers may care to recon-

Figure 7.14:

Percentage of Democrat voters in the last 8 mayoralty elections.

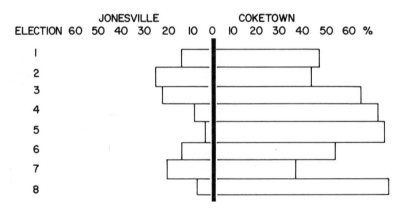

struct their own matrix for the above display to check for themselves that they have grasped the general idea of what is involved.

Another type of simplified pictorial depiction of correlations is as follows. The latest provincial election in Manitoba involved some fifty constituencies; there were four political parties and many in-

---

[4] For ample illustration of this method of depiction see Berelson *et al*, "Political Perception", pp. 72-85 in Maccoby, *Readings*. (This passage is an extract from the book by Berelson *et al*: *Voting*, U. of Chicago Press, 1954; see chapter 10 for greater exposition.)

dependent candidates competing. In a strikingly simple and direct presentation, local newspapers showed the results as a map of the constituencies color-coded in five colors, each constituency colored according to the code for the party affiliation (or lack of it) of its elected representative. The basic general idea is simple enough. Some form of structural framework is erected such that, within it, different things can be shown in pictorial terms. A series of pie charts is perhaps the simplest and commonest way of doing this.

COLLAPSING MATRICES

In a way, one of these 'in-the-big' matrices is rather like a hornet's nest. Once it is taken to pieces, a buzzing confusion results as its mass of tiny occupants comes shooting out in all directions. Now there is the problem of coping with them and of trying to estimate what their movements suggest should be done. It is easy enough to move down from a general level of analysis. The initial matrix is simply broken into pieces and each of these turned into a matrix consisting of a detailed study of what was previously a piece. There are now 4, or 8, or 16 times the original quantity of findings. But these new masses of findings cannot be summed up without moving back up again to a more general level of analysis. So it is necessary to know how to climb back up, as well as how to climb down. The investigator needs to have at his disposal ways of combining, simplifying, or marshalling the welter of details produced when he moves from in-the-big analysis to analysis of detail. Basically, he can do this in one of two ways. He can uncomplicate the data, thus allowing trends or outlines to show through more clearly, either by cutting down the number of matrices or by simplifying the individual matrices internally.

The number of matrices is cut down by a process known as 'collapsing' them. This means not employing two matrices to demonstrate the correlations between one thing and two others. Rather, details about this 'one thing' are entered into the cells of the matrix which sets out the correlations between the other two things. Thus two matrices are collapsed into one by making that one do the work of two. An example will show most clearly what is meant.

Supposing the task is to find out what is really going on in the phenomenon known as 'the brain drain'. The investigator wants to discover what kinds of brains are going where, and whether over time their migrating flocks are growing in numbers.

Figure 7.15:

TYPE OF GRADUATE
1945

	Arts	Science	
UNIVERSITY OF ORIGIN — Oxbridge — Employed at home (U.K.)			with other years (1950, '55, '60, '65, etc.) each
or away (out of the British Isles).			represented by another pair

Arts   Science

	Arts	Science
Redbrick — Home		
Away		

of 2 x 2s.

North American readers may not all be quite sure which British universities these terms refer to. Oxbridge (Oxford and Cambridge) is to Redbrick what the Ivy League is to the state universities. Some of the older and more prestigious 'other universities' (London, Edinburgh, Manchester and so on) may, like the Big Ten, not be included in Redbrick in some people's accounting. They are included here for the purpose of obtaining a dichotomy or simple two-way split.

Such matrices can be collapsed simply by totting up all graduates and expressing the number from Redbrick as a percentage of this total. Then percentages thus gained are inserted into the cells of the matrices which remain. Note that *something* has to be put into the cells anyway, and also that in all cases it is possible to work out the percentage of Oxbridge graduates from that of the Redbrick ones. The number of matrices can thus be halved without losing any information:

Figure 7.16:

1945

	Arts	Science	
Home	% Redbrick	% Redbrick	others for
Away	ditto	ditto	1950, etc.

Consider another couple of illustrations to drive the point home. How could some of the matrices discussed earlier be collapsed? Refer back to figure 7.8 for a moment. Supposing I want to include in that analysis a further investigation into the themes which appear on the coinage. I would have to do it this way:

Figure 7.17:

	Emperor	Senate	Army	People	
			Themes pertaining to		in Nerva's coinage
Gold					
Silver					plus a matrix
Orichalcum					each for the
Copper					other emperors

I could collapse the six matrices — one for each emperor — which would result from the above into one large matrix in one of two ways. I could in each case express the themes relating to the senate as a percentage of all the themes considered, or I could color-code each category of theme and express the four theme categories as a succession of four differently colored numbers — or bars. I could then enter this percentage figure in each of the cells of the original matrix of figure 7.8. Alternatively I could total up all the issues on which a given theme appeared, whatever the metal in which it appeared. I could simply list these totals, or I could express those on the gold as a percentage of those on all other metals. Or I could express those on precious metals as a percentage of those on all metals. Or I could present a series of differently colored numbers, the colors coded to indicate gold, silver, etc. Any of the latter three courses would again give me one matrix, as follows:

Figure 7.18:

THEMES	Nerva	Trajan	Hadrian	Antoninus	Aurelius	Commodus
Emperor						
Senate						
Army						
People						

Consider just one more illustration to make sure of the general idea. Refer back to figure 7.7 for a moment. Supposing I wanted to have, as entry-headings running down the left hand side of the boxes, *aspects* of the 'issue' under consideration. What would I do with the categories 'favorable or unfavorable presentation'? Well, I could include in the cells information as to attitude. I could put a tick when the writer is favorable, and a cross (or simply nothing) when he is not. Or, if the cells contain numbers indicating the numbers of passages in which there are references to the aspect concerned, I could color-code the numbers: green for favorableness, red for the reverse.

Again, this procedure means that I can analyze for a further characteristic or attribute without increasing the size of the matrix already in use. I have done so by taking the details which could be arranged in two sets of matrices and squeezing them into one set. I have collapsed two matrices into one.

DICHOTOMIZING

The commonest way of collapsing the analysis of a characteristic, category or what have you is as follows. Define that characteristic as in one state or another: pro or con; senatorial or anti-senatorial; Republican or Democrat; high or low; Conservative or Labour. This is known as 'dichotomizing' (cutting in two). Then simply enter the figure for *one* of these two states of the thing in question as a percentage or fraction of the overall total of occurrences of *both* states. Thus the one number provided tells the reader two things. Now this process can be used to make entries into the cells of a matrix which correlates two other things with which this characteristic is in some way connected.

SIMPLIFICATION OF MATRICES

Collapsing matrices can simplify a plethora of detail by reducing the number of matrices used in an analysis. But the complexity of the findings can also be reduced by simplifying the matrices themselves. Simplification is achieved by reducing the number of divisions in the criteria which are used to form the matrix. This step means fewer subdivisions, and thus less complexity within the matrix itself. The illustration generally given goes something like this:

Figure 7.19:

PARTY MEMBERSHIP

		Right Wing	Left Wing	Independent
DEGREE OF ACTIVITY	High	'GOOD' PARTY	MEN	INDEPENDENTS
	Medium	INDIFFERENT	PARTY MEN	APOLITICALS
	Low			

The superimposed heavy lines and the capitalized names within the matrix indicate how the original 3 x 3 matrix has been simplified into a 2 x 2.

The criteria used to differentiate among the people being examined are those of support of party, and political activity, respectively. Although in actual fact a graduated range of such support and activity obviously exists, each can be simply divided into two gross divisions, containing high support or high activity in the one division and everything else in the other. If a ranked (high, medium, low) series is cut into two (high and not high), the result is a more rough and ready division, clearly. The 'not-high' part has 'moderately highs' as well as 'lows' in it, and so is not a 'pure' division. So fine discriminations are sacrificed among the data in order to obtain a clear, large-scale set of partitions within those data. The point however is that often an analyst can be *too* finicky. Drawing too many fine distinctions can prevent him from seeing that many of them are just subtypes of a few major types. Simplification, then, is a tactic aimed at letting the gross, large-scale differences in data stand starkly out.

To see how it works, and to get another illustration of the tactic, take one of the previously used matrices and see how it could be simplified. Refer back to figure 7.8. The list of emperors could be split into 'Good' Emperors (good from the senate's point of view that is) and 'Bad' Ones. The list of metals could be split into 'precious metals' and 'others', the former most likely being of interest to senators, the latter to the lower orders. This simplification reduces a 6 x 4 matrix into a 2 x 2: figure 7.20. This is an enormous reduction in complexity, and very considerably increases my chances of seeing patterns in the data. If I am handling several 6 x 4 matrices, it may in fact be the only way in which I will be able to take in the overall implications of the serried ranks of figures confronting me.

Figure 7.20:

		'GOOD EMPERORS'			'BAD EMPERORS'	
	Nerva	Trajan	Antoninus	Aurelius	Hadrian	Commodus
PRECIOUS Gold						
METALS Silver						
OTHERS Orich-alcum						
Copper						

As above, the heavy lines and capitalized lettering indicate the 2 x 2 which has been superimposed on the more complex (6 x 4) original matrix.

NUMERICAL REDUCTION OF PROPERTY SPACES

Besides this process of simplification, there is another — known as the reducing of property spaces (=cells). In general this is done in one of two ways. It can be done numerically, by assigning numbers when it is deemed wise to states of the categories being used. Or it can be done pragmatically, by rule of thumb. This happens when the analyst says to himself: "Well, in effect I've got three (or four, or whatever the number may be) classes of things in these sixteen cells. So I'll reclassify in a simpler way, using these actual groupings which I've found to exist." Look at some examples to see how to perform these two operations.

First, numerical reduction is achieved by assigning numbers to states or rankings within categories. This is not usually a very satisfactory way of contrasting major aspects of those data. Please refresh your memory of figure 1 in chapter 6 by referring back to it. It is a very big matrix, somewhere in the order of 20 x 7. Now imagine that I have to cope with four of these, one for each of four authors. I want to establish what the issues are which receive most attention in all four and, in particular, which issue gets top priority treatment from each author. Actually, *eight* matrices were involved, as each writer was analyzed in two matrices. One was a micro-analysis, dealing with his treatment of the events of Marius' career. The other was a macro-analysis, dealing with the major associations which Marius had for him.[5] Each issue is rated in seven ways. Four of these are quantifiable. I could decide that five or more mentions is a high frequency of mentions in a given writer's practice, whereas one mention is low. This distinction gives me a scale of high (5 or more), medium (4 to 2) and low (1) frequency of mention. I can scale 'extensiveness of treatment' or 'strikingness of diction' or 'numbers of literary figures' in the same way. I can now score 'highs' as three points, 'mediums' as two, and 'lows' as one. Using this scoring system I can easily establish the top three, or five or ten issues in each writer's treatment of the life and doings of the historical personality involved. To pick out the top scores, I have only to sum along each line (called 'row') in the matrix and enter up the score at the right-hand edge, then check on the final figures. I can do likewise for the other three writers and make a consolidated matrix out of my findings. In it, any overlaps or disparities among the various writers' emphases will speedily become apparent. Numerical reduction is in fact the quickest way of sifting through such a mass of data for this kind of information.

You may remember the device known as the 'attention score', discussed previously. This is capable of being adapted to other uses, of course. But, as described, it is in the form intended for use on newspapers. It consists of analyzing the presentation of an item of news in terms of its type of headline; position on leading page; column width and length; size of typeface; and number of illustrations. All these things could be scored with the same system as has just been described in the last paragraph. Then the sums also described there could be done. Thus this tactic of using numbers to score data gives a relatively straightforward and uniform way of cross-comparing any number of issues in any number of writers, no matter how many or how complicated are the matrices involved.

Such assigning of numbers can be helpful with simpler problems, too. Consider figure 7.18. It involves themes. Some of these themes occur quite infrequently. They may appear on only one issue. Others occur time after time, with minor changes, on issue after issue. Some occur on gold coins, which were issued as far as modern scholarship can tell in small numbers. Others occur on copper coins which came out in vast strikings. One occurrence of a theme on a coin in a limited issue can hardly be allowed to count for as much as thirty-seven

[5] For some matrices illustrating the present subject under discussion see pp. 16-18 of "The Changing Picture of Marius".

occurrences (with minor variations) of another theme in a series of gigantic issues. There is no *objective* way of evaluating this disparity. But, again, I can rank issues into large, medium and small, and occurrences of themes into frequent, moderately numerous, and few. This ranking can be done in terms of the practices of each emperor. I can now 'score' each theme accordingly as the issues in which it appears rate in regard to these criteria. Although this scoring is arbitrary, it is uniformly done. So the arbitrariness can be regarded as the price to be paid in order to get a unifying measuring device. The numbers this device produces will readily enable me to cross-compare degrees of emphasis behind the emperors' coining policies.

So numerical reduction provides us with a sort of rough and ready measuring-rod. By using it, some sort of idea of the comparative magnitudes or importance of the various details which have been piled up by detailed multivariate analysis can be quickly obtained. But it is very far from being a precision instrument. Suppose I am using the four sets of criteria discussed three paragraphs back. Any item can score either 3, 2 or 1 on each of these four sets. This gives a matrix with 81 cells and a scoring system ranging from 12 to 4. There is only one way of getting 12 points or 4 points in this serried array of cells. But there are 19 ways of getting 8 points, 16 of getting 7 or 9 points, and 10 ways of getting 6 or 10 points. (The reader may care to check on this, to see how good his skill with 2 x 2s has by now become. The four aspects which are being rated are: frequency of treatment, extensiveness of discussion when touched upon, strikingness of diction employed and numbers of literary figures. All are rated as either high, medium or low; 'high' scores 3, 'medium' 2, and 'low' one. No allowance has been made, in this exercise, for nil scores; these would, of course, further complicate the picture in practice.) A score of 8 can thus represent any one of 19 different combinations of rankings on the four criteria concerned. The same score could thus be applied to two very different things.

One way of getting round this difficulty consists in weighting. The investigator decides that, on criterion 2, the scoring will range 6:4:2, and on criterion 3 it will be 9:8:7, and so on. But he is now importing value judgements as to the importance of a criterion into his scoring system. If his value judgements do not happen to be the same as those of the writers whose work he is scoring, his decisions will result in a set of wrongly ascribed emphases.

Numerical reduction, then, gives only an extremely rough guide to emphases. It can help with an initial sorting of data into approximate degrees of importance and so on. A bulldozer can help clear the site for an archaeologist, but he will not use it on the close work of the dig itself. Similarly numerical reduction must be used with discretion.

PRAGMATIC REDUCTION

Pragmatic reduction, the other way of simplifying things, is a very powerful technique indeed, when circumstances are such that it can be used. It involves separating an array of cells into a smaller number of 'types', each comprising a combination of cells. There is quite a good chance of being able to do this, for those who think about it. Suppose the job is to examine writers' attitudes in regard to a number of issues. Now attitudes, observably, range along a graduated scale from one extreme to the other. But, basically, an attitude is either strongly held, or held with qualifications. A man with strongly held attitudes on one issue is likely to have them on others, just as a more tentative attitude is also likely to be in force on several issues rather than on only one. But then again, occasionally people with odd quirks are found. So some of the cells in the matrix will be much more in use than others. Moreover, the combination of properties that goes with a certain cell may be quite like that which goes with another, and the two can be treated as a type. But the easiest way of seeing what is involved is by working through an example.

A psychobiographical study could be done much as Isaacs goes looking for "Scratches on our Minds" in *American Images of India and China*. The matrix would be formed by inquiring into how various aspects of a woman's life situation (down) are presented (across). One might look at man:wife or wife:male relatives relationships; mother:child relationships; women and work; women and the vote, and so on. 'Looking' would involve seeing what was said, and in what quantities and frequencies; what types of incidents tended to occur in conjunction with such discussion; what artistic associations (films, books, etc. mentioned in connection) were found in proximity, and so on. There would be one matrix for each writer. The matrices would be split into groups, one group for each class (social, educational, or what have you) of writers. The idea is to see whether the above groupings reveal any trends in ways of viewing the woman's life-situation; specifically, to see what difference social class (or education or whatever) makes.

Suppose a literary researcher engaged upon a psychobiographical study has a group of British novelists of the '50s and he wants to see how their attitudes relate to their class background, or schooling, or somesuch. He decides he will look at their views on women, adolescents, and out-groups in order to classify their attitudes. Now, on women, views might range from those of militant support of women's rights to attitudes advocating that "a woman's place is in the home." Maybe these two positions could be characterized as high and low respectively. A midway position might be that which holds that such and such a profession should be open to women *now* — an empirical, non-theoretical aim to improve the status of this particular under-privileged group, realistically taking regard for the current state of affairs. I will leave the definitions of a similar range of attitudes on teen-agers to my individual readers, but possibly this same type of ranking (militant crusader, pragmatic step-by-step improver, belittling reactionary) might enable us to categorize our writers' attitudes to non-whites as 'high' 'medium' or 'low'. This ranking produces the following 27-cell matrix:

Figure 7.21:

Attitude to non-whites

		High			Medium			Low	
		Attitude to women			Attitude to women			Attitude to women	
		Hi	Med.	Low	Hi	Med.	Low	Hi	Med.	Low
Attitude to adolescents	High									
	Med.									
	Low									

There is still the job of ranking these writers by class background or whatever. Class background will involve at least 6 categories: upper upper, lower upper, upper middle, lower middle, upper working and lower working. This ranking is going to produce a consolidated matrix of 27 x 6 cells. Such a complex matrix is likely to cause plenty of difficulty and so it will have to be simplified somehow.

Look at our 27-cell matrix. Liberals will be found there; these will be people who score 'high' on all 3 counts, or, if not that, then 2 highs and 1 medium. Plot them in as L. There will be authoritarians too. They will be the reverse of the liberals — 3 lows or 2 lows and 1 medium. These are the polar extremes. What about the man in the middle, the realistic pragmatist? He is going to score 3 mediums or

2 mediums and either a high or a low. It is convenient to call such people 'realists'. Authoritarians are plotted in as A, realists as R. Figure 7.21 can be reworked as 7.22: just a bank of property spaces. Here it is below. Keep an eye on it. Ignore the letters not talked about yet. Filling up, isn't it? The type liberal has taken up 4 cells; so has the authoritarian; the great middle majority has taken 7. That is more than half the cells used up by only 3 types.

What is left? Some confused people (C): they score one high, one medium and one low. There are six such combinations of scores. Two types are left, both people with quirks — they have 2 highs and a low or 2 lows and a high. The latter are, maybe, authoritarians who have the good luck to have had really deep and meaningful relationships with a woman or women (or had a non-white friend or friends, or know some adolescents well). So, in one regard, this type of person has become more sympathetic to others' problems. Call him an eyes-opened (E). This leaves the disillusioned liberal (D). Maybe he has had an unfortunate experience with a woman (or a non-white person or an adolescent). Three reactions are possible: "It takes all sorts to make a world" (incident forgotten); "This woman is poison"; "Women are dangerous". He has chosen the third. Or make up your own story. Anyway, there it is: he has a problem. But the matrix of 27 cells has been reduced into six personality types:

Figure 7.22:

Attitude to non-whites

	Attitude to Women			Attitude to Women			Attitude to Women		
Attitude to adolescents	L	L	D	L	R	C	D	C	E
	L	R	C	R	R	R	C	R	A
	D	C	E	C	R	A	E	A	A

The enormous simplification which results from such reduction means that data can be worked on much more easily. Results will stand out more clearly, and the investigator has strategically selected among the data in such a way as to enhance his chances of perceiving patternings there. When the data, or his ingenuity, allow him to use this technique, it will prove a most useful method of simplifying and clarifying his overall analytical procedure.

FUNCTIONAL REDUCTION

Perhaps, in closing this section of the chapter, I should briefly mention a tactic which is called 'functional reduction'. Sometimes some of the cells in a complex matrix are empty, or for some reason can be regarded as being empty. Think of the issues in copper in figure 7.10 for example. Still better, because the categories of high, medium and low stand out so clearly, is table 1 in "Political Legends

Figure 7.23:

		NUMBERS OF DIFFERENT LEGENDS
SINGLE METALS	Orichalcum	20
	Silver	10
	Gold	7
	Copper	4
COMBINATIONS OF METALS	Gold, Silver, Orichalcum	18
	Silver, Orichalcum	9
	Gold, Silver	5
	Gold, Silver, Orichalcum, Copper	5
	Silver, Orichalcum, Copper	4
	Gold and Orichalcum	2
	Orichalcum, Copper	1

on Hadrian's Coinage."[6] These aspects of the matter can be ignored and attention confined, for the rest of the analysis, just to the issues which remain. In this way, as a function of producing a matrix, the complexity of the analysis has been reduced. In the proposed psycho-biography, for example, it is almost certain that nothing will be found in the boxes for lower working class, and probably nothing in those for upper upper. This situation will cut 6 categories down to 4.

It is always worth being on the lookout for a chance to reduce the complexity of analysis by functional reduction. But this type of reduction depends on the material on which the analyst is working, not on his skills in working it. So knowledge of this tactic does not give him as much ability to manipulate his material as does knowledge of pragmatic reduction. There is always the possibility that he

[6] *The Turtle*, 6, 1967, p. 295.

may be able to use *both* pragmatic and functional reduction in the one piece of analysis. He could in the psychobiographical example just considered. There, pragmatic reduction would cut 27 property spaces down to 6 types, and functional reduction would eliminate two unused categories out of six. These forms of reduction used in combination thus change a very confusing 27 x 6 cell matrix into a 6 x 4 one which is readily comprehensible.

CONCLUSION

So then, if the task is to provide a framework within which masses of details can be readily contrasted, this is how it is done.[7] This framework enables distinguishing between levels of analysis — for example, 'in-the-big' as opposed to detailed analysis. It also enables moving at will from one level to another. Further, the framework compels researchers to think out all the possible combinations of things implied in their initial question. As the discussion on 'substructuring' showed, it thus helps to improve the questions posed. There are ways of reducing the complexity of the matrices which are produced when using this technique. Thus the technique can be flexibly adapted to suit particular problems.

The following chapter is going to outline ways of manipulating problems so that the technique can be used upon them. Actually, it soon comes to be used almost automatically, when circumstances require. To help get into the habit of using it, it is a good idea to examine others' use of it carefully. When a writer is about to set out the framework of a study involving multivariate analysis, before reading on, try to set out how *you* would do it. After reading, close the book and try to reconstitute in detail how he went about it. It does not take long to get the hang of it. Incidentally, this is a technique highly suited for use with punch cards and a card-sorting machine. Those machines tend to be relatively little used in these computerized days, and so you can often jump a long queue waiting for access to a computer programmer, and run off your study yourself, cheaply.

---

[7] This is not the only use to which multivariate analysis can be put. Rather, it is only the simplest and most basic of a long series of increasingly complicated ways of using the technique. Two articles which may help you on your way, if you wish to proceed further into this series, are: P. F. Lazarsfeld, "Evidence and Inference in Social Research" in D. Lerner (ed.), *Evidence and Inference*, Free Press, 1958, and Lazarsfeld, "Interpretation of Statistical Relations as a Research Operation", pp. 115-25 of Lazarsfeld and Rosenberg (eds.), *The Language of Social Research*.

An Arts criticism of the technique is that it 'assumes a spurious homogeneity among the data.' Now it is, of course, easily possible to produce nonsense findings if the technique is applied to atypical, or improperly grouped, materials. Classicists and Medievalists have many horror stories about such things. A huge find of the coins of a particular emperor in an archaeological dig at a particular trading site suggested that enormous issues were put out by the emperor in question at one point. Fortunately, however, a casual reference in an ancient writer to that emperor's army having over-wintered at the city in question indicated that what is involved is a mere freak of over-representation in survival. The practice of considering massive runs of data (i.e. the total output of an emperor's entire reign, in conjunction with the total output of a dynasty) reduces the risk of undue influence of such freaks of overrepresentation. Furthermore, the pages of the basic handbooks on the source materials generally proliferate cautions on the nature and representativeness of their data.

Whenever there is a mass of data produced by some fluke of chance, and, by using the technique, a generalization is made from such data, that generalization will be unsound. But *whatever* technique is used to analyze a faulty sample, the result will be skewed. Seeing that the data can fitly be used involves sampling (see chapter 5). It is true that skill in drawing a sample is vital to multivariate analysis, because such skill enables making maximum use of source materials. The larger the amount of data used, the better, because oddities within it have more chance to cancel one another out. Sampling errors tend in fact to *obscure*, not fictitiously to create, overall trends.[8] But, though it is vital to multivariate analysis, sampling is a separate stage preceding it. Any analytical technique can be only as good as the sample on which it is based. This is a truism, not a special point of weakness unique to multivariate analysis.

Multivariate analysis is the tool which allows investigators to analyze very large amounts of data without being simply overwhelmed by them. Now, in practice, what happens when the normal Arts scholar is confronted by a huge mass of data? The traditional impressionistic approach consists of picking out the 'striking' details ('striking' to the particular impressionist involved, that is), and arguing a 'likely' case from some selection, intuitively chosen. This approach results in the construction of a thesis which has probability, but not provability. What multivariate analysis does in such cases is to set the data out so that any one part of them can be compared with

---

[8] See McClelland, *The Achieving Society*, p. 61.

any two (or more) other parts, to see what the interconnections between these parts are. Thus a series of hypotheses can be tested, one after the other, in the light of *all* the data.[9] Try naming another technique currently used in Arts-type studies which provides such comprehensiveness.

[9] A single indicator of some classification or other is never fully representative; so analysts generally consider several. This consideration involves posing more than one question. See Lazarsfeld on "the interchangeability of indices" in his article "Evidence and Inference in Social Research."

8

Applying Multivariate Analysis and Beyond:
Matching Patterns in Data

INTRODUCTION

This chapter is very largely about how to use multivariate analysis while conducting a content analysis. Its first section concerns the business of deploying the matrices typical of multivariate analysis when analyzing in fine detail. Various ways of coaxing source materials into such matrices are discussed. There is special emphasis on thinking of a multivariate analysis in pictorial terms, as these make for greater clarity. An illustrative example is set forth at length, to show the consequences for the content analysis as a whole of casting the source materials into this framework of matrices. There is also a discussion of standardized categories which fit such a framework.

The second section concerns the use of the framework of matrices typical of multivariate analysis to plan a content analysis as a whole. Correlating data generally involves multivariate analysis. A specimen research design is discussed, to show how to plan a content analysis so that it will correlate its findings. There is also discussion of shifting levels of analysis and of reduction and simplification of analytical layout. A series of major forms or uses of content analysis, all involving multivariate analysis, is discussed during this section.

The third section then proceeds beyond multivariate analysis into the matching of patterns as a way of analyzing or cross-comparing complex clusters of data. There is a discussion, using a Venn diagram, of the logic-of-the-situation type of approach necessary in analyses of contiguity. Then a series of different patterning devices, for imposing order within chaotic data, are reviewed. Finally, some devices for economically recording and displaying vast amounts of data (and correlations among them) are discussed. With this, the chapter ends. It will, I hope, enable readers to correlate complex data with much greater ease and skill.

Section 1: Multivariate Analysis at the Level of Data Extraction.

If we can set our data out in the patterned way discussed in the previous chapter, we can see what goes with what, what is there in surprisingly large proportions, what is not there, and so on. 'But', you may be thinking, 'the kind of writing *I* have to work on just don't come in easy-to-count combinations. And they're works of artistic creativity, so these methodical patternings just don't occur in them.' Actually, it is very rare indeed for *anyone's* subject matter to take a form which readily lends itself to this type of formal, systematic inquiry. So, besides knowing how to carry out the inquiry, it is really wise also to know how to prepare written (or even painted) material so that such inquiry becomes possible. No matter how good a cobbler may be, if he is confronted with a live cow and a pair of worn shoes, he will be unable to turn the former into a neatly-mended pair of the latter. This intermediate phase of the operation, that of turning the live cow into leather as it were, is the first step in an irreversible succession of steps. Those who cannot take it will never be in a position to go on to the last step. In what follows, a variety of ways of going about this business of 'turning a live cow into leather' are outlined. Some form of one of them may be applicable to your problem, or may give you an idea which you can develop to handle your problem.

REDEFINING THE QUESTION

The easiest way of manoeuvring the subject matter around so the matrices of multivariate analysis can be used is by redefining the question. Take an example which shows how this works. I was once asked to talk on 'what are the current trends in Classical scholarship?' Now this is such a huge topic that an hour's talk on it could well act more like a Rorschach test than an informative lecture. In a Rorschach test, a person is confronted with a sprawling mass of detail, in the form of an irregularly shaped blotch, and asked what he sees there. As there *is* no recognizable thing depicted in it, anything he 'sees' comes out of the promptings of his own unconscious. So, in my case, to select this aspect or that could well have indicated to the audience merely where my own interests lay. Such selection, that is to say, may not indicate aspects of this complicated body of work which would be generally agreed by a cross-section of my colleagues to be outstanding within the field. So I decided to redefine the question in communications terms. Who says what to whom, through what channel, and to what effect? I decided, that is, simply to take the main Classical journals and see what they were talking about. Decision on this matter brought a whole spate of sampling problems sharply into focus. What *were* the main Classical journals, which years should be chosen, and what should be considered (e.g. articles only, or reviews too)? I decided to take the top two American and top two British journals, so that I could examine international, as well as national, trends.[1] Thus the articles in the journals could be regarded as bits of information in a stream pouring through the journals as channels. Now some kinds of 'bits' are more countable than others. So I defined the bits to be studied as the names of books and articles dropped by the scholars in writing the articles involved.

I could now ask the following questions: Are scholars relying for their information on books or on journal articles? Are there differences in national practice in this matter? Has the current practice always been in vogue? Not bad for a simple 2 x 2:

Figure 8.1: 1945

Reading:	American	British
Books	574	242
Articles	321	233

(with other matrices for the years 1955 and 1965)

I could also ask whether scholars, of either national group, now or in the past, were reading in disciplines other than their own. The answer turned out to be 'No'.

Figure 8.2:

Work from fields of

	Anthropology	Economics	Political Science	Psychology	Soc. Psych.	Soc. Anthro.
'45 Amer.						
Brit.						

And I could ask: Does, or did, the country of origin of a publication affect its chance of being 'perceived' by either group?

[1] See "Problems and Prejudices in the Humanities", *Bulletin de l'Association Canadienne des Humanités*, 20, 1969, pp. 30-31.

Figure 8.3:

National origins of publications:

	American	British	French	German	Italian	Others	
Books	99	159	62	209	16	29	(In the American journals
Articles	154	39	20	76	9	23	for 1945)

Thus, by redefining the question, I was able to select highly quantifiable data. And, by a strategic choice of questions, I was able to produce a factual basis for discussion of issues of major importance.

STRUCTURING THE SITUATION

But it often happens that such freedom to redefine a question is lacking. The task may be to produce a study of an historical personage, for instance. In such cases, there are ways of visualizing the problem which readily lead to setting out the subject matter in a form suitable for multivariate analysis. The strategy in this case, then, consists of defining the situation in a certain structured way. You may remember the strategy already outlined (figure 6.1): the major stages of the man's life, together with the major events of his career, are listed in chronological order. This exercise produces a list of categories, to run down the outside left of a matrix. Across the top run the categories: mentioned at all, in how much or little detail, with error or inconsistency, with literary figures, with striking verbiage, with bias, etc.

However, this may well be too exhaustive a method of inquiry. If the job is to compare the picture of Disraeli in ten contemporary writers, and to do so along with other things in the course of a busy term, there will have to be some way of focusing on only the major items in his career. Or the job may be comparing views on an issue, rather than a personality. What generally happens in such cases is that there appear a number of issues or aspects which ought to be looked into. The questions then arise: Are these the only issues to consider? Are they the major ones? Would other people also think that these, in particular, should be investigated? Well, suppose the investigator thinks of these issues or aspects in terms of a Venn diagram (overlapping circles). He decides that the importance of an issue will be indicated by the size of the circle he attributes to it. He can indicate its salience — how much it was *perceived* as important or striking — by putting the more salient issues on top of the others. He can indicate issues or aspects which are interlinked by positioning them close together in the resultant heap. He can play around with this heap — adding, repositioning and so on — until he produces a configuration which, quite subjectively maybe, he feels to represent his picture of the matter *in these terms*. This is a very easy way of depicting, arranging, and re-arranging all these things. The following is the kind of figure which results:

Figure 8.4: ISSUES IN THE CAREER OF MARIUS,
           DEPICTED AS A FORM OF VENN DIAGRAM.

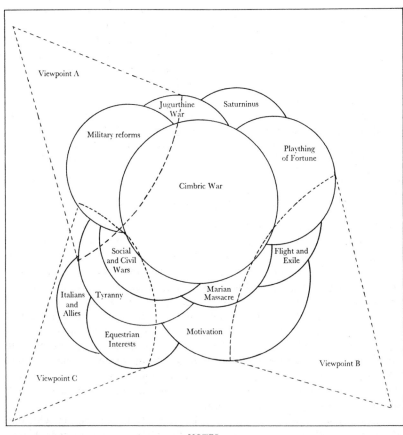

NOTES

The circles indicate things about Marius on which one would expect comment in any full depiction of him. Centrality and uppermost position indicate salience; size and top-most position importance. Salience of any one issue is relative to overall patterning of emphases. This diagram is my impression of the relative importance/salience of *these* issues in the source tradition as a whole. In an actual full-length picture (e.g. Plutarch's) relative emphases tell a great deal about the writer. In a picture reconstructed from asides, the writer's selectivity indicates issues felt important/salient (*if* any pattern emerges).

KEY: A — shows Marius primarily seen as a military figure, as the great man shaping history.

 B — a negative picture of Marius (stressing his flight, massacres, Fortune, vicious motivation) seen in terms of socio-political forces, as shown for example by Lucan, of the first century A.D. rhetorical school.

 C — the modern view, stressing business interests, widening of franchise to Italian groups, as in the Badian-Carney-Gabba view.

This way of conceptualizing the matter as a whole will make a researcher very highly aware of problems of degrees of emphasis, what to include, whether certain things are interlinked and so on. It also gives an easily visualizable yardstick against which to measure other people's views. For it is easily convertible into a matrix. The 'aspects' mentioned become a list of categories, downwards on the left. The characteristics — importance, salience and interrelatedness — become another list (frequency and extensiveness of treatment, strikingness of diction, connections with other issues) running across the top.

It is now possible for the researcher to refer to a number of standard works on the personality involved, and see how well his definition of the situation agrees with theirs. When he has made the changes indicated, he will have produced a testing device, independent of his own idiosyncrasies and of the documents to be considered. This device is important, because to see what *isn't* in those documents necessitates being able to acquire a larger, overall viewpoint from somewhere.

PATTERNING THE DATA

Yet another way of preparing data consists of imposing a pattern on them to see what results. This process is rather like sieving a bag of flour for weevils. There are different forms of sieve, some with larger holes than others, some with specially shaped holes. You choose the one that will let everything else go through except what you are interested in. Take an instance to see how this works. I wanted to look at the awareness of sickness, disease and death in non-medical circles in antiquity.[2] I was interested in the sorts of things which writers took for granted or mentioned in passing, as well as in any specific comments they might have. Here is how I built up my 'sieving' device. It involves passing the same material through a number of different 'sieves', so that I could speedily sort out the data into heaps, each consisting of a specific type of data.

When a writer refers to illness, it is generally in connection with one of three basic issues: disease; people who diagnose or treat it and their ideas; or things which are used in connection with keeping or making people well. The following depiction represents this very simple, basic way of looking at the matter:

[2] For a paper "A Pre-industrial City through Contemporaries' Eyes: Content Analysis of Views of Rome", delivered at the 1968 meeting of the American Political Science Association; see pp. 9-12 thereof.

To sort all the references in a group of writers into these three very large categories is a relatively speedy matter. Where a passage should be considered in more than one of these categories, it is simply so arranged. But it is also marked in some way to show that it has been taken into account more than once.

I can now expand my basic categories into a systematic framework of reference: see figure 8.6. I can take the heap of references to 'disease' and sort them into (a) diseases which are given a specific name and into (b) symptoms which are vaguely assigned. This sorting limits the number of decisions, and, in consequence, the subjectivity attendant upon any one counting operation. The first selecting procedure merely sorts out references to diseases, as opposed to references to doctors or medical facilities. The second concentrates upon these references to disease, already identified, and sorts them into *either* references to named diseases *or* generalized references to symptoms, etc. The third selection procedure then sorts the diseases into an alphabetical list of diseases mentioned, with a count of their frequencies. A fourth selection procedure does the same for the symptoms. Figure 8.5 indicates schematically how the analysis proceeds:

Figure 8.5: A DECISION TREE

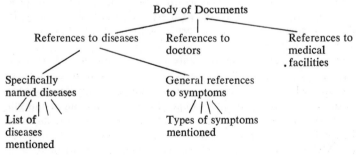

The objective is to avoid the situation in which it is necessary to make a large number of interrelated decisions about each one of a stream of details. An analyst will overload his discriminatory capacities, tire, and perform unevenly if he does this. So it is wise to manoeuvre things so as to make relatively simple decisions ('Is it such and such, or isn't it?') at each of a number of decision points. In this way, better strategy in spacing out the decisions which have to be made permits making them faster, and with uniform standards of judgement. Moreover this method has the advantage, when several persons are classifying the data, of pinpointing areas of disagreement or haziness in classification.[3]

If I have writings which come from two different periods, I can compare the two sets of diseases and symptoms, to look for differences. This possibility applies whether such differences involve matters of increased sophistication in identification or knowledge of diseases, or matters of emphasis, or what have you. Readers should be able to visualize the two matrices involved (list of diseases downwards at left, ways of conceptualizing them across, at top) without a table. The way the analysis has been cast readily facilitates multivariate analysis, as is evident. The same type of procedure can readily be followed in dealing with the other two categories (doctors and facilities), in terms of the items related to them in figure 8.6.

Figure 8.6, then, represents a patterned way of looking at the data. This type of layout is often seen in books and newspapers. It is used when someone is analyzing a system, when there is an interweaving of connections (including circular chains of causation) rather than a single sequence of one thing resulting from another. This layout can be used for a wide range of such relationships. It gives a framework of reference, or, if you like, a patterning of linkages or interrelationships. One body of writing can be compared with another in terms of how each stands in relation to this framework. Or, to revert to my previous imagery, here is the sieve through which to pour first one, then the other, body of writings. Alternatively, it may be regarded as a sort of master pattern, against which different but complex things can be compared.

A number of different types of analysis can be conducted with the aid of this device. First of all, it can be used, as it stands, as a set of categories with which to perform a content analysis. For this purpose, its little boxes are converted into categories for the left-hand margin. But this type of format itself confers certain advantages on the analysis. It is 'open-ended': new boxes can be added if the source material suggests it. 'Code of ethics', for instance, was most strongly suggested by my material. Also the format suggests certain interconnections (shown in the figure by the dotted lines with arrows), and thus the

---

[3] See in general, *Content Analysis*, pp. 138-40.

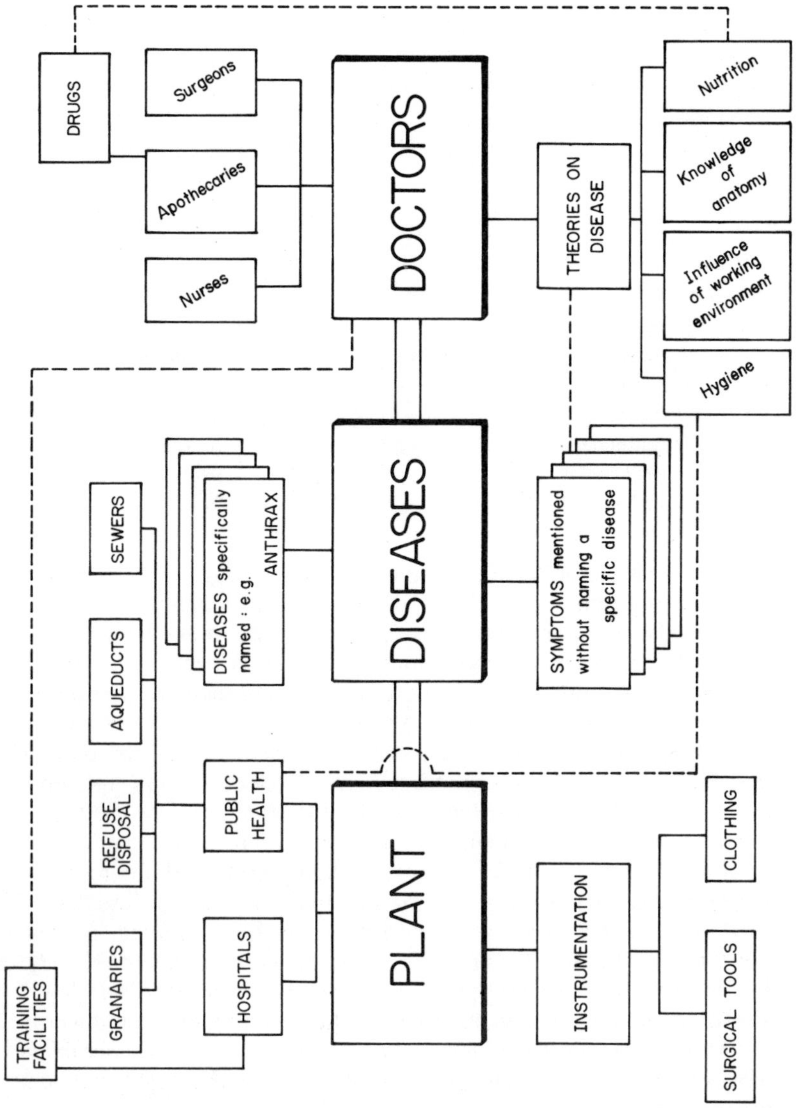

Figure 8.6: CONTENT ANALYSIS CATEGORIES SET OUT AS A SYSTEM.

query: does the source also make these connections? The format thus encourages a dialectic between analyst and his source material.

Thirdly, there is more than one way of using this framework to compare two bodies of writing. One has already been suggested: a straightforward content analysis, using the labels on figure 8.6 as categories. This system can be used for comparing a body of writing from an early period with another body from a later one. But the framework can also be regarded as containing a pattern of emphases, if looked at 'in the big':

Figure 8.7: A SIMPLIFICATION OF THE SYSTEMS DIAGRAM

	Facilities	Diseases	Doctors
Matters immediately connected	Buildings	Symptoms	Personnel
Matters ultimately connected	Services	Conceptual tool kit for describing diseases	Theories on the causes of sickness

Each box in this matrix can be reconstituted from figure 8.6, of which it is a simplification. The boxes can each be regarded as representing an issue area. Each of a series of contemporary writers can now be compared with his fellows, to see how the overall patterning of emphases and omissions correlates in each issue area. This is a way of getting to the heart of a very complicated matter in an uncomplicated direct and uniform fashion.

Finally, the figure makes an excellent visual layout for data. It is possible to color code for frequency of mention and for emotive language used when mention is made. Or all those little boxes which received only infrequent entries or entries of fleeting significance can be omitted. In this way, for each writer being examined, a diagrammatic abstract summarizing his pattern of emphases can be created. This kind of thing is called a profile. Profiles can be compared, if they are not too complicated, by simply running an eye over them. If they are too complex for this treatment, they can be rearranged, as described above, as cells in a matrix and simplified by numerical reduction. In this way, the analyst can survey at one glance the vast assemblage of data, now reduced to manageable proportions by this highly economical use of symbols.

This is an elaborate way of going about reaching the findings. It is very costly in terms of time and effort. Hence it is justifiable only if employed in a major study. If such detailed findings are not needed, a simpler research design would be more appropriate. For it should be kept in mind that the objective of content analysis is to do as *little* counting as possible. So the best research design is the one that produces the appropriate data most economically. And, in this case, there are quicker ways of obtaining similar bodies of data if findings at a more general level will prove adequate.

Suppose the purpose is merely to assess the pattern of disease at two points in history. Use is going to be made of the unconscious assumptions and incidental side references, as well as the specific comments, of two groups of novelists, dating respectively to each of the points in time involved. The tactic of employing a diagram to bring the inquiry to a focus is a good idea in this case too. Unless the novelists are of very recent vintage, they probably will not know of, or, anyway will not think in terms of circulatory, glandular, nervous or respiratory *systems*. Their observations will be at a much lower level of sophistication. They will tend to think of the body from the outside, and in terms of bodily regions. So if the 'diagram' is a little drawing of a stick-man marked off into zones (head; chest and throat; stomach; back; sexual organs; arms and legs), their observations will feed into it more readily. This device is very easily turned into a matrix by listing the zones as the left-hand side categories. It will be possible to pick up overall trends from data so grouped.

But it will obscure certain types of relationship amid a welter of detail packed into the matrices. A second way of visualizing what the findings represent will be needed. Think back to the stratagem of using the modified form of Venn diagram. Imagine a number of discs, each containing the name of a disease or of a symptom associated with a particular bodily area. The analyst could use *his* knowledge of respiratory or alimentary systems and other aspects of medicine to sort these discs into interrelated configurations: colds, rheums, bronchitis, pleurisy, and T.B., for instance, would indicate afflictions of the respiratory system. To organize the data diagrammatically, these discs can be used as a cluster of individually separate circles linked by lines.

This collection of discs constitutes an 'ideal type' model of how the topic might be treated. It alerts the analyst to the potential range of varieties of items, of interrelationships among them, for consideration. It provides him with a framework in terms of which he can uniformly analyze extremely variegated bodies of data. It is in fact a pictorial form of an elaborate 2 x 2 matrix. The discs are the subject matter categories, running downwards at the right. Their connecting links and emphasizing features are the presentational categories, running across at the top. However, the discs (etc.) are only a notational system. The researcher commences with a blank sheet and plots in such symbols (i.e. discs, each indicating that the illness it represents has been mentioned) as are suggested by the source materials. Thus, heaviness of outline might indicate frequency of mention; size of circle, length of treatment when mentioned; and hatching might indicate striking diction. A dotted line could be used to link two circles when one disease or symptom tends to be mentioned in proximity to another in the source material. If mention of one always leads to mention of the other, an arrowhead can be used to indicate this sequence. If diseases or symptoms are specifically linked, a solid line can be used to link the circles, again with an arrowhead if appropriate. Discussion of the sociogram and the propositional inventory later in this chapter provides further illustration of this type of diagram. It is easy enough to rearrange such a pictured configuration as a matrix. Now the incidence of such troubles in one period can be compared with those of another. I found that there was a great dropping away in diseases of the alimentary type in the second period of classical antiquity which I studied. The introduction of aqueducts and bathing facilities on a massive scale were probably responsible.[4]

This device, with its interconnected circles, thus enables checking out different types of patterning in the findings. For those patterns can sometimes come in a vaguely defined and scattered way. The analyst himself may, initially anyway, be as unaware of trends they represent as are the writers who are inadvertently providing the data. So the above *two* different varieties of 'sieving' operation will usually have to be employed one after the other. The two modes of analysis are complementary. The same body of data can be processed in two different ways by using them. When findings converge or overlap, proportionately stronger arguments can be based upon them.

STRUCTURING THE SAMPLE

Finally, the enquiry can be cast into a form which facilitates multivariate analysis by the way in which the materials to be used are selected. This procedure employs some version of what is known in survey analysis as the panel method, most strikingly illustrated in the voting studies cited in chapter 7. Here is a much simplified account of how this method works. An event is selected which is of major importance for the group of writers being studied. The event has to act as a watershed: things must be significantly different after it from what

---

4 See "A Pre-industrial City through Contemporaries' Eyes," p. 10.

they were before it. The same questions are then asked of the writers, in regard to work that dates before the event, and other work which dates after it. Now it is possible to tell what that event *in fact* meant to such people. This meaning is indicated by what they did and thought (the books they wrote, etc.) after it, compared with their actions and thoughts on related matters prior to it.

The method is generally used in studying the thoughts and actions of a selected group (panel) of voters before an electoral campaign begins, while it is on, and in a follow-up after voting has occurred. But Isaacs has used what is in effect this method in his book *The New World of Negro Americans*.[5] Here he examines what Africa means to a group of writers at a succession of points in time. These points are so chosen that one comes before, then the others each follow, one after another, a series of events of great significance in and for Africa.

If the question requires working with diary-keepers or letter-writers, the selection from their writing can be made by choosing material dating to the periods before and after some epochal local event or series of events. When I was studying what life was like in an ancient city, to get some idea of how people's experience of city life changed over time, I chose writings from two periods. One fell just before an enormous improvement in public services and facilities, in regard to policing, fire fighting, flood controls, housing controls, public baths, shopping arcades, libraries, water supplies, parks and public amusements. The other fell just after the improvement had been carried through. Patterns of crime, disease and sex, I found, all altered.[6] The strategy of selection involved in the panel method is capable of being widely and flexibly used, once the enquirer has grasped it and seen a few imaginative developments of its initial application.[7]

AN ILLUSTRATIVE EXAMPLE

So far there has been consideration of four strategies, four ways of creating order in written documents so that multivariate analysis can proceed. The *question* can be redefined so that its new form elicits details in a structured way. Or the *situation* can be redefined so that a basic structuring underlies all subsequent analysis. Or a patterned

[5] See chapter III, especially part 1, "The Hazy Presence".

[6] "A Pre-industrial City through Contemporary Eyes", pp. 8-15.

[7] Let me recommend two studies in this connection: G. H. S. Jordan, "Popular Literature and Imperial Sentiment: Changing Attitudes, 1870-1890" in Canadian Historical Association: *Historical Papers Presented at the Annual Meeting*, 1967, pp. 149-55, and U. P. Burke, "A Survey of the Popularity of Ancient Historians, 1450-1700", *History and Theory*, 5, 1966, pp. 135-52.

framework can be used to extract data from the documents. Finally, the structure, or systematic order, can be imposed by the way the *sample* is selected. These strategies concern different stages of the process of content analysis. Now it is time to come right down to practical details, by following a strategy through to its application in practice, in tactics. Take a common type of content analysis and see how it can be arranged so that multivariate analysis of the data it produces can be easily possible.

Suppose the task is to compare textbooks. It may be to contrast French-Canadian with English-Canadian textbooks, or American with Canadian. Or it may be to see to what extent the textbooks of one period present their material in a different fashion from that of their predecessors of an earlier period. In such a case, everything turns on a redefinition of the question. The investigator can say: "Here are the critical issues; I'll compare the textbooks in regard to the way they present these issues." All he now has to do is to extract the details concerning the presentation of these issues in a uniformly patterned way, and then his matrix is established. The 'issues' can run down the outside left and the 'forms of presentation' along the top. Figure 8.8 indicates how this might be done. The discussion in chapter 5 on sampling, as this concerns the comparison of textbooks, indicates how to go about all the other matters involved.

It may be felt that this is all very well, but that, while it will indeed cope with a detailed project, it hardly helps when help is most needed, at the point of making a purchase on the bookshop floor. For this task, a much quicker process is required. The following suggestions should help with a decision of this kind. You can adapt them to suit your own purposes.

Two checks are advisable. An in-depth probe will reveal how well the textbook copes with detail. A probe of its breadth of coverage will show how thoroughly it covers its period. The first requires at least *two* spots at which to make spot-checks. (Treatment of any *one* issue might be atypical of the book as a whole.) So two issues are taken and a list of items which should be discussed in any competent treatment of either is prepared in advance. Such preparation will give a little matrix which will go on a 5" x 3" card which can be carried in a pocket. The list will run down the left (using the 5" length of the card), and the textbooks can be listed across the top as A,B,C . . . Another such card can record two, or possibly three, telltale items in regard to which the textbooks can be contrasted. These are: overall fullness of treatment in pages; (possibly) the number of major items mentioned in each as a fraction of the number of which mention ought

Figure 8.8: MATRIX FOR COMPARISON OF TEXTBOOKS

FIRST WRITER, FIRST GROUP OR PERIOD

FORM OF PRESENTATION

ISSUES	How much bulk?	Range of viewpoints considered	'Social forces' or 'great men' explanations?	Issues clearly† understood?	Issues coherently‡ presented?	Striking language, figures, etc.	Value judgements	How much emphasis?
1	*							
2								
3								
4								
5								

* The dotted line is meant to enable the analyst to contrast the treatment accorded to one side of the case, issue, or conflict with that accorded to the other.

† By 'clearly' is meant 'avoidance of error and presentation of all the major aspects of the issue.'

‡ By 'coherently' is meant 'without inconsistency and in a narrative which is presented sequentially and with logical ordering of its main points.'

to have been made; and up-to-dateness of bibliography (how many of the works cited were published in the last 5, or even 10, years?). To ascertain overall fullness of treatment, all that is needed is a skeletal outline of the main epochs within the period supposed to be covered. A textbook on Roman history will have to cover the early, middle and late Republic, and the early, middle and late Empire, for example. Once the outline of epochs has been constructed, the task becomes simply to record how many pages each textbook accords to each of them. The enquirer can also jot down the number of recent books cited in the bibliography for each epoch. It is positively amazing what such quick tests do reveal.

The difficult part of all such approaches, of course, consists in choosing the issues. This is not easy before the period is known. But anyone can ask the appropriate faculty member or some advanced students what the important issues are. Or he can look at past examination papers, or essay topics, for the course involved. It pays to check into issues of *secondary* importance (for example Sulla rather than the Gracchi, and Vespasian rather than Augustus), as the author is almost certain to have given full treatment to well-known controversies. As to the skeletal framework, the course description should indicate the main epochs within the period it covers. If it does not, inquiries can be made, as suggested above in regard to the issues. It is as well to take the precaution of identifying personalities or issues which constitute cut-off points, breaking the overall period down into epochs. Sometimes authors do not distinguish epochs, or have their own, unusual ways of demarcating such inner boundaries. They must be compared uniformly, however. So there will be need for the ability independently to impose a uniform set of time-divisions, or divisions by topic, on whatever works are to be considered.

STANDARDIZED CATEGORIES

The more complete and more elaborate comparison of textbooks outlined in chapter 5 is, however, the one which provides the best illustration. In practice, we can manoeuvre things so as to employ multivariate analysis on material which, initially, does not seem at all suited to such analysis. The discussion in chapter 5 shows how thoroughgoing are the consequences of any attempt to cast the analysis in terms suitable for producing the matrices of multivariate analysis. But it also provides a highly adaptable basic framework for dealing with a type of problem which is of frequent occurrence. In my history method seminars, where students have complete freedom in selecting their projects, it is always the case every year that several opt for this kind of application of the technique. What is more, they tend to produce the most technically competent projects, indicating that this makes a good starting point when they are learning to use the technique. This can be said of no other variety of application of the technique, although the biographical runs it a fairly close second.

If this framework is generally adopted, with adaptations to suit the particular demands of each individual project, we will have gained for ourselves a set of what is sometimes termed 'standardized categories', and a set, at that, cast in a form suited to multivariate analysis. We have now seen two examples of such categories, neither of them at an advanced level of analytical sophistication. One concerned reconstructing a writer's image of an historical personality, or comparing images which had been reconstructed. The second, the one just discussed, concerned comparing the way issues are presented in textbooks. We have also seen that, in certain issue areas (such as the study of fictional populations in journals), there exist categories of proven usefulness for their investigatory power. These too can be cast into the form of a matrix, by employing them as subject-matter categories (down) used in combination with categories relating to features of presentation (across). For instance: frequency and length of mention, number of literary figures used, intensity of diction and feeling, etc. See the categories running across the top of the matrix in figure 6.1.

Standardized categories provide a ready-made analytical infrastructure applicable to a particular variety of problem or issue area. If a question can be redefined to use such categories, a predetermined strategy, worked out down to the details of its tactics, will be made available for use. Unfortunately there are not very many sets of these standardized categories. That limitation at least makes it easy to remember those which do exist, and what they can do. There is, however, at least one other set. This is considerably more sophisticated than those so far discussed and its scope and range are much greater.

This set of standardized categories comes in connection with an overall framework of analysis within which individual or group characteristics can be evaluated.[8] The categories occur in three tables. The aim of the analysis is to assess the ways in which an individual, or a group, draws his, or its, conclusions.

[8] See chapter 14 of *Communication Content*: E. S. Shneidman, "Logical Content Analysis: An Explication of Styles of Concludifying." The bibliography at the back of *Communication Content* lists further work by Shneidman on this most important topic.

One table sets out the various aspects involved in reasoning a way to a conclusion. Another does the same for the possible ways of arguing a case, termed 'cognitive manoeuvres'. In some respects all men reason alike. In others, groups of men have been conditioned to reason in a particular way. In yet others, individual peculiarities are strikingly evident. A subject's speeches or letters or what have you can be scored in terms of these tables. An individual personality's normal practices are thus obtained. Once the investigator deals with more than one person (as he must in comparing viewpoints or assessing group views), the list of 'cognitive manoeuvres' becomes a matrix. But, whether he has to cross-compare or not, a pattern in using items from that list becomes apparent in the case of each person under analysis. Any such pattern of modes of reasoning points to underlying beliefs about order and causation necessary to make sense out of that pattern. It also indicates the psychological characteristics necessary to support such a fashion of reasoning about reality.

A third table lists psychological traits known to relate to the various types of reasoning listed in the first two tables. The pattern of modes of reasoning which kept being plotted into the first two tables is now related to the patterns of psychological traits set out in the third table. The patterning behind an underlying *psycho*logical manoeuvre thus becomes clear. A broadly based interpretation of the subject material, in terms of a body of psychological theory built upon practical findings and independent of the content analyst, is thus produced. This interpretation can be cross-checked for validity by testing other parts of the documentary material to see whether there are continued manifestations of the characteristics which this analysis imputes to the subject (or subjects).

Section 2: Multivariate Analysis at the Level of Research Design.

The set of standardized categories just discussed spans two levels of analysis. One is the close, detailed analysis involved in the process of extracting the data. The other level concerns the overall strategy of analysis, or research design. Multivariate analysis can be employed at both of these levels. So far, indeed, consideration has been given to the use of the matrix, typical in multivariate analysis, as applied to the fine detail of an investigation. But such matrices can nest within a larger one, which sets out the overall framework of comparison, at the macro-analytic (in the big) level. All but the simplest of studies — any study, in fact, which involves more than one correlation of data — will probably require planning in terms of multivariate analysis at the level of overall strategy.[9] This probability will appear best in considering an example.

AN EXAMPLE OF A RESEARCH DESIGN

Supposing I wish to examine the policy of the British Conservative Party in regard to law and order and the European Common Market respectively. To establish what that policy was, two things would first have to be done. I would have to establish the range of policy options (to see what the Conservatives chose to emphasize and ignore, as well as include). This would best be done by contrasting their policy with that of the other parties (Labour and Liberals). Also, I would need to be able to separate electioneering issues from basic planks in the platform. So I would have to look at pre-election and post-election policy declarations. This work produces a giant matrix as a framework or overall outline for my study. Across the top are the categories: Party I, II and III; down the side are those of Time I and II. Now in each cell of that matrix nests another matrix, this one dealing with detailed analysis. This time the categories that run across the top are: press releases for the media in general (I) and speeches to professionally concerned groups (II). Down the side run: categories detailing the policy options first for the law and order platform (I), then for that on entering the Market (II). I can now compare pronouncements by party leaders.

It is simply not possible to design such a study without using some form of multivariate analysis. Analysts simply have to know how to go about correlating data in order to check more than one factor against another. Shifting from one level of analysis to another is also quite likely to involve use of this technique of analysis. Consider an example, involving such shifts, to see why this is so. The example involves a content analysis cast in systems terms and conducted by Gerbner.[10]

A SYSTEMS APPROACH TO CONTENT ANALYSIS

Gerbner's work on our 'common symbolic environment' — the ocean of words in which we swim — has produced a framework for examining our cultural climate. His thesis is that a precondition of the emergence

[9] For instance, when Holsti provides an illustration of a research design, it is cast in these terms. See *Content Analysis*, pp. 37-40. The example which follows in the text, incidentally, owes its inspiration to Holsti.

[10] "Cultural Indicators: The Case of Violence in Television Drama". This study has been selected as an example because of the significance of its content, as well as for its superb control of content analysis as a technique.

of public issues or debates involves this 'common symbolic environment'. The latter consists of commonly shared understandings nurtured by the media among mass publics. This is produced by a message system (the outpourings of the media), which is regulated by the institutions of corporate industry and politics. Together these act to cultivate public awareness. So, before assessing the meaning of the response of an individual or a group, it is necessary to know the assumptions underlying that response and generated by the media. Thus the key to a culture is the shared understandings through which public debate is carried on.

Gerbner has evolved a framework for the analysis of a message system: see figure 8.9.

Figure 8.9: DIMENSIONS, QUESTIONS, TERMS, AND MEASURES OF MESSAGE SYSTEM ANALYSIS (from "Cultural Indicators: The Case of Violence in Television Drama", p. 21; reproduced by permission of the author).

Dimensions:	EXISTENCE	PRIORITIES	VALUES	RELATION-SHIPS
Assumptions about:	WHAT IS?	WHAT IS IMPOR-TANT?	WHAT IS RIGHT OR WRONG, GOOD OR BAD, ETC.?	WHAT IS RELATED TO WHAT, AND HOW?
Questions:	What is available for public attention? How much and how frequently?	In what context or order of importance?	In what light, from what point of view, with what associated judgements?	In what overall proximal, logical or causal structure?
	ATTENTION	EMPHASIS	TENDENCY	STRUC-TURE
Terms and measures of analysis:	Prevalence, rate, complexity, variations	Ordering, ranking, scaling for prominence, centrality, or intensity	Measures of critical and differential tendency; qualities, traits	Correlations, clustering; structure of dramatic action

This is in fact a matrix of the type common in multivariate analysis, or rather a whole interconnected series of such sets. This fact is obscured because the framework comes as one component part of a gigantic systems analysis which operates at several levels. This book has presented only one illustration of a systems approach using content analysis so far, and that was a very simple example. So, while considering this particular instance of multivariate analysis, also take a look at this more typical example of a systems approach employing content analysis.

What Gerbner ultimately wants to do is to see how three things — corporate institutions, the message systems produced by the media, and the ideas and assumptions in people's heads — all interact upon one another. This is, if you like, the most advanced level of his analysis. It is where he is studying the complex interweavings of some things which are themselves very complicated. However, before he can study this, the most advanced or topmost level of his subject, he has to have certain facts. These can be gained only by studying his subject at the next most advanced level, that second from the top. He therefore has to investigate, one at a time, the complex inner workings of *each* of the three things whose interactions constitute his most advanced level of study. Figure 8.9 shows how he sets about analyzing one of the three, namely the media-produced message system.

Figure 8.9, then, represents an overall analytical framework. It can be used to analyze the total output of messages from any society's mass media. It identifies the strategic dimensions, those by whose analysis the key characteristics of that message system can be laid bare. It outlines the questions and the methods with which to do the analysis. Each dimension acts as a category of inquiry. Together these categories provide a systematic battery of questions, which provide findings progressively building one upon the other. At the finish, an overall, interrelated set of findings has been produced which shows how the message system is working, and what its basic assumptions are. Gerbner, you will remember, wishes to establish a set of monitoring devices which can quickly, and *early*, identify the building up of social tensions, as these begin to well up subliminally in the mass preconscious. If this set of standardized categories can do that, it can certainly be used — by social historians and others — to investigate movements of thought and belief in the past.

This matrix is in fact so enormously wide in its range of applicability that other, smaller matrices can nest within it. For the concept of 'a message system' is at a rather advanced level of generalization. It is next to the topmost one being used, in fact. This means, in practice, that it has to be broken down into more specific component subconcepts if it is going to be examined in detail. Levels must be shifted yet again, to a less abstract level. For instance, it is necessary to establish what is actually in the message system (across) in regard to a particular group of issues (down) before going on to ask the other questions at the level of greater generality indicated in the overall outline framework. By this time, i.e. by looking at statements on specific issues, the analyst is looking at a part of one of the three things whose processes of interaction form the subject matter of the study. And he will find himself looking at a set of standardized categories now that he has arrived here. Let me explain.

Gerbner wants to know what is in the message system in regard to 'Patterns of Life'. So he selects an area that has been much studied by specialists in mass communications, namely 'The Fictional World' — in this case 'of the T.V. Drama'. Since so much attention has been lavished on the study of the 'populations' of such fictional worlds, a great deal of expertise in conducting such analyses has been built up. It is known, for instance, what are the kinds of methods which produce quick and sure findings economically from masses of documents. A theme, 'Life Styles', focuses analysis. An interaction unit, 'Who whom?' (insert 'kills', 'does violence to', 'ignores', 'is friendly to') enables counting operations to be performed. And a series of categories sorts the findings in ways known to produce results. First, socioeconomic status: interactions among age groups, classes, and ethnic groups are looked at. Then in- and out-groups: relations within, and between, each are examined. Then time-perspective: possibly an actual example might best illustrate this category. Gerbner looked at 'The World of Violence/Non-violence' (depicted on T.V.) as projected into the past (where 90% of the dramas were characterized as falling into the category of the World of Violence), the present (75%) and the future (100%).[11] The general applicability of such sets of standardized categories to other areas of study than the mass media (e.g. novels) is obvious; so let me turn to belaboring the less obvious.

While examining this illustrative example, something has been seen of how a systems approach works, when it is using content analysis. One level builds upon another. It is planned as an interrelated combination of inquiries. It relies on a series of mutually supportive methods of analysis. For instance, the study of corporate institutions (another of the 'three things' whose interaction was the subject matter of the study) could be conducted by employing the various forms of analyses generally described as 'approaches to decision making'. The insights generated within the field of study known as 'bureaucratic theory' would also be drawn upon. Thus content analysis would be only one of a battery of analytical techniques all being deployed within the systems approach.

[11] This part of Gerbner's study is of gripping, not to say spine-chilling, interest. See "The Case for Cultural Indicators", pp. 18-20.

I do not propose in this book to go into the business of constructing such systems analyses. That is another subject, and a very complicated one.[12] But it is worth pointing out, at this juncture, that this tactic of building one study upon another is a very useful stratagem.

CUMULATIVE CONTENT ANALYSIS

Such a process is known as cumulative content analysis. Now that we understand how multivariate analysis works, we should be easily able to follow the steps involved in cumulative content analysis. Take a straightforward application as an example, to see what is involved in practical terms.

There is no contemporary biography of Marius, a famous soldier *cum* politician of the late Roman Republic. I reconstructed what was virtually such a biography by collating all references to Marius in Cicero's voluminous writings.[13] This work was done by setting up a maximal list of career events and associations, on the lines of the micro- and macro-analyses already outlined in discussing the comparison of biographical materials. Once this analytical infrastructure was set up, it was of course available for repeated use. So I did the same thing with another voluminous writer of the next century, Valerius Maximus. I then went on to do the same thing for Plutarch (a writer of the *next* century) and for John the Lydian (four centuries later).[14] There was thus built up a series of systematically collected, coherent sets of data — if you like, a little data-bank.

The following investigations were thus rendered possible. First, by using the above picture of Marius as a yardstick for comparison, I was able to observe what happened to its component parts at various points in antiquity. These writers are all *litterati*: scholars of wide reading and, in fact, recognized by their contemporaries as being outstanding in this respect. Thus I could ask: what did the well-read man of each of these

[12] Possibly the best book currently available on systems theory, for a non-specialist who wants to read his way into the subject, is Buckley's *Sociology and Modern Systems Theory*.

[13] In "Cicero's Picture of Marius". At this stage, incidentally, I had not yet heard of content analysis, and so thought that I had evolved a new technique of analysis.

[14] See the studies "The Picture of Marius in Valerius Maximus" and "The Changing Picture of Marius in Ancient Literature" respectively. I did not learn of content analysis until after I had completed the study concerning Valerius Maximus, and it was only after learning of it that I thought of the cumulative study. So the description in the text implies an overall plan which I would nowadays automatically think of, but which, at that time, I evolved only gradually.

periods add, change, drop or re-emphasize as he 'told all' about Marius?[15] Now Marius' career was long and tortuous, and heavily involved in politics. So I could ask, secondly: how well did each subsequent age know and understand its history of Marius and the crucial age he dominated? Some moderns have very pronounced views as to how politics worked in Marius' day, upon what could be called the political culture of his times.[16] There is dispute as to whether this political culture remained after Marius' day. So, by examining how well later writers understood that political culture, I could assess how similar — or how foreign — it was to that of their own times. And, thirdly, I could see which of the component parts of the 'picture' got full treatment in these writers and which were skimped. By relating these findings to what is known about writers whose work centres on the component parts involved, and writers also whom the analyzed authorities claimed to be using, I could thus assess which of these writers survived, and how influential they variously were, from period to period. This assessment gave information on scholarship and the survival of written communications in antiquity. (From a rather poor sample. There need to be several writers of this sort from each age to establish the viewpoint typical of that age. The sad fact is that they just have not survived.)

The framework on which such analyses are based is really very simple. The overall outline involves time periods (across, top) and whatever is being investigated (down). Suppose the latter is political culture. I can list aspects of that concept in forms relevant to Roman Republican practices (down). Inside the outline framework thus formed nest smaller matrices. Each matrix lists those aspects of Marius' career relevant to any aspect of the 'political culture' concept (down). The nesting matrix also has categories for the language, value judgements, etc., used by the writer in mentioning these aspects of Marius' career (across). Writers of different periods give prominence to different aspects of Marius' career, within the terms of the 'political culture' concept. Moreover, they comment on them in different ways. All this information can be easily cross-compared by employing this

15 Some of this is set out in matrix form at pp. 16-18 of "The Changing Picture of Marius".

16 The work that springs to mind in this connection is R. Syme's *The Roman Revolution*, Clarendon, 1939 (see especially chapter 2). For the concept 'political culture' (a most useful aggregation of ideas for anyone wishing to compare different societies, or the same society at different stages), the work that springs to mind is that of Pye. See L. W. Pye and S. Verba, *Political Culture and Political Development*, Princeton, 1965, chapter 1, or Pye, *Aspects of Political Development*, Little, Brown, 1966, pp. 101 & 104-5 (and cf. 40-48).

framework. Alternatively, if *sources* are bring investigated, I can list those thought influential for, or writing on, the period (down). Within the outline framework thus formed (time periods across, sources down), the nesting matrices are inserted, as follows: Type of use made of source (acknowledged, unacknowledged, echoes, etc.) is listed (down). So are the subject matter categories in relation to which such use is made (across). This arrangement will show which writers are influential (and whether this is at first or second hand) and for what kinds of matters. Again, the overall framework reveals patterns with a clarity which could not be achieved in any other way.

This is not a difficult analytical procedure. I used Marius' career and associations as a theme with which to collect data. I then used that theme to cross-compare the data thus produced. The procedure involves two stages. In the first stage, a series of 'pictures' are reconstructed from different time-periods, methodically, uniformly and fully. In the second stage, these pictures are successively contrasted, by applying one uniform array of questions, to see how they differ. Various theories about the causes of such differences are checked in process. This is done by seeing whether the changes involved in any one case are of a nature which the theory would explain. Until the reconstruction of the first stage has been accomplished, it is just not possible to see patterns in, or any *systematic* divergences (however gross) among those pictures. The wood just cannot be seen for the trees. Thus cumulative content analysis is a procedure in which the first stage produces findings which can enable a fresh batch of questions to be put at the second stage. It is in this sense that the inquiry can be said to build upon itself. Use of multivariate analysis helps it to do so.

PSYCHOBIOGRAPHY

Another form of content analysis, that which aims to generate findings which will overlap, can also be best discussed now that multivariate analysis has been explained. Take psychobiography, for instance. It concentrates on perceptions commonly prevalent because implanted by a childhood socialization which has affected a whole generation in common. Suppose, instead of inquiring into the unique thought-world of one highly a-typical individual, similarities in the thought-worlds of groups of more ordinary people are investigated.[17]

[17] Basically, though a formal psychobiographical framework is not employed as such, this is what Isaacs is doing in *Scratches on Our Minds* and *The New World of Negro Americans*. As the former work was heavily based on questionnaires, however (whereas the latter analyzes written work), the latter is of more relevance to would-be content analysts thinking of some form of psychobiographical study.

The analyst might take ten nineteenth century writers — novelists may-be, five of conservative and five of more liberal views. Then he takes an issue — the status of women, say. He can break this issue down into more manageable aspects (duties to father/husband; rights against same; independent acts thought proper; etc.) He next finds out what each writer has to say on each aspect. He can now, by a consolidated matrix, compare the views and assumptions which all his novelists share, then those which all the conservatives share, and finally those which only the liberals share. It is even possible to tell which views are unique to an individual, and thus a-typical. Now he can proceed to a similar examination of another issue (social change, for instance). He can finish by assessing what sort of readers the writers were aiming to reach. This job is done by looking at such things as library borrowing statistics; volume, price, and sales of books published; and so on. It may even be possible to find some evidence of their readers' reactions.[18]

A quick review of the research design of such a study will enable readers to see how multivariate analysis helps in getting it up. In overall terms, there are two categories across the top, where five writers of conservative views are being compared to five of a more liberal bent, and two running down: the issue-areas 'views on the status of women' and 'views on change'. This comprises the giant matrix within which the others nest. For there has to be a separate matrix to examine the details of each writer's treatment of each issue area. Thus 'views on women' involves a series of subject matter categories, running down, and a series of categories relating to presentation, running across. Even the four-cell overall matrix outlined above would involve twenty such nesting matrices.

Twenty is too many. Some form of reduction will be necessary if trends are to stand out in all this welter of detail. Numerical reduction, effected by weighting the presentational categories, should cause the most salient subject matter categories to stand out. Some will run across the board (i.e. occur in all writers). Some will occur in the conservative writers and not the others, and vice versa. Individual peculiarities will stand out. A consolidated matrix can now represent these trends. A single matrix will suffice for the issues which are uniformly salient. Two will be necessary to distinguish issues salient for right and left respectively. Reduction in fact results in such simplification in

---

[18] Jordan tries to do the latter in his study "Popular Literature and Imperial Sentiment", mentioned above. Incidentally, he did not know of content analysis at the time of writing that study, and attained the level of analytical sophistication so evident there by his own individual efforts. Yet, even at this stage, he subsequently found the literature on content analysis enormously helpful.

the presentation of voluminous and complex data that it is possible to study even two or more periods in this way and still present the findings with clarity. Study of several periods enables the assessing of changing values, climates of opinion, or what have you.

But the study described initially above is aimed at presenting the picture of these aspects of reality as seen by a certain class in this particular society. The analyst in this case also has data on the values and the practices thought normal within that class, and on the ways in which communications flowed within it. He may even be able to add to our scanty knowledge of the history of the family, if he has used the interaction unit and inquired into their perceptions of how families in fact got on together. Information on the history of the family is in fact very far from being as full as it might be. All kinds of unhistorical stereotypes are bandied about, as part of the conventional wisdom on the subject.[19]

What a man defines as reality is real in its consequences for him, as has been seen. So these images of social 'reality' which have been gathered represent the *'facts'* — the modes of behavior current at the time, the climate of opinion if you like. The analyst has thus reached through to the texture of the human relationships within which his writers lived.

RUNNING CONVERGING TESTS

No matter what form of content analysis has been used, it will be necessary to make some kind of cross-check upon the validity of its conclusions. As seen, it takes several measures — qualitative as well as quantitative — to establish significance. Equally, the most convincing demonstration of the validity of an interpretation comes when findings from one analysis after another all produce the same kind of data. A content analysis can be planned so that it will produce converging findings. Very often multivariate analysis can help.

The basic idea behind the converging tests is that of establishing the central core of findings which keep turning up no matter which way the source materials are analyzed. The shaded area of overlapping in the following Venn diagram shows what is meant:

[19] See R. Fletcher, *The Family and Marriage in Britain*, Pelican, 1966, chapters 2 and 3, and page 205. This state of affairs is partly due to the lack of the conceptual and analytical equipment, among historians, requisite for this variety of social history. Hopefully, the present book may do something to remedy this situation.

Figure 8.10: OVERLAPPING FINDINGS.

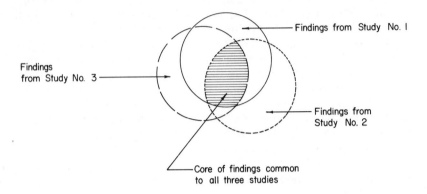

Discussion so far has touched on three procedures for going about this business of producing findings which will overlap and thus show what is central and what is peripheral to the inquiry. These are the test-retest procedure, multiple confirmation, and multiple operationism. The first is a simple stratagem, but the second two are not. Consequently they can benefit from being cast in the framework usual in multivariate analysis.

MULTIPLE CONFIRMATION

The test-retest procedure involves dividing the sample into two at the outset. Then the content analysis is rerun on the second sample, to see whether similar findings eventuate. Multiple confirmation is merely an extension of this stratagem, which consists of seeing whether source material not analyzed in the first study turns up similar findings. In multiple confirmation, however, different but related source materials — i.e. more than one other variety — are successively checked. The illustration of this technique which is generally cited involves an attempt to establish the main psychological values of Hitler's Germany by examining German plays, songbooks, handbooks for youth organizations, speeches, newspapers, and even stamp illustrations.[20] Now, to distinguish between the values common to German society in general and those peculiar to Hitler's variety of it in particular, it is necessary to assess the period prior to Hitler's Germany as well. This requirement means six categories for source materials and two for time-periods; a

20 See Webb and Roberts in *Communication Content,* p. 321.

twelve-cell matrix. Each cell will contain a matrix for detailed analysis of its source materials, involving categories for value analysis (down) and for analysis of presentation (across). These nesting matrices, however, can be simplified and consolidated by reduction, as in the psychobiographical study just outlined.

Analysis of converging trends thus means checking correlations and hence means multivariate analysis. Consider Gerbner's study of violence in the mass media, for instance.[21] It considers films in which schools, teachers, or students play a large part, then films centring upon culture heroes, then television dramas. It also compares the films on these topics put out by different national groups and at different points in time. Such complex cross-comparison cannot be done without the framework provided by multivariate analysis to control the proliferating data. Or consider the so-called flip-flop control(!) which involves analyzing not only another sample of source material but a slightly different set of questions. The example cited studied children's drawings and found that Father Christmas was drawn larger and more out of scale before Christmas than after. This effect was not mere pre-Christmas euphoria; other figures were not exaggerated in this way when the children were induced to draw them. Witches, on the other hand, *decreased* in size before Hallowe'en.[22]

MULTIPLE OPERATIONISM

However, the most dramatic confirmation occurs when findings from different types of analysis, as well as different types of source materials, complement one another. The illustration generally quoted is of the case where a questionnaire inquiring what topics were of public concern produced the same findings as a content analysis of 'Letters to the Editor' of newspapers.[23] In basic outline such a study involves two major sets of categories. One is constituted by breaking down the issue-area 'topics of public concern' into a list of component issues or themes. The other is constituted by the establishment of time periods to show the changing content of public awareness. The content analysis is then conducted, and the questionnaire administered, in terms of this framework.

[21] See "Cultural Indicators: The Case of Violence in Television Drama", pp. 16-20.

[22] Webb and Roberts again (a delightful study, this): *Communication Content* pp. 323-325.

[23] *Ibid.*, 321; on the technique in general, see Paisley, *ibid.* pp. 285-86 and *Content Analysis*, pp. 16-17 and 83.

This is, in essence, a very simple strategy and easily applicable — with a little imagination and ingenuity — to a wide range of problems. For instance, in my study of "Problems and Prejudices in the Humanities", I examined major Classical journals to see whether contributors were reading mainly books or journal articles, whether the national origin of a publication affected its chances of being cited, and whether these scholars were reading across the boundaries of academic disciplines. The same questions were then put to Classical books published by major university presses, to check on the findings of the study of the journals.[24] Findings from questionnaires administered to Classicists and others attending learned conferences contained complementary data.[25]

Section 3: *Beyond Multivariate Analysis: Matching Patterns*

THE LOGIC OF CONTIGUITY

Behind this strategy of searching for overlaps in the findings, so as to show what goes with what in the sources, there is a certain type of analytical logic, the 'logic of contiguity'. A brief outline of a study using it will best illustrate what is meant. The study had to do with assessing the validity of two opposing schools of thought in regard to a certain writer's delusions.[26] As a result of their impressionistic readings, one school maintained that these delusions were the product of homosexual impulses. The second school, on the other hand, held that ambisexuality was at the bottom of it all. In general terms, here is how the content analysis proceeded.

First, the major points of reference in the writer's thought-world in connection with his delusions were established: himself, God and the sun. Secondly, the two schools' viewpoints were reduced to their basic essences, to enable them to be compared with a stark simplicity. If the former view is correct, all the above symbols ought to have masculine connotations; if the latter, then feminine connotations should be found. Thirdly, all passages containing these three words were culled from the text. An equal number of passages centring upon

24 "Problems and Prejudices in the Humanities", pp. 33-34.

25 Actually, it did not occur to me, at the time, to use the findings from these questionnaires. They were conducted in N.S.W., Australia, and never brought to publication owing to my leaving the country. These ways of checking on the validity of studies are only 'obvious' once they have been pointed out.

26 See J. Laffal, "Contextual Similarities as a Basis for Inference", in *Communication Content*, especially pp. 167-70. The determination of what constituted each term's associational field, and also the correlation of the various fields, involved sophisticated mathematical operations, it should be observed.

words strongly associated with masculinity and femininity were like-wise culled. As step four, the words used in association with the three crucial words were examined. So were words associated with symbols which were clearly masculine and feminine respectively.

It was thus possible to compare the associational field of each key word, one at a time, with that of the other key words, then with that of masculine, and then of feminine, symbols. In this way, for each word, and both concepts, the frequencies of words or concepts in its associational field stood revealed as a pattern. It was thus possible to see whether the associational field of the word 'sun' was similar to that of the concept 'maleness' or to that of the concept 'femaleness'. The latter proved to be rather more the case. See figure 8.11, a Venn diagram, which indicates the respective amounts of overlapping.

Figure 8.11: THE LOGIC OF CONTIGUITY:
AN ILLUSTRATION.

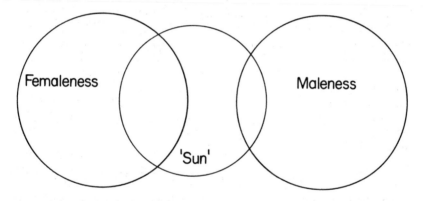

Moreover, the overlaps between the associational fields of 'sun' and 'God' could be similarly compared. They were found to be very slight: for the victim of the delusions, 'God' was predominantly a male symbol. Thus *neither* school of thought was upheld in its contentions.

Basically, three steps are involved in this procedure. The points in dispute (key concepts and their interrelationships) have first to be established. Outside criteria against which to judge them have next to be established. Then the relationships claimed by either side are assessed in terms of these criteria. In more specific terms, the pro-cedure goes as follows. First is established precisely what each school of thought claims: what terms are involved and what relationships are posited between the terms. In this case, one school held that God and the sun were male *and not female* symbols $(A,B=X\overline{Y})$, whereas the other maintained that they were *both* $(A,B=XY)$. Secondly, what constitutes a male symbol and what a female one for this writer is established: what kinds of associational field does each have? The associational field of each of the terms in dispute is also determined. The investigator can now proceed to the third stage: to examine whether the relationships between the terms, as claimed by either school, in fact hold good. The findings are: $A=X\overline{Y}$, $B=\overline{X}Y$; $A\neq B$; thus neither viewpoint is justified by the facts. The whole business is rather like comparing two configurations with a master pattern to see which in fact resembles that master pattern.

PATTERN MATCHING

There is nothing very novel about this idea of pattern fitting. It is just a little more carefully thought out than what we are all used to, as will appear from the following illustrative examples. The first involves a type of pattern fitting that many readers will have themselves employed at some time or other. The next is a little more sophisticated, but obvious enough. The one after that is not quite as obvious. The fact is that we are here dealing with a type of analytical procedure that we are all vaguely familiar with. Most of us, however, have never considered what its potential could be if it were methodically developed to the full. Many will be surprised to learn how far the various Social Sciences have gone in their development of this procedure.

FROM MAP TO COGNITIVE MAP

The first example may come as something of an anticlimax. It is certainly obvious enough: it is a map. All of a writer's geographical references are plotted on to a blank map, one containing only the outlines of major land masses. Then the results are contrasted with a 'proper' map, one produced by a specialist geographer. It can thus be seen how the patterns in the writer's mind 'fit' those of reality. All very obvious? Consider an actual case studied, to see what this 'very obvious' form of pattern fitting can turn up.

The case studied was that of John the Lydian, a Byzantine bureaucrat of the sixth century A.D.[27] He was a voluminous and discursive writer, ideal for this kind of study. Writers whose work is confined to

---

[27] See chapter 6 of my *Bureaucracy in Traditional Society*.

a restricted theme, or who do not survive in bulk, cannot be meaningfully analyzed in this way. Their reticences are of no significance, and no one can form an adequate picture from their few geographical allusions. John's geographical references were in fact plotted on to *three* blank maps. On to the first were plotted all references datable to the 'Classical' era (effectively c.850 B.C. to 284 A.D.); on to the second went all those relating to the Dominate (285-518 A.D.); and on to the third went all those relating to his contemporary times (519 to the 550s A.D.) Briefly, the first, or 'Classical', map revealed a world of cities, around the shores of a Mediterranean whose focal points were Italy and Greece, in that order. The second, or map of the Dominate, revealed a less city-filled world, comprising the Mediterranean and Near East, and focused on the latter. The third, or contemporary map, revealed a world of tribes and mountains, stretching from the Caucasus to the British Channel, with Anatolia as its heartland but with the Mediterranean no longer at the focus of attention.

What had changed was the focus of attention, which had shifted from cities and the Mediterranean area to tribes and the area of the Black Sea. The frequency and the salience of items mentioned indicated the change. The map was seen as a military man would see it, not as a civil administrator or someone interested in Church affairs would have viewed it. Its key features were strong points, not trade lines or administrative regions. There was little attention paid to the difference between urban and rural living conditions. John oriented himself, in describing Philadelphia (his home town) and Constantinople (the city in which most of his working life was passed), in a very distinctive way. Such an orientation recurred elsewhere only in regard to Antioch. Upon examination, the line of road connecting Antioch with Constantinople was found to be unique in its mapping, comprising the only tract of terrain receiving — when all John's scattered asides were considered together — detailed attention right along its full length.

Shifting levels to look at major assumptions implicit in, rather than the details of, these maps, I found that 'Rome' changed for John (who lacked a sense of national identity, incidentally). Initially she *was* — her Empire comprised — the civilized world, with a scatter of barbaric tribes dimly and intermittently visible at her outer edges. But contemporary Rome was one of a concert of powers in a balance-of-power world. Natural forces worked only disaster upon this world. Out-groups, negatively perceived, hemmed it menacingly around. An astrologer's star map stretched above it, influencing its various regions.

Thus, by testing this particular pattern against others, I could answer a number of questions. What kind of map was John himself using? Probably not Ptolemy's, in spite of his claims. How typical is John's picture of the world when compared with that of his contemporaries? It is quite, quite different from that of Cassiodorus, a contemporary, but from the West. How does it fit with what moderns assume the picture of the world in the sixth century to have been? This is difficult to say, given the haziness of those assumptions. John's presuppositions about out-groups and about natural causation yield valuable insights into his personality. For he lived in a threatened, darkling world. Cassiodorus, his contemporary in an objectively much more menaced Western part of the Empire, had a much more cheerful view of 'reality'.

Apparently, young animals have an 'orienting reflex' built into them to help in the all-important business of getting their bearings. So all of us have gone about this business of orienting ourselves long before coming to the age, and use, of reason. Thus many of our attitudes towards geography and topography are psychological rather than logical. And we tend to think about such things in pictures.[28] So not merely is the map a very useful master pattern, but approach to a man's thought-world at this level is likely to admit us easily into his sub-conscious, where we can find out things about him that concern his thinking on other matters than geography. For a brilliant study in thus effecting entry into the minds of modern town-dwellers, Lynch's *The Image of the City* is recommended.[29]

PERSONALITY SYNDROME

This underlying psychological imprint, which our mental 'maps' of our surroundings bear, links this form of pattern fitting to the next. But the next type is not just 'used in awareness of' underlying psychological forces; it focuses squarely upon them. It takes a personality syndrome as its master pattern, and checks to see whether the patternings in the data correspond to that pattern. A personality syndrome is a cluster of characteristic attitudes, beliefs or acts, found by researchers always to go together in a patterned set of behavioral activities.

Here is how it works. If a man is an authoritarian, he will take a predictable position on an entire series of *psycho*logically connected

[28] This fact emerges very clearly from Isaacs' book *Scratches on Our Minds*.
[29] Authorities as eminent as Bruner speak highly of the stimulating effect of Lynch's work on the visual power and subtlety of students exposed to it: see *Toward a Theory of Instruction*, p. 34.

issues: God, the fatherland, morality, position of women, sexual behavior, art, duties towards parents, toughness, attitudes towards out-
groups, deviants, change, and chance.[30] Similarly, a set of characteristic
propensities, though these are much different, will be found in the
personality of a man with a high 'need to achieve'.[31] The analyst will
either find this pattern, or syndrome, in the man's writings, or he will
not. It is too distinctive to be missed, once the analyst knows what he
is looking for, if it is there.

Similarly, open and closed minds, it would appear, differ in the
ways in which they each reject beliefs they do not hold; in the amounts
known about such beliefs; and in the coherence with which beliefs
actually held are put together. 'The world' is differently seen as
'friendly' in one case, 'hostile' in the other, and authority figures are
endowed with different influence, relative as opposed to absolute.
Time perspectives differ too, the latter being much more narrowly
focused than the former.[32] It is thus possible to make inferences
as to a man's personality from the way in which he holds his beliefs.
One very interesting study even considered the closed-mindedness of
a *group's* reactions, as indicated by the dogma emanating from a
series of Councils involving decisions on matters of belief, against a
background of differing amounts of threat to that group from its environment.[33] This kind of approach is capable of being extended for
use in a variety of situations. For instance, its syndrome of characteristic activities can be used as telltale evidence of the basic philosophy
of a political party, whatever the latter's verbal declarations as to
its intent.[34]

THE CONCEPTUAL DICTIONARY

In a way, then, the syndrome is the equivalent of the map which
was used in the first illustration to show how to go about 'pattern
fitting'. Indeed, psychologists speak of 'cognitive maps' in this connection. And, in a way, the third example also, which involves what
its users call 'conceptual domains',[35] is a form of word map — a map

[30] See Adorno *et al.*, *The Authoritarian Personality*, e.g. pp. 255 ff. (on the
'F scale') and 543 ff. (on Thematic Apperception Tests).

[31] See McClelland, *The Achieving Society*, e.g. pp. 39-46 and 210-40.

[32] See Rokeach, *The Open and Closed Mind*, pp. 31-53.

[33] *Ibid.*, chapter 21 ("The Effect of Threat on the Dogmatization of
Catholicism").

[34] See P. Selznik, *The Organizational Weapon*, Free Press, 1960; e.g. pp.
vii-xi & xiii.

[35] See Laffal, *op. cit.*, in *Communication Content*, pp. 162-4 for what follows.

of the linguistic universe comprising all the written output of a given people at a given period.

In this case the master pattern is a conceptual dictionary, something rather like a thesaurus. This is created in the following way. Words are first grouped by common elements of reference into concepts which must be readily recognizable by external judges. It then emerges that some of these concepts or groups of words are very close to one another. They keep occurring apropos of much the same kinds of other groups of words or issues. These associating groups are therefore classed all together under a broader, more general idea or theme, which comprises all the concepts involved. This theme is known as a 'conceptual domain' (see figure 8.12). Typically, the language of any period contains only a limited number, less than 200, of these conceptual domains.

Figure 8.12: A 'CONCEPTUAL DOMAIN'.

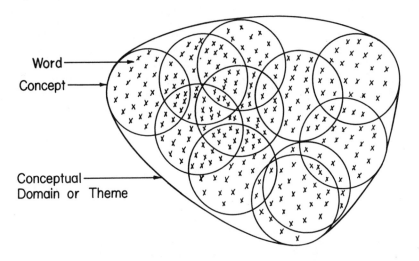

Once it has been established what the conceptual dictionary is for any given speech group, the analyst can then take any one of the writers of that group and contrast *his* conceptual domains, or even concepts, with those which that dictionary shows to be normal for the group. All the idiosyncrasies of his usage now appear. It becomes possible to see the words which *aren't* there, and those which are over- or under-represented. And this is happening on a scale so large that the writer is not even aware of the patterns in his usage which such a device can reveal.

Here is a much simpler application of a somewhat similar approach. In comparing the language of schoolboys of middle-class and working-class home backgrounds in regard to the way both used adjectives and adverbs, the list of the 100 most commonly used English words (McNally and Murray, *Key Words to Literacy*) was employed to eliminate all which that list contained. The results showed "a clear tendency for the middle-class boys to use a wider variety."[36]

SOCIOGRAMS

Another way of using the master pattern is as a form of grid, constructed so as to allow different patterns to be plotted on to it. Take a simple one to start with. It is known as a sociogram.[37] It is used for plotting out the patterns of relationships within a group. It works as follows. A questionnaire is administered to a group, asking its members to name their best friends, closest working associates or some such. Suppose each person has been allowed to indicate a first, second and third choice. Heads are now counted. Anyone who is named by someone else as his first choice is scored 3 points for being so named. A second choice gives the person so named 2 points, a third 1 point. The analyst can now establish the 'choice stars', the popular people who receive most choices and points, and the group's wall-flowers, those who receive least of both. But he also has information on the number of times a person is chosen (a points score can be run up in different ways); on mutual choices, and on converging choices. This is enough to identify friendship groups or cliques, as in the following figure, figure 8.13 which is based on the following choices:

Bill	chose Joe, Charlie & Norm;
Charlie	chose Joe, Norm & Harry;
Fred	chose Norm, Joe & Charlie;
George	chose Harry, Joe & Fred;
Harry	chose Bill, Charlie & Joe;
Joe	chose Charlie, Harry & Bill;
and Norm	chose Harry, Bill & George.

---

[36] *Social Class*, p. 110.

[37] There is a good straightforward discussion of sociograms in a special section on them in L. Broom and P. Selznik, *Sociology*, Harper & Row, 1968, pp. 170-75.

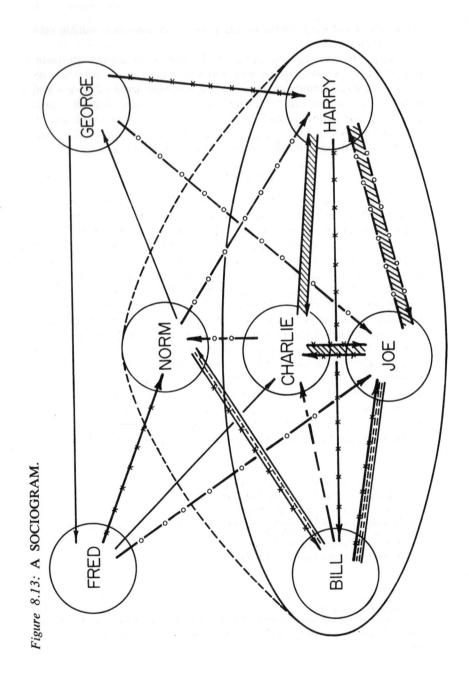

Figure 8.13: A SOCIOGRAM.

The figure is composed of circles (to represent the persons involved), arrows (to indicate who chose whom) in various thicknesses or colors (in this case three, to represent first, second and third choices), hatching (to represent mutual choosings) and some form of oval (to enclose the areas of intense interaction). The investigator identifies the 'choice stars' and locates them centrally. He then tentatively positions those who have named the 'stars' as their first choice in relation to those stars. Mutual choice creates the strongest link; higher scorers are assigned the more central positions, and arrows should be kept from crossing one another, as far as this is possible. The choices made by the stars are now plotted. This step should identify the maximum-interaction groups. The wallflowers are now positioned on the border relative to their choices and choosers.

Quite complicated patterns can be identified with this framework of arrows and circles. It is how overlapping directorates among a corporate elite are traced and demonstrated, for instance. Once the patterns of close relationships have been established, enquiry can be made into the characteristics of the persons within them (as opposed to those who are not so included). Different symbols can be assigned to indicate each important characteristic. In this way an inquirer can investigate further aspects of the relationships which have been discovered by the sociogram in the first place or stage.[38]

'All very well,' you are no doubt thinking, 'but I'm not going to be dealing with questionnaires.' No, but you might be analyzing patterns of family interaction in novels or mass media, for purposes of literary or social history. Using a sociogram for such a purpose will make it possible to visualize complexities and aspects of relationships that can be 'seen' only diagrammatically. Use words to try to work them out and the analysis simply cannot be followed through. The words will get in the way, by making the exposition too complicated. Take an example to show what is meant.

Suppose I have a public figure who is a prolific letter writer (Cicero, for instance). I want to find out whether he is the time-serving opportunist contemporaries sometimes make him out to be. One way of checking this is to see whether he changes his friends with his circumstances (he rose from obscurity to political and social eminence).

---

[38] The classic among such studies explores the extent to which personal relationships affect the communication of scientific information. Sociograms are used as indicated in the text. See Menzel and Katz, "Social Relations and Innovation in the Medical Profession", in Maccoby's *Readings*, pp. 532-45 (for illustrations of sociograms in use, see pp. 535 and 540).

I can identify two quite distinct periods in his life — before and after, as it were. I can now content analyze the letters of each period and record my findings in terms of, and upon, the one uniform framework, consisting of a sociogram. It will be a rather special variety of socio-gram. It will centre upon my subject and locate his intimates, friends and acquaintances (his enemies likewise) within concentric circles (his intimates — friends or foes — in the middle).

I can now map out the cliques which he did (and *didn't*) belong to, by tracing the relationships among persons so named. If I wish, I can even compare Cicero's version of who knew whom with the versions of others as to who were in these cliques. I can also ascertain the characteristics of persons in each zone, assigning different symbols to designate literary, political or social notables, for instance. I can even give these persons some kind of rating on the standing they enjoyed among contemporaries in each of these fields. Thus, at a glance, I can now compare Cicero's network of acquaintance at each of two (or more, if I so wish) periods. If I suspect that he is choosing his acquaintances for ulterior motives, I can evolve a system of signs to identify the range of characteristics which would accord with such motives, and make up both sociograms in terms of this system. This exercise will quickly, economically, and dramatically prove or refute my point.

Thus what we have called the master pattern does the following things. It helps organize material. It focuses attention on a particular group of details inside a mass of other details. It makes it more easily possible to compare complicated bodies of data. So it will provide a focus, and some categories, for a content analysis, and help make sense of the detailed findings of that analysis. It is an analytical framework of a sort which is naturally suited to be incorporated in a study that employs content analysis.

GENEALOGIES

There is another such pattern, related to the sociogram but more complex, which can do correspondingly more complex things. This is the genealogy, as used by the ethnographers.[39] It is used like this. First the family trees of a particular selection of households are each individually established. Then various characteristics of the persons featured in each family tree are represented diagrammatically on second copies (and third, fourth, etc., as needed) of the originally

[39] For a really good illustration of this technique in action, see C. R. Bell, *Middle Class Families*, Routledge and Kegan Paul, 1968, chapter 5.

constructed tree. The trees from one class or region are then compared to those of another class or region. It can now be seen, plotted on to the copies of the originals, how the symbols group for each class or region, and how they tend to be differently patterned for the different classes or regions. It is as though a pictorial version of a 2 x 2 is being used, in a way.

Suppose the genealogist is interested in literary or social history. He wants to establish, by content analysis of a group of novels or letters, how families of a certain period tended to behave. The genealogy, used to direct his content analysis, will catch up an enormous amount of detail. First, with it he can discover just what degrees of kindred were thought of as constituting the family in his documents. A mass of interrelated details — the genealogies of ten families, let us say — can be represented in ten diagrams, taking only five pages. Once these facts are in, he can start comparing the characteristics of the genealogies of one class or period with those of another. How geographically scattered was each one? Within a genealogy, what characterized those members who kept in touch, as opposed to those who interacted less frequently or closely? How does the family on his tree behave on important occasions — births, marriages, deaths? Are current ideas about the status of women (involving matrilocality, say), in the period represented by his documents, borne out by female patterns of behavior in these respects? Clearly, if the history of the family is to progress, those investigating it will have to be able to perform this kind of analysis with ease.

PROFILING

While on the subject of literary or social history, there is another, quite different, form of master pattern which can also be profitably used in a content analysis. This is known as 'profiling', and here is how it works. Suppose the task is to explore the life-styles, or personality characteristics, of the personages of a fictional world — in the novels of a given period, say, or in its films, or, as in our illustration, in its television dramas.[40] The basic problem is one of an overabundance of detail: readers may remember the earlier image of the mouse being buried under a stream of grain pouring from a sack. A way has to be found of enabling the overall patterns, hidden by this wealth of detail, to emerge. And they must do so in some uniform way, so that they can be contrasted.

[40] See Gerbner, "The Case for Cultural Indicators", pp. 27-29, and figures 2.4. The classical study is M. U. Martel and G. J. McCall, "Reality Orientation and the Pleasure Principle: A Study of American Mass-Periodical Fiction (1890-1955)", pp. 283-334 in Dexter & White, *People, Society, and Mass Communications.*

This is where the master pattern or grid comes in. It consists of a number of personal characteristics. These are arranged as a series of 'dimensions' (continua linking opposing extremes). Thus a character can be young or old, usual or unusual, incompetent or efficient, attractive or unattractive, emotional or unemotional, logical or intuitive, rational or irrational, violent or non-violent. Each dimension is divided into a number of segments, the same number for every dimension. Thus the continuum ranging from 'very young' (1) to 'very old' (7) is divided into seven stages. Dichotomous attributes (male/female) can be included as well, if this is necessary.

The population of the fictional world is now divided up into the types of person to be compared. The profile drawer then takes the first of his types and finds the mode (or most frequently occurring instance) for each of the characteristics shown as dimensions, or lines, on the grid. He now draws a line connecting the different points on each of the lines of the grid. The resultant line is the 'personality profile' for the (modal) type of person he is investigating. He can also assess whether the type tends to be male, generally speaking, or female. He now proceeds to do the same for the other types, but draws differently colored, or differently marked, lines for each successive 'profile'.

In this way, nine different kinds of data on each of more than three hundred fictional characters can be reduced to four different profiles (lines) on a grid. Thus, overall trends can be very simply and clearly outlined. Such profiling also provides an economical way of examining the influence of a series of different factors affecting the fictional population involved. For instance, Gerbner considered the characterization that went with different roles; that which distinguished killers from those killed, and that which went along with a happy, as opposed to a sticky, end. In each case the fictional population is divided into the groups related to the factor whose influence is to be considered: roles; killers/killed; happy/sticky ending. Then, by means of a set of personality dimensions, a modal profile is established for each group. Finally the profiles are compared, to identify overall differences. Profiling provides an economical way of outlining the influence of different factors. Also, it facilitates comparison of the influence of these different factors. Looking through its lenses, it is quite easy to see the wood despite all the trees.

THE PROPOSITIONAL INVENTORY

As this pattern-fitting business becomes more elaborate, it also becomes less generally applicable. It changes from a broad general approach into a specialized technique, tailor-made to suit a particular problem. Look at an example of such a highly specialized technique to round off this series of examples, this pattern-fitting topic, and this chapter. The technique goes by the name of the 'propositional inventory'.[41] It enables the discovery of the values of different groups at a particular point in time. It does so, however, by examining how mass media of differing persuasions react to a specific issue. Only some of my readers will be concerned with this type of problem and have this type of source material available. Still, it is just conceivable that it might be extended to investigate the reactions of novelists of differing persuasions (or readerships!) in regard to a certain type of incident, issue or situation. For completeness' sake, our series of examples will be rounded off by examining an instance of this advanced stage to which the business of pattern-fitting has evolved.

This illustration involves the following incident.[42] A French school-teacher and his wife, who was ill, were being baited by some young pranksters under cover of darkness. To scare the boys off, the teacher fired off his gun at random, mortally wounding one of the boys by accident. The teacher took the boy to hospital, then called the police. The treatment of the incident by the press of the Left, Right and commercial Centre is the object of the study. Its aim is to uncover the underlying assumptions of these groups on social issues, and to see how these interrelate.

First, then, the discussion of the incident by each newspaper is divided up into the various assertions made during that discussion. Each assertion is then reduced to a proposition, or generalized statement. The propositions which result are then sorted into categories, descriptive of themes, tendencies, or aspects of the subject matter of the debate. The propositions in each category are in this way arranged into passages, each labelled with a phrase which indicates the general nature of the passage:

> "A heart-rending affair";
> "Unjust conditions";
> "Good man, terrible accident";
> "Not a political case";
> "A national disgrace".

[41] For the case-study and description of the methodology on which my account is based, see *ibid.*, pp. 30-32 and figure 5. (The later version of this paper does not retain the discussion of the propositional inventory which featured in this earlier version.)

[42] This incident is discussed in Gerbner's paper, "Ideological Perspectives and Political Tendencies in News Reporting", *Journalism Quarterly* 41, 1964, pp. 495-508.

Each passage occurs in all three sectors of the press. So the analyst could calculate how much space was given by the press as a whole to a given passage, and then work out what percentage of this total was made up by the statements of each sector of the press.

A 5 x 3 matrix results, in fact. This frame acts very much as did the grid for plotting profiles in the last example. The analyst could now obtain a profile of each newspaper's performance, and he could also gain an overall picture of the pattern of emphases in each *sector* of the press. He could compare each newspaper with all the others, one by one, in terms of their respective profiles. The resultant overlaps enabled him to place the papers of the centre in relation to the others. In more general terms, he could see the sociopolitical viewpoints favored and disliked by the leftists and rightists, and, further, show how greater extremism (towards Right or Left) affected the viewpoints in question.

What this technique does is impose a pattern on a welter of highly diversified data. This pattern enables the data to be categorized uniformly in a set number of ways. Categorization in turn enables 'profiles' of large sectors of the sources to be reconstructed. Comparisons are thus facilitated, and the effects of a number of different factors can be separately assessed. Readers who think back will realize that the first two of these statements could be said about the pattern-fitting involved in the use of a map as a master pattern. A propositional inventory, however, involves the use of not one, but two master patterns, one after the other, and in such a way that the first creates the second. First of all the grid has to be constructed. Then, when it has compendiously marshalled the data, profiles of the various individual newspapers are constructed from it and compared, as a second-stage operation. Let me not try to develop the chapter into greater complexities than this.

9

Fitting the Components Together:
Applying Analytical Infrastructure
And Theory: A Recapitulation

If you aspire to some skill in commenting upon literary, historical or social events, you will need a certain amount of competence in the basic techniques of handling written material. If you can also analyze pictorial materials methodically, your commentary will be able to consider a greater range of data and in greater depth. Unavoidably, such commentary will involve the following fundamental problem: when you have an hypothesis, how do you examine your data to see whether they support it or not? Content analysis is a basic technique evolved to deal with this problem. There is no other of such wide general applicability.[1] You will need to be competent in its use. As a basic tool, a good literary craftsman will use it with easy familiarity, along with his other tools of analysis and synthesis. It is the poor craftsman who hates — or, even worse, is ignorant of — his tools.

COMPONENT TECHNIQUES

The snag with this tool, however, is that it is so flexible; it is difficult to get a clear idea of what it is, and, consequently, of all the ways in which it can be used. Basically, it is just a bundle of analytical techniques grouped loosely together. Each user makes these up into a combination specially shaped to suit his highly individual

---

[1] Others may exist, but they are more specialized. Moreover, there is only one — C. Lévi-Strauss' structural study of myth — that springs at all readily to mind. See his *Structural Anthropology*, Basic Books, 1963; for a 'reader', see E. Leach (ed.), *The Structural Study of Myth and Totemism*, A.S.A. Monograph No. 5, Tavistock, 1967, or M. Lane (ed.), *Structuralism: A Reader*, Cape, 1970.

purposes. Hence all sorts of variants on the one basic form have been evolved. We have considered the following varieties in this book, for example: classical, computerized, critical, cumulative, logical, non-frequency, systems-oriented and theoretically oriented. (All technical terms used in this chapter have been discussed elsewhere in this book; track them down by referring to the Index of Matters, where they are all listed.) To make matters worse, content analysis is now regularly being used in conjunction with other social science techniques, either to form its categories or to produce converging findings. So it is essential to have a clear idea of its main, basic outline. Figure 2.2 and the discussion thereto provide such an outline.

The bundle of techniques involved in content analysis concerns how to go about establishing categories, context and counting units, measurements of data which these produce, and the sample. Together these present a variety of forms of posing questions. But this is not a nice, orderly series of steps. Instead, each affects the other; they all have to be taken into account simultaneously. It is necessary to keep trying out different combinations. A change made to one will involve a succession of modifications elsewhere among the others to counter-balance it. Getting a group which will work thus involves a circular process. It generally means a series of exploratory pretests, known as a pilot study, which forms the preliminary phase of the content analysis operation.

In figure 2.2, 'phase' has been used instead of 'stage' in order not to confuse this discussion with that of cumulative content analysis. Really the difference is one of level. Any content analysis involves a procedure consisting of pretest, data extraction and checking back. A cumulative content analysis involves using this entire procedure to establish a set of findings from one batch of documents. These findings are then turned into questions and used in *another* (entire) content analysis procedure upon a second batch of documents. Thus each stage of a cumulative content analysis involves all the phases described in figure 2.2.

Though it suggests ways of posing or reformulating questions, content analysis will not tell what question to ask. Moreover, questions increasingly tend to be asked against some theoretical background. Again, this background is not provided by the technique, of itself. What happens is that questions are asked in the light of a body of work which suggests certain leading ideas. This work helps, in particular, by suggesting categories, or complementary methods of inquiry. But it also helps, generally, by providing guidelines during the period of testing comprised by the pilot study.

Once the pilot study has established the final form of the analytical infrastructure, the second phase, that of extracting the data, gets under way. When the sample has been decided upon, counting units and context units can be used to sort data into categories. There are various methods of assessing the weight or importance to be assigned to individual pieces of these data. The data can also be grouped first in one combination of categories, then into another, by multivariate forms of content analysis, if establishing correlations is wished. Together, these operations constitute the procedure of data extraction. Source materials may be made to undergo several of these sievings at this phase of the analysis, as the analyst probes different aspects of the subject matter, or employs quantitative, qualitative, or contiguity analyses, one after the other. These overlapping inquiries aim to produce complementary or corroborating findings.

From the data or findings produced in this way, the analyst makes the inferential leap to his conclusions, thus proceeding beyond the second phase of the operation. Inferences are not governed by, nor are they part of, the technique of content analysis, but the technique does aim to provide help in validating them. One way it validates inferences is by turning its conclusions into questions, and asking those questions of another sample of its source material, to see whether similar findings again result.[2] The aim is, basically, to produce converging findings. These can also be produced in two other ways. The same question can be put to different but related bodies of source materials. Or another analytical technique can be used upon such materials in conjunction with the original content analysis. This checking-up process constitutes the third phase of the operation. All three phases, when taken together, amount to the technique of content analysis.

COUNTERS TO CRITICISMS

In a limited sense, content analysis can be termed 'scientific': it abides by the logic of inquiry and of evidence evolved for psycho-social phenomena. But it is no impersonal, experimental procedure of automatic applicability. Observably, an old hand at content analysis uses the technique better than a newcomer does. It is an art. Moreover, however expert a person may be in applying the technique, he cannot content analyze *any* set of documents for *any* purpose. He

[2] Another way is by demonstrating that there is some standard of comparison, preferably externally provided, against which to check conclusions. See Holsti in *Content Analysis* pp. 102-103, or in *Communication Content*, pp. 116-7.

has to know a lot about the background of the issues he is inquiring into and the documents he is analyzing, as well as about the technique itself. As elsewhere, with content analysis too, "discovery favors the prepared mind." The more known about questions, documents and technique, the greater the versatility and sensitivity in analysis, and the greater the ability to see the implications of findings.

A common reaction is that this is no way to handle literature. In fact, however, scholars *have* used the technique to investigate literary questions, and with meaningful results. Certain aspects of any body of literature can be examined only by looking at that body as a flow of communications. For the properties of a collective may not be reducible to the sum of the properties of each of the individuals who constitute it. For instance, no one member will exhibit all the linguistic traits common to his speech community. No one program, no one T.V. station even, exhibits all the patterns common to the 'world' of telecasting in which it and its competitors operate. Moreover, with this technique it is possible to ask new questions, or look in new ways at old problems, and so reveal meaningful aspects which previously could not be analyzed. Consequently, content analysis is going to be increasingly employed in literary studies.

An even commoner reaction comes in the form of the contention that content analysis is 'only an elaborate form of what we all do anyway.' As has been seen, in a way this statement is true. A mature scholar who has been working on literary documents in a disciplined way will recognize in the technique an extension, generalization and formalization of what he has been doing. Such a person can absorb what is involved in content analysis with incredible rapidity. In one case I have seen this happen in the course of *one* seminar. The paper to be discussed at the seminar had been circulated well in advance, and there had been some discussion in conversation prior to it; but full exposition of content analysis as a technique (with diagrams to illustrate and under close cross-questioning) occurred only at the seminar. The scholar involved was Dr. Donald Earl of the Department of Latin in Leeds University. Such a person, however, never, in my experience, delivers himself of the above contention. The person who does is in need of help, though he may not appreciate it (at least in the form of the 'help' outlined in what follows).

If someone merely recounts the various procedures involved, his recitation will be accompanied by a counter-incantation of *we-all-know-that*s. To enable such a knowledgeable person to discover just how much he in fact knows, questions are necessary. This matter has already been raised in the first chapter. There, however, discussion was limited to presenting the points which could be followed by a reader without a knowledge of content analysis. By this point, it is to be hoped readers will be able to appreciate the significance of failures to answer the following more complex battery of questions. They probe into two areas: the first involves the analytical infrastructure of the technique; the second, its interdisciplinary nature.

First, then, can he *within thirty seconds* (or minutes for that matter) draw a diagram setting out how to solve our bag of marbles problem? Can he outline an alternative model to the psychoanalytic model or personality, or the maximization of profit model of an economic system? Can he briefly sketch a way of contrasting perceptions of perceptions, where a metaperspective and a meta-metaperspective are involved? Try setting out the substance of that sentence concisely without using either term. A metaperspective is your opinion of someone else's opinion of something (B -A on X). A meta-metaperspective is — you guessed it — that someone else's opinion of *your* opinion of his (the former someone else's) opinion of that something (A -B -A on X). The terms come from the Laing book on interpersonal perception.

Secondly, time-budgeting: what books has he read, and what lectures or conferences has he attended, in disciplines other than his own in the last three (or six) months? What friends and acquaintances has he in any three Arts and any three Social Science departments? There lies a chance to practise with a sociogram. Also bibliography: ask him to name a *total* of five books dealing at least in part with methodology, from the following disciplinary areas: Anthropology, Economics, Political Science and Sociology. See what he knows about some major figures who have shaped the thought-world of the social sciences—Gordon Allport, Jerome Bruner, Talcott Parsons, Max Weber (or whoever).

Anyone who goes around giving a lot of help of the above nature may find that he has to brush up on his reading in the 'how to win friends' area. The experience should, however, convince him of how far 'we all' are from being aware of the problems which content analysis has been evolved to deal with.

QUESTION-POSING

While on the subject of questions, however, let us examine the relationship between content analysis and the asking of questions. Only when this relationship has been clearly understood will the limitations of the technique become plainly understandable. In the first place, content analysis cannot be used to 'go fishing'.[3] That is to say, content analysis cannot be used to probe round among a mass of documents in the hope that a bright idea will be suggested by such probing. Content analysis gets the answers to the question with which it is supplied. So results of the content analysis depend on the skill and strategical sense with which the question is put. But the question comes first: content analysis will not provide it. Ask a superficial question *via* a content analysis and all that will be obtained is busy-work if it is a manual content analysis, GIGO ('garbage in, garbage out'—a computer operators' saying) if it is computerized. An oil rig strikes oil only if it is well positioned.

It might be said that roughly 80 per cent of the responsibility for the success of a study resides in this business of thinking up the initial question. Ten percent resides in having enough knowledge of content analysis to put the question in a way that will get meaningful results. And the other 10 per cent resides in the diligence put into the work of carrying the study out. Without knowledge of content analysis however, nobody is going to produce a study that is 90 per cent successful. Rather, he is all too likely to have one that is 100 per cent a failure.

The role played by content analysis is a subordinate one, then. But it is crucial all the same, because it provides a battery of techniques. These give the freedom to inquire into a previously un-dreamed-of variety of aspects of the initial question. They provide a rich variety of ways of reformulating questions so as to make them capable of producing findings which can be substantiated. Thus content analysis enormously expands our capacity to formulate questions. Knowledge of its potentialities vastly increases the range of 'the possible', precisely at the point where it pays most to have such an increase.

For some people, analytical problems involve such complexities and such delicate nuances of meaning that it is difficult to understand the nebulous questions which they pose — or the allusive hints in which their 'findings' are conveyed. A tendency to mystification is a feature of a particular style of viewing things.[4] Yet other people can ask complicated and subtle questions of bewilderingly confusing source materials in a way which makes the import of their questions clear, and which yields findings of a striking clarity and immediacy.

---

[3] This is made abundantly clear by Holsti in *Content Analysis*: see pp. 27, 41, 48, 67 and 94 (and cf. 151-2).
[4] See *The Image*, p. 10 and Lane and Sears, *Public Opinion*, p. 16.

Think of Lynch's treatment of 'imageability', for example. When this clear-headedness occurs, it is immediately recognizable, and brings with it an intellectual exhilaration that is memorable.[5] Quite simply, there is nothing to beat a bright idea turned into an inquiry conducted with penetration and clarity. And it is content analysis which makes the latter part — and thus the whole — of this combination possible, when someone is analyzing documents or paintings or the like.

In regard to question-posing, it is not generally realized that a content analyst means something very different by 'a sophisticated question' from what the average history or literature scholar means. In these disciplines, there is a tendency to equate complexity in a question with sophistication. But a question of simple form is not necessarily unsophisticated, any more than a complex question is automatically sophisticated. A pair of examples will show what is meant. They represent the kind of questions that are frequently re-garded by Arts scholars as unsophisticated and sophisticated respec-tively. Both are assessed from a content analyst's viewpoint.

The first question is of this kind: "How did Justinian, Lydus and Procopius regard social change?" The question is posed by breaking down the fuzzy concept 'social change' into countable component parts: images of the past / present / future, motivations imputed to beneficiaries, and so on. This is the process of atomizing described in chapter 2 ("Controls on Subjectivity"). This question, when so posed, is known to tap unconsciously held views of considerable psychological significance — in the form of assumptions about causation, human relationships, and such matters. Moreover, it is known that there are certain patterns in perceiving such things which relate to known per-sonality syndromes. Further, techniques have been elaborated for probing into this particular issue area. The question, then, though simple in form, forces assumptions of fundamental significance into the open, and is capable of being rigorously posed. For a content analyst, it is a sophisticated question.

The kind of question that tends to be regarded as sophisticated in Arts scholarship goes somewhat like this: "Did so-and-so write his history of that war, in the form in which we now have it, to impress such-and-such a dignitary?" Such a question involves assessment of

[5] A common reaction on reading Part 1 of *Centuries of Childhood*. The audience's reaction to Jordan's paper, "Popular Literature and Imperial Senti-ment" was of this nature, too (not a typical reaction to a paper at one of the big conferences). I am not claiming that either author was consciously using content analysis, though their approach is obviously very like the classical variety. I merely wish to give examples of this quality of clarity in analysis.

motivation and situational pressures as well as ticklish sampling problems. Consider what this means.

First, autobiographical information on both 'so-and-so' and 'such-and-such' is needed, preferably including some indication of how 'so-and-so' perceived his work to impress 'such-and-such'. Such information is not always available. Even when it is, it cannot be proved that the inferred motivation was that which in fact actuated the writer in question. The other question avoided this impasse by describing perceptions (rather than inferring motivations) of an issue. That issue was chosen, and then investigated, in such a way as to relate those perceptions to various patterns known to characterize given personality types (i.e. there was a theoretical frame of reference behind the study).

Secondly, it is necessary to establish the situational pressures on 'so-and-so' at the time of writing. There are no rules to tell what kind of situational pressure makes most, or least, impression. If the scholar 'makes allowances' for the effect of this or that factor, he is simply cheating. He has to *show* how 'so-and-so' was affected by a given factor. Nobody can presume to 'know'.

Thirdly, to assess 'the form in which we now have it' he will need evidence of other drafts, and a considerable body of other writings by 'so-and-so' in order to establish divergences from that writer's practice when he was not trying to impress. Again, such data is not always available. And impressionistic analyses which aim to establish the intent of a communication from internal evidence, observably, rarely agree.

Consequently, from a content analyst's viewpoint, a question of this sort is most definitely *not* a sophisticated question. Its very complexity makes it impossible to ask this question with methodological rigor. It involves insuperable sampling problems. Its inferences are based on the questioner's own unsystematic inductions from his personal experience. Hence it has to build from one guesstimate to another to reach its conclusions. It can produce only a possible (at best a credible) answer. No other person working on the same source materials need ever reach closely similar conclusions. The content analyst, on the other hand, is aiming to keep his own idiosyncrasies and subjective interpretations to a minimum, in order to produce findings which someone else would get from the same source materials. To be sophisticated, in his view, a question must be framed so as to make this result possible. It must also, of course, focus on a significant issue.

This predilection for 'operational' questions can be taken too far, however. There is such a thing as an overharsh scientific superego.[6] By this term is meant a preoccupation with doing only those studies which have the most immediate face validity, based on the most quantitative of methods. This type of obsession gave to early studies employing content analysis — and, consequently, to the technique as a whole — something of a bad name. For there was a tendency to ask only the kinds of questions that the most narrowly quantitative applications of the technique could cope with. Hence there developed (and has persisted) a stereotype of the content analyst as the man with a predilection for 'counting for counting's sake'.

This is a gross misrepresentation of actual practice. A fundamental aim of the technique is that of devising ways of obtaining documented findings while doing the *minimum* of counting, and doing it in the most economical way, at that. Moreover, a superficial question, even if it is investigated with the most exquisite prodigies of technical analytical virtuosity, will still yield only superficial results. A penetrating question, on the other hand, even though it may be paired with a relatively unsophisticated form of content analysis, can yield deeply significant results.[7] We are not after analytical virtuosity for its own sake. Rather we want to discover what we need to know about analytical techniques if we are to tackle the problems which are our overriding concern. It is the payload carried, rather than the fashionableness of the carrying vehicle, which is our prime concern. The Arts part of the dialogue between Arts and Social Sciences consists largely in trying out social science theories and techniques and reporting back on how well they work. Thus, wide-spread use of content analysis in Arts studies could be of considerable significance in the further development of the technique.

Questions come to us intuitively, out of knowledge of, association with, and concern for the issues involved. Application in working on them is a matter of moral fibre, resolution, or what have you. But, for knowledge of content analysis, we cannot just summon up our

[6] For the term, and some penetrating insights, see D. Riesman's "Comments" on Berelson's paper "The State of Communication Research" in Dexter and White, *People, Society and Mass Communications*, pp. 514-5.

[7] As, for instance, in Lawton's content analyses of schoolboys' essays and group discussions, at pp. 111-26 of *Social Class*; or in Gerbner's use of simple, quantitative measures, at pp. 18-20 of "The Case for Cultural Indicators". It is a basic tenet of content analysis not to strive for a quantifiable answer at the cost of making question superficial. See *Content Analysis*, pp. 11-12 (and cf. p. 194).

inner resources. We have to go beyond them, to *learn* about it, if we want to make it ours to call upon. It will not just come out of the blue.

However, that superego mentioned above, in the form of cautiousness brought about by knowledge of the technique, can be of service. It can give us an early warning, as to when source materials are not adequate for analytical purposes, or when a line of inquiry is going to be fruitless. Though it widens the horizons of the possible, it also makes it fairly clear just what is (and *isn't*) comprised therein. But there is a difference between rational caution and letting fashionable questions lead us on a drunkard's search.

When we are in dire analytical straits, when we are doing the equivalent of making a raft to carry us in safety from a sinking ship to a distant goal, our prime objective must be to make the kind of raft that will do the job, not the one that will win the 'designer of the year' award. My assumption here is that most content analyses will be carried out on the 'bread and butter' projects of the normal working week — the course-work essay, the position paper summarizing a mass of memos, the review and suchlike. These typically have to be done in a hurry, under pressure of work. Obviously, when we are in the business of boat-building as such (i.e. getting a thesis launched), we will take more care over the theoretical side of the research design. Even in such cases, however, I take it, we should be prepared to undertake 'weak' forms of content analysis if these are the only ones applicable to the problem under consideration. These matters were discussed in the fourth sections of chapters 2 and 4, where the strong and weak forms of content analysis were considered.

DEFINING THE ANALYTICAL SITUATION

Prior to question-posing, however, comes the business of defining the problem. Indirectly, content analysis can considerably expand our sensitivities in this area too. For to understand what content analysis is currently aiming to do, we must have some acquaintance with work on the psychology of cognition. Our attention is therefore necessarily drawn to the influence of selective perception and of frameworks of reference. Let us quickly review how these in turn relate to the questions we pose and the forms of content analysis we then employ. Gerbner has an excellent diagrammatic representation of how a document is related to the events it describes. This is here reproduced, with permission, as figure 9.1.[8]

Figure 9.1: A GENERAL MODEL OF COMMUNICATION.

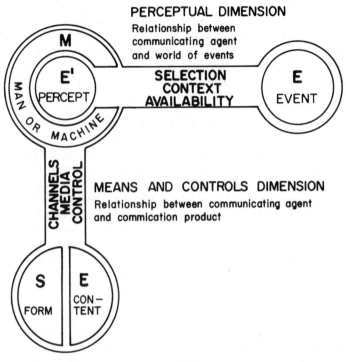

The diagram sets out what happens when someone perceives an event — a riotous assembly, say. Certain features in that event are more striking than others (availability). It occurs against a background of previous happenings, such that certain of the things which ensue at the assembly have a special significance (context). Given his previous experiences, our observer's sensitivities are particularly acute so far as certain things — violent acts, perhaps — are concerned (selection). When our observer communicates his impressions, the form which his communication takes will further affect what is communicated. A satirical essay makes a different vehicle for conveying

8 For the original diagram, and an excellent discussion of it, see pp. 484-88 of Dexter and White, *People, Society and Mass Communications.* A longer explanation occurs in "A Framework for the Study of Communications", mimeo, Annenberg School of Communications, U. of Pennsylvania, 1961. See also p. 177 of *AV Communication Review*, 4, Summer 1956.

a message than does an historical monograph, for instance (channel). So different messages are conveyed. A private letter differs from the newspaper column containing a 'special observer's report' (medium). There may well be institutional, corporate or political pressures restricting what is reported (controls). The actual message will be presented as the rules of its genre suggest and as the writer's literary capacities allow (form). Its content will be shaped largely by things like that writer's point of view, even by his physical health and social background. It is this end product, which Gerbner aptly terms a 'social event', on which the content analyst has to work. For him it becomes an 'event', in terms of the diagram, and so the whole process is repeated when he in turn writes about it.

Content analysis makes us consciously aware of the interlocking complex of analytical problems involved in investigating such a 'social event'. Content analysts have always been very alert to the need to check back into the assumptions basic to the questions with which they must operate. As figure 2.2 shows, the pilot study aims to force us to think about these problems of filter and framework. The development of theoretically oriented content analysis is so important because it requires us to tie the questions which we intend to pose to some theoretical background. Figure 9.1 sets out the sequence of steps that came before the message, or 'social event', was arrived at. At the heart of this process are the facts that the observer first selectively perceives events, and then reconstructs what he has chosen to see according to some patterned way of viewing them, perhaps involving an image, model, or ideology. Theoretically oriented content analysis requires us to take this process into account in setting up our analytical infrastructure. It requires us to show how such processes are related to what we are looking for in the data. It also requires us to justify the relationship which, we claim, exists. We might, for instance, be claiming that a writer's excessive preoccupation with, and the stand he takes upon, certain issues indicates an authoritarian disposition. We must in consequence be able to confirm the connection between these attitudes and the personality syndrome allegedly involved. This confirmation will involve applying some criterion which is independent of our analysis.[9]

Two levels of analysis are thus involved in a content analysis. The first is straightforward: analysis of the content of the message or documents or whatever (see figure 2.2). The second is more indirect. It involves analysis of the events that led up to the creation of that

---

[9] See Paisley in *Communication Content*, p. 283.

message (figure 9.1 relates). Content analysis aims to save us from overloading our critical capacities. It provides an analytical infrastructure, or strategy of investigation, to deal with the first problem. And forms of the technique, such as critical or theoretically oriented content analysis, also aim to provide a range of strategies for thinking about these underlying secondary problems.[10]

It is easy enough to show how the first, straightforward level helps in thinking about analyzing something. Think back to the discussion of the paper on "Propertius, the Parthians and Propaganda". Knowledge of the range and type of approaches employed by content analysts in propaganda studies enabled me to focus clearly on the speaker's analytical infrastructure. The technique thus imparted the ability to take up a critical posture even in dealing with the verbal exposition of an original thesis. It enabled, in short, distinguishing with ease between message content and organizational infrastructure, and thinking about the latter in comparative terms.

The second level has been added to help with the business of putting questions in terms of some body of theoretical work. This level may involve theories about personality, bureaucracy, comparative politics, communications phenomena, or what have you. This possibility in turn means that, to exploit the full potential of content analysis, the questioner will have to read further into the Social Sciences. Arts students usually require a reference work so that they can follow up links between content analysis and various other social science approaches. One very convenient form of reference work which social scientists have evolved is the 'reader'. This is a book which breaks up a disciplinary area into its main component subfields and provides a section on each. The section generally comprises an overview of the sub-field involved, plus some classics of its literature — epochal articles, or chapters from books. Hence the Maccoby reader was put on the bibliographical Short List. Arts students seem to find it particularly helpful, so readers should have, in it, a good introduction to this type of reference work. Thus (partly), this book claims to be only an introduction to content analysis. My assumptions are twofold. One is that awareness of what is going on in various social science disciplines is essential to anyone engaged in studying how people communicate. The other is that the Arts and the Social Sciences constitute complementary, not contradistinctive,

---

[10] I owe the idea of "strategies of thought" (and much else in this chapter) to Bruner, who is of opinion that the drawing of attention to such things should begin very early, because they are so basic to understanding. See *Toward a Theory of Instruction*, pp. 95-6.

thought-worlds. What we bring to it from one of them helps us to see more deeply into the other.

Now one way in which work in the Social Sciences differs from that in the Arts is in time-budgeting when a research project is in process. A far larger amount of time seems to be spent by the former on the business of actually setting the project up, or defining the problem. And the greater proportion of this time is spent on locating the questions to be asked so that they relate to some body of theory. Theoretically oriented content analysis involves this kind of approach. Once an analyst has oriented his questions in this way, he automatically gains a host of advantages. All kinds of related issues, sub-questions, possible categories and norms for comparison appear. Awareness and sensitivities are expanded by exposure to a storehouse of insights built up and checked by *others.*

Moreover, the analyst is kept in conscious awareness of the importance of images or models of reality for the thought-worlds both of the writer of the document(s) involved and of himself in analyzing it (or them). And this second or indirect level involved in content analysis also encourages him to think of the whole business of analysis as itself proceeding at various levels. Think back to either figures 2.2 or 9.1. This consciousness of multiple levels of significance enhances our capacity to keep such levels distinct and to move between them at will, whether what is involved is multistage sampling, cumulative content analysis or shifting levels to probe into unconscious levels of a writer's expression.

The brutal facts are that, without some form of guidelines to help in the complex business of analysis, confusion or skewing (resulting from the inadvertent cutting of corners) is bound to result. Nobody will think his way through all of the above complexities, starting from scratch, just for one analytical problem, even if it is thesis-size. An analytical infrastructure produced unaided simply has no chance of being as sophisticated as one produced in knowledge of the work that has been done on content analysis. And how many of these factors affecting a writer's thought-world is anybody *in fact* going to take into account while conducting a detailed examination of a text impressionistically? Content analysis involves both a cluster of analytical techniques and a network of guidelines. The latter tie the whole complex to related findings relevant to significant background factors — motivation, institutional framework etc., as the case may be. Content analysis calls attention both to individual analytical problems and to their overall relationships to one another. It represents the compiled work of many men and women who have thought long and hard on this complex problem. It saves time and gives access to a huge store-house of analytical techniques and insights. Can anybody afford *not* to use it?

RELATED SOCIAL SCIENCE APPROACHES

Perhaps it would be as well to indicate just what are the main areas in which content analysis is strongly linked to a particular social science discipline. First, then, it very often happens, when we are engaged in a literary study, that we have to pass a judgement which involves an assessment of personality. For even though we may not be occupied with a study of a biographical nature, we often have to appraise decisions or crises in which personalities played a prominent part. People have more sense nowadays than to trust to 'common sense' or intuitive appraisals of personality functioning in such circumstances. But there is a tendency among Arts people to equate Psychology with Freudianism. There is much more to current Psychology than that, and it can only add depth to our understanding of psychosocial events to know, at least in outline, what is going on in various fields of personality theory.

Awareness of what is going on over the boundaries of other disciplines (even when these border on one's own) is still the exception rather than the rule, in the Arts part of academe at any rate. There are signs and stirrings of change in this respect, of course. But the pace of development, and the proliferation of sub-specialties within the various social science disciplines, make it difficult for outsiders fully to grasp the overall significance of work being done there. This is especially the case with a discipline which is developing as vigorously as is Psychology.

We do not merely use personality theory to interpret the dynamics revealed in our source materials. We also use it to interpret and improve the functioning of our own understanding of ourselves. And, if we can make more complete or more sensitive use of our own capacities, if we improve the processing unit as it were, all of our subsequent processing operations — interpretive, analytical or what not — will thereby also be improved. Consequently, knowledge of what is going on in work on the psychology of cognition is of the utmost strategical importance. Such work, after all, is reshaping our ideas on how we do our thinking. Nothing can be more basic or productive of greater development than the gaining of new insights into the thought processes.

Moreover, it is becoming increasingly evident that language is much more than a tool with which to think; it is part of the thought processes themselves. So attention given to work in psycho- or socio-linguistics can give much the same kind of results as that paid to work on the psychology of cognition. Indeed, these fields are all interlinked. To look at it the other way round, a cumulative deficit is incurred if we fail to inform ourselves about basic new insights in the above fields. A series of new insights is rapidly being spawned by, and is developing from, the initial discoveries there. Thus, standing still means dropping back, relative to the moving front of informed awareness in these regards.

A cumulative deficit is a lack which produces an increasingly serious series of other inadequacies. As a situation develops, the person suffering from the deficit progresses at a slower pace, thus falling ever further behind the advancing front of development. His inadequacies now compound his difficulties, as each successive problem calls for ever greater resources to cope with it.

And really, when a scholar's business is with words or images — as a content analyst's must be — discoveries about characteristics of the processes of communication produce insights and information complementary to that business. It is difficult to see how anyone can justify failure to monitor what is being said by the communications specialists. For people working on topics involving a mass public, even in the form of novels, it is sheer ineptitude not to be informed of related developments in the field of Communications.

These areas, then, are clearly linked fundamentally to content analysis as a technique. Content analysis of the disciplines to which the users of the technique belong, conducted into any recent bibliography on content analysis, will show this connection quite clearly. The departments which seem to give most emphasis to the *teaching* of content analysis as a research tool are Communications and Sociology.[11] Other areas will be indicated by each investigator's own specialized concerns. If these interests touch upon social history, Social Anthropology or Social Psychology as well as Sociology are obvious areas to inquire into.[12] For those interested in other times or other

[11] See Barcus, "Education in Content Analysis", *Communication Content* p. 548.

[12] The obvious starting point for such inquiries is with a 'reader' for the appropriate subject area. There is quite a variety of such readers, so it seems better to counsel each reader to pick one for himself rather than present a short list of titles. However, it is useful to know about the A.S.A. series, published by Tavistock. It consists of monographs published by the Association of Social Anthropologists of the Commonwealth, and contains some most interesting works (for instance I. M. Lewis (ed.), *History and Social Anthropology*, 1968, No. 7).

cultures, the work in the field of Comparative Politics will probably be very useful.[13] It is not just a case of such scholarship having made a variety of cross-cultural models available, important though this contribution is. It has also evolved powerful and economic ways of contrasting complicated and very different institutions, etc. Decision-making, for instance, is one of these 'ways'.[14]

At a less general level, there are a number of specialized techniques which are most useful as analytical devices and which are not difficult to comprehend. It will pay anybody well to gain enough familiarity with these to be able to see where and when to use them in ordinary everyday work. Sociogramming is one. Model building is another. The latter is particularly important, as people tend to fixate upon models. My experience in the English universities of 1969-70, for instance, has been that Parsonian action theory still retains a dominant position in much of the thought-world of the Social Sciences.[15] Only by being able to view models relatively dispassionately, as various strategies for organizing thought, can scholars escape from the embraces of some one particular model, and thus be free to realize the potential of new ones — or realize the failings criticized in old ones.[16] This is a matter wherein it is particularly important not to have to rely on others to detect the significance of new ideas. Finally, the growing body of work on the analysis of interactions and roles holds rich promise for all who are in the business of analyzing literature. And for others, too: such studies, at another level, have led to a wholly new way of thinking about international affairs, for instance.[17]

[13] There is such a wealth of material in this field that anybody may simply become bewildered as to how to enter it. In my experience, Arts students have found G. A. Almond and G. B. Powell, *Comparative Politics: A Developmental Approach* (Little, Brown, 1966) helpful and assimilable. It belongs to a series, in Comparative Politics, which the reader may find it useful to know about.

[14] One of the earliest accounts of what decision-making is seems still to make the most intelligible introduction to it: R. C. Macridis, *The Study of Comparative Government*, Random House Studies in Political Science No. 21, 1955. For a more recent survey, see W. Edwards and A. Tversky, (eds.), *Decision Making*, Penguin, 1967.

[15] For a critique of Parsons, and a step beyond equilibrium models, see Buckley, *Sociology and Modern Systems Theory*, chapter 2.

[16] See Young, *Systems of Political Science*, pp. 10-11, 94, and 97-102. The various 'systems approaches' of his chapters 3 to 6 constitute a series of large-scale models, each coping with different conceptual problems.

[17] See (C. A.) McClelland's *Theory and the International System*, and Deutsch's *The Analysis of International Relations* — both highly stimulating pieces of work.

It is because of its links with work in the above areas and specific techniques therein that content analysis is no longer viewed, nowadays, as a little specialism all away on its own in a corner somewhere. Insights originating in the above fields can be used to help shape a content analysis. Or the investigator may want to use a content analysis in conjunction with some other form of analysis as a part of his overall scheme of operations. It is now seen as one tool in a set, complementing and being complemented by the others. Developments in the disciplinary areas mentioned above have in fact been instrumental in resolving some of the problems long troubling content analysis as a technique.

CATEGORIZATION

For instance, a difficulty experienced in the early stages of the development of content analysis involved the forming of categories. There were no rules on how to go about category formation. This difficulty has been largely dealt with, however, by the practice of orienting a content analysis so that it relates to some body of theory, or to theoretically informed findings. Theories of personality — that on authoritarianism, for instance — will suggest categories for the investigation of a writer's attitudes or thought-world. Theories on bureaucracy will do likewise for those who want to inquire into the operational code of a bureaucracy in another age or society. A concept such as 'political culture', from the theoretical field of Comparative Politics, will provide a series of categories.

For anyone working on the mass media, the findings of scholars who work in what is termed the 'Communications' field will suggest categories. Such scholars have even produced what are virtually standardized categories for the analysis of the 'fictional world' of this or that medium. Sets of categories exist which have proved their usefulness in analyzing issues which are frequently investigated: value systems, propaganda, stylistics, and so on.[18] Moreover, for certain commonly recurring problems some standardized categories have in practice emerged. These come at various levels of sophistication. Some involve simple comparisons of textbooks or biographical material. Some involve complex comparisons; see the discussion of logical content analysis in chapter 8.

Furthermore, models can be employed to suggest categories. Various types of model can be so used: ideal types (both varieties thereof), cross-cultural, and postulational models spring readily to

[18] See *Content Analysis*, pp. 104-116.

mind. The analyst simply turns the major component sub-units, around which their creators have built such models up, into his categories of analysis. He can even use a sociogram or genealogy to generate categories. Both of the latter, for instance, will identify in-groups and out-groups. He can set these up as categories (reading down). Then he can categorize them in turn, in terms of appropriate socio-economic — or other — characteristics, to form yet other categories (reading across). For those who cannot devise a way of employing any of these frameworks of reference to provide their content analysis with a set of categories, it is always worthwhile reading through the various bibliographies which list studies involving applications of the technique. Such applications are by now numerous enough for there to be considerable likelihood that someone has attempted a similar line of investigation or type of problem to that on which any novice investigator is engaged. If so, he has someone else's system of categories to set him rethinking his own.

COUNTING

A relatively common fallacy is that content analysis involves 'mere quantification'. Now the fundamental aim of the technique is to provide a documented body of findings. After all, the whole idea is being able to pinpoint the evidence on which conclusions are based. And how *does* anybody argue if not by citing evidence? Unsubstantiated generalizations will not advance any case far. Of course, sometimes content analysis is used to establish frequencies of occurrence and so on. But to imagine that this is all that the technique can do is thoroughly to misconceive its potentialities. As the discussion on counting indicated, using a ratio scale $(0,1,2,3\ldots)$ is only one of many ways of counting.

For instance, non-frequency content analysis aims to discover the single telling clue (or omission) which of itself tells a whole story. Critical content analysis overpasses details on or from individuals to look at the implications behind trends. Logical content analysis seeks to generate patterns and compare them cumulatively with other pattern-revealing frameworks. Sometimes all that an investigator is looking for when employing a content analysis is 'everything which concerns a certain issue-area.' The objective is to find out what *kinds* of things such an inquiry turns up, not their frequencies.[19] One im-

---

[19] An example of such a form of inquiry occurs in chapter 10, "The Contemporary Views of a Traditional Bureaucracy", of *Bureaucracy in Traditional Society* (Carney) where an attempt is made to discover what a top-level and a middle-level bureaucrat conceived their respective jobs to involve.

portant variety of assessment, in fact, involves looking for associations. Its questions are of the form 'what goes with what?' or 'is this or that *pattern* there?'

In fact, then, what is involved in content analysis is the extraction of data, in all kinds of forms and all kinds of circumstances, to answer all kinds of questions. Its most attractive feature is that it can do so much more than just count frequencies. A person is lucky if his analytical problem does not involve a complex data-extracting procedure. For, generally, crude frequency counts will reveal only simple, gross differences. Subtle differences need sophisticated means of showing them up. This technique brings with it an extensive range of complicated measuring procedures, and is amazingly adaptable in facilitating their use.

It should be noted that many versions of the technique assume familiarity on the part of the user with multivariate analysis, in one or another of its forms. Understanding of at least the rudiments of this technique of analysis (which is even more basic than content analysis) is necessary, in order to be able to use the latter flexibly.

Various types of diagram can help in gathering an analytical framework together. Such diagrams, once they have served this purpose, can be subsequently reconstituted as 'maximal' versions of themes, or as matrices or master patterns for purposes of comparison. The ability to visualize problems in pictorial terms, as well as in words, can be a great help to an analyst. Very often, after all, the producer of the source materials had pictures in *his* head while writing.[20] And sometimes it is positively unhelpful to try to think in a form of words — when analyzing patterns of interactions, or metaperspectives, for instance.

INFERENCE

In looking at a communication, we can see only the middle link in a chain which leads from intent through content (the communication) to effect. Any conclusions drawn from the 'content' part about either of the other two must be based on inference. Inference, like categorization, is well known as a problem area in content analyses. It has consequently received much attention. The best strategy evolved to date for improving the validity of inferences reached through a content analysis involves planning a series of analyses. These are so

[20] As in chapter 6, "John's Picture of the World around Him", *op. cit.* (discussed apropos of the use of the map as a patterning device in chapter 8 of this book).

Figure 9.2: A COMMUNICATIONS FLOW.

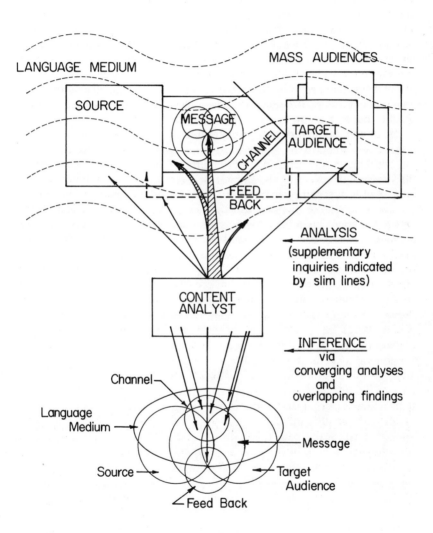

designed that they produce overlapping or converging findings if the hypothesis being tested is valid. The simplest variety of this family of strategies involves running a back check, using a second sample, to see whether findings similar to those obtained in the first content analysis are obtained in the second. The most elaborate variety involves multiple operations, of this nature: different techniques of analysis are used on differing but related materials, to produce converging findings. These varieties are polar extremes: others of their family (such as running three or more differently angled content analyses on the same material, and so on) fall in between.

Thus, in dealing with the intent-content-effect sequence, inferences about either intent or effect become much more valid if some form of the above strategy is used. It helps to visualize that sequence as a flow of communications, as in figure 9.2.

This flow can then be regarded as a system of action or set of interworking parts. Data on other parts of it than those involved in the message are also analyzed, not necessarily by a content analysis, in a search for complementary or converging findings. These might involve discovering personality characteristics of the communicator and of 'average' members of the target audience, or reactions to the message on the part of the audience, or even the communicator's reactions to his audience's reactions as expressed in private correspondence, for instance. Two examples of studies investigating the effect of message content were cited earlier in this book. They were Jordan, "Popular Literature and Imperial Sentiment", and Burke, "A Survey of the Popularity of Ancient Historians". Both are very competent pieces of analysis. They each use a form of this type of approach; the approach outlined here is a more fully developed version of what is found in them. Jordan did not know of content analysis at the time of writing; Burke knew of "Content Analysis" and of *Trends in Content Analysis*. Also, it has been systematized: it provides an organized framework within which to deploy a variety of analyses at different levels.[21] It thus constitutes a model, or overview in large-scale, easily visualizable (and memorizable!) terms, of the analytical possibilities inherent in the total situation.

Often, however, much as we would like to operate in this way, there simply is not the requisite abundance of documentation available. When documentary materials are more limited, the above strategy cannot always be adopted as a check on the validity of

---

[21] It is in fact cast in terms of a systems approach: compare it with Easton, *A Systems Analysis of Political Life*, pp. 12 and 29-33.

inferences. It then becomes a matter of devising some criterion against which to judge the validity of findings. This matter has also occasioned much attention and ingenuity on the part of content analysts, in the form of discussions of norms. There are various ways of constructing a yardstick against which to judge the significance of what is found in a single body of data. Different types of models — ideal types, postulational, cross-cultural — can be brought in. Or maybe a body of theory — on personality, say — can be adduced to show the meaningfulness of the patterns found by the content analyst in the data. There are sampling problems too, when data are less abundant, which can affect the validity of inferences. Normally, we can take several batches of data, and treat the others as a control group to set off against the one on which we are working. If there is only the one batch, then its own internal norms have to be established, so that it can itself be used as a control, to be set off against specific (allegedly special) passages from within it.[22] It should thus always prove possible to appraise the findings of a content analysis critically and comparatively as a means of checking the validity of its inferences.

PAYOFFS

It is also possible critically to appraise the results to be gained by using content analysis, as compared to more impressionistic 'methods'. Perhaps it would be appropriate to conclude this chapter with such an appraisal. There are three things to be done with a content analysis, as has been seen with figure 2.7. What is really in a welter of detailed documents can be described. Hypotheses can be tested. And the validity of conclusions can be improved. Whatever special benefits are to be gained from this laborious way of doing things can now be examined.

First then, description. This is not just a matter of counting frequencies. With content analysis 'what's really there' — and what *isn't* — can be discovered. 'What's really there' very often, under unremitting and impartial analysis, turns out to be rather different from what an impressionistic reading allows a researcher to presume to be there. This is particularly likely to be the case if complex or lengthy documents are involved. For instance, the authority on the bureaucracy discussed above (A. H. M. Jones) holds that it was the devotion to their duties of middle-level officials which enabled the bureaucracy of Justinian's day to function. Top-level officials are seen as somewhat

[22] See Hall in *Communication Content*, pp. 156-57.

dilettante, if not parasitical.[23] Detailed study, however, shows that the middle echelon officials thought almost exclusively in terms of their bureaucratic interests, and tended to overexact taxes unless restrained by the men of the upper levels. Here there was more political sense, and some identification with wider public interest. Thus the relationship of the two levels was symbiotic.

Noticing that some one thing, or pattern of things, is not present is generally a matter of luck, so far as impressionistic reading is concerned. With content analysis at his command, however, the investigator can design an analytical infrastructure that will automatically detect 'what isn't there'. A maximal version of a theme, or a matrix, or a master pattern, will do this job for him. And he can focus on things which are not there in any specific form — for instance, patterns of interaction — using one particular type of counting unit and the techniques for categorization that go with it, as described in chapter 6. Anyone who is unaware of this battery of techniques simply cannot cope with analyses of this degree of subtlety and complexity. New types of investigatory activity, then, become possible through the technique.

This extra reach is possibly most strikingly evident where analyses of non-verbal materials (pictorial, musical, etc.) are concerned. For the new ways of conceptualizing interaction units, themes, and pattern-matching provide recording units, categories, and correlating devices suited for application to such non-verbal materials. The development of contingency analysis, with its emphasis on associational fields and complex interrelationships, is particularly well adapted for such application. Together, these developments enable analysts to quantify their inquiries into material whose analysis hitherto was not considered feasible. Thus content analysis opens up new kinds of materials to investigation. It makes it possible to obtain converging findings by analyzing non-verbal material which is complementary to verbal material. It makes it possible to study a culture systematically and quantitatively through its paintings and drawings.[24] Careful, measured description of such materials is simply not possible without the analytical infrastructure and controls on subjectivity in assessing emphasis and other factors which content analysis provides.

---

[23] A. H. M. Jones, *The Later Roman Empire 284-602: A Social, Economic and Administrative Survey*, Blackwell, 1964, p. 606.

[24] See *Centuries of Childhood*, pp. 33-49 for an illustration of what is meant; or, better (a content analysis proper is involved), Aronson's study "The Need for Achievement as Measured by Graphic Expression."

It often is not appreciated, but meticulous description in terms related to specialized bodies of theory and knowledge is basic to the development of any field of inquiry. Such descriptions are much rarer than is generally realized. They do not just happen accidentally. Impressionistic approaches, for instance, do not produce studies which can be depended upon, because nobody can be sure exactly which materials an impressionist has investigated, and what he had in mind while doing so. Content analysis, on the other hand, constitutes a method which can be guaranteed to produce precise and systematic descriptions.

When you think about it, a striking feature of work in Arts is its scattergun nature. Within a single issue area, one study will simply run alongside of, or at a tangent to, the next. Indeed, their relationship may be almost non-existent. This non-convergence is bound to happen, in many cases, with impressionistic work for, to produce cumulative findings, a great number of analytical techniques is a prerequisite. And these must be available at the level of detailed analysis and simultaneously at the level of overall planning. It is in practice very difficult to construct all of these alone, working independently and from scratch. Content analysis, however, makes available a sequence of analytical techniques. Each has a range of special-purpose variants, and there are guidelines for combining them. Consequently it is easier to think in overall terms in planning an investigation. The investigator is not distracted and overwhelmed by having first (or concurrently) to construct a series of interrelated analytical techniques suitable for use in detailed terms. Hence a well-thought-out research design becomes a practical possibility. Using the technique of content analysis in fact encourages thinking in terms of overall planning whether it is a matter of combining content analysis with (or within) another technique of analysis or cumulatively combining one content analysis with another.

Of course, not all studies should aim at producing cumulative findings. All that is meant is, to be in analytical control of a situation, the investigator has to be able to produce such studies when needed. As things stand, he likely is handicapped, merely for want of the requisite analytical expertise.

So it is that content analysis makes possible projects of a much larger scale than is usual in impressionistic work. For, as has been seen, a content analysis can build upon itself. It can also generate little data-banks of methodically accumulated findings which can be built upon. Moreover, content analysis can bring large-scale projects within the bounds of the possible. Interscorer reliability can be controlled, which makes it possible for a piece of work to be split up and farmed out. This advantage is crucially important, since a content analysis can now be employed merely as one segment of a larger, overall systems-type approach. Equally important, however, is the fact that, with a tool like content analysis to use, a neophyte in a discipline can become meaningfully engaged upon significant issues within that discipline at an early point.[25] At the everyday level, this possibility makes an enormous difference even to the kind of classroom projects which can be attempted. At a more advanced level, the technique thus brings the possibility of planning, in long-range yet detailed terms, to develop a field of inquiry. This type of planning occurs significantly less in Arts than in other areas, largely because it is difficult to do it without methodical techniques of inquiry. Knowledge of content analysis should therefore considerably increase the ability of people in Arts to deploy a strategy of investigation when they feel it to be necessary.

This is not an argument for committee-mindedness, but for increased ability to organize our working capacities. Suppose we want to open up a neglected area in a field. Hodgetts, for instance, speaks of a "bland consensus version" of Canadian history, which "brushes aside the conflict of opinions."[26] Suppose we want to produce a revision of Canadian history from this neglected viewpoint: How do you go about it, as things stand? Commission one man, to report back a lifetime later?

Besides making long-range planning of cumulative research possible, content analysis also, as has been indicated, enables investigators to probe into non-literary materials: pictures, for instance, or music, or films. As well, it enables all sorts of investigations to be conducted into materials formerly not easily or regularly utilizable for such research. The unconscious assumptions of the Fathers of the Church can be investigated to see what they tell about specific aspects of social history, for instance. Or children's comics may be used to trace what is happening to a people's views on imperialism.[27] And the technique is applicable not only to modern writings, although its strongest applications may well be there, where the data are more abundant. It can be used on all kinds of source materials, and for all kinds of investigations. (The analysis of people's images of reality

[25] On the importance of this point, see *Toward a Theory of Instruction*, p. 155.

[26] *What Culture? What Heritage?*, pp. 24-5 & 99.

[27] As Jordan did; see pp. 150-53 of "Popular Literature and Imperial Sentiment".

forms, possibly, the strongest area of application for the technique.) Indeed, it is highly probable that its application to some of the pre-modern subject areas will make it possible to tackle new problems, or investigate new aspects of old ones, thus reinvigorating the whole climate and area of inquiry. It will also constitute an alternative mode of inquiry, vying with, as well as complementing, those already established within each subject area — such as prosopography in Classics. Consequently, it will be seen as a competitor and threat by some individuals and schools who have a heavy investment in estab-lished approaches. Finally, the gradual build-up of studies employing content analysis has produced a specialist literature on the technique, constituting a repository of findings and analytical ideas. Researchers can draw freely upon it, and so enlarge their overall analytical capaci-ties. The technique should thus enormously expand our potential areas of investigation.

A side-effect of the intensive reading required in content analysis is the acquisition of an unusual degree of familiarity with a text. That is unusual, being impossible to attain except when under the discipline of having to conduct a detailed inquiry uniformly and meticulously, to achieve a specific goal. The prolonged concentration involved sharpens sensitivities and induces a special depth of awareness. After all, with a content analysis, the investigator is putting into his work on a text something of the same quality of intense sustained effort, bearing the overall requirements of the text in mind, as did its author. It is only for those working at this pitch that the finer features of the organizational infrastructure of a text become visible.[28]

What anybody sees in a body of writing is a function of what he brings to it. And content analysis adds to what the investigator nor-mally brings to it. A price has to be paid for this hypersensitivity, it must be admitted. A person can look with such intensity at some things only by omitting to take others into account. But, after all, this is the price which any form of analysis exacts. With an impressionistic approach, it is possible to keep changing the focus of attention in a way that is impossible when conducting a content analysis. In fact, all arguments in favor of the grasshopper mentality, as opposed to concentration, will hold for impressionistic reading, as opposed to con-tent analysis. It should, however, be noted that some varieties of content analysis allow for the expansion of the analyst's focus of

[28] I am indebted to Mr. E. Harrison, of the Department of Classics, Leeds University, for this idea. His methods of work are exceedingly close to what is now termed classical content analysis, and his comments arose from personal observation based on this work.

attention during the course of the analysis. The left-over list attached to the conceptual dictionary allows such development, for instance. So does cumulative question-posing going with a systems framework adapted as a set of categories, as in figure 8.6.

But the main advantage with content analysis resides in the fact that the analyst is *conscious* of, and deliberate about, focusing his attention. Thus he is alive to the possibility of distortion, and he thinks in terms of running several assessments. Hence an unusual depth of self-awareness normally accompanies any study employing content analysis.

The second objective of content analysis was that of testing hypotheses. Nobody can use content analysis for case-making. The technique uncovers *all* material relevant to the search, without regard to what the discoveries imply for anyone's established position — including his own! Actually, 'hypothesis testing' has come to mean more than checking on a hunch or some random question of the investigator's own devising. Generally, something rather more systematic is involved. For the technique enables posing some very sophisticated questions, and they can be related to theoretical viewpoints, or frameworks, resulting from work independent of the worker's own. A postulational model, for example, can be turned into a most elaborate set of counting units and categories. In this way, the most intractable of materials can be tested for what was originally the most nebulous of questions. Moreover, theoretically oriented applications of the technique have done much to show how to relate questions and the validity of conclusions.

The very format of a content analysis in practice puts us under pressure to think out the implications behind our questions fully. After all, the question has to be elaborated to an extent that makes it a fitting partner for its analytical infrastructure, even if only to devise some worthwhile categories. Such elaboration cannot be managed without relating the question to some major theory or body of work. It is thus no accident that the current trend is away from the superficialities of frequency counting. The in-depth questionings associated with critical content analysis[29] are likely to be increasingly a feature of future applications of the technique. It is thus almost inevitable that some theoretical hypothesis will influence most investigators in posing their questions.

The third objective in using the technique was that of facilitating inference. This task sometimes is a matter of an elaborate plan of investigation that enables the investigator to produce a series of con-

[29] See Gerbner's remarks at pp. 486-97 of Dexter and White, *People, Society and Mass Communications.*

verging findings. But perhaps the most spectacular instances of 'facilitated inferences' occur with the use of cumulative content analysis. In such cases projects are designed in stages. The first stage establishes patterns from one set of data. The second stage turns these patterns into questions and directs them at quite a different body of material. The findings from this operation enable the researcher to perform cross-comparisons of yet other material, at the third and final stage, asking related but different questions. With this strategy of investigation there is a form of conscious, flexible control at a number of levels, providing the capacity for long-range, detailed planning, of a scope barely possible in an impressionistic approach.

Fundamentally, the advantages conferred by familiarity with the technique are these. Any scholar is led to adopt an impersonal investigatory frame of mind when inquiring into texts. As stated above, it is not possible to use content analysis to champion a cause, because it will extract all the material *against*, as well as for, the case. And it tends to produce surprise findings. Hence the only frame of mind that is comfortable, when applying the technique, is a relatively detached 'Let's wait and see' attitude. Also, access is gained to strategies of thinking which facilitate complex and long-range planning of analysis. In a way, content analysis is a state of mind. It involves a predisposition not to take for granted what may be buried under a mass of words. Many of us have this predisposition anyway. You would not have read this book in the first place if you did not have some such attitude, for instance. But a content analyst must also have an easy familiarity with a complicated body of knowledge and practices. Content analysis is, in a way, like typing or driving a car: nobody can master the technique involved merely by reading about it in the abstract, but only by practice. It is as well to keep this analogy in mind when starting to use it, incidentally. It is not advisable to launch out upon complicated studies until a certain basic degree of competence has been acquired from the experiences of carrying out simple assignments.

Familiarity of this sort has to be consciously and deliberately acquired. No one has *this* 'in the first place'. Once gained, however, it combines with the above-mentioned predisposition to produce craftsmanship in the analysis of words.

Everyone will be familiar with analyses built upon the impressionistic extracting of striking passages, followed by generalizations inferred from them in an inductive, unsystematic fashion based on personal experience. Such impressionistic analyses may be tricked out in verbal finery. There may be a sophisticated literary style, brilliant anecdotal illustrations, an enormously well-stocked vocabulary, and the ability to exploit it by selecting striking turns of phraseology. But do not confuse skills in word magic — verbal or presentational — with analytical capacity. Impressionism is the starting point, not the culmination, in analysis. It takes application and disciplined work to pass beyond this initial stage, however. Some of us never do. The aim of this book has been to take the reader a step or two along the way towards greater than impressionistic analytical competence. The shrewder your criticisms of it, the more effective this book will have been.

A successful writer on content analysis never fails to rouse a following — *all* critics.

APPENDIX

APPLYING CONTENT ANALYSIS
TO SYNOPSIZING, ABSTRACTING,
AND REVIEWING

Readers will all be familiar with the sinking feeling that comes when we have to read up for a project or to familiarize ourselves with a new field. Much new information has to be taken in, and made our own, so that it will spring immediately to mind when we have to use it. Yet, as we all know from seeing people produce book reports, it is very rare that this job is well done, even when it is only a *single* book which has to be so digested.

Possibly the sinking feeling occurs in its most acute form when we have to decide, actually at a lecture or seminar, how full and of what sort our notes are going to be. There are just so many things to decide. How are we to get through the material as fast as possible, yet not miss anything, and at the same time retain the maximum amount possible in our memory? We are going to be inundated with new facts and with new ways of handling those facts. New facts can simply be fitted into the older ones we already have. But, taking in new ways of handling facts is the equivalent of rebuilding the ship while at sea, a much more difficult feat. And, amid all these jostling new ideas, how are we to pick out the *radically* new ones?

These situations keep recurring right through our lives. We have a choice between three courses. First, we can compound our problems by waiting until the situation crops up before trying to think out a strategy for coping with all of these different yet interrelated decisions. Secondly, we can evolve a strategy before becoming involved in the crisis of deciding. In this way we can do one thing at a time. We can think out a way of coping with these difficulties when not under the pressure of having actual difficulties on top of us demanding all our attention. Or, thirdly, we can pretend that the problem is not there, and cope with each situation 'off the top of the head' as it arises, without bothering about a 'strategy'. This approach means that we never show our 'true' form, because we never marshal all our resources to deal scientifically with the cluster of problems. This appendix is written for readers interested in the second of the above choices. It reviews, and elaborates upon, some common strategies used to deal with this problem.

Now the problem is all too common, and so we are all fairly familiar with various ways of meeting it. Consider what is usually done in a situation where someone has to read his way through a certain number of books to familiarize himself with a topic. Generally, one of two things will happen. He will either make notes on each book, or he will put pencil-markings, either in the margins or as underlinings, in each book. Now there is nothing like making extensive notes for achieving thoroughgoing familiarity with a book. But, in practice, it takes so long, and it takes so much out of a person. We simply cannot contemplate doing it for a large number of books.

The pencillings are at the other extreme, if you like, of this note-taking continuum. It scarcely slows one down at all to make them while reading. The snag is that they mean so little. All they indicate is that something in the passage adjacent to them is significant for some reason. They 'mean so little' in another way, too. Apparently, retention in the memory is connected with what a person is doing at the moment when the material is read. If he is merely reading, the material registers only marginally. If he is doing something with his hands to record what he is reading, then the material registers more strikingly. In proportion to the meaningfulness of the activity, each person remembers the material the more clearly.[1]

Consider these different approaches as different ways of processing inputs of data which stream through the mind as a flow of through-puts. What kind of end-product, or out-put, does each give?

If anyone simply reads, hoping to remember, so much material is being so rapidly fed into the memory that only a confused residue remains — vague impressions, from Heaven only knows which of several sources. At the other extreme, pages of notes, written up or typed out as a detailed abstract, give excellent recall. But nobody can abstract enough to do all the reading which has to be done — at least, not do it at the speed it has to be done if attention and enthusiasm are to remain high.

Pencillings help a little. For a short while after reading a book, they help its striking passages to remain in our memory and to be located in the book. But the writer's thought does not become reformulated in our own words (and thus it does not become a part of our own familiar mental property) when we merely put a pencil mark by a striking passage. This is the crucial difference between pencilling and abstracting. In the latter case, the writer's material is taken and rendered into forms of thought and expression familiar to ourselves. Our minds master his. With pencillings, we are simply swept along whither the writer wills. We are not forced to make his thoughts meaningful in terms of our own body of knowledge. So they do not become ours, and consequently they soon fade from mind.

[1] See C. A. Mace, *The Psychology of Learning*, Pelican, 1962 ed., p. 41 (the whole of chapter 3 is in fact relevant).

Clearly, some intermediate strategy — between pencillings at one extreme and abstracting at the other — is required. What we want is something that will let us take in new material as rapidly as is consonant with retaining its key points in our memories. Those readers who know of it may well be thinking of the *Schlagwort*, or 'Striking Word', system in this connection. It works as follows. The crucial word or concept in a passage is used as a key. It is put as a heading on a 5 x 3" card. On the card can be entered either a simple page reference to the book in which the passage occurs, or a brief synopsis of the passage followed by this page reference. The key words thus produced are next put in alphabetical order in a 5 x 3" card index. In the blank spaces flanking the reference word at the top of the card, can be inserted cross-references to related concepts elsewhere within the index.

For convenience, the details of the book are abbreviated (e.g. Carney, *Content Analysis* could become *CA*). An alphabetical list of these abbreviations, each abbreviation followed by full details about the book concerned, is then kept, as a separate card index, for use along with the *Schlagwort* system.

We now have a reference system that is much superior to sheafs of pages of abstracts. Additions can be made to it. For instance, other passages from other books relating to a particular crucial concept can be recorded subsequently on the initial card or on a second card with the same concept as its reference key, but marked '2'. New cards containing new concepts can be inserted. Filing and searching operations are easy — a thing which cannot be said of typescript pages, for these may each contain a multitude of filable items or important points.

Readers who have used this system will, however, be thinking ruefully of some of the snags that are involved. For instance, we must remember what the key words are. Over the years, and as the card index grows, this task is not always easy: our interests shift and change. It is necessary to be using the system all the time if all its many keys are to be at the forefront of our awareness, and there is a point at which it just gets too big. Also, although we can simply list page references under each 'striking word', it does not pay to do so. In order to be able quickly to review the point behind each such reference, we really must enter some details of the passage involved. This entry involves almost as much time as a straightforward abstract in the form of pages of notes. Finally, the system is not as flexible as it at first appears. We can add to it easily enough. But, if we want to make a fundamental change in the 'Striking Words', we meet all the difficulties inherent in trying to reconstitute any elaborate system of cross-reference. And it is quite probable that some such changes will have to be made. All it needs is a new insight, which indicates either that we should break up an important concept into several component parts, or that we should redesignate some such concept in other words. We will immediately find to what extent concepts come webbed together in clusters which are all somehow or other associated, like frogs' spawn.

Rewriting twenty-odd sets of cards every so often is a task for someone with more time than people tend to have.

Let us move from the *Schlagwort* system and the abstracting end of this range of activities down to the 'pencilling' end. For, as some of my readers may well be thinking, there is yet another stratagem located thereabouts. Instead of just pencilling in a line running down the side of a paragraph or underneath a phrase or sentence, we can use a set of symbols which will indicate what is in the passage and how important it is. Obvious enough, but not as unsophisticated as you might think. For, using the awareness acquired in the course of conducting a content analysis or two to help us evolve a set of symbols, we will very soon have the equivalent of our own special shorthand system at our disposal.

We will be operating with a limited, and therefore easily rememberable, range of symbols. These will compel us to retranslate the writer's words and thoughts into our own, but we will be able to do so in the very briefest form. We will also have the various marks as a form of index. A snag is that we will normally have to own the books which we mark. Marks gently put on with a soft lead can be rubbed out without a trace, so a researcher might possibly use this stratagem even if he has a book to review which is not his own. The number of books involved in a year's study is not likely to be so great as to make this practice prohibitively expensive, especially in this age of paperbacks. With practice, an investigator should be able to operate at something greater than 80% of normal reading speed, yet end up with at least the key points retained in his memory and a permanent index of all relevant points at his fingertips. In practice this stratagem has so many advantages in comparison with the others that, once its implications are grasped, it is usually adopted as the workhorse for all operations of this type.

As an experiment, enquire around among your friends to find who is using some such set of symbols. There will probably be several such people. Get them to describe their sets. Then compare the results. You will probably find that things are as follows. People start with quite simple sets, shaped to deal with particular problems. But the sets tend to grow and develop with use. They come to be usable for a more general range of tasks, in fact. And, though no two sets are alike, they all tend in common to have symbols for certain types of things. We will now try building up a set of symbols of our own, using other people's experience to help us get started, to see where it leads us.

First, then, and most obviously, a set of symbols will be needed to serve simply as descriptive indicators. We will want to be able to indicate that a particular bibliographical reference identifies an important book, for instance. Or there may be a particularly well-chosen phrase that we want to remember: we will need a mark to locate its line in the text. We will want to be able to do likewise to show where a particularly telling point has been made. And it will be enormously helpful to have symbols which can indicate levels of increasing importance: such as 'important', 'very important', 'very important indeed', for instance. These can go around other signs to indicate the degree of importance of such signs. Thus we can circle a sign as a mark that it is important, and shade the circle if it is very important.

We could even put the whole passage inside a ruled oblong, if it is very important indeed.

Other things for which people all seem to have symbols of one sort or another, in this part of their symbol systems, are as follows: example, illustration, summary/summation, back reference and enunciation of a general principle. It may also prove helpful to be able to distinguish between a major point, a case involving two alternative points and a list of points (in a summary or typology for instance).

Signs for 'negative', 'absent', and 'anti-' will be found necessary too. These also can be combined with other signs, to make the latter more specific.

Already, one fact has emerged. If we can *combine* symbols, we can represent a great many more things without adding to our basic collection of symbols. Used only by themselves, independently, three symbols can designate three things. Used in combination, the same three symbols will provide another dozen designatory combinations. Once the full significance of this elementary tactic of combining symbols is appreciated, these 'signs in the margin' cease to be a mere list of indicators and become a kind of shorthand system. This is a major insight into, and development of, our symbol set.

Symbol sets tend to have signs denoting various semantic matters: when coming upon a writer's definitions of his basic concepts, for instance, some way of indicating that point, and what is involved will be needed. And here is where to apply the principle just learned about combining symbols. For, by simply adding a number after the symbol for a definition, different *kinds* of definition can be designated. For instance:

d_1 ('Historically, the word had the following meanings') historical definition;

d_2 ('When he uses the word, he's always talking about such and such') definition in terms of actual usage;

d_3 ('When he uses the word, it's always in a context with such and such a mood') psychological definition;

d_4 ('When such and such happens, you've got [the word]') operational definition.

s_1 There will also be found a need for a sign indicating that an assumption of the writer's is nestling in the lines opposite.

s_2 Another useful sign is one indicating that a qualification or criticism of something or other in a text has been found.

$s_2 s_1$ A combination of these two symbols gives a little combination saying: 'Here is something contrary to what one might expect.' This combination will be found very useful when an investigator is reading his way into new material.

v, vj   Almost inevitably, too, some way of indicating a viewpoint or a value judgement will be wanted. Reading someone else's work always brings home how much his viewpoint differs from our own, how much his way of perceiving things is affecting what it is he says he is seeing. This difficulty occurs particularly, of course, if this 'he' is talking about psycho-social events. Now, as it happens, work on the psychology of creativity indicates that creative persons tend to be unusually aware of the way in which their ways of perceiving reality are distorting that reality. So our symbol system will do well to have some kind of symbols to tell us when this kind of thing is going on. Let us call these 'symbols to do with the psychology of perception.' We will probably find we want a way of

Fr, Fa, v, designating a frame of reference, a focus of attention, a viewpoint, a world
v, view (fixed belief about some basic human or physical relationship), an
i, i,, s₃ image, a stereotype, and a psychological (rather than logical) reaction.

People seem, too, to evolve symbols to indicate the ways in which writers go about reaching their conclusions. These vary, from a sign which simply says 'analysis is going on here,' to a range of signs which indicate different types of analysis — deductive, inductive, comparative, converging and so on.

In case it may prove helpful for readers to have some idea of the sort of thing that tends to be involved here, a list follows. The first one or two concepts will probably be found in most elaborated symbol systems. But this list is unusually elaborate, as result of my preoccupation with techniques of analysis. Though far from perfect, it may show others where to start to develop their capacity to annotate distinctions between different types of analytical operations.

Common, then, to many sets of symbols are signs for: analysis ($\emptyset$); question (Q); comparative (cf.); empirical analysis by a practical test ($\emptyset_1$) & deductive ($\emptyset_o$).

More highly elaborated symbols:

inductive analysis (-- -- -- --); profiling (-- -- -- --); analysis by rating on ideal types/polar extremes (o-- -- --o); time series analysis (-- -- -- --); ranking ($\vdots$); analysis in terms of a developing situation, over time (-- -- -- --) — see figure A2, below. Convergence analysis ( ); circular causation ( ); chain of causation ( ); logical tree ( ); trend analysis ( ); Venn diagramming ( ); other forms of overlapping ( ); multivariate analysis (xy^t); analysis via mean, median, mode (LCD).

There are other areas which will tend to be developed, as a general rule, in any set of symbols which has been at all well elaborated. Communications phenomena and models are instances. But the areas detailed so far are the major and most generally represented ones. So let us pause to consider what they have to tell us about this way of performing synopsis or abstracting.

Now, first of all, we have looked at this business very much as a content analyst would. We have looked for underlying regularities. We have chosen to group signs in terms of the areas in which basic things occur, according to our experience in the analysis of language. We have also tended to cast our set of symbols in a way that suggests categories and quantification. This line of approach can be pushed a little further. Clearly, by analyzing the contents of a symbol set, we can determine the preoccupations of its user. Put the other way round, a symbol set can be specially built to perform content analysis for us as we go about our abstracting. Let me go into these matters in more detail, to explain what I mean.

It should be clear that, once certain basic matters have been coped with, a set of symbols can be elaborated in any way desired. So the overall set of symbols, and the way they are used, will tell a lot about the annotator's preoccupations. It is not just a matter of which symbols are used. Also significant are the statistics indicating which of those symbols are most frequently used. There are various categories — denotative, semantic, psychological, analytical, etc. — and different degrees of use — high, medium and low — within each. Think of all this as a 4 x 3 matrix. It is an easy matter to go through a marked book and assign each symbol to its category and frequency. This sorting establishes patterns of usage. That certain symbols are particularly dear to their user is indicated by the fact that he makes so many of them. For 'content' is largely put into a book by the interests of the person reading it: the same book can, observably, mean two different things to two different readers.[2]

Now, a person's use of his symbol system is not altogether under conscious control. There are too many signs, and people generally read too fast for self-consciousness. Yet each leaves behind him a trail of marked books. It is thus possible to probe into our own subconscious. Looking back, we become horribly conscious of just what we saw — and all that we failed to see — in a particular book; of how crude our ways of abstracting were. We can see the areas in which growth has occurred — and whether it is still going on. We simply compare the full range of the symbol system at an earlier point with its range at a later point. New signs indicate growth. Areas specially prolific in new signs indicate the 'cutting edge' of awareness. Currently, in my own symbol system, for instance, signs relating to transactionalism (to do with one person's perception of someone else's perception of something or other, and so on) are beginning to proliferate in this way.

It is even possible to probe around among the areas of awareness currently identifiable in a symbol system, to locate blind spots, and then to devise ways of filling them in. Awareness of the ways in which we are going about abstracting gives a control over it which makes it into an altogether different and more sophisticated progress. Try it for a month or so. You — and it — will never be the same again.

---

[2] See Krippendorff, at page 70 of *Communication Content*, and page 13 of Gerbner's "The Case for Cultural Indicators".

Just as we gain a heightened awareness of our own frame of reference, so awareness of the frameworks of others also becomes immeasurably more sensitive. Suppose we are operating a system geared to pick up definitions, viewpoints and assumptions, and the author does not define his terms, does not spell out his assumptions, and lets his viewpoint interfere with his interpretation of his data. That system will expose such weaknesses starkly. A lecturer in a seminar, if he is performing so, is like a burglar setting off one silent alarm after another by going through a series of beams of invisible light. Method, or lack of it, is quickly and clearly signalled. So is radical novelty. A predetermined system cannot cope with it. What generally happens is that the first time someone meets an instance of it, he forces it into his frame of reference. But the subconscious is unhappy. It baulks violently, the second time. By the third occurrence at the very latest, he is consciously aware that he has to do some rethinking of his system, no matter how inconvenient this prospect may be.

Think what this means when reviewing a book. The reviewer goes through at fairly high speed, yet is left with his own index. He has only to flip back through the pages to identify all points at the 'very important indeed' level (or at the 'very important' level, if he wants a more comprehensive review). He can then see what sorts of things tend to occur most frequently therein. The thickness of the clustering of symbols tells much about the relative importance of this or that chapter, or, indeed, of the book as a whole. More than this, a special symbol system can be made just for use on the book — a kind of miniature content analysis, geared specifically to the things the book *ought* to be discussing. The reviewer next reads through with all speed, then goes back and counts heads in the various categories. This is not the way to become a popular reviewer, maybe; but this reviewer can be sure of his facts. There is nothing quite so pathetic as to see a person presenting a book review challenged by the quotation of counter-instances, to have his generalizations crumple as they are shown to be based on partial consideration of the facts. It is even more embarrassing if this happens in print, and if you are the reviewer. A system will very rapidly pay its way, then, once it has been developed past the early, teething stages.

Think also of what this means for an investigator reading his way into a field. He can decide in advance what are the new insights which he wants to acquire, and devise a set of symbols that will make him sensitive to them when they crop up. My own symbol system, for instance, is, compared with others I have examined, very lavishly developed as concerns signs for analytical techniques. I have been deliberately trying to expand my skills in this area, so have created a fairly sensitive 'early warning system' to detect what is being done in this regard by the writers I am reading. If these writers really want to drive home points that I have not anticipated, I will still be made aware of it, because the unanticipated novelties will not enter my symbol system. Lynch's book is one I remember in this connection. I have never had to do so much rethinking of my symbol system for any other single book. Others too seem to have been similarly influenced by Lynch's work.[3]

This has been a brief look at the bare bones — the basic symbols — of a suggested system. We have also looked at some of the things which can be done with it. This appendix can conclude by considering further how any researcher can make a system of his own. For, fundamentally, your system has to be of your own making. No one else has quite *your* set of interests or problems to investigate. Unless you make it for yourself, gradually, by trial and error, it will never be your intimate possession, springing readily to mind. However, you can build it much more soundly and quickly by paying attention to what others have done.

That trick of putting a number after a letter will be remembered. It enables various aspects of the concept symbolized by that letter - 'definition', say — to be separately identified. Now, this is a principle which can be extended. Suppose someone finds that, within the general conceptual area designated by a symbol, various aspects repeatedly have to be separately identified when he is abstracting. The master symbol can be developed accordingly, adding numbers to designate these related or associated concepts. This trick saves having to introduce wholly new symbols. It also allows the system room for internal growth as it matures. Thus the range of things which can be represented can be enormously increased while keeping the total number of symbols within memorizable bounds.

Consider an example which shows how this principle works. Start with the concept 'image'. This general conceptual area can be further elaborated by specifying important derivative ideas within it:

Figure A.1: A CONCEPTUAL AREA

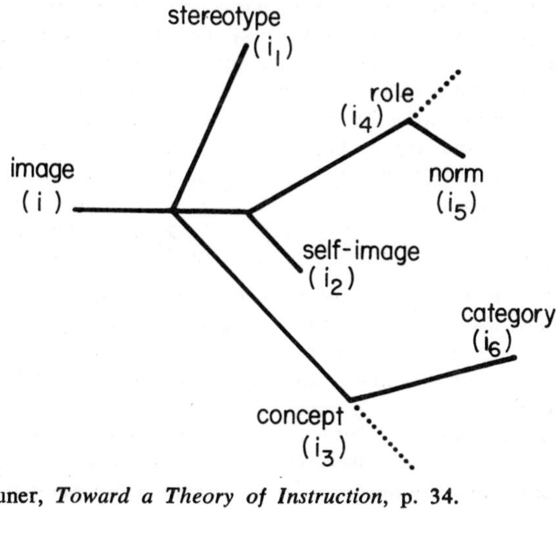

[3] See Bruner, *Toward a Theory of Instruction*, p. 34.

This kind of thing can be done with most such basic conceptual areas. If it cannot, then the basic concepts have not been thought out well enough; they should be thought through again.

While it is not wise to be overeager to add a new concept, there is no need to worry about doing so, either. It will be found that a mind can hold only a certain number of bits of information. There can be increase in the size, but not the number, of the bits. So the new concept has to fit into the structure of the system. And it has to 'work', by proving repeatedly useful. If it does these things, then it will be retained without effort. If it does not, it won't, no matter how much effort has been put into keeping it. The symbols have to earn their keep. There is no room for freeloaders in our overpopulated consciousnesses.

Readers will each shape his or her own system according to special interests. These, of course, no one can predict. But the following general guidelines may be found useful. First, if you start with the minimum number of symbols, then the actual needs experienced in your reading will suggest others to you. This cautious beginning is better than starting with a numerous preordained set of symbols, for you may get into the habit of using them clumsily in your reading; you will be still too inexperienced to spot it quickly if one or more of them is not working very well. Secondly, it may pay to regard the areas already shown to be well represented in most symbol systems as growth points. You can expect it will be necessary to make up symbols for concepts relating to such growth points. You can do this against a background of awareness of others' experiences and of the general principles involved. Thirdly, your symbol system will probably undergo an initial period of quick growth. It will then grow rather slowly, in fits and starts, as particularly seminal books have to be encompassed by it. Fourthly, it will help if you monitor it. A check every three months to see what is happening to it will tell you a lot about yourself, as well as about your system. Fifthly, you may also find it helpful to run a cross-check in the form of a reading tally. You can keep such a tally on a monthly basis by maintaining a reading list scored by a points system — so many points for a book, as against one point for a journal article, or individual chapter in a book, for instance. Such a tally helps keep up your in-put of reading material, if only by showing you how much less of it there is than you supposed. It also gives you some idea of how fast you are getting through your reading, so that, in the light of this knowledge, you can start planning your reading ahead.

Readers will probably average between five and ten major books in a year's reading. As these are generally available in paperback, purchase should not be beyond the bounds of feasibility. Hence the drawback to using such a symbol system — that one has to own the books involved — is not insuperable.

I have referred only very briefly to two other 'growth areas' which, experience indicates, you may well want to develop. These concern the concepts of models and communications. It should prove helpful to be aware of the following specific points, which are discoveries arising out of practical experience. If you are reading books on social or psychological topics, then you will quite certainly want a symbol to indicate 'theory' and another to indicate 'model'. Apart from the fact that your own mind employs frameworks of reference to deal with abstract ideas, the writers whom you read will be actually talking about such frameworks, referring to them as models or theories.

Some signs to distinguish between various types of systems will also prove to be required, almost certainly. Will you want to distinguish between static, structural-functional systems (and even, within such static systems, between structures and interrelationships), and dynamic, cybernetics-type systems?[4] If you are dealing with communications phenomena, you will probably experience a need to be able to symbolize a communications network. It will also, probably, prove highly convenient to have symbols for the following concepts, which are featured prominently in communications theory or its analysis:

category, content analysis, decision-making (as a theoretical framework), feedback, pay-off, semantic field, target audience, and theme.

There is one final matter. This is most often brought up in discussions commencing: "If only someone had told me in the beginning . . . ." When stated, especially before you have experience in operating a symbol system, it seems too simple and obvious to be of much significance. You have a choice between using either recognizable letters or little pictograms (which is why I have referred to 'symbols' throughout the discussion). Pictograms have the initial disadvantage of not being familiar. But this unfamiliarity soon vanishes. They have the lasting advantage of enabling you to think yourself free of words in at least parts of your thought processes. Diagrams can relate to things without the disturbing emotional undertones from which words, of their nature, can never win freedom.[5] Moreover some things may be inexpressible in a single word (and therefore by a single initial letter), but easily representable by some simple diagrammatic form. And it is as easy to elaborate a basic pictogram-concept, with or without the use of numbers, as it is to elaborate upon a basic concept tied to a letter.

---

[4] There is an excellent discussion of the evolution of the general idea which is here termed 'systems', in Buckley, *Sociology and Modern Systems Theory*, chapter 2. Chapters 3 to 6 of Young's *Systems of Political Science* provide a description of the different varieties of systems approach currently in use.

[5] On the different types of thinking facilitated by diagrams as opposed to words, see McLuhan, *The Gutenberg Galaxy*, pp. 77-79.

Figure A.2: A PICTOGRAM
DEVELOPED

KEY:

(a) Analysis of trends or occurrences in a series of happenings over a period of time.

(b) Analysis of same on either side of a watershed event.

(c) Analysis of trends against the background of a developing situation or crisis.

(d) Cycle of phases in a maturation process.

(e) Continuum between two polar extremes.

(f) Two axes, enabling two-dimensional plotting between two sets of such extremes.

(g) Ranking order, series arranged between high scores (top end) and low ones (bottom).

(h) Yardstick/criterion (r a n k i n g order used as basis of comparison for a series).

(i) Geo-historical survey or the like (comparison of events in a range of countries over a period of time).

(j) Profiling (rating of composite set of scores on a number of interrelated dimensions).

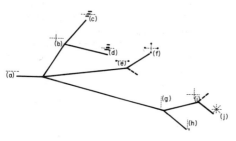

You may, however, choose to use letters. Actually, what is generally done is to use a mixture of both pictograms and letters. In any case, if you are using letters, it is possible, by using different sorts of letters, to step up the suggestive power of a symbol system. Thus you might, for instance, employ the letters of our own alphabet, in the lower case, for simple descriptive signs, reserving the upper case for signs of a psychological nature. You might use paired letters to indicate some special variety of theoretical or analytical approach (CA - content analysis, DM - decision making, SF - semantic field). You might use letters from another script — Greek for instance, or Russian — to pick out conceptual areas upon which you particularly wish to focus, that of semantics, for instance, or of modelling.

From all this, it should be clear that such a set of symbols is a superb general-purpose tool for abstracting, reviewing or synopsizing. This is not to suggest that you should use only one of the methods of abstracting considered in this appendix. Indeed, for convenience in circumstances of frequent, rapid reference (or for an easily portable reference-system), you may want to constitute a special purpose *Schlagwort* system. This might record the key points identified in a sub-field of specialist 'literature' by a symbol system but scattered through a large number of books.

From the few general principles given in this appendix you can work out your own special set. And that set will be an interrelated body of analytical constructs, not just a list of notational devices. For there is much practical and theoretical experience behind these few general principles. Moreover, to use the system, you have to force the writer's message to relate to your framework of reference. Omissions and inadequacies are thus revealed, as well as strengths and novelties. As a consequence, much is retained in your memory, even on a single reading of a text. And, in the process, you construct a permanent index for later use. This symbol system, in fact, gives you more retention, with less loss of speed, than does any other of the procedures considered in this appendix. It is also the most flexible and easy to live with. Furthermore, it enables you to direct your inquiries even when starting out into an unknown field, and also to monitor many of your hitherto subconscious assumptions. It is the logical outcome of the knowledge you will by this time have gained of how to conduct content analyses.

BIBLIOGRAPHY

T. W. Adorno, E. Frenkel-Brunswick, D. J. Levinson and R. N. Sanford, *The Authoritarian Personality*, Harper, 1950.

G. W. Allport, *The Nature of Prejudice*, Doubleday Anchor, 1958.

G. W. Allport and L. J. Postman, "The Basic Psychology of Rumor", in Maccoby *et al*, *Readings in Social Psychology*, pp. 54-65.

G. A. Almond and G. B. Powell, *Comparative Politics: A Developmental Approach*, Little, Brown, 1966.

P. Aries, *Centuries of Childhood: A Social History of Family Life*, Vintage ed., 1965.

E. Aronson, "The Need for Achievement as Measured by Graphic Expression" in Atkinson, *Motives in Fantasy, Action and Society*, pp. 249-65.

—see under Lindzey.

J. E. Atkinson, ed., *Motives in Fantasy, Action and Society*, Van Nostrand, 1958.

R. F. Bales, *Interaction Process Analysis*, Addison-Wesley, 1950.

F. E. Barcus, *Communications Content: Analysis of the Research*, 1900-1958, (unpublished) Ph.D. thesis, U. of Illinois, 1959.

——Appendix: "Education in Content Analysis: A Survey", pp. 539-54 in Gerbner *et al*, *Analysis of Communication Content*.

F. Barron, *Creativity and Personal Freedom*, Van Nostrand, 1968.

A. H. Barton, "The Concept of Property Space in Social Research", in Lazarsfeld and Rosenberg, *The Language of Social Research*, pp. 40-53.

—see under Lazarsfeld.

R. A. Bauer, I. de S. Pool and L. A. Dexter, *American Business and Public Policy*, Atherton, 1963.

C. R. Bell, *Middle Class Families*, Routledge & Kegan Paul, 1968.

L. Benson, "An Approach to the Scientific Study of Past Public Opinion", *Public Opinion Quarterly* 32, 1968, pp. 522-67.

C. Bereiter and M. B. Freedman, "Fields of Study and the People in Them", in Sanford, *The American College*, pp. 563-96.

B. R. Berelson, *Content Analysis in Communication Research*, Free Press, 1952.

——"Content Analysis" in Lindzey, *Handbook of Social Psychology*, vol. I, pp. 488-522.

B. R. Berelson and M. Janowitz, eds., *Reader in Public Opinion*, Free Press, 1953 ed.

B. R. Berelson, P. F. Lazarsfeld and W. N. McPhee, *Voting*, U. of Chicago Press, 1954.

——"Political Perception", in Maccoby, *Readings in Social Psychology*, pp. 72-85.

H. Bloch, "A Revolution in Classical Scholarship?", *Journal of Hellenic Studies* 88, 1968, pp. 136-7.

K. E. Boulding, *The Image: Knowledge in Life and Society*, Ann Arbor ed., 1961.

E. A. Bowles, ed., *Computers in Humanistic Research*, Prentice-Hall, 1967.

L. Broom and P. Selznik, *Sociology*, Harper & Row, 1968.

J. A. C. Brown, *Techniques of Persuasion: From Propaganda to Brainwashing*, Pelican, 1963.

R. Brown, "Models of Attitude Change", pp. 1-85 in the following:

R. Brown, E. Galanter, E. H. Hess and G. Mandler, *New Directions in Psychology*, Holt, Rinehart & Winston, 1962.

J. S. Bruner, *Toward a Theory of Instruction*, Norton ed., 1968.

J. S. Bruner, J. J. Goodnow and G. A. Austin, *A Study of Thinking*, Science Editions, N. Y., 1962.

L. Bryson, ed., *The Communication of Ideas*, Harper & Row, 1948.

W. J. Buckley, *Sociology and Modern Systems Theory*, Prentice-Hall, 1967.

R. W. Budd, R. K. Thorp and L. Donohew, *Content Analysis of Communications*, Macmillan, N. Y., 1967.

U. P. Burke, "A Survey of the Popularity of Ancient Historians 1450-1700", *History and Theory* 5, 1966, pp. 135-52.

A. W. Burks, "Icon, Index and Symbol", *Philosophy and Phenomenological Research* 9, 1949, pp. 673-89.

T. F. Carney, "Cicero's Picture of Marius", *Wiener Studien* 73, 1960, pp. 84-122.

——review of W. C. Helmbold and E. N. O'Neil, *Plutarch's Quotations*, *Journal of Hellenic Studies* 82, 1962, pp. 168-9.

——"The Picture of Marius in Valerius Maximus", *Rheinisches Museum für Philologie* 105, 1962, pp. 289-337.

——"The Words *sodes* and *quaeso* in Terence", *Acta Classica* 7, 1964, pp. 57-63.

——"Commentary on a Psychoanalytical Study of Alexander the Great" in *Proceedings of the Second Annual Great Plains History Conference*, U. of Manitoba, 1967, pp. 88-95.

——"Political Legends on Hadrian's Coinage: Policies and Problems", *The Turtle* 6 (5), 1967, pp. 291-303.

——"The Changing Picture of Marius in Ancient Literature", *Proceedings of the African Classical Associations* 10, 1967, pp. 5-22.

——"A Pre-industrial City through Contemporaries' Eyes: Content Analysis of Views of Rome" (mimeo) paper to the 1968 meeting of the American Political Science Association.

——"How Suetonius' Lives reflect on Hadrian", *Proceedings of the African Classical Associations* 11, 1968, pp. 7-21.

——"Content Analysis for High School Students", *Quarterly of the Manitoba History Teachers' Association* 1, 1969, pp. 3-17.

——"Problems and Prejudices in the Humanities", *Bulletin de L'Association canadienne des Humanités* 20, 1969, pp. 27-48.

——"The Emperor Claudius and the Grain Trade", paper delivered to the Northern Great Plains History Conference, 1969 (mimeo, Department of History, U of Manitoba).

——*Bureaucracy in Traditional Society: Romano-Byzantine Bureaucracies viewed from Within*, Coronado, 1970.

J. B. Carroll, *Language and Thought*, Prentice-Hall, 1964.

A. V. Cicourel, *Method and Measurement in Sociology*, Free Press, 1964.

D. F. Cox, "Clues for Advertising Strategists" in Dexter and White, *People, Society and Mass Communications*, pp. 359-94.

E. H. Dance, *History the Betrayer: A Study in Bias*, Hutchinson, 1960.

J. Deese, "Conceptual Categories in the Study of Content" in Gerbner *et al*, *Analysis of Communication Content*, pp. 39-56.

W. Delany, "Development and Decline of Patrimonial and Bureaucratic Administrations", *Administrative Science Quarterly* 7 (4), 1963, pp. 485-501.

H. Delatte, "Key Words and Poetic Themes in Propertius and Tibullus", *Revue* (International Organization for Ancient Languages Analysis by Computer) 3, 1967, pp. 31-79.

K. W. Deutsch, *The Nerves of Government: Models of Political Communication and Control*, Free Press, 1963.

——*The Analysis of International Relations*, Prentice-Hall, 1968.

L. A. Dexter, "Communications — Pressure, Influence or Education?" pp. 395-409 in the following:

L. A. Dexter and D. M. White (eds), *People, Society and Mass Communications*, Free Press, 1964.

J. T. Dorsey, Jr., "An Information-Energy Model", in Heady and Stokes, *Papers in Comparative Public Administration*, pp. 37-57.

K. Dovring, "The Annals of Science: Troubles with Mass Communication and Semantic Differentials in 1744 and Today", *American Behavioral Scientist* 9, 1965, pp. 9-14.

M. Duverger, *The Idea of Politics: The Uses of Power in Society*, Methuen ed., 1966.

D. Easton, *A Systems Analysis of Political Life*, Wiley, 1965.

H. Eckstein, ed., *Internal War: Problems and Approaches*, Free Press, 1964.

W. Edwards and A. Tversky, eds. *Decision Making*, Penguin, 1967.

S. N. Eisenstadt, "Bureaucracy and Bureaucratization", *Current Sociology* 7, 1958, pp. 99-165.

A. E. Ellis and F. A. Favat, "From Computer to Criticism: An Application of Automatic Content Analysis to the Study of Literature" in Stone *et al, The General Inquirer*, pp. 628-38.

E. H. Erikson, *Childhood and Society*, Norton ed., 1950.

R. R. Fagen, *Politics and Communication*, Little, Brown, 1966.

M. I. Finley, "The Ancient Greeks and their Nation: The Sociological Problem", *The British Journal of Sociology* 5 (3), 1954, pp. 253-64.

R. Fletcher, *The Family and Marriage in Britain*, Pelican, 1966.

J. A. Garraty, "The Application of Content Analysis to Biography and History" in Pool, *Trends in Content Analysis*, pp. 171-87.

A. L. George, "Quantitative and Qualitative Approaches to Content Analysis" in Pool, *Trends in Content Analysis*, pp. 7-32.

G. Gerbner, "A Framework for the Study of Communications", (mimeo) Annenberg School of Communications, U. of Pennsylvania, 1961.

——"Ideological Tendencies and Political Perspectives in News Reporting", *Journalism Quarterly* 41, 1964, pp. 495-508.

——"Images across Cultures: Teachers in Mass Media Fiction and Drama", *The School Review* 74, 1964, pp. 212-29.

——"On Content Analysis and Critical Research in Mass Communication", in Dexter and White, *People, Society and Mass Communications*, pp. 488-99.

——"The Case for Cultural Indicators, with Violence in the Mass Media as a Case in Point", (revised) paper to the American Political Science Association's 1969 meeting (mimeo), Annenberg School of Communications, U. of Pennsylvania, 1969.

——"Toward 'Cultural Indicators': The Analysis of Mass Mediated Public Message Systems", in Gerbner *et al, Analysis of Communication Content*, 123-32.

——"Cultural Indicators: The Case of Violence in Television Drama", *The Annals of the American Academy of Political and Social Science* 388, 1970, pp. 69-81.

G. Gerbner, O. R. Holsti, K. Krippendorff, W. J. Paisley and P. J. Stone, *The Analysis of Communication Content*, Wiley, 1969.

B. Glad, "The Role of Psychoanalytic Biography in Political Science", (mimeo) paper to the 1968 meeting of the American Political Science Association.

D. H. Goldhamer, "Towards a More General Inquirer: Convergence of Structure and Context of Meaning" in Gerbner *et al, Analysis of Communication Content*, pp. 343-54.

F. I. Greenstein, *Children and Politics*, Yale U. Press, 1965.

C. S. Hall, "Content Analysis of Dreams: Categories, Units and Norms" in Gerbner *et al, Analysis of Communication Content*, pp. 147-58.

C. S. Hall and R. L. Van de Castle, *The Content Analysis of Dreams*, Appleton-Century-Crofts, 1966.

E. T. Hall, *The Silent Language*, Doubleday, 1959.

S. I. Hayakawa, *Symbol, Status and Personality*, Harcourt, Brace & World, 1953.

——*Language in Thought and Action*, Harcourt, Brace & World, 1963 ed.

G. Heady and S. L. Stokes (eds), *Papers in Comparative Public Administration*, U. of Michigan, 1962.

H. Heckmann (ed.), *Elektronische Datenverarbeitung in der Musikwissenschaft*, Regensburg, 1967.

R. L. Heilbroner, *The Making of Economic Society*, Prentice-Hall, 1962.

J. H. Hexter, "The Loom of Language and the Fabric of Imperatives: The Case of *Il Principe* and *Utopia*," *American Historical Review* 69, 1964, pp. 945-68.

A. B. Hodgetts, *What Culture? What Heritage?*, Ontario Institute for Studies in Education, 1968.

O. R. Holsti, *Content Analysis for the Social Sciences and Humanities*, Addison-Wesley, 1969.

——"Content Analysis" in Lindzey and Aronson, *Handbook of Social Psychology*, vol. II, pp. 596-692.

——Introduction to Part II ("Aspects of Inference from Content Data") and

——"A Computer Content-Analysis Program for Analysing Attitudes: The Measurement of Qualities and Performance", both in Gerbner *et al, Analysis of Communication Content*, pp. 109-121 and 355-80 respectively.

C. I. Hovland (ed.), *The Order of Presentation in Persuasion*, Yale U. Press, 1953.

C. I. Hovland, I. L. Janis and H. H. Kelley, *Communication and Persuasion*, Yale U. Press, 1957.

L. Hudson, *Contrary Imaginations: A Psychological Study of the English Schoolboy*, Pelican, 1966.

——*Frames of Mind: Ability, Perception and Self-Perception in the Arts and Sciences*, Pelican, 1970.

D. Hymes, ed., *Language in Culture and Society: A Reader in Linguistics and Anthropology*, Harper International, 1966.

H. P. Iker and N. I. Harway, "A Computer Systems Approach towards the Recognition and Analysis of Content" in Gerbner *et al, Analysis of Communication Content*, pp. 381-405.

R. Inglehart and R. Schoenberger, "Communications and Political Mobilization", (mimeo) paper to the 1968 meeting of the American Political Science Association.

A. Inkeles, *What is Sociology? An Introduction to the Discipline and Profession*, Prentice-Hall, 1964.

H. A. Innis, *The Bias of Communication*, U. of Toronto Press, 1951.

H. R. Isaacs, *Scratches on Our Minds: American Images of China and India*, Day, 1958.

——*The New World of Negro Americans*, Viking, 1963.

I. L. Janis, "The Problem of Validating Content Analysis" in Lasswell *et al, Language of Politics*, pp. 55-82.

I. L. Janis and S. Feshbach, "Effects of Fear-arousing Communications", *Journal of Abnormal Social Psychology* 48, 1953, pp. 78-92.

A. H. M. Jones, *The Later Roman Empire 284-602: A Social, Economic and Administrative Survey*, Blackwell, 1964.

G. H. S. Jordan, "Popular Literature and Imperial Sentiment: Changing Attitudes, 1870-90", Canadian Historical Association, *Historical Papers presented at the Annual Meeting*, 1967, pp. 149-55.

A. Kaplan, *The Conduct of Inquiry: Methodology for Behavioral Science*, Chandler, 1964.

E. Katz, "The Two-Step Flow of Communication: An Up-to-date Report on an Hypothesis", *Public Opinion Quarterly* 21, 1957, pp. 61-78.

E. Katz and P. F. Lazarsfeld, *Personal Influence: The Part played by People in the Flow of Mass Communications*, Free Press, 1955.

—see under Menzel.

E. Kitzinger, "The Cult of Images in the Age before Iconoclasm", *Dumbarton Oaks Papers* 8, 1954, pp. 82-150.

N. Kogan and M. A. Wallach, "Risk Taking as a Function of the Situation, the Person and the Group" in Mandler *et al, New Directions in Psychology III*, pp. 113-278.

K. Krippendorff, Introduction to Part I ("Theories and Analytical Constructs") and

——"Models and Messages: Three Prototypes" both in Gerbner *et al, Analysis of Communication Content*, pp. 3-16 and 69-106 respectively.

A. Kuhn, *The Study of Society: A Unified Approach*, Irwin-Dorsey, 1963.

J. Laffal, "Contextual Similarities as a Basis for Inference" in Gerbner *et al, Analysis of Communication Content*, pp. 159-74.

R. D. Laing, H. Phillipson and A. R. Lee, *Interpersonal Perception: A Theory and Method of Research*, Tavistock, 1966.

M. Lane, ed., *Structuralism: A Reader*, Cape, 1970.

R. E. Lane, *Political Ideology: Why the American Common Man Believes What He Does*, Free Press, 1962.

R. E. Lane and D. O. Sears, *Public Opinion*, Prentice-Hall, 1964.

H. D. Lasswell, "The Structure and Function of Communication in Society" in Bryson, *The Communication of Ideas*, pp. 37-48.

——"Why be Quantitative?" and

——"Detection: Propaganda Detection and the Courts", both in the following:

H. D. Lasswell, N. Leites and associates, *Language of Politics: Studies in Quantitative Semantics*, Stewart 1949 (M.I.T. re-issue 1965).

H. D. Lasswell, D. Lerner and I. de S. Pool, *The Comparative Study of Symbols*, Hoover Institute Studies, Series C, Number 1; Stanford U. Press, 1952.

——see under Lerner.

D. Lawton, *Social Class, Language and Education*, Routledge & Kegan Paul, 1968.

P. F. Lazarsfeld, "Evidence and Inference in Social Research" in Lerner, *Evidence and Inference*, pp. 107-38.

——"Interpretation of Statistical Relations as a Research Operation", pp. 115-25 in:

P. F. Lazarsfeld and M. Rosenberg, eds., *The Language of Social Research*, Free Press, 1955.

P. F. Lazarsfeld and A. H. Barton, "Qualitative Measurement in the Social Sciences: Classification, Typologies and Indices", in Lerner and Lasswell, *The Policy Sciences*, pp. 155-92.

E. Leach, ed., *The Structural Study of Myth and Totemism*, Association of Social Anthropologists' Monographs Number 5, Tavistock, 1967.

D. Lerner, *The Passing of Traditional Society*, Free Press, 1957.

——, ed., *Evidence and Inference*, Free Press, 1958.

D. Lerner and H. D. Lasswell, eds., *The Policy Sciences*, Stanford U. Press, 1951.

C. Lévi-Strauss, *Structural Anthropology*, Basic Books, 1963.

I. M. Lewis, ed., *History and Social Anthropology*, Association of Social Anthropologists' Monographs Number 7, Tavistock, 1968.

G. Lindzey, ed., *The Handbook of Social Psychology*, Addison-Wesley, 1954.

G. Lindzey and E. Aronson, eds., *The Handbook of Social Psychology* (second edition), Addison-Wesley, 1968.

K. Lynch, *The Image of the City*, M.I.T. Press, 1960.

R. Lynn, *Attention, Arousal and the Orientation Reaction*, Pergamon Press, Oxford, 1966.

G. J. McCall and J. L. Simmons, *Identities and Interactions: An Examination of Human Associations in Everyday Life*, Free Press, 1966.

C. A. McClelland, *Theory and the International System*, Collier Macmillan, 1966.

D. C. McClelland, *The Achieving Society*, Van Nostrand, 1961.

E. E. Maccoby, T. M. Newcomb and E. L. Hartley, *Readings in Social Psychology*, Holt, Rinehart & Winston, 1958 ed.

C. A. Mace, *The Psychology of Learning*, Pelican, 1962 ed.

M. McLuhan, *The Gutenberg Galaxy*, U. of Toronto Press, 1962.

J. McNally and W. Murray, *Key Words to Literacy: A Basic Word List*, London, 1962.

R. C. Macridis, *The Study of Comparative Government*, Random House Studies in Political Science, Number 21, 1955.

G. Mandler, P. Mussen, N. Kogan and M. A. Wallach, *New Directions in Psychology III*, Holt, Rinehart & Winston, 1967.

N. N. Markel, *Psycholinguistics: An Introduction to the Study of Speech and Personality*, Dorsey, 1969.

M. U. Martel and G. J. McCall, "Reality Orientation and the Pleasure Principle: A Study in American Mass-Periodical Fiction (1890-1955)", in Dexter and White, *People, Society, and Mass Communications*, pp. 288-334.

H. Mattingly, E. A. Sydenham and others, *Roman Imperial Coinage*, Spink, London, 1923 following.

E. J. Meehan, *The Theory and Method of Political Analysis*, Dorsey, 1965.

H. Menzel and E. Katz, "Social Relations and Innovation in the Medical Profession: The Epidemiology of a New Drug", in Maccoby *et al*, *Readings in Social Psychology*, pp. 532-45.

R. K. Merton, A. S. Gray, B. Hockey, and H. C. Selvin, *Reader in Bureaucracy*, Free Press, 1952.

L. T. Milic, "Making Haste Slowly in Literary Computation", in Bowles, *Computers in Humanistic Research*, pp. 143-52.

G. Miller, "The Magical Number 7, plus or minus two: Some Limits on Our Capacity for Processing Information", *Psychological Review* 63, 1956, pp. 81-97.

R. B. Miller, *Statistical Concepts and Applications — A Nonmathematical Explanation*, Science Research Associates, 1968.

J. C. Mitchell, "The Concept and Use of Social Networks", pp. 1-50 of:

J. C. Mitchell, ed., *Social Networks in Urban Situations*, Manchester U. Press, 1969.

R. E. Mitchell, "The Use of Content Analysis for Explanatory Studies", *Public Opinion Quarterly* 31, 1967, pp. 230-41.

F. Mosteller and D. L. Wallace, *Inference and Disputed Authorship: The Federalist*, Addison-Wesley, 1964.

J. E. Mueller, "The Use of Content Analysis in International Relations" in Gerbner *et al*, *Analysis of Communication Content*, pp. 187-97.

P. Mussen, "Early Socialization: Learning and Identification" in Mandler, *New Directions in Psychology*, pp. 51-110.

——see Mandler.

R. C. North, O. R. Holsti, M. G. Zaninovich and D. A. Zinnes, *Content Analysis: A Handbook with Applications for the Study of International Crisis*, Northwestern U. Press, 1963.

D. M. Ogilvie, "Individual and Cultural Patterns of Fantasized Flight" in Gerbner *et al*, *Analysis of Communication Content*, pp. 243-59.

I. and P. Opie, *Lore and Language of Schoolchildren*, Oxford U. Press, 1959.

C. E. Osgood, S. Saporta and J. C. Nunnally, "Evaluative Assertion Analysis", *Litera* 3, 1956, pp. 47-102.

W. J. Paisley, "Identifying the Unknown Communicator in Painting, Literature and Music: The Significance of Minor Encoding Habits", *Journal of Communication* 14, 1964, pp. 219-37.

——Introduction to Part III ("The Recording and Notation of Data"), and

——"Studying 'Style' as a Deviation from Encoding Norms", both in Gerbner *et al*, *Analysis of Communication Content*, pp. 283-6 and 133-46 respectively.

K. Polanyi, C. M. Arensberg and H. W. Pearson, *Trade and Market in the Early Empires*: *Economies in History and Theory*, Free Press, 1957.

I. de S. Pool, ed., *Trends in Content Analysis*, U. of Illinois Press, Urbana, 1959.

I. de S. Pool, H. D. Lasswell, and D. Lerner, *Symbols of Democracy*, Hoover Institute Studies; Series C, Symbols: Number 4; Stanford U. Press, 1952.

N. Postman and C. Weingartner, *Linguistics*: *A Revolution in Teaching*, Delta, 1966.

G. Psathas, "Analyzing Dyadic Interaction" in Gerbner *et al*, *Analysis of Communication Content*, pp. 437-458.

L. W. Pye, ed., *Communications and Political Development*, Princeton U. Press, 1963.

——*Aspects of Political Development*, Little, Brown, 1966.

L. W. Pye and S. Verba, eds., *Political Culture and Political Development*, Princeton U. Press, 1965.

J. Raben, "Content Analysis and the Study of Poetry" in Gerbner *et al*, *Analysis of Communication Content*, pp. 175-86.

A. Rapoport, "A System-theoretic View of Content Analysis" in Gerbner *et al*, *Analysis of Communication Content*, pp. 17-38.

D. Riesman, "Comments" (on B. R. Berelson, "The State of Communication Research") in Dexter and White, *People, Society and Mass Communications*, pp. 512-516.

F. W. Riggs, "Agraria and Industria: Toward a Typology of Comparative Administration", in Siffin, *Toward the Comparative Study of Public Administration*, pp. 23-116.

——*Administration in Developing Countries*: *The Theory of Prismatic Society*, Houghton Mifflin, 1964.

——"Bureaucratic Politics in Comparative Perspective", *Journal of Comparative Administration* 1, 1969, pp. 5-38.

E. M. Rogers, *The Diffusion of Innovations*, Free Press, 1962.

N. Rokeach, *The Open and Closed Mind*, Basic Books, 1960.

N. Sanford, ed., *The American College*, Wiley, 1962.

I. G. Sarason, *Personality*: *An Objective Approach*, Wiley, 1966.

G. Sartori, *Democratic Theory*, Wayne State U. Press, 1960.

E. G. Schachtel, "On Memory and Childhood Amnesia", chapter 2 of Talbot, *The World of the Child*.

N. Schidt and B. Sveygaard, "Application of Computer Techniques to the Analysis of Byzantine Sticherarion Melodies", in Heckmann, *Elektronische Datenverarbeitung*.

W. Schramm, ed., *The Science of Human Communication*, Basic Books, 1963.

S. Y. Sedelow and W. A. Sedelow, Jr., "Categories and Procedures for Content Analysis in the Humanities", in Gerbner *et al*, *Analysis of Communication Content*, pp. 487-500.

H. Selye, *The Stress of Life*, Longman, 1957.

P. Selznik, *The Organizational Weapon*, Free Press, 1960.

E. S. Shneidman, "Logical Content Analysis: An Explication of Styles of 'Concludifying' ", in Gerbner *et al*, *Analysis of Communication Content*, pp. 261-79.

W. J. Siffin, ed., *Toward the Comparative Study of Public Administration*, Indiana U. Press, 1957.

G. Sjoberg, *The Preindustrial City Past and Present*, Free Press, 1960.

B. Snell, *The Discovery of the Mind: The Greek Origins of European Thought*, Blackwell, 1953.

P. J. Stone, "Confrontation of Issues: Excerpts from the Discussion Session at the Conference", in Gerbner *et al*, *Analysis of Communication Content*, pp. 523-37.

P. J. Stone, D. C. Dunphy, M. S. Smith, D. M. Ogilvie, *The General Inquirer: A Computer Approach to Content Analysis*, M.I.T. Press, 1966.

R. Syme, *The Roman Revolution*, Clarendon, 1939.

T. Talbot, *The World of the Child*, Doubleday Anchor, 1968.

R. F. Terwilliger, *Meaning and Mind: A Study in the Psychology of Language*, Oxford U. Press, 1968.

J. D. Thompson, *Organizations in Action*, McGraw-Hill, 1967.

T. P. Thornton, "Terror as a Weapon of Political Agitation", in Eckstein, *Internal War*, pp. 71-99.

S. Ullman, *Semantics: An Introduction to the Science of Meaning*, Blackwell, 1962.

C. A. Valentine, *Culture and Poverty*, U. of Chicago Press, 1968.

L. S. Vygotsky, *Thought and Language*, M.I.T. Press, 1962.

E. Webb and K. H. Roberts, "Unconventional Uses of Content Analysis in Social Science", in Gerbner *et al*, *Analysis of Communication Content*, pp. 319-332.

M. Weber, "The Essentials of Bureaucratic Organization: An Ideal-Type Construction", in Merton, *Reader in Bureaucracy*, pp. 18-27.

T. D. Weldon, *The Vocabulary of Politics*, Penguin, 1953.

D. M. White, "The 'Gatekeeper': A Case Study in the Selection of News", in Dexter and White, *People, Society and Mass Communications*, pp. 160-71.

—see under Dexter.

R. K. White, *Value-Analysis: The Nature and Use of the Method*, Libertarian Press, N. J., 1951.

B. L. Whorf, *Language, Thought and Reality*, M.I.T. Press, 1956.

R. Williams, *Britain in the Sixties: Communications*, Penguin, 1962.

——*The Long Revolution*, Pelican, 1965.

R. Wohlstetter, *Pearl Harbor, Warning and Decision*, Stanford U. Press, 1962.

A. G. Woodhead, "Thucydides' Portrait of Cleon", *Mnemosyne* 13, 1960, pp. 289-318.

O. R. Young, *Systems of Political Science*, Prentice-Hall, 1968.

Index of Matters